DAYS

Memories, Journals, Stories, Letters and Poems

ROSEMARY PRIMONT OKUN

Published by Classical Music Today, LLC

Copyright © 2016 Rosemary Okun
Foreword © 2016 Michael Primont

All rights reserved.
Printed in the United States of America
First Edition

No part of this publication may be reproduced in any form without the written permission of the author, except for brief quotations in reviews.

"Perhaps Love"
Words and Music by John Denver
© 1981 Chrysalis One Music / BMG Ruby Songs
All Rights Administered by BMG Rights Management (US) LLC and BMG Rights Management (Ireland) Ltd. (IMRO),
a BMG Chrysalis company.
Used By Permission. All Rights Reserved.

Published by Classical Music Today, LLC
Edited and designed by Kerry Grimes

ISBN-13: 978-0-692-80836-8
ISBN-10:   0-692-80836-1

For my loving husband,

Milton Okun,

who shared this journey with me.

CONTENTS

Foreword ... IX

STORIES AND POEMS

How Many Times	13
Street Symphony: Queens Village, New York, 1932	13
First Memory	15
Time	16
First Christmas Memory	17
Dear Mother	20
All The Years	21
Real	21
The Last Nap	22
Buttercups And Violets	25
The Irish Connection	25
Parcheesi	27
Anatomy	28
Honesdale	28
Three Good Reasons	31
At Fifty	32
Grandchildren	32
Michael	33
Autobiograhy - Rosemary Okun	34
Fourth Of July	38
Charity Begins	39
Dear Cousins	47
Gustave Primont	61
Grandpa	63
Hollis	64
Grandma	65
Poem – Grandma	66
Golden Anniversary	66
What To Wear	69
Will And Leah	69
Aging	74
Real Meaning	75
Days	76
October	77
October Dream	77
Fire	78
Imperfection	82
Inspiration	83
Hershey's Kisses	84
Uncle Gus	86
Uncle Willie	90
Andy	95
Crutches	96
Alcohol	96
Purpose	99
Art	100
Déjà vu	100
Pretending	101
Hell	102
Aunt Elvira's Visit	103
Convents	114
Parties	115
Shopping	118
Aunt Mamie	120
Pets	122
Homer	129
Our Cat Is Different	131
Typewriter	132
The Decision	133
A Mother's Love	133
My Time At Time-Life	135
There Are Smiles	138
In The Meantime	149
First Date	157
Happy Anniversary	161
L'auberge du Père Bise	166
1984 Olympics	166
Afterlife	169
One Day	171
Notes To A New Word Processor	171
Love Happens	174
Evelyn	179
Independence	201
Anyone For Seconds	211
Thanksgiving	212
First Love	218
The Movies	221
The Piano	235

Christmas Declarations	238	Memory	350
Another Christmas	245	It Hurts Now	355
Some People Satisfy	247	Three P.M.	357
The Godsils	247	Will At One	358
Uncle Percy Godsil	248	Heritage	359
Of Relative Cleanliness		Sister Age	360
And Godliness	252	Litany	362
Faith	257	Thursday's Child	363
Dear Milt	258	Life	365
Milt	259	Greenwich Village	365
Will's Funeral	260	Old Friends In The Village	369
First Things First	266	Just Desserts	370
I Have Been Touched By My Death	267	On Grief	373
Mom And Dad	267	Whose On First	374
In Absentia	269	Lists	375
Where Is	273	I Showed Him My Poem	377
Names	273	You Never Know	379
Of Tutus And Splints	274	On Her Birthday	380
Wilson's	279	In Memoriam	381
Thanksgiving For All	282	Debt	388
I Gave My Big Rug		The World	389
To Andy And Julia	284	Mickey	390
Cousin Sue	284	Hold The Mayo	392
Letter To Myself	287	Possessions	392
And What Of Today	287	Jean	396
Depression	289	Lizzie	404
June Night	289	We Were There	405
Elizabeth Rose Sparks	296	Easter	408
The Gifts They Gave	301	Aunt Vera	410
Frozen	307	Letter To Mary Litchult	414
Only For The Trying	308	After Reading Anne Sexton	427
Jewelry	309	Bicycles	429
The Silver Ring	309	The Growler	432
Talloires 1	319	The Birth Day of Motherhood	439
Life Is A Babka	320	Jenny	440
November Again	323	Getting Closer	452
Thanksgiving Again	325	Dad Old	455
Physics	325	Happy Birthday	470
My Dearest Milt	332	Letter To An Old Friend	471
Growing Up	333	Dîa De Los Muertos	477
Talloires 3	338	The Grandkids	484
On Being An Artist	341	Origins	490
An Impossible Task	345	Streetscene	495
Crossroad	346	The More It Changes	495

It's A Mystery	502
Animals With A Difference	512
Perhaps Love	518
November	523
November Dream	526
A Gift From Rose	526
Great Divide	531
Insomnia	532
About Love	535
Before The Storm	536
List Of Ingredients	537
Women And Books	538
Grandpa	542
The Cooper Union For The Advancement of Science And Art	544
At The Opera	547
The View From Here	548
My Self	553
In Desperation	554
Habit	558
Mysteries	562
Bedroom	563
A Woman	568

Manus, Iris and Morty: 371, 377
Morris, Madeleine: 382
Okun, Andrew: 172, 238, 292, 444
Okun, Emily: 443
Okun, Julia: 293, 446, 447
Okun Sparks, Jennifer: 172, 238, 245, 260, 295
Okun, Will (grandson): 442
Price, Elinor: 195, 233, 286
Primont Dinegar, Jean: 300, 423, 504, 516, 520
Primont, Michael: 187, 197, 199, 204, 209, 299, 338, 349, 394, 397, 426, 428, 437, 441, 448, 453, 467, 474, 476, 477, 480, 485, 489, 507, 513, 521, 528, 540, 543, 546, 552, 555, 556, 557, 559, 560, 561
Reitter, Bob: 373
Reitter, Rose: 19, 24, 297, 344, 373, 562
Robinson, Carol: 481
Shapiro, Fran and Irv: 193
Sparks, Peter and Wendy: 178
Sparks, Elizabeth, "Lizzi": 442
Straus, Dorothy and Leonard: 336, 340
Witkin, Joan: 401, 534

UNTITLED JOURNALS

33, 34, 94, 246, 258, 288, 291, 294, 289, 302, 323, 342, 349, 356, 469, 470, 478, 487, 509, 517, 549, 563, 565

LETTERS

Baird, Marian: 289, 319, 3720 373, 441, 555
Bender, Betty: 51, 403
Chatelain, Jacques and Assunta: 353, 381, 383
Domingo, Placîdo: 469
Geringer, Eda: 315
Henrion, Mickey: 384, 391, 491
Howard, Diane: 449
Josephs, Peggy: 399
Kaiser, Hannah: 385, 387
Karpan, Molinda: 298
Litchhult, Mary: 276, 414

Michael Primont and Rosemary Primont Okun, Annecy, France, C. 1975

FOREWORD

I was born during the postwar housing shortage in 1946. When my father returned from overseas, he and my mother moved in with my aunt Rosemary's parents. When I arrived, I was the first grandchild in the family.

Rosemary Primont was eighteen and still living at home. She and my mother were almost the same age, so the two of them had lots to share-including me. Rosemary was born in 1928 at home in her parents' upstairs bedroom in Queens Village, twenty miles and a world away from Manhattan. She was the third child of Walter Primont, a bossy, fun-loving milk salesman, like many of their neighbors, they were Catholics. Rosemary's brother (my father) Mike was eight years older, and her sister Jean was five years older. They were like most families: a gluey mix of love and dysfunction.

My first clear memory of Rosemary is from when I was five years old and spent a weekend on the Jersey Shore with her and her first husband. When I returned home, my father solemnly informed me that his sister was a beatnik. I could tell by his disapproving sneer that this was meant as a slur. But I had a different impression. I saw a lithe beauty, with straight dark hair that reached her shoulders, and a soft, sweet smile that embraced me. Unlike my father, she had no harsh edges or visible calluses. And unlike anyone else in our family, she was exotic, graceful, soaring. I thought beatniks were wonderful.

Years passed, and tensions between my father and his parents kept us from seeing his family except when he was away and my mother would take us on the subway to visit my grandparents at their ice cream parlor in Manhattan. These visits were fun for Peter and me, but rare, and usually lasted just a couple of hours. We visited Jean a few times a year, but we almost never saw Rosemary, who at the time lived in New Jersey.

I saw Rosemary at my grandmother's – her mother's-funeral. Nana was buried next to my grandfather, a World World I veteran, in the Long Island National Cemetery. The following summer, I was on a trip to France while in college, adrift, trying to find my way in the world after surviving a stint in the army and Vietnam, when I stopped off to visit Rosemary, her new husband, Milt, and their children, who were living in London. I was unprepared for the deep connection that struck both of us when we finally met as adults. Even though we were apart for most of my life, it felt as if Rosemary had always been there.

In 1975, to answer my incessant questions about our family, Rosemary began to send me long letters filled with memories of her childhood in the 1930s and 1940s. We continued to get together whenever possible, and we corresponded for almost forty years while she made homes in London, Talloires, New York, and Beverly Hills, and I tramped to Burgundy, Rome, Los Angeles, Palo Alto, Seattle, Beijjing and Vancouver. She also kept up a correspondence with many friends and with her growing family.

Depression-era Queens Village and the adjoining town of Hollis, where her family moved in the 1940s, were tightly packed neighborhoods of small homes with pianos in parlors and oversized radios that broadcast tinny voices, static, and music from faraway places. Children of that time were "to be seen but not heard," and roles and rules were assigned according to one's place. Most girls were expected to marry, have children, and be active members of their local parish. A few who "heard the call" would become nuns. Close friends of your parents were addressed as "aunt" or "uncle," and the bulk of life was confined to the neighborhood, the parish, and, for the Primonts, the local American Legion post.

Try as they might, the nuns at Rosemary's school were unable to mold the sensitive, picky child into a conforming Catholic, but instead left her with a nagging sense of guilt. She would forever feel like a misfit whose shortcomings were there for all to see.

After high school, Rosemary somehow escaped to Manhattan and The Cooper Union to study art. There she was exposed to a wider, richer world of ideas than had ever reached Queens Village or Hollis. At twenty, she married a fellow art student. A few years later, her daughter Jenny was born. By the age of twenty-seven, Rosemary was single again, living with the secretarial skills that she'd picked up in high school. By this time, she had begun to experience bouts of depression, an affliction that would stay with her for the rest of her life. Contrary to her image of herself at the time, and perhaps more under the influence of the nuns than she realized, Rosemary set her goal to find a new father for Jenny and new husband for herself. And that's when she got lucky! Along came Milton Okun, a tall, handsome, gentle folk musician. They were married in 1958, and have been together ever since. Milt adopted Jenny, and then he and Rosemary had a son, Andy. They now have three grown grandchildren.

Milt was born in Brooklyn, of Russian immigrants. His father worked as a civil engineer for New York City, and his mother ran a summer camp in the Adirondack Mountains. A gifted musician, Milt trained to become a concert pianist but was forced to give it up after losing two years of practice due to a kidney disease he contracted before the advent of antibiotics. He has had a storied career as a teacher, performer, arranger, musical director, producer, and music publisher. In 1960, Milt and a close friend, Robert De Cormier, founded Cherry Lane Music, Inc. Early on, De Cormier sold his interest in the company to concentrate on a career as a choral conductor. Cherry Lane grew to become a leading independent music publishing company by the time of its sale in 2011. Milt has played a key role in the careers of artists as diverse as Peter, Paul and Mary, John Denver, and Placido Domingo, and has earned numerous gold and platinum records. In 2010, he was elected to the Songwriters' Hall of Fame. For more than ten years he was a board member of the Los Angeles Opera. An opera lover since early childhood, he is currently studying Italian at the age of ninety in order to better follow the lyrics.

Through their fifty-plus years together, Rosemary has been the organizer of their many homes and voyages. She also stepped in and took the reins of Cherry Lane for a year when they discovered that the person to whom they'd entrusted the job was not following their instructions. At the age of fifty, she finished a bachelor's degree in English, and then a year later earned an MFA in creative writing. After that, she learned to speak fluent French. At the age of eighty-four, she published a collection of her poetry and drawings, titled *An Imperfect Life*.

Rosemary's writings to me about people who inhabited her childhood released a treasure of grace, insight, and humor in stories, letters and poems. Her written memories are like brushstrokes that evoke a vivid portrait of her and all the people she has loved.

I will never be able to fully express how grateful I am to Milt and Rosemary for welcoming me into their lives. They extended their hands to me a long time ago, when I needed it most and our hearts have been joined ever since.

———Michael Primont

HOW MANY TIMES

How many times
have I told my listeners
the story of my life
oh, we laugh to hear the jokes
I've told, the entertaining
to a round of applause
and the sad times, bad times many
oh, we cry lightly over those
and they wring their hands with me
my listeners
tell us again they say
and I tell them
again

STREET SYMPHONY: QUEENS VILLAGE, NEW YORK, 1932

At five in the morning, Charlie the milkman with his horse and wagon rattled into the street, bottles clinking, hooves clip-clopping, until they reached the house of a customer. The horse slowed as Charlie jumped off the wagon, and without waiting for the driver, eased toward the next house at a bride's pace. Charlie ran with quick steps, put the bottles on the stoop, picked up the empties, and dashed back to the wagon. Sometimes the horse forgot to act like a bride and took off, with the milkman running down the street calling "whoa" after him. Then voices sang out "quiet" in the dark, and moments later horse and driver returned, clinking and clip-clopping down the street to continue the day's deliveries.

    Alarms rang. Mothers got up, dressed, called to children to wake up. People yawned, faucets ran, toilets flushed. Iceboxes and refrigerators opened and closed, and kettles of water rattled on stoves. Passing cars honked "kookookakooga." Women said goodbye to husbands and schoolchildren, and called out instructions to children playing outdoors.

Dogs barked in house after house as doorbells rang when salesmen made their rounds selling magazines and vacuum cleaners. Two blocks away the Long Island Railroad trains went over the railroad ties in rhythmic intervals, and locomotives made long hoo-hooing sounds when the driver blew the whistle.

Cool autumn winds blew crisp leaves off the maples for dogs to dig under, and children flung themselves into piles of crackling leaves before fires burned them into white snapping leaf smoke.

On gray winter days falling snow muffled all sound to near silence. Shovels scraped and threw, scraped and threw. Cars ground out a beginning, like victrolas starting to play, while some men cranked and others pulled at throttles. On cold sunny days the coalman's boots crunched prints in alley snow where he went to send coal whooshing through cellar chutes into wooden bins. Bare branches whipped and slapped bits of ice against windows and into gathering drifts.

Spring brought bird songs and bicycle bells, shouts of children freed from winter clothes, the metallic scrape of roller skates on the sidewalk. There was a beating of carpets, a rubbing of windows, and digging sounds of renewal in gardens.

Through open windows in summer, women could be heard singing with the radio. Breezes shook leafy branches on the maples, and hollyhocks and honeysuckles drew noisy bees. The coalman, now an iceman, with great hunks of ice melting under brown burlap on the back of his truck, used his wooden handled pick to chop out frozen blocks of ice for housewives, then shaved off slivers for the children to suck on. Horse-drawn carts with iron wheels grated slowly through the street, led by men shouting "straawberrries, straawberrries, waatermellonnn" no matter what they were selling. Garbage pails thunked. Lawnmowers sliced and tossed. Gates groaned and slammed. Babies cried.

Each mother had a special song to call her children home. It was a friendly tune, unless she was annoyed about something. No child mistook another's call for its own, but some children ran home while others dallied until the calls became less musical, and a harsher note was sounded. Some seemed tone deaf. Their mothers walked up and down the street calling in voices of resignation.

On summer evenings, adults sat on front steps, cigarettes and cigars glowing in the dark, gossiping and sharing pitchers of ice tea and lemonade. People laughed and sang songs. Metal tops on glass jars opened and closed for captive fireflies. Young children played running games—kick the can, giant steps, hide and seek—and shouts of "home free all" rang out.

Family by family the street went to bed. Doors closed, locks snapped shut, and outside noise subsided. People whispered, snored, shifted under bedcovers, made love. Sometimes sounds of fighting broke the stillness as a man came home singing, too drunk to care, and his wife tried to hiss him quiet. Sometimes there were cries of a woman giving birth.

Houses creaked in the night. A dog barked. Someone sighed. A hungry baby cried. Until the only sounds were those in dreams, as much a part of the music as the rest. □

FIRST MEMORY

Clinging to the side of the crib crying, I saw my brother passing by in the hallway. I reached out to him, waving my arms to be picked up. He stopped in the doorway and smiled at me. He was dressed for school, and when he came close to the crib, I grabbed his shirt.

"Wait a minute. Don't cry. I'll see if I can take you out." He stuck his head out the door and called down, "Hey, Ma, the baby wants to come out of her crib. Should I bring her down?"

I didn't hear the answer, but I held my arms out to him, hopping a little on the soft mattress, until he came over and picked me up. "See, I told you not to cry."

His ten-year-old body was thin and felt different from my father's. I could feel myself rocking a little as he balanced me up by his shoulder. I liked him. He was nice. He didn't want me to cry. He carried me downstairs and I guess the day went on like most others. □

TIME

Time had a shape. Mornings were at the bottom. Seven o'clock was when my mother and father woke up. That was the bottom of the shape exactly. Then came eight o'clock, a little above seven. I ate breakfast at eight. After that came eight-thirty. That was when I left to go to school. Then the day went up to noon when I came out the school door to go home for lunch. Each hour or special time had its place on the way up the day. Three o'clock was for playing after school, and six o'clock was different from everything else, because that was when we ate dinner, and nighttime started. The day went on up after dinner, to bedtime, then to midnight. That's when it started down to the next day, though the real end of the day might be one o'clock in the morning when my mother scolded my father for coming home late from the American Legion, or from the bar around the corner where he'd been out having a good time with his friends. He only stayed out till four o'clock once or twice a year when there was a special party. Four o'clock was the time no one was awake to know about it. It was close to where six began to curve around to the beginning of morning at seven o'clock. It was hard to sleep to ten or eleven because that was too far up, and it was so light outside.

Yesterday and the days before that were always in back of me. To think about them I had to turn around inside myself and look at yesterday, then the day before and then the day before that. Days were like a pack of cards, thin and sitting one in back of the other, waiting to be separated and looked at, to be got into in that dark and hazy way. If I tried, I could see and hear everything that had happened, and taste and smell what was in those days. I just had to look very hard and let myself be there. □

August 1, 1976
Alpine Drive, Beverly Hills

Dear Michael,

    I'm very happy the coat was welcome. It gave me pleasure to think of it keeping you warm. You really did get across to us what the climate would be like in that part of France. I'm still trying to get used to the house in L.A. I think my problem with it is made up half of resentment at being forced to move when I didn't want to and half of discomfort at being in such large rooms. I think we must all have space requirements that are individual, and mine are filled in rather small quarters. We went to Aspen over Thanksgiving with the children because Milt had to work on a TV show with John Denver. We stayed in a pleasant small condominium—all the luxuries—but small. I felt great. Didn't love being immersed in the show business scene, but I loved being in that small space with my family.

    It's December and coming up to the holidays and I miss my mother and my father. I miss Christmases past and snow outside that crunches when you walk on it. I miss looking in the windows of small houses at Christmas trees with tinsel at night. Michael, I miss it all and I'm sad.

    I haven't written anything in six months and I don't know how to start again. Should I send this letter? I'd like to because I want there to be one person somewhere to whom I can write the truth.

    Be well, and we will see you in the spring, at which time I should cheer up.

    Love,
    Rosemary

FIRST CHRISTMAS MEMORY

The Christmas tree was too big. It stood like a false furnace in the corner of our small living room and reached up into the second story through the stairwell. The star at the top was like a beacon to the people in the upstairs hall, telling them that the tree was waiting for them to come down and be warmed by the colored lights and the reflections in the gold and silver of the ornaments.

The tree was so tall it had to be tied to the banister to keep it upright. I was too young to put any of the breakable ornaments on the tree, but they let me join in the fun at the end when it was time to put the tinsel on.

"Just put on a few pieces at a time and spread it around like this." My mother placed some tinsel in my hand and showed me how to do it. I put one piece on and then another then threw the rest in a heap on one of the branches and turned to get more.

"No, no, a few at a time, love," and she gave me another handful.

"Now, that's done," she said, "Let's go to the kitchen and have some hot chocolate." She and Mike and Jean left the room and I stayed where I was, sitting on the stairs and looking down into the tree. It was wonderful.

I wasn't allowed to use the big black handled scissors, but they were next to me on the step up near the second floor. They were so big I had to use two hands to pick them up. I circled them around in the air making them open and close. Then I saw the brown twine that tied the tree to the banister and I decided to cut the end off it. Then I cut some more, and then some more, and when there was no more to cut off the end, I stuck the scissors through the banister and cut the cord itself. The star on top scraped across the ceiling and the tree landed with a crash across the living room floor. It was interesting.

Mother came running into the living room, with Mike and Jean after her. "My god, what happened?" she asked, "maybe it wasn't tied tight enough, Mike." They didn't ask me what had happened and I didn't think to tell them. The top of the tree had to be cut off where it bent when it went across the ceiling. I watched as they put the tree back in the pail of dirt and Mike tied it to the banister again, this time with instructions to make sure there were enough strong knots to keep it up. They swept up the broken ornaments and straightened out the tinsel.

Then they went back to the kitchen, and I went up the stairs again to where Mike left the scissors. I didn't bother cutting the ends of the twine, but went straight for the cord between the tree and the banister. The tree was shorter now and went down faster. This time I waited by the steps, the scissors in my hands, and there was no question of how and why the tree was falling.

I was surprised that Mike and Jean were furious. Mother scolded me for touching the scissors. "You mustn't play with scissors." She tried not to laugh. "What will Daddy say when he hears you cut down the tree twice?" □

> August 10, 1976
> Alpine Drive, Beverly Hills

Dear Rose,
Beverly Hills is worth a good long chat over tea and coffee but that will have to wait. Meantime, let it be said that I love it...when I'm not working my ass off, which isn't often. There has been more work connected with this move than with any of the last three.

Every time I read your poem I find things that I didn't see before, and that's what it's all about. I wonder if they're the things you meant to say...You've written a poem...given a gift to a friend...pleased me terrifically... and taught me how to search again and again for more than surface pleasure in words.

This was a good move. If we can be happy, we'll be happy here. And if we can't, we'll have given it great effort. It's a compromise between London and Chappaqua. I'm not depressed the way I was back east. I miss you and Mickey Randolph and Mickey Henrion and a few other people, but I know our friendship will survive in spite of distance. There's a point where friends become family and it doesn't change feelings. I think about all of you a lot. It's funny isn't it? All my really good friends are women. There are men I like but never in the same way. At one time I would have said that sex made it impossible to be friends with men, for me at least, but I no longer think that. It's just that I've achieved companionship without strain with a few people. None of us compete with each other or with other women as far as I can see. I don't know any men who aren't involved with what their image is to the world, namely, to other men...

We have a little Kerry Blue to keep Pokey company. They romp all day in our fake Connecticut backyard. Little Bear loves it just the way he did London, Greenwich, and Chappaqua. He's a very insensitive cat, which must mean that we're not too neurotic or he's dumber than I think.

Be well, and give Bob and the boys my best.

Love,
Rosemary

DEAR MOTHER

You died four years ago. I miss you so. I haven't even the comfort to know you exist in a form I can understand anymore. You would have shuddered when you were alive if anyone had told you that but because you died without pain, I no longer shudder at the thought of death myself and face it with nothing more than sadness at what I will never see or know of the people I love.

Andy just walked into the room and announced, "My mind is a blaze of numbers." I love him so. You wouldn't recognize him now he's so big. He is still the tender gentle boy you loved so much and gave so much to, just grown larger. You died a few days after his tenth birthday and Jenny's nineteenth. She's a woman now with a life of her own and very happy. She's a marvelous cook, takes after you, and enjoys feeding people the way you did. But she's everything you and I never were, Mother, because in her time she can be anything she wants to be...and she wants to be so much. She's an artist, the way we thought I might be, and a photographer and a creator...assertive, warm, intelligent, and sensible. May she always be strong.

My children are as nice as they are partly because you loved them so. All your warmth and love, the food you prepared and fed them, the diapers you wrapped around them so kindly, your hands as you touched them, your smile as you cooed and spoke to them, your devotion to their being alive and well. They may not remember it but somewhere in their souls you left an impression that marks them for life and they'll give that kindness to some other lives before they're done and never know why. Thank you.

And thank you from me for what you gave me back there in Queens Village, the food, the warmth, the soft breasts to lean against, the sweet forehead to put my cold hands on, to know I was appreciated. Thank you, Mother.

Rosemary

ALL THE YEARS

> All the years
> the birds sang
> outside my window
> that fresh spring sound
> that woke my soul
> and made me glad
> Woke my soul today
> to childhood
> sunshine mornings
> when food was given
> and love was mine
> without asking

REAL

"Mommy, suppose you aren't real."

"What do you mean, dear?"

"Suppose everything I see is my imagination." I followed her around the room as the bed was being made, watching her strong arms lift the mattress to tuck in the clean sheets.

She didn't say anything, and I leaned against the side of the bed, fingering the down pillow, waiting for an answer.

"Move out of the way. I'd like to get out of here." Her hands felt strong and firm as she pushed me away from the bed. Feeling me watching her, she asked, "What is it, dear?" She leaned over and looked at me.

"Mommy, suppose nobody is real and they're just my imagination. Maybe everything is just pretend inside my head." My mother looked worried and I went on, "What if there's no food or sky or house and I'm imagining everything. Maybe you're not real either, just somebody in my head."

While I was talking I moved close to my mother trying to see if when I touched the printed housedress, it would be there, or would it just be air now that she knew the secret. No, through the fabric, I could feel her fat, warm leg, and I patted her arm. Looking up at her face I saw a closed expression around her eyes as she picked up the pillow and plumped it firmly on the bed and said, "Don't think things like that. It will make you nervous. Come on, let's go do the other beds." □

THE LAST NAP

I remember the last time my mother tried to make me take a nap. I must have been four years old, because it was midsummer and I was on her bed in our house in Queens Village. I've taken thousands of naps since, but that was the last official childhood nap.

"Take your nap, like a good girl. Then you can have milk and cookies."

I looked up at her. "I'm not tired, Mommy." I knew it was no use, but I pleaded anyway. "Do I have to take a nap?"

"You need a nap. Now go to sleep."

Her voice was firm and pleasant and I turned on my side so I could look out the window. The sun was still high in the sky and shone through the leaves of the maple trees in front of the house. They wavered gently each time a small breeze went by, patterns shifting, light green and dark. I could hear the older children playing outdoors. I crept to the window to see what they were doing. My sister Jean and her friend Mildred were playing on the front steps. I could hear their muffled voices, so I strained against the screen with the side of my head to see if I could hear what they were saying.

I heard my mother coming up the stairs and I jumped back on the bed and pulled the sheet up to my chin. I shut my eyes tight pretending to be asleep as she walked past the room. I sighed. I wasn't tired and I didn't want to take a nap. Hearing me, she came into the room. "Can't you get to sleep? You'll be so tired you won't be able to stay awake until dinner."

"I'm not tired."

"Come sit on my lap, and I'll rock you to sleep the way I used to, when you were a baby."

I threw off the cover, took a soft pillow to pet, and climbed up onto her sloping lap. She leaned back in the rocker and cuddled me in her arms. While we rocked, she began to sing a lullaby that I liked:

> Sail baby sail
> Out upon the sea
> Only don't forget to sail
> Back again to me

She sang the words in her timid, tuneless voice. I felt her large, warm breast under my head and her strong arms around me. While she sang she looked off into the distance, and following her gaze, I could see a boat with a loved child in it. The water was dark blue and someplace far away it was nighttime where the child would go to sleep. I looked up at my mother's face, at her pink skin, fine and soft like a child's. I tried to get closer to her. I would never forget to come back to my mother no matter how far away I went.

She rocked and I asked quiet questions. "Did your mommy sing that to you?"

"I don't remember my mother, but I guess she did. She must have sung something to me." She looked at me and smiled.

"Why don't you remember?"

"I was a little girl when she died. I was too young to remember."

"Did you sing to Mike and Jean?"

"I sang to all three of you. I used to sing a song to Mike when he was a baby. Let me see if I can remember the words." Her smile became brighter.

> Hush little baby, don't say a word
> Mama's gonna buy you a mockingbird

I closed my eyes and thought about her rocking my brother. I could hear a special sound in her voice as she remembered him when he was little. I opened my eyes and she gave up. "I guess you won't take a nap today. Maybe you don't need one any more. You're getting to be a big girl now."

I was happy I wasn't going to have to take naps any more, and I still got the milk and cookies. But I was sad that my mother didn't have a mother to sing her to sleep. It was hard to imagine. I wanted to make it up to her but didn't know how, so I kept the knowledge of what she hadn't had inside me, and it made me love her more. □

October 22, 1976
Alpine Drive, Beverly Hills

Dear Rose,

I hope the classes are going well, and yes, I would like to see the poems I've helped to make possible through your volunteer teaching at the juvenile facility. It makes me feel great to think of you opening so many new things for so many children.

I'm taking an incredible class called Making Grammar Work with a marvelous former high school grammar teacher, now writer. She is very exciting and is using work by Faulkner, Hemingway, Dylan Thomas, etc. to illustrate what can be done if you're willing to throw yourself into the fray. I love every minute of it. That's not strong enough—I'm high on it. We bring in things that we write or have written in the past for her to see and to be analyzed by the class. I'm catching on to what I am not making clear, and after that I may actually learn to embroider a little.

I'm also going to a group-counseling course for women interested in returning to work. It's fascinating and informative. We've taken tests—personality, interests, and occupational—and my highest score naturally was homemaking. So what else is new? It's nice to know that the thing I've done for the last twenty-five years is what I like to do best. It is interesting though to see yourself on paper, if not particularly cheering. I have the feeling that I'd better take a hard look at what I am and make the best I can out of it. I wanted to see if there was anything in there that said "you'll be a lousy writer, lady," but, of course, it didn't say that. It did say I couldn't do many other things and expect to enjoy myself. The only occupation that came up as a possibility for me that I liked was speech pathologist. That I think I would like and am very suited to.

Amazingly, Leah and Will are happy as clams in their new abode, a nice hotel with all kinds of disgruntled elders and a lot of activities, a staff of waiters who almost throw the food at them, and a great apartment. We'll see how long it lasts. Write, say hello to Bob and the children.

     Love,
     Rosemary

BUTTERCUPS AND VIOLETS

If you hold a buttercup under your chin, it makes your skin shine yellow, and that means you like butter. Jean says, "Buttercups make you hungry."
I like yellow roses with pink on them. Mother likes them too. But when she goes to a party in her black fuzzy dress, she wears a white flower that's very smelly.

Dandelions are pretty. They make your hands yellow if you squeeze them and then my mother says, "Wash your hands and get them clean before you eat." I like when dandelions are white puffs and you can blow them away in the air.

25

Jean says you can tell if your boyfriend likes you when you pull the petals off a daisy.

Sometimes I pick some flowers for my mother, but when I put them in a glass of water, they don't stay up. They get all wilted and knocked over, but she likes them anyway and she puts them on the windowsill so she can see them. Aunt Frances gave me a cookie with a violet and purple sugar on it. That's the only flower I ever ate. □

THE IRISH CONNECTION

"Can I come on the swing?"

"Don't let her on." The biggest boy stepped over and stood in the way. "Who are you?"

"That's Rosemary," said Mary.

"I wanna swing too," I said.

"What for?"

"Cause I wanna ride."

"Go home."

"You better let her on," Mary looked up at her three visiting cousins. They were older than she was. "My mother'll get mad."

"Go home, you. Look at her. Crybaby."

"I am not a crybaby." My face was twisting and my mouth turned down. "My uncle's a policeman and he's gonna arrest you."

"So what. My cousin's a policeman and he'll arrest him."

"My other uncle's a policeman too and he'll arrest him. So there too."

"Your uncle is not a policeman, is he, Mary?"

"Yes, he is." Mary's brown eyes were wide. Her cousin Eddie was big, almost as big as Mike, and she was afraid he might hit her, but she had to tell the truth. "Her two uncles are policemen."

"And my aunt's a nun," I said, "so you better let me on the swing."

Eddie gave up, and moved aside. "Okay, let her on." A nun was serious. □

PARCHEESI

Mike and Billy Wilson were playing Parcheesi.

"Can I play too?"

"Nah, you're too little." Billy pushed my hand away from the board and threw the dice.

"I wanna play."

"Okay." Mike pushed his straight red hair out of his eyes and made room for me next to him. I stuck my hand in and picked up the dice from the board.

"She'll ruin it. Look what she's doin'."

"She can play one game with me. Here, let me show you."

I liked the colors on the Parcheesi board, best of all blue. And the leather cup to shake the dice in. I held it out and shook it, listening to the sound of ivory clatter inside the hollow container. It did something to the dice when you shook it. Everybody shook it that way.

"Come on, throw the dice," Billy was whining now.

"Leave her alone, she's just a little kid."

"She can't move there. That's cheating."

"I wanna go there." Now I was whining. "Can I put it there, Mike?"

"Yeah, you can put it there. Go ahead."

"That's stupid."

"She's my little sister and I can let her win if I want."

Mike patted me on the shoulder and I glared at Billy, who was getting up from his chair in disgust. I threw the dice once more and moved to the end of the board with a sideways look at Mike to see if it was okay.

"See, you won," he said, and I glowed at him with pleasure. I knew I hadn't won but I was happy to get to the end of the game first. My brother didn't let that mean boy win instead of me. As I went back into the house I could hear Billy complaining, "That's stupid. You let her win?"

"Aw, you're stupid. Let's go do somethin' else." □

ANATOMY

My father has me on his lap, trying to coax me to eat. It's a Sunday meal—meat, mashed potatoes, peas, carrots, and dessert. So far I've eaten mashed potatoes, one piece of carrot, five peas, and one bite of meat.

And I'm finished.

There's a general clucking and muttering around the table. "She has to eat, Walter." That's my mother speaking.

"That child doesn't eat properly. What's the matter with her?" That's Grandma.

"I ate everything on my plate." That's Jean. She always eats everything on her plate. Nobody pays attention to her.

Dad takes over. "Here comes the choo-choo. Up the hill, down the valley, and into the tunnel." He carries the spoonful along the pretend tracks. I'm charmed by the game; open my mouth to a spoonful of peas, when the train reaches the tunnel. Before I know it, the train is on its way again. This time with potatoes. I like potatoes. And then carrots. I'm chewing and swallowing. Now I see the next spoonful is peas.

I turn my head aside and mumbling through almost closed lips, "My pea box full." I shake my head NO and Dad pretends to be hurt. In my mind I see that down in my throat there's a pipe with small boxes attached to it, like the ones for wooden matches. The boxes are different sizes and the pea box is very small. □

HONESDALE

I was three years old when I graduated from my crib to the double bed with my sister Jean the night we came home from Honesdale, Pennsylvania, at the end of the polio-ridden summer of 1931. My family never took vacations, but we went to Honesdale that year because my father decided that my mother, sister, brother, and I should get out of New York during the epidemic. Besides, it would be a great way for us to learn about roughing it on a farm.

And it was rough—a bare light bulb hanging over the linoleum covered kitchen table, a smelly outhouse occupied mostly by bees, a cast iron pump that pulled up water from the well out by the barn and a bull that kept wandering by to bellow at the back door.

I don't know what the adults did for baths, but the older kids took theirs in a galvanized tub on a scruffy lawn. It was the kind of tub that suburbanites used for washing their dogs or chilling beer at picnics. I was still small and skinny enough to take mine in a pail. Baths were not a problem for my father, who only came down to see us on Saturday and left on Sunday. They were a problem for my mother and any relatives my father happened to bring with him to leave for the week. He was big on relatives and friends, and we never knew who would spring out of the passenger side of the car. Often it was Grandma, who emerged cranky and complaining, or Grandpa, ready with a smile and a pat on the shoulder. Sometimes it was Dad's Armenian friend Vic, who spent the weekend repairing everything that had broken down during the week.

I spent more than one day that summer with everyone in the kitchen and Grandma demanding to know what my mother was going to do to get rid of the stray bull in the yard. Why didn't she call the Police? With nothing more than a worn-out old broom as a weapon and no telephone in the house, Mother would clamp her jaw and refrain from saying all the things she might have said, like "You'd never know Grandma grew up on a pig farm in upstate New York."

Uncle Ed and Aunt Edith were with us one day when the bull came to call. Uncle Ed had lost a leg from the knee down when he was run over by a trolley at the age of twelve. Aunt Edith always looked as if she might faint whenever there was any excitement, so they weren't likely candidates for helping to get rid of the bull. When Uncle Ed picked up the broom and started for the door, Aunt Edith screamed, "Oh, Eddie," and Grandma hissed at him, "Think of your leg," then scowled at my mother. It was okay to send my mother out. She was only a daughter-in-law.

So my mother took the broom from Uncle Ed and went out on the porch waving it and saying "shoo" to the hulking beast, who backed up a foot or two to survey the scene and continued eating the grass. A few minutes later, my brother Mike and his friend Billy Stengel sneaked out another door and found the farmer who owned the bull. "That bull wouldn't hurt anybody," he said, and made a joke about city folks and brooms.

"Take him home," my mother said without smiling, "and don't let him back this way again." She still held the broom. "I've got young children here, and if anything happens to them, you'll know about it."

When the bull wasn't frightening family and friends, Mike terrified Jean, telling her that the bull would chase her because she had red hair. Poor Jean spent a lot of time ringing her hands in fear that summer, racing past the farm where the bull was fenced in.

Sundays were the highlights of the vacation. My father piled us all in the car and we went to church in town. I don't remember the church or the town, but afterward we always stopped at a small country store and had Mello Rolls, a kind of gluey ice cream tube wrapped in paper and stuck in a cone. It was fun to peel off the paper, and when they softened, they didn't run. If Grandma was with us, she complained about my father spending all that money, and Grandpa smiled behind her back and bought himself a pack of Luckies.

One Sunday my father treated two other kids in the store to Mello Rolls. They were standing next to the freezer looking hopeful, and he never could offer treats to us without giving some to any children nearby. After grilling my father as to why he would buy ice cream for children he didn't know, the owner of the store asked him if he would like it if he caught us taking treats from a stranger. To which my father replied that if he was up to anything fishy he certainly wouldn't have brought his wife, his three children, his seventy-year-old parents along with him, to say nothing of choosing a store filled with people, all of whom were probably related to the kids. He just thought they might like some ice cream, and it wouldn't be nice for them to have to watch us eat ours in front of them.

We came back to Queens Village that September, back to small-town life on the fringes of the most cosmopolitan city in America, as unaffected by proximity to Manhattan as any town in the Midwest, but it was advanced civilization to us compared to Honesdale. Back to the ice cream truck jingling past the house every day, Bohack's grocery store on the corner, sidewalks to skate on, and bathrooms with bathtubs and toilets. □

THREE GOOD REASONS

It can't be that we moved to California two years ago to the day. It's 1978, and I'll be fifty next week. In 1976 I was forty-eight. I didn't like that. It sounded aging and morose. Fifty sounds better. It's an easy number to remember, not wishy-washy and uncertain. I wonder if sixty will sound better than fifty-eight.

I looked through the list of suggested exercises for the class, and what seemed stimulating yesterday seems insurmountable today. I don't care about the first time that I suspected my parents were not all powerful. I'm trying too hard to appear self-sufficient to my own kids. My poor parents' lack of omnipotence was the least of their problems...

I must be cheering up, because I can think of three things that have impressed me so greatly that the image of those moments changes my feeling about being alive. Each is different but there must be a link. The first was an August landscape in South Dakota. If one looked full circle, there were thunderstorms, sunshine, blue sky, soft clouds, murderous storm clouds, and finally a rainbow. The earth was deep red brown and the fields were a soft, silky flaxen color. Barns and farmhouses were small, and neither poor nor prosperous.

The second was the first time I saw Jenny. It was late afternoon on a sunny October day and the maple leaves outside the hospital window were turning. The nurse held her up, a small bundle at the foot of the bed that moment. Amazing, one second to have no feeling, and the next to love, with all its ramifications of joy, fear, and pleasure, for the rest of your life.

The third moment I will not forget was a glimpse I had of the golden statues at the Tutankhamen exhibit. For the first time, I understood men's preoccupation with gold. There's more to it than just status and power. Gold, when used in art in a way that allows the beauty of the metal to show, may possibly be the best material to work with. The Tutankhamen statues were crafted with such excellence and were such a marriage of material and form that they may be the most beautiful visual things that men have ever created. I do not expect to see any greater art than that.

Almost no one lives to be a hundred but there is something about fifty that makes me feel I have started the second half of my life. Perhaps I will die tomorrow and the second half began when I was twenty-six, when Jenny was a year old, when my body was young and strong and the worst ailment I thought I'd ever have was blisters from a sunburn. □

AT FIFTY

>Smiling at the ease of softening
>at the touch and kindness of each other
>we are a feast
>of joy and boredom
>more pleasure than trial now
>Sad knowing at the end
>there will not have been enough.

GRANDCHILDREN

I just had a nice conversation with Michael. I love him. I decided this morning that instead of his being my first child (I was nineteen when my sister-in-law had him and I got to take care of him), he was actually more like my first grandchild.

A grandchild is a baby you adore. You cuddle and play with it. You feed it, wipe its chin and its bottom, and it runs to you because you're special in its life. You quote its clever sayings to friends, show its picture, get on the floor and play horsey with it. You bring it presents and candy and call every day when it has the measles. Then its mother and father take it home and put it to bed and you read a book or go to the movies and pick up your real responsible life and have nothing to do with whether the baby wakes up at three in the morning with a nightmare, or becomes a bank robber when it grows up, or needs its teeth straightened.

A grandchild is the dessert of life. No strains or tensions between you, no need to deny the use of the car, or to enforce a curfew. Just love and smile, love and hold, and love, and say goodbye.☐

MICHAEL

I was wrong
I have a friend
Something I gave him
In his childhood
Never forgotten by him or me
Bound us together
It was love I gave him
Arms that held him
Spoonfuls of food
Apple juice
And a hearing ear

Journal
June 27, 1978
Alpine Drive, Beverly Hills

I feel as if I should say something important in this journal. So I write. And what comes out? Complaints, trivia, sarcasm, humor. The day I can't find something to laugh about or make fun of, I will sink under the senselessness of it all. I have sad days of introspection when everything drags. Today seems a day of nothing important in any direction.☐

Journal
June 28, 1978
Alpine Drive, Beverly Hills

We have an owl living in our yard. I know he lives there at night because he hoots when it's dark. It's a funny sound. I wonder if you're up close can you hear a "t" on the end of the "hoo." Our owl doesn't sound the "t" or else we are too far away to hear it. The sound is a translucent soft gray. It must be that I associate the sound with the pictures of owls that I have seen. We were very disturbed when we moved here two years ago and discovered this owl spent so many hours at night vocalizing. A few times I wanted to call out, "Quiet, I know you're there," and I think Jenny did shout something at it one time. Now when I wake up during the night and hear him, I don't pay any attention at all. The hoot is only a small part of the background noise for sleep. It blends very well with snoring, barking, and creaking. □

AUTOBIOGRAPHY
June 29, 1978

Happy birthday! I'm not one age. I'm every age I ever was, and today is a good day. I like being fifty. I liked three, four, and five. Six was bad news. School. Left, right, prayers on knees, Sister Superior, Father Herchenroeder, forgetting. Reading was good. Seven was difficult, getting along on the playground, big sister. I fell in love with Jerry Brady. Now that was good. Eight, long walks to school, singing, dancing, and playing detective on the way. I can't do math and I can't write. School gets worse. Nine, ten, eleven. By this time I know every tree outside every window at school, much less about what's happening inside. I never fail anything, but no one, including me, knows why. I can draw, and it is the only means of communication between the outside world and me. If I can't write, my mind wanders most of the time, and I don't get along in the schoolyard. At least on Fridays we get an eight-by-ten sheet of yellow paper, and I can draw. And my drawing is usually the best one up on the board. Sometimes as a bonus I get another piece of paper, but the second drawing is never as good.

Twelve, I become a hypocrite. I smile and talk to a girl who is silly because her best friend is giving a Halloween party and I want to go. After the party, all night long in my dreams, I am dancing with Jerry Brady and my hair is in curlers. All night long, in reality, I take the curlers out of my hair, and then put them in again when I wake up.

Thirteen, hypocrisy becomes habit, and I make what a thirteen-year-old calls friends.

Fourteen, with relief I leave grammar school. Less hypocrisy and more feeling. For years I have been reading the same books again and again. Although I am intimately acquainted with Nancy Drew, Judy Bolton, Bomba the Jungle Boy, and Tarzan. I live on Prince Edward Island with Anne Shirley at Green Gables and I am Emily of New Moon.

Fifteen. Now I am ready for romance. I read a copy of *The Moon is My Undoing* for a whole year, turning from the last page to the first, a chain reader of one book. The war is on. Except for a vague uneasiness about my brother somewhere in the Pacific, I am untouched. I think uniforms on young men are beautiful. I don't know that explosives kill and people die. My school principal, Sister Rose Gertrude, is a maddened general in an army of Catholic administrators and frightens me more than Hitler or Mussolini. The war would end sooner, so we say, if only we could send her to the front.

Sixteen. I think I am in love. I go steady. I hold hands, kiss, and have romantic dreams. He goes into the army, and we write letters every day.

Eighteen. I fall in love. I am in love, and I am very unhappy. He is Protestant and I am Catholic. The Montagues and Capulets have nothing on the ill will flying between the two households, unfortunately only one block apart. Slander, snubs, and threats, assisted by mutual incompatibility, make misery of the next three years, taking my mind conveniently away from Auschwitz,

Buchenwald and Hiroshima. Anesthesia wears off and a horror at being human takes over.

Twenty, twenty-one, art school, work as a legal secretary. I marry an artist. Meaninglessness. Depression. Dostoevsky. I want a child.

Twenty-five. My daughter is born. She is the most beautiful person in the world. Nothing has ever meant anything to me before Jenny.

Twenty-seven. I leave my husband. I am depressed to the point of suicide. Only Jenny makes me live. I walk through life unhappy. I am a depressed mother, a depressed secretary, a depressed student and teacher of modern dance. I have read Proust, Joyce, and Flaubert, and I see nothing in any of them that cheers me. I find a therapist who tells me I have nothing to be depressed about, so I rediscover hypocrisy. Now that I smile again, I go to parties. I meet Milt and we marry. I am thirty, in good health, pretty. My daughter has a father. I am still romantic. And still depressed. So I find another therapist.

Thirty-three. My father dies a horrible death, prolonged and undignified. Brutal to watch. I cannot avoid it. I have disliked him since I was six, but when he dies, I cry for days. I cry for him and for myself and for all that can never be between us. I cry for my grandfather, and my aunt, and my Uncle Arthur, all of whom I loved, and whose deaths I ignored because I was being romantic and depressed.

Thirty-four. One night I wake in terror. I ask myself what I am so afraid of. I answer "death." I am not less afraid but at least I know. I have a son, and my mother comes to live with us. I love my children and my husband and my mother, but life is not what I thought it would be. *The Ladies' Home Journal* and *Anne of Green Gables* have not prepared me properly.

Thirty-six. I begin to paint. We move to the suburbs. I learn to play paddle tennis. I am a good cook. I sew. And drive a car to the dentist, dry cleaner, and supermarket. Jenny is twelve and looks at me with cold eyes. She puts a sign on her door that says "a blank expression" and no one enters without knocking. I discover Peter De Vries, Agatha Christie, and Thomas Hardy, and rediscover James Joyce, Marcel Proust, and *Anne of Green Gables.*

Thirty-nine. Kindergarten and the knowledge of death crush my son. He is diagnosed schizophrenic. He is not, but until I know, I do not think I can live. Assassinations, napalm, riots, looting. Our home is an oasis of pretended calm, an eye of a storm, as we protect him from what he cannot bear.

Forty-one. I no longer play paddle tennis and do not enjoy the growth of trees. I hate the war and feel Dostoevsky has written my life story. I am tired.

Forty-three. We move to England. Vietnam goes on and I gain perspective. I relax. I read papers. I go to movies. I love the opera. I learn as I watch my mother die that I am no longer afraid of death. It can be peaceful and unaccompanied by terror. It is life I fear.

Forty-five. Jenny is grown, an artist, and easier to like now that she is no longer convinced that I am her enemy. We communicate through our drawings. I start to write. I have never enjoyed anything as much. I write of the room where I was born. My mother. My father. My brother and my sister. The town. The trees. The books. The school. Aunts and Uncles. Milt and my children begin to know me as I begin to know myself.

Forty-six. We return to America. I like and do not like it. Milt is overwhelmed by the sight of his parents aging, his own mortality, and the uselessness of everything he does, and it is my turn to be the strong one.

Forty-eight. We move to California. I go to school. I find I like studying. I like the students. I like the teachers. I am appalled that I like getting A's. I no longer care that I am middle-aged.

Forty-nine. A friend graduates and I go to the ceremony. Someone gets honors and I think "how nice." Someone else gets highest honors and I am consumed with envy. I am back in the first grade, watching Sister give Gertrude May a gold star when I have just gotten a silver one. I return from graduation furious that I will not achieve outstanding honors. My family laughs because they know that as I joke about it, I am grinding my teeth. Maybe I should reject life credit, credits from art school, start at the beginning, and get straight A's.

Fifty. Milt has made it possible for me to enjoy my birthday. Across from my desk, he has hung a plaque on the wall that makes me smile as I read:

ROSEMARY OKUN
Highest Honors
June 29, 1978

FOURTH OF JULY

Firecrackers. Cherry bombs, roman candles, and sparklers. My father used to bring home a cardboard carton of firecrackers every year, and the day before the Fourth of July, after dinner, he would make my mother and the three of us children sit on the back stoop while he performed his annual macho feat of driving my mother crazy. Through the whole operation she would be panicked, not her usual style at all, saying, "Walter, don't hang on to it so long. You'll blow your hand off. Walter, watch out. I don't want to have to wait on you for the rest of my life because you don't have any arms left. For heavens sakes Walter, why do you buy those things? Get rid of them. Please." My brother always laughed and wanted to try some himself, but my father would only let us have the sparklers, so Mike would leave, grumbling and muttering. Jean always wanted to be off with friends, watching their fathers shooting off firecrackers, though they never had as many or as loud. That left me to sit and cower with my mother; sure something dreadful would happen to my big laughing father...

Most of the sparklers were saved for after dark when we sat on the front stoop talking to neighbors. Children gathered hungrily around as Jean and I lit one sparkler after another and my father made us share them. "You got to. They don't have any." Mother stayed irritated all evening. My father ignored the Depression, spending money on firecrackers, ice cream, and drinks all around. Some of our neighbors were poor and were probably glad when he treated their children along with his own, but poor or not, they all thought he was crazy to spend his money on foolish things when times were so hard.

If he ignored the Depression, I didn't know it existed. There was always food to eat, and surprises, and ice cream, cake, candy apples, and Hershey's kisses. I never felt poor; in spite of having little money, I grew up thinking there was plenty to go around and I'd never go hungry. □

CHARITY BEGINS

When asked by my mother why he had brought home two King James Bibles, a version that Catholics weren't permitted to read, my father explained that the salesman looked hungry, and admitted that along with buying two Bibles, he had also given the young man a quarter to buy breakfast. Dad never could resist a well-told sad story. This was during the Great Depression, and many of the stories were true, so life was full of temptation for him. My mother, often an unwilling partner to his kind deeds, wasn't ungenerous, but his way of doing things without considering the consequences for the rest of us was a constant irritation and burden for her. He'd bring people home for dinner, and then leave it to her to figure out how to feed them.

Dad was easy prey for anyone who wanted to get rid of an animal. Tell him it was slated for the pound, and it was scooped up and carried home. Our cat Mickey came to the house in a cake box, put there by the clever baker who wheedled my father into saving a helpless kitten from drowning. The box had a red ribbon tied round it, either by the baker as a bonus or by my father, who hoped to convince Mother that the cat was both a present and a good substitute for apple strudel.

One day Dad brought home a Doberman Pinscher that had been kept chained for the first two years of its life in the back of a store by a local storekeeper. Dad gave the man a lecture on cruelty to animals and fifty dollars, and then brought the dog home. Off the leash for the first time in his life, the dog jumped on the dining room table barking in rage and ecstasy, and then proceeded to terrorize everyone except my father. We thought it was because Dad had rescued him but that was giving the dog too much credit. It turned out that along with being six foot and weighing two hundred fifty pounds, Dad wore a belt, and a belt was the weapon the storekeeper had used to beat the dog. We made this discovery when Dad went to hitch up his pants that first day, and the dog flew through the dining room window. We felt lucky a few years later, when a friend of Dad's wanted a watchdog for his lumber company. After he promised not to keep him tied, and not to beat him, the dog, his chain, and a month's supply of dog food were passed on free of charge. Momma would have paid a second fifty dollars at any time to get rid of him.

The house next door to us consisted of two small apartments and was rented to a succession of tenants my parents disapproved of. Since there was a shared yard and driveway, they decided to buy the house and clean the place up. The ground-floor tenants were the Cobins, notorious in the neighborhood for Mrs. Cobin's slatternliness and Mr. Cobin's inability to hold a job. They had appeared on the block one day, Mrs. Cobin, black hair hanging limply over her round red cheeks, and Mr. Cobin, hungover and unemployed. They had two plump little girls, never quite clean, who resembled their parents, one, the mother, and the other, the father.

My parents bought the house for a small down payment and a very large mortgage. When the first month's rent came due, my father crossed the narrow driveway, firm in the decision to raise the rent from seven to ten dollars a month. He and my mother figured that would be a quick way to get rid of undesirable tenants. He was a long time coming back. Upon his return, he stood in the doorway, looking defensive, as he tried to explain to Mother why he hadn't collected the rent, and why he ended up lending the Cobins ten dollars instead. "Walter, you fall for every sob story you hear. You were supposed to tell them they had to pay the rent or get out."

"But Mary how could I? I mean, they have no food in the house. And the kids are hungry and crying. They didn't have anything to eat for dinner." Dad's face was contorted. "I know he's a bum, but I just couldn't do it."

My mother got up and went out the door, saying, "Well, I can." She came back five minutes later, went straight to the kitchen, and took the remains of our dinner over to the Cobins.

Over the following six months, my father lectured Mr. Cobin on the evils of drink, and Mother threatened to throw Mrs. Cobin out if she didn't keep the house clean. In that time, the Cobins paid a total of ten dollars in rent. Mrs. Cobin left garbage in the driveway, and Mr. Cobin stayed hungover. At last, armed with righteous anger and a listing of empty apartments in the local paper, my mother forced them to move three streets away. They left loud in their praises of Dad, and told their new neighbors that my mother was unreasonable. Several disastrous times Dad cosigned notes for friends who couldn't pay back the loans. If they could have, they wouldn't have borrowed the money in the first place. So in order to pay back the loans and feed the family, Mother was forced to perform the miracle of the household loaves and fishes with my father's salary each week.

And it wasn't just people who needed money or pets in need of a home. Every once in a while we'd wake up to find one of his friends sleeping on the couch in the living room. Our house was small and the living room was more of a path between the front door and the dining room, so a guest was a big event. And always an inconvenience. I don't know what Harry Lopez did for a living, but it didn't always pay, because he spent at least three days a year on our couch. "But, Maryanne," Dad would say, "Harry's down on his luck, and his landlady won't let him in his room." Harry was a short dapper man with a waxed mustache, always dressed in a kind of flash thirties style, light jackets with thin stripes and two-tone pointy shoes. My mother usually cut Harry's visits short by telling Dad that he could "lend" Harry the money to pay his rent. Harry left, rejected and sighing that my mother was "the best cook in the world." So good was she, that after each stay on the couch, he found it hard to go back to boarding house food and showed up regularly for meals, until my mother would force herself to let him stand and watch us eat a whole meal without offering him a bite.

There was a suicidal wife named Muriel, who ran away from her drunken husband and spent two weeks in our living room after she called my parents threatening to jump under a subway train one Saturday morning. My mother was all for saving her, but was less enthusiastic when Dad told Muriel she was welcome to use the couch as long as she needed it. Muriel took Dad at his word, and when her husband called in tears each day to apologize, she refused to speak to him. Two weeks later, Mother told her she didn't have to go home to her husband, but she had to go someplace else, and soon. Muriel called him to come and get her, crying that Mother was cruel and inconsiderate, and husband and wife took off in his old Studebaker, angrily denouncing my parents for interfering in their lives by letting Muriel stay in the first place.

Dad never learned. Mother managed as best she could and forgave him, knowing that things would be solved in accordance with her philosophy of "everything comes out in the wash." Neighbors adopted the extra kittens and puppies. The Bibles sat, dusted but unread, on a shelf in our living room. Harry's landlady always took him back. Even the loans were paid off eventually. But one day Dad did something so bizarre that it looked for a while as if it might make a permanent change in our household.

One morning, I was eating breakfast when I heard Mother call out, "And don't bring her back here." Dad answered in a tone of hurt innocence as he went out the door, "Aw, Maryanne, don't be silly."

"Never mind, don't be silly." She came into the kitchen. "It would be just like him to show up here with her this afternoon."

She poured herself a cup of coffee and began to cut up a sugar bun. The cat crawled up the back of her chair to take a swipe at each bite as she lifted it to her mouth. "Go away, Mickey," she said, shaking her shoulders and leaning her back against him until he gave up and jumped to the floor. Sugar buns, the food he was weaned on, were as dear to him as they were to Mother, but that day she was being selfish.

"Who were you talking about?"

"Oh, a cousin of your grandmother's you never met."

"What's her name? And why would Dad bring her back here?"

"Margaret O'Donnell. There were two of them, Margaret and Kathleen." She scowled. "Kathleen died the other day, and your father's gone to the funeral with your Uncle Ed. And you never know what he might do."

Five hours later Uncle Ed's car pulled up to the front of the house, and Dad got out and whispered to my mother, "Maryanne, she had no place to go."

"You fool, now you've done it," Mother hissed.

Margaret was all in black. Dusty black coat, black crepe dress, and black buckled shoes. Even her suitcase was ancient rough leather that had once been black. Her eyes flickered in my mother's direction, and then shifted to my father. "Walter said it would be all right, didn't you, Walter?"

Now that he could see my mother's face, he wasn't so sure any more that it was all right, but he tried to look casual. "How do you like your tea, Margaret?"

"Lemon and sugar, please."

My sister Jean and I sat next to Margaret on the couch making conversation. Then I went off to find the cat so she could meet him. When I offered to let her hold Mickey, she drew back, her dry wrinkled face showing distaste, and said, "I don't like cats."

In the kitchen I could hear my father and mother. "I just couldn't leave her. You should have seen the place they were living in. It was a hovel. And Kathleen was the one with the pension. Margaret has nothing. She had no place to go."

"What are we going to do with her? You know no one in your family ever liked her."

"Just give it a try, Maryanne, maybe it won't be so bad."

"What makes you think she'll be any better at eighty than she was at fifty? It doesn't work that way, Walter. If she was terrible all her life, she'll be dreadful now."

Dad came back into the living room, his expression sulky. Here he'd brought somebody home to live with us, and my mother was going to spoil it. Maybe he should have put Margaret in a cake box and tied a red ribbon around it. I wondered if my mother would be able to maintain her reputation for hard-heartedness when faced by the gaunt black-clad figure of my father's fourth cousin. For by this time the family relationship had been explained to our satisfaction by Uncle Ed.

"She was Ma's third cousin, daughter of her second cousin on her father's side, so she's your father's fourth cousin," as if she wasn't Uncle Ed's own fourth cousin as well. When he saw my mother's face as she carried in the tea, he got up and said, "Thanks, Rosemary, but Edith's probably waiting for me. I'd better go."

She gave him a cold look, then turned to Margaret and tried to smile, "I'm sorry, Margaret, but I don't have any lemon in the house. Would you like milk?"

It was the spring of 1940 and Mike was in the Navy. I'd been using his room since he enlisted. That afternoon, Margaret, with her wrinkles and her small suitcase, was settled into my brother's room, and I moved back in with Jean. Dad brought up a wooden rocker from the basement and put it in the room so Margaret would have a place to sit in privacy if she wanted. For a few weeks things went well. She did what she could to be helpful. Not much, but Mother was satisfied if she straightened her bed and peeled the potatoes for dinner. Jean and I brought her lemons for her tea, my mother bought her two pretty light-colored dresses to cheer her up, and my father joked about finding her a beau.

Margaret was quiet and watchful. She seldom spoke unless she was spoken to. She was so modest that she wouldn't go to the bathroom in the middle of the night without putting on her dress and shoes. Dad was unable to resist asking if she didn't need the shawl as well, and she said she would wear it if he thought it was necessary.

Every afternoon, in the living room, she would loosen her long, still-dark hair, and with a small smile sit combing it down over her back and shoulders, like an ancient siren parked on a plush couch waiting for a shipwreck.

When Mike came home on leave, he slept on a mattress on the floor of the dining room. Margaret was charmed by his sacrifice. She insisted he was a hero and baked a cake for him. She dusted imaginary lint off his shoulders and polished his shoes, taking on the role of a flirtatious older cousin. Jean and I teased him, and my father laughed. My mother's lip curled in amused displeasure as she watched Margaret at work.

Mike loved it. He pretended to take her seriously and brought her candy and flowers. The day he left to return to his ship, she cried and advised him "to hope for the best, expect the worst, and take what God sends."

After Mike left, Margaret changed. It was as if she had given him all that was left of her good will. She was morose. She spent more time in her room. I caught her hitting the cat with a broom. She began to lock him in the cellar when we were out. When my parents were home, she smiled. When they were out, she walked through the house muttering and glaring at Jean and me if we got in her way. She began to complain that we were messy, eating too much, and making too much noise.

Margaret was lectured on being patient with children. We were given lectures on being patient with old people. After school we changed our clothes and left the house immediately, and the cat spent most of his time visiting our next-door neighbors. Each week was worse than the week before.

Whenever her anger became too great, she would go upstairs, climb into the rocker, and recite a litany of her hate. Day after day, as long as my parents were out of the house, Jean and I could hear the wooden runners creaking on the bare floor, and her voice grumbling complaints about us.

"Brats. I didn't come here to wait on them. Peanut butter. Jelly. Take the salt and pepper shakers off the table. I'll tell Walter on them. That cat should be killed. Walter won't let them treat me that way."

Over the weeks, the monologue took on religious overtones. Margaret began to include Mother in her complaints.

"God will punish her. Make the bed. Take the salt and pepper shakers off the table. Who does she think she is? It's the devil in her."

When Dad was home, Margaret sat lamblike and smiling, but one day he came home unexpectedly and was horrified by the loud thumping and angry muttering coming from her room. It was like having Medea in her old age, rocking off steam upstairs, and calling on God to avenge her, now that she was too old to do it herself. Hearing his seventy-eight-year-old maiden fourth cousin calling his wife a bitch and his two daughters bastards was such a shock that he rushed out of the house, leaving the problem of Margaret, like most other problems, to my mother to solve.

Six months after Dad brought Margaret home from her sister's funeral, Mrs. Kelly, a widow from the neighborhood, stopped my mother and said, "Mrs. Primont, I understand you have a woman living with you who might be interested in a job babysitting. Since my husband died, I have to work. My son is only ten years old, and I need someone in the house to give him breakfast in the morning, and keep an eye on him when he gets home from school."

"Well, I don't know, Mrs. Kelly. Margaret's a problem. She's cranky, and she doesn't like children. I don't think it would be a good idea."

"I've been trying so hard to find someone, and I'm getting desperate." Mrs. Kelly was beginning to cry, tears running down her cheeks. "Billy's too young to be by himself so much of the time. I wouldn't expect her to do more than dust and make the beds and do the dishes. And I'll pay her ten dollars a week, plus room and board."

"I'll send her around to you, Mrs. Kelly, and you can speak to her yourself. But I want you to know, if you hire her, and she goes to live with you, you'll have to be responsible for her. She can't come back to us."

The offer presented Mother with a problem. Margaret was dreadful. But what could my parents do with her? She was in the house. She was a distant unloved relative. My father had offered her a home, and now he was as anxious as the rest of us for her to be gone and never come back. But the thought of a ten-year-old boy being under her care was disturbing. "Mrs. Kelly, I think you should think hard about it before you decide. She's a bitter old woman. She doesn't like children, and she hates cats."

"I don't have a cat."

"Well, then just make sure you don't let her have a rocker in her room."

Three days later Margaret was elated. We heard her upstairs talking to herself in a tone of malicious glee. "God will punish them. Put away the salt and pepper shakers. It's the devil in her. That cat should die." Without a goodbye or a thank you, she packed her shabby black suitcase, picked it up with the ease and strength of a twenty-year-old, and marched triumphantly around the corner.

"Well," said my father wagging his head as if he were remembering something long forgotten, "Ma always said Margaret was a terror."

From Mrs. Kelly we heard occasional stories of Margaret's crankiness, but never a word from Margaret herself. We were as dead to her as her sister Kathleen, and if she passed us on the street, she never said hello.

Soon life closed over her time with us, smoothing out the unpleasantness, the way water does rough sand on a beach after a storm. The rocker went down to the basement, the cat stopped acting as if the house was haunted, and Jean and I began to invite friends over again.

Harry Lopez still managed a few days on the couch each year. There were always the unexpected guests at the table and the unwelcome calls from the bank after Dad cosigned a note for a friend. That was just a part of life. But after Margaret, Mother never let Dad go to a family funeral, unless she went with him. □

DEAR COUSINS

Let me introduce myself. My name is Rosemary Primont Okun, and I'm a first cousin of your father. We moved to California twelve years ago, and every time we went to San Francisco I would look in the phone book hoping to see the name "Primont." I knew that my cousin Arthur, or Little Arthur as we used to call him, lived in Palo Alto for a while after he was married. The last time I saw him was probably at his sister Margie's funeral in 1947. It seems my nephew Michael looked in the right phone book and found you. There must be some primitive instinct that works in us all that makes us want to search out our roots and branches, to recognize in another face a smile or a mannerism that flowers on the family tree.

Michael called the other night and told me he had spoken to you, and that you would like to see some pictures of your grandparents. Your grandfather was my father's eldest brother, my godfather, and my favorite relative. I have only one son and I named him Andrew Arthur after my Uncle Arthur.

I wonder how much you may know about the side of your family that gave you your name. If you meet any other Primonts they are probably relatives, because as I understand it, the name, French in origin, was something like Primout and I can hear my grandfather pronouncing it— Primoo—and saying that after his parents (your great-great-grandparents) lived in the United States for a while, they got so tired of people not being able to pronounce the name correctly they changed it to Primont—not much easier to pronounce, but definitely unique.

I told Michael that I have very few pictures of my father's family and wouldn't like to trust them to a commercial lab for copying for fear of losing them. However, thanks to the copier in the next room, I was able to make you some reasonable facsimiles, and in the case of a couple of the group photographs, the copies are better than the originals.

As to family history, Grandpa (my grandfather and your great-grandfather, Gustave Primont) told me that he was born two years after his parents emigrated from France. They were from the region of Alsace-Lorraine. Grandpa died at eighty-nine in 1948, so he must have been born in 1859 and they must have arrived in America about 1857. He remembered seeing a parade of Civil War soldiers when he was a little boy. He had an older brother named Arthur whom I met only once when I was very young, and they were both in their eighties. That Arthur was rounder and fatter than Grandpa and seemed pretty cheery. I don't know why I never ever saw him except for that one time. Maybe they didn't get along, or their wives didn't like each other. Whether there were any other children I don't know. I think that branch of the family lived in New Jersey. And I think that Grandpa may have been born on Staten Island. I do remember meeting one of my father's second or third cousins on the French side of the family. Her name was Edmae Sabatier. So possibly there were some shoemakers in the family or else they were just related to us by marriage.

At some point, Grandpa's family moved upstate to Saratoga, New York. My brother said that Grandpa's father was a tinker and a peddler. That would be logical for that time and place since upstate New York was mostly agricultural, and tinkers and peddlers were a necessary part of the scene.

Grandma, whose name was Margaret Donahue, was from a farming family outside Saratoga. I remember when I was six years old visiting some relatives on a farm on the way back from Niagara Falls. Someone in muddy boots and overalls tried to coax me to stick my hand through a fence and pat some gigantic hairy pigs in a sty. That was the first time I understood I wasn't a good sport.

Grandma also had some elderly spinster cousins living in New York, one of whom my father once brought home from a funeral. I wrote about her in a story, "Charity Begins," that I've enclosed and that about says it for Grandma's family as far as I can tell you about them. I think one of Grandpa's first jobs in New York was for Cartier, the French jewelers, where the perfect French he learned from his parents in his childhood was a source of great pride to him, though he didn't pass his knowledge on to his own children. He taught me a few words in French when I was little and always liked telling me that because his accent was so good, one of the French jewelry repairmen at Cartier had asked him what part of France he was from. He worked at Cartier for many years, toward the end as doorman, and was given a diamond stickpin when he retired.

One of the stories Grandpa used to tell was about the day of the blizzard of '88 when he had to walk home about twenty blocks from work. His eyes shone when he talked about the strength of the wind and how he wasn't sure he'd make it. Last year I came across a picture taken after the storm and finally understood what it must have been like. Cartier is seven blocks away from where the picture was taken. The boy in the picture could be your grandfather who must have been about that age. Grandpa was living with us at the time of the 1947 storm. He sat by the radio listening to the news, chortling each time the announcer said the winds weren't strong enough to call it a blizzard. The blizzard of '88 was his moment and he kept saying, "It's bad, girl, but it ain't a blizzard."

Grandpa was a sweet, good man. He was probably prudent. In appearance, he was the quintessential Frenchman one finds sitting in cafes in small provincial towns in France, face tanned and wrinkled, bald with a sprinkle of close-clipped white hairs on top of his head and a fringe over his ears and around the back, a large, slightly hooked nose, and an expression of kindly amusement at his own foolishness and that of everyone around him. He was of moderate height with a small potbelly that seems to have been inherited by my son Andy, and Michael and his brother Peter. He was also the source of the bunions scattered here and there among the family members. He was a really nice, kind man, loving to his children and grandchildren and devoted to his wife, which was good because although her husband and children loved her, I don't think anyone else very much did.

Grandma was all Yankee. She ruled her family like a dictator. The only time I remember her smiling in the twelve years she was alive after I was born was once after a holiday dinner at her house. She and Grandpa and her five children played a game of Euchre, her favorite card game, on the round oak dining table, while the daughters-in-law and the grandchildren sat around and watched or did whatever the rest of a family does at a time like that. There was a Tiffany lamp hung low over the table, and I can still see Grandma's face under it, with all the down shadows making her look even more ominous. At one point she gave a choked-off chuckle of laughter and said, "Ha," as the corners of her mouth turned up for a few seconds over a good hand. It was such a rare occasion that her five children teased her for a few minutes for having accidentally smiled.

I didn't like Grandma, though possibly the older grandchildren who knew her when she was younger may have had more pleasure in knowing her. I was the youngest in my generation, ninth and last, and she had probably used up whatever pleasantries she had in her before I arrived. Also, I looked like my father and he was never her favorite.

Grandpa and Maggie, which is what Grandpa called Grandma, had five children, Arthur, Gus, Ed, Walter (my father), and Elvira, in that order. They were very clannish and close-knit, and when they were together everyone else was excluded, not out of unkindness, but by the outsider's sense of not belonging. My impression of it was like of one of those cells you draw diagrams of in a high school science class: Grandma the most important-looking spot in the middle of the cell, Grandpa and the five children moving around her inside the circle, grandchildren and daughters-in-law wandering around the outside, enjoying looking in or wishing they were somewhere else.

I remember hearing your grandmother Annie and my mother speak scathingly about "the Primonts" while "the Primonts" were milling around two feet away from them not noticing a thing they said. It's true that all four sons married, and three of them—Arthur, Gus, and Walter—had families and homes of their own with only Ed and his wife living in the same house as Grandpa and Grandma. But the moment the original family got under the same roof, it was always the same. They were a sort of club unto themselves.

I think they got their sense of humor, those who had one, from Grandpa, and their most striking characteristic, the complete conviction that they were right—at all times—from Grandma. Maybe this was the most irritating characteristic to the daughters-in-law if not to the grandchildren, some of whom, myself for instance, could have been clones of the originals. In our branch of the family, Michael and I are the two extreme examples of the trait, so consequently we get along very well, neither one the least threatened by the other's rightness.

Whenever the family got together they sang and made music. That was one of the ways families entertained themselves before the advent of radio and television. Luckily, they were very musical. Elvira, a music teacher, played the piano and the accordion well and often, and almost any other instrument that came into her hands. Ed played the mandolin, Gus the ukulele, and Grandpa the banjo. My father, who was untrained, could play the piano by picking out the chords and always sang harmony. Arthur may have played an instrument at some time or another, but I don't remember him doing anything but singing. They all sang. Except Grandma. She just sat in her beautiful old, oak rocker and kept her eye on everything. I'm tempted to say beady eye. At some point they always sang "When You and I Were Young, Maggie" to please Grandma. It must have pleased her, because they always sang it, and Grandpa would say, "Do you remember when I used to sing that to you?" Then she'd harrumph, and if she was pleased I couldn't tell you. But they were all pleased. And something I never thought of until this minute. After Grandma died, the whole family never got together and sang again. Their apartment was rented to someone else, the piano went to someplace else, and Grandpa moved upstairs to stay with Ed and Edith.

 Grandpa and Grandma had only three things in their house to interest a small child. First, there were the two beautiful old oak rockers with simple hand-carved backs. They were good for heavy rocking if you could keep it quiet enough not to attract Grandma's attention. Then there was the stereoscope. You looked through a pair of glasses at two nearly identical pictures side by side and when you got them in focus, you could see a scene in three dimensions. The one they had must have been in their possession from before the 1900s, and there were lots of snow scenes, forest glades, and cityscapes.

 When the pleasure of looking at them wore off, there were the family albums, kept next to the stereoscope in Grandma's hope chest on the sun porch. They weren't like photo albums today. These had curved covers made of worn, burgundy velvet, held closed by decorative metal clasps. They were from the time before ordinary people had their own cameras, so the photographs were taken by professional photographers and placed on beautiful thick pages made like mats and edged in gold. When the albums were closed they had a kind of regal appearance. The photographs were of Grandpa and Grandma when they were young and their friends and relatives, all posed in the nineteenth-century manner. The picture I remember best was one of Grandpa and Grandma on their wedding day with Grandpa sitting and Grandma standing up very straight next to him in her dark-blue wedding dress with its hundred buttons on the back and leg-of-mutton sleeves, him solemn, and her looking just as prim as she did when I knew her fifty years later. She wore the same dress, with some alterations to the seams, at the Mass celebrating their fiftieth anniversary.

As I wrote that sentence I suddenly remembered that I distinguished myself at that Mass. I was the flower girl, and as I marched down the aisle in the procession, I began tossing the flowers from my basket a few at a time right under Grandma's feet and was hauled into one of the pews before I could throw the basket as well. There were a lot of hissed "don'ts" and "what did you do that for?" and many tears from me.

The albums don't exist any more. In a fit of depression and grief a few weeks after Grandma died, Grandpa destroyed all of the photographs and then threw the albums away.

Your grandfather, my well-loved Uncle Arthur, was married to your grandmother Annie, whose surname I never knew. I think she was Irish. She must have been pretty when she was young, because she was still pretty in a jolly, old-fashioned kind of way when I knew her in her fifties and sixties. If there was a Mrs. Santa Claus, Aunt Annie could have been her sister. She was very fat, not unusual in those days for a woman with five children, and had a heavy, breathy laugh and a cheerful smile. When I think about her today, I can hear her voice, not with a brogue, but saying very Irish-sounding things, talking about her children with affection, but with a pretense of not complimenting them, or sometimes saying, "Aw, go on, Walter," and putting her hand up in a mock gesture of rejection when my father said something outrageous.

Uncle Arthur and his family lived in the Bronx and he used to come and see us, sometimes without the family, just stopping by to say hello; so I knew him better than your grandmother and their children, whom we only saw once a year at our house, maybe once a year at their house, and sometimes when we all happened to visit Grandpa and Grandma at the same time. Arthur visited his parents often, but without the family. Today the trip from their old neighborhood to ours in Queens would take half an hour but in those days it took a few hours.

Arthur's oldest child, the oldest grandchild, was called Chubby. She was born around 1910 and may have been named Annie after her mother but was lucky enough to get a nickname all her own and escape the "Big Annie, Little Annie" routine the rest of us had to endure. There was Big Arthur and Little Arthur, Big Walter and Little Walter, Big Rosemary and Little Rosemary. Grandma called Grandpa "Gus" and their second son "Gussie" and Gussie's son "Little Gus."

Chubby was my favorite cousin because she made Margie and Dorothy stop teasing me about my flower throwing the day of the fiftieth anniversary celebration. Chubby was beautiful in a classic English-Irish way, with a fair complexion and soft, red-blonde hair that she wore in flat, marcelled waves coming down around her face. She never married, having fallen in love with someone "unsuitable" whom her parents forbade her to marry. Being a good Catholic girl, she obeyed them, and then proceeded to live at home in pleasant martyrdom, making them pay for their interference for the rest of their lives. Maybe no one else proposed to her, or no one that she liked, but she was a spinster by the time I was five and old enough to remember her and that was what she stayed.

I think Margie was the second-oldest daughter. Aunt Annie was short, but Uncle Arthur was six four, and so, I think, was your father. The four girls were probably close to six feet tall and, except for Claire, were very heavy like their mother. Margie was the prettiest, with dark brown hair and very arched eyebrows. Her skin was clear and she always seemed to be laughing. She was sarcastic, very, very sarcastic. It took courage to tangle with her verbally. She left me pretty much alone. I was too young to be a target, but she used to work my father, sister, and brother over each time they got together. My father, being one of "the Primonts" and, therefore, always "right," would look at her in amazement for daring to question his rightness. She probably felt just as right as he did, but since she was so much younger than he, and a girl, he was a little miffed by her uppityness. She married a nice man named Ed Bertero, and after a few years of marriage and the birth of three children, she died, six months after her father. Chubby took on the task of mothering Margie's children. After some years, because she had the responsibility for the children and the household and only the status of housekeeper, Ed offered to marry her, perhaps out of loyalty, family love, or gratitude, but Chubby refused, preferring martyrdom—or independence, depending on how you looked at it. I liked her enough to think it was independence. My sister, who knew her, better than I during those later years, says that Chubby said she regretted her decision. I know she loved the children and on some level probably loved Ed too. I know she thought of the children as her own.

The next sister, Dorothy, was even more sarcastic than Margie without the good looks to take the sting out of her words. I kept out of her way as a little child for fear of what she might say. She was the only one who didn't think I was too small for a verbal whacking. I never went anywhere without carrying a book to read, so I could always avoid Dorothy by losing myself in some corner, coming up now and again for some cookies and patting from Chubby. Dorothy became a nun, so after a while we seldom saw her.

Claire was blonde and soft looking. She wasn't beautiful like Chubby and Margie, with regular features, but she had an appeal the others didn't have, and did much less verbal sparring. She looked more like your father and her father, and probably had a gentler side. She was friendlier with my sister and brother, who were closer to her age, and when the families were together, Claire and Jean and Mike often stayed together.

Arthur, your father, was a distant figure to me. He must have been twelve or thirteen when I was born. When I was six years old I proposed to him, sure he would wait for me to grow up. I remember Chubby and Claire trying to explain to me that cousins couldn't marry each other, while Arthur stood laughing and blushing as they teased him about me.

Your grandfather Arthur was a New York City policeman. My mother said he had a reputation for being the only cop in New York who always paid his way on buses and trolleys and wouldn't accept a free cup of coffee from anyone. If you knew New York, you would know what that said for him. It was as corrupt then as it is now, though less impersonal. His beat was outside the Public Library at 42nd Street and Fifth Avenue, and he was such a gentle, good man that people went out of their way to say "hello" and "how are you?" to him. After he retired, people who knew that my father was Arthur's brother would stop him on his salesman's rounds and ask to be remembered to Arthur.

A radio commercial for Philip Morris Tobacco featured a midget who came out dressed as a page (most radio shows were performed before live audiences), and at the beginning of the commercial he would sing, "Caaall forr Phiillip Morrriss." He became a friend of your grandfather's, and every time he'd pass 42nd Street and Fifth Avenue in his limousine when Arthur was directing traffic, he'd shout out "Caaall forrr Arthurrr Priiimont" and have everybody shouting and hallooing to him and Arthur.

On the other hand, his brother Gus, also a policeman, was something else, a sad case. His brothers and sister, and even my mother who didn't much like him, said that as a young man he had been lots of fun, all jokes and good humor, until he was injured while on traffic duty. The injury was to his head, and he had about nine operations to remove pressure and fragments of bone in his brain. He got violent headaches, and his behavior was usually mean and ugly. His parents and family were always patient with him, and no one was permitted to criticize him in front of them.

When Aunt Jenny died, Gus scandalized the family by marrying a Protestant divorcee named Margaret, who I thought was wonderful but demented for having married him. The ladies in the family, like Grandma, Aunt Edith, and even my mother, were caustic and said Margaret only married Gus for his disability pension, but gradually, in spite of being divorced and different, she won their goodwill, just in time to divorce him on grounds that I suspect had to do with violence. Gus then proceeded to marry a short, wispy, middle-aged blonde named Helen, a European refugee with a squeaky voice and a thick accent who probably figured that after Hitler, Gus didn't look so bad. I remember one family occasion when all the kids were hysterical with laughter, saying that Helen kissed like a vacuum cleaner. It was sad but true. However, she was so eager to please and took such good care of Gus that eventually the family forgave her for being so unappealing.

Little Gus was a few years younger than your father, and probably came to a bad end. Dorothy, in a fit of sentimentality a few years ago, came across some Primonts in the Brooklyn phonebook. She dialed the number, and after explaining who she was, got the distinct impression her call was unwelcome. I seldom saw Little Gus, and my last memory of him is that at the age of thirty, now calling himself Pete, he talked my father into giving him a job (I think he'd just gotten out of jail for some petty crime, and he may have racked up such a record under the name Gus that he decided to start anew). Within two days' time, he conned Grandpa, then eighty-six years old, out of twenty dollars by telling him that the young woman he had just married hadn't known she was pregnant until she went to the hospital with a stomachache and came back with a baby. Then he fiddled sixty dollars away from my brother's wife, and the next day stole about fifty from my father, and that was the last we saw of him. Doesn't sound like a number you want to dial when you're in a strange city and have nothing better to do?

Then there was Uncle Ed. I think Ed and Elvira were the only two of the children in your grandfather's family to finish high school. My father went to work when he was twelve, and I suspect Arthur and Gus did too. Ed graduated from high school and got an office job as a bookkeeper because he was run over by a trolley when he was twelve and lost half his right leg. He had a fascinating, but not very comfortable, wooden leg. The money the insurance company gave for the accident paid for a two-family house in Ed's name in a good suburban neighborhood, and was the reason the family could move out of Hell's Kitchen. It was an uninteresting ugly box of a house, painted yellow, and smelling of absolute, implacable cleanliness. By the time I was born, Ed was bald, set in his ways, and married to Aunt Edith.

Ed and Edith kept company for ten or fifteen years before they married, because Edith, who worked as a secretary, had an elderly mother to take care of. There's a picture of her in uniform during the First World War, so perhaps she did some kind of volunteer work. Edith was old-fashioned, not just prim and proper in a kind of belated Victorian sense. Even to a young child she had an aura about her of otherworldly puzzlement, as if she'd walked through a door into the wrong century and was sure that someday, if she just pretended not to notice how strange everything was, she'd accidentally find her way back to wherever it was she came from. There was something antique about her, delicate lace collars, drooping shirred dresses, slightly quavering timid voice. And something strong. She was tall, taller than Ed, and while she had pale, delicate, Irish fair skin and she moved quietly, her movements had a certainty of purpose.

I heard many remarks I wasn't supposed to hear or understand to the effect that Ed and Edith probably hadn't slept together because they wouldn't have known what to do. Our common ancestors were not kind. No wonder Edith liked the children on her own side of the family better than on ours, and even Ed seemed to favor them.

If the rest of the family looked on Edith as a kind of ladylike cipher, Ed loved her totally. He used to call her "Deede," and his voice always sounded warm and understanding when he said it. They lived a serene and sober life that suited them. They both worked—and saved. I suppose they were the only ones in the family who had the habit of saving. It was during the Depression, and saving was much easier for a couple with two jobs and no children.

Uncle Ed was methodical and probably self-conscious and shy, or maybe secretive, at least with his feelings. Most of the time he had a slight smile on his face, which would occasionally turn into a large smile if someone said anything funny, though even then there was a quality of pessimism about his smile that said "be careful, the situation may change for the worse at any moment." He could make jokes and amusing remarks, but always in a self-deprecating manner, so that if no one laughed, he could perhaps pretend that he hadn't meant to be funny. He was usually more of an appreciator than an instigator of fun. For some reason or other, he called me Max when I was little. I used to become indignant and say I was a girl not a boy, and he would raise his eyebrows, always with a small smile, and say he didn't know that. I think it was the closest to the family habit of teasing that Ed could muster.

I finally understood Ed when I was nineteen and decided to paint my bedroom and he explained his philosophy of house painting. He told me that every three years when he decided the house needed painting on the outside, he would start at the upper southwest window and then continue painting according to some plan he'd worked out years before. He knew exactly on what day he would be painting each window and door, when the first coats and when the second, in the two weeks it took to paint the house. That was a kind of order I'd never encountered before or even imagined existed.

Stability and order were never part of the salesman's bag of tricks, and if Ed was the family bookkeeper, my father Walter was the family salesman. Walter was indiscriminately generous and childishly impulsive. He couldn't bear to see anybody needing anything. He loved to sing and dance, joke, and be with lots of people. He was bossy, opinionated, and mercurial. My mother Rosemary was the disapproving rock he anchored himself to in order to keep himself from sinking in the storms he created. Compared to the rest of the family, he was off the wall. He and Gus had been close friends until Gus's accident, and Dad could never understand why we couldn't forgive Gus's miserable behavior. Maybe Gus had been more like him than the others. He wasn't when I knew him.

In 1916 your grandfather already had a family, Gus was a mess, and Ed had his wooden leg, so Walter was the only brother to fight in the First World War, and he became the flag waver of the family, though they were all pretty staunch patriots.

Walter loved his parents and brothers and sister, but I don't think they approved of him. He was too flamboyant. He was too everything. He had no middle ground. Today, psychiatrists would say he was manic-depressive. Where some people who suffer from the disease go for months and even years without periods of depression, his moods changed from gay to sad many times in a day. Life was often painful because he felt too much, and his children and wife bore the brunt of it.

He was a natural leader, and had a way with words, a prodigious memory for almost everything he ever saw or heard, and a sense of discretion about his experiences that made him a wonderful storyteller. He was also a great mimic. Like the rest of the family, he was honest and patriotic, and unlike them, irresponsible and irreverent. He was a registered Democrat who always voted Republican. In other words, he was a contradiction. I could go on about him, but that's another story, one for my children and grandchildren.

Elvira was the baby of the family and the only girl. She could do no wrong. First of all, she was a nun, a Dominican Sister, and that put her beyond criticism. She was allowed one visit home each year, and the whole family, including the grandchildren, gathered at Grandpa and Grandma's in Hollis for a celebration dinner. Grandma always roasted a big leg of mutton, rare, with brown gravy, mashed potatoes, and lots of vegetables. At the end there were always a couple of pies, a cake that Aunt Edith made—very neat and iced perfectly with no extravagant drops of chocolate escaping. And, of course, music.

Elvira was a funny kind of nun. She never lost her New York Hell's Kitchen accent and said "yeah" and "no kiddin'." She was never a spiritual kind of person, though I've no reason to doubt the sincerity of her religious dedication. Grandma felt betrayed when Elvira went into the convent, and for all anyone knew, was the reason for Elvira's decision to enter. In those days, as an unmarried daughter, she would have been expected to stay home and live under her mother's thumb. And Grandma had quite a thumb. As it worked out, her family could visit her once a month and she only went home one day a year, even though her convent was only an hour away. So once a year, she had a day of complete freedom, at least from ten a.m. to six p.m., a lot of family gossip, and a glass of beer, which she loved, with her family. She played the piano and accordion to their applause. When she said goodbye at the end of the day, she didn't look unhappy to be leaving, but sometimes cried because her father and mother cried.

Elvira, like Ed, nearly always looked as if she was smiling; only she laughed and joked often. It was as if she had some secret pact with life to always see the funny side of things.

So there are the Primonts as I remember them. I'm sorry I don't know more about your grandfather and grandmother except how much I liked them. I hope you like the pictures and I'm sorry there aren't more. I realize this is a very long letter and probably way more than you may have wished to hear, but it's been fun for me to write it. How does one end a letter to relatives one hasn't met? Perhaps I should just say,

Love from a second cousin,
Rosemary Primont Okun

GUSTAVE PRIMONT

My father's father was born on Staten Island in 1859 to French parents who were recent immigrants from Alsace-Lorraine. He was just old enough in 1865 to remember seeing a parade of soldiers back from the Civil War marching in New York City.

It occurs to me in the year 2001 that even though I loved him, I never thought to wonder if he had a middle name. His wife called him Gus and his five children called him Pop, but I only thought of him as Grandpa.

He was a pleasant presence in my childhood. Unlike my grandmother, he liked my mother and used to walk the few miles from his house with his unclipped poodle Sugar on the leash to visit over a cup of coffee and some of my mother's apple pie. I remember Grandpa sitting in the kitchen laughing and shaking his head while they gossiped. He was a short thin man who always wore a vest and whose potbelly was decorated with a gold watch on a chain. He had a fringe of white hair low over his ears and around the back of his neck, and there were single hairs, always cut short, growing at random on his bald head.

I never heard him yell at anyone, and the closest he ever came to scolding me was one time when I teased Sugar, whose temperament was more like Grandma's than Grandpa's. Sugar was fifteen at the time, and I was the last grandchild, so like Grandma, Sugar had had a bellyful of grandchildren by the time I came along.

When Grandma died, I remember seeing my father and Uncle Arthur leading Grandpa out of their bedroom, crying and leaning on them for support. When I asked my mother why he was crying, and she said it was because Grandma had died, I couldn't understand why anyone would cry about Grandma. I don't remember her smiling at me.

Grandpa lived with Uncle Ed and Aunt Edith after Grandma died, and when he couldn't take care of himself anymore because he had cataracts, he came to live with us. My parents were working and I went to school at night, so I cooked his meals and took care of him during the day. I was twenty then, in love and unhappy. Very unhappy. He was eighty-nine. He'd broken his hip and was confined to bed. We were upstairs in his room. It faced south, and outside the sun shone on snow caught in the branches near the window. Grandpa was in a wheelchair, fussing with the food set on a tray in front of him.

"You know I don't like them this way." He poked at the undercooked vegetables with his fork.

It was true. I did know it. But down in the kitchen, closed in my own unhappiness, I let my hands go about the business of preparing his food without thinking. I couldn't think of him, only of myself. I sat on the rumpled covers on his bed with my back against the wall and made an effort to look at him. He was almost blind, bedridden now and alone for most of the day. I felt sorry for him, but when my eyes shifted to the snow outside the window, I began to cry, not for him, but for me. What had happened? Everything was going wrong, and life seemed a terrible mistake, all pain and little pleasure. Tears ran down my face.

"Don't cry, girl. I'm sorry I was cranky. I didn't mean to hurt your feelings." He peered at me through his thick glasses. I started to tell him that I wasn't crying over what he said, but he continued, "It's disappointing when the food's not right, you know." He sighed. "If the food's not right, there's nothing else. I can't read the papers any more." He glanced down sadly at his plate, but in the moment that he faced me, I saw a look that seemed half contentment and half apology that his words had affected me. Somebody cared enough to cry when he complained.

So I didn't tell him it wasn't his fault. I moved to the edge of the bed and held his hand with its fine ancient skin so smooth to touch. "I know you didn't mean it, Grandpa." I was glad he thought he'd made me cry because I could tell it made him feel he was still important. And it was true. His fingers stirred in mine and he murmured, "That's a good girl."

We stayed that way for a while, me stroking his hand, and when the late afternoon shadows began to fall across the curtains, I kissed him and put him back to bed. I put his glasses on the night table beside him and asked him if he'd like to listen to the radio. He said he didn't care. I turned it on. I picked up the tray and left him, wondering what he was thinking as he turned stiffly on his side, faded brown eyes staring unseeing at the wall. □

GRANDPA

From the sun porch, we could hear Grandma's false teeth clicking in her mouth as she muttered her irritation into her wrinkled chin.

"What's the matter, Maggie?" Grandpa called out, "What's the matter with her, Walter? Go see."

"It's okay, pop. Just a little fuss about nothing."

"Are you sure?" Grandpa was anxious. "Something must be the matter."

He leaned toward the radio and said to me, "Imagine that, girl. You can hear what he's saying, all the way from Chicago."

I crowded close. "Can I listen too, Grandpa?" The radio was a flat wooden rectangle with little silver tubes, some wires and a small speaker sitting on top of it. I frowned the way he did and put my ear close to the speaker. There was funny noise and a skinny, wiry voice coming out.

"Be careful, girl, that's my radio that the kids gave me for my birthday. Didn't you, Walter?" He smiled with pleasure. "Let's turn it off; we don't want to waste it." He pushed the switch, detached the aerial from the windowsill, and shuffled into the kitchen to soothe Grandma. We could hear small chuckles and cooing's, and then we heard him say "C'mon, Maggie" a few times in a coaxing tone. He came back to the sun porch, winked at me.

His smile and the wink gave me courage to say, "Grandpa, can you show me that funny picture machine that makes everything look real," and we went off hand in hand through the kitchen to the living room to find the stereopticon. □

HOLLIS

Remember green and white linoleum
scrubbed to sterility till we lived there
thirty years of perfection, erased in a week

Remember the apple tree outside the kitchen window
and white curtains, dotted swiss, stirring
Remember Aunt Mamie sipping tea
and Grandpa, old blind eyes and oak cane
eating eggs fried in fat, denying the pressure cooker
Remember the gray car, and love the first time,
sadness and pain

Remember dreams and Gibson Girls
the Blessed Virgin
priests, prayers, and betrayal
Remember Hollis
October leaves and apples, always apples

GRANDMA

"I'm hungry. Can I have peanut butter, please?"

"Have some bread and jelly. Bread and jelly is good for you."

Grandma stalked to the pantry a few steps away. I watched her unwrap the bread. I was the ninth grandchild, not yet formed into the proper family image, at least not as far as Grandma was concerned.

She put the bread and jelly on a plate and set it on the table, frowning at me to signal it was time to eat. I edged over to the table looking at the generous helping of grape jelly and sat on the chair in front of it. I hated jelly. It was sticky and too sweet. I didn't like bread either, unless it was under peanut butter or brown gravy, but I took a lick of the jelly and a bite of the crust, my mouth puckered in distaste.

"Why don't you eat it? You asked for something to eat." I sat on the chair gulping back fear. I was afraid of Grandma.

"Speak up, girl, why won't you eat?"

"What's the matter, Ma?" My father walked through the kitchen on his way to the back sun porch where Grandpa was sitting, leaning close to the radio. "Something wrong?"

Bright and cheery, not a trouble on his mind, he smiled with affection at the oldest and youngest females in his family.

"I gave her bread and jelly and she won't eat it."

"Maybe she's not hungry." He leaned over me and said, "You'd better hurry and eat it or I'll swallow it before you get a chance." I looked at his big smiling mouth and picked up the bread and offered it to him. He laughed and took a big bite, enjoying the bread and the joke. "I guess she's not hungry, Ma."

My mother walked in just as Grandma was saying, "You spoil her, Walter. She should be made to eat what's put in front of her."

My mother frowned. "What's going on?"

"She wanted something to eat, and now she won't eat it."

"She doesn't like bread and jelly," my mother said. "I don't have peanut butter," Grandma complained. "Besides, she should eat what she's given. If she's hungry, she'll eat."

"She'd have to be starving to eat bread and jelly, and she's not starving yet." Mother was annoyed with us all, annoyed with me for not liking bread and jelly and for looking less than perfect in front of Grandma, annoyed at my father for smiling and sidling out to the sun porch, and annoyed at Grandma, who had always disapproved of her.

"It's good food. Maybe somebody who's not so fussy will be happy to have it." Grandma grunted. "If she was my child, she'd eat that or nothing." □

POEM-GRANDMA

When I was born
Grandma was too old
to make new friends
We were strangers
who sometimes met in the hall
Grandma believed
children should be grateful
and apologize when accused

Visiting Grandma was no pleasure
for a child who didn't like jelly bread

GOLDEN ANNIVERSARY

The morning of Grandpa and Grandma's golden wedding anniversary was sunny and bright. Grandpa wore a tuxedo, rented for the occasion. As always, his gold watch chain dangled across his stomach. Grandma's dark blue wedding dress was taken out of its trunk and carefully altered, the leg-of-mutton sleeves made smaller and the material from them used to let out seams. She carried flowers given to her by her children.

Mass was going to be said in Amityville, in the parish where Aunt Elvira taught school, and Elvira was given permission to play the organ at the celebration. Just before she started to play "Here Comes the Bride," my mother put a basket of flowers into my hands and gave me a gentle shove in the direction of the altar. "Remember, walk slowly. Now go." I started down the aisle, followed closely by my cousin, Chubby, the maid of honor. I could feel my new Mary Janes sliding on the linoleum floor, and I looked down in fascination at their shining blackness. Chubby leaned over and hissed, "Rosemary, look where you're going. Walk straight ahead!" Four years old and not used to performing, I looked up at her, surprised to see the sunshine pouring through the stained glass windows of the small church. A window was open, and there were pink blossoms on the tree outside. A bird sang, and a light breeze came in.

One of Arthur's girls, Margie, leaned into the aisle laughing, her arched eyebrows and deep blue eyes looking a little fierce. "Go straight ahead, silly," she whispered. "You'll fall down if you don't. And start throwing those flowers."

Chubby took my hand, and we walked the rest of the way down the aisle together as I scattered rose petals on the floor. Then we sat in a pew at the front of the church. I turned around, looking for my mother. When our eyes met, she frowned and glared and I looked quickly away. Uncle Arthur, the oldest son, had the honor of escorting his mother down the aisle to where Grandpa waited for his wife, a look of great pleasure on his face. The ceremony was short. The old people renewed their vows, taking each other again as man and wife. The granddaughters in their new dresses, purchased for the day, sat spread among the guests like colored flowers, thinking they would never get old like their grandparents, wouldn't want a golden wedding party, and certainly wouldn't wear a funny dress like Grandma's. I heard them talking about it later. Their wedding dresses would be white and they would wear veils and their grooms would be forever young.

Outside the church, as people came up to congratulate Grandpa and Grandma, the scene was cheerful and happy. Everyone milled around, greeting and kissing. I stayed with Chubby, letting her defend me from the criticism of my performance. Even Grandma had something to say about it. "I told you she was too young.

You should of let somebody else do it—Claire or Jean." Her crabbed voice showed her discontent with such lack of discipline in a grandchild. "What were you doing?" I couldn't answer, so Chubby did it for me. "Aw, it worked out all right, Grandma. She's just a little girl, you know. And she looks so pretty. I'm sure nobody noticed." I clung to her more tightly after that.

Poor Chubby found it hard to get away from me, even to go to the bathroom, and had to promise to come right back.

Everyone rode back to Hollis. Elvira, who at that time could only leave the convent once a year, was given special permission to go home for the party after Mass, though with instructions to be back by four o'clock. The house was decorated with ribbons and flowers. Wooden boards on trestles were set up in the basement. They were laden with food made by the daughters-in-law, and a special wedding cake with a bride and groom on top was bought at the bakery. One of the girls made a blue dress for the bride so it would look more like Grandma. I looked nervously at the small figure of Grandma perched on the cake, as if it might start scolding me. I was happy when the cake was cut and the miniature bride and groom went upstairs to be cleaned of icing and put away in a drawer as a souvenir. ☐

WHAT TO WEAR

Everything (sartorially speaking) has been so stirred together since the sixties that one can no longer look around and say, "That man is a lawyer," or "She's a housewife." Clothes are no longer badges for professions. We went to a picnic yesterday in a friend's backyard in Santa Monica. Most of the people were dressed motley casual because the host is a retired musician and his wife is an architect and painter. The ones who stood out were interesting to muse about. There was a tall, handsomely beautiful blonde woman who turned out to be a musician teaching at one of the state colleges. She wore a sexy white blouse with a ruffled V-neck collar and a black skirt. It was probably what she would wear playing in an orchestra, or it would have done for a saleswoman in 1950 in a very expensive Fifth Avenue dress shop, the kind of place where the women who work in the shop are more elegant than the customers. There was a ballet teacher, long-necked, hair in the obligatory bun at the farthest point up and in back of her head. She was out of keeping in a dusty rose denim jeans suit. She looked like a receptionist. There was a doctor—a general practitioner—who looked as if he'd been weeding in the garden. I wouldn't have known what he was if I hadn't heard him calling his service.

The funniest combination of man and clothes was a building contractor who I took to be a sculptor or a psychiatrist. He had on a turquoise shirt with a sailor collar, white duck pants, pottery jewelry on a string around his neck, and lots of curly hair on his chest and crinkling down from a part dead center on his head and reaching to his shoulders. He seemed to be strutting even when sitting or standing still. He had ruddy skin, befitting a contractor, and lots of muscles. Best of all, he had a handlebar mustache, and when he talked he lifted his head and stuck out his jaw as if in an effort to get the words past all that hair. Milt and I wore what we've always worn. Our uniforms don't seem to vary much from year to year. When new fads take over he doesn't notice, and I don't get around to them. □

WILL AND LEAH

So much has happened in these last years. Andy off to school in England, grown up and still very young for his age. I think he will be like Milt, who was almost but not quite an adult at thirty-three when I met him.

I want to write about so many things, the past, today, tomorrow... What shall I choose? I feel I must tackle the subject of Leah and Will, but that requires a grand digression on the subject of Leah and myself, which of course leads to the all-important one of mothers and sons, specifically, Jewish mothers and sons.

Leah was born in a Russian shtetl, Tschedrin, in about 1890 to a family of many brothers, sisters, aunts, uncles, and cousins. I never thought to ask at what point in her life she decided to marry Will, who was her first cousin, her mother's brother's son. My picture of Leah as a small child was of a little girl with iron determination to get her way in everything. When, early on, she came up against the shtetl fact of a girl's inferiority, she turned all her energy and drive to out-manipulating everyone she came up against.

She had a lot of problems. What the shtetl woman needed was cunning, persistence, and people to manipulate. Also, she was undoubtedly limited by, to use the current term, learning disabilities. I remember several things from the first night I met her: her deep tan and deeply wrinkled face, the hard speculative look as she inspected me, and the fact that she called her husband "Okun" as if he had no first name. Later I learned that she could never get the names of her husband and two sons straight, so Okun was the only name she was sure would be right, but she got everybody's name wrong. For years she called a friend of ours Shirley though her name was Charlotte. She called my son Michael, the name of her other grandson. Sometimes she called him Milton or Dan (Milt's brother), and I was always Beth, Dan's wife, who was often called Rosemary.

Whatever her shortcomings, she arrived in the new world at the age of eighteen determined to be on top, and the hell with the heads and hearts she crushed getting there. She tyrannized an entire retinue of cousins and siblings to the extent that I never heard one of them criticize her until the day we all went to see Will and her off on a trip to Europe. I was standing with everyone on the observation deck and as the plane wheels lifted, the rest of the company turned to each other like a football huddle and began to say things they wouldn't have dared to say had she still had her feet on U.S. soil.

We have pictures of Will and Leah, very young, and very much a couple. They loved each other. He loved her; he loved her all through their years together. And until five years ago, when her senility became unendurable, he wanted only to be with her. Then his own physical and emotional frailty became too much for him to overcome.

She alienated her son Dan. Milt loved her and never allowed himself to be bothered by anything she said or did. He became a model of apathy and silent sulks. He could deflect any situation that displeased him by turning a blank face and mind to it.

Leah was dreadful to Dan's wife, Beth. I don't know how she treated her during the courtship, but I heard that on the morning of the wedding, Leah closeted herself with Beth and informed her that since Dan was marrying beneath himself, Beth would have to make a supreme effort to raise herself to his level of excellence. She then proceeded to make herself obnoxious by constant inspections of closets, dresser drawers, garden shed, and desk, in fact, any place closed or hidden in their lives. She rearranged the refrigerator, criticized, carped, nagged, and manipulated, until they gave up all possibility of living in New York and moved to North Carolina, where they saw her for a few weeks at a time several times a year.

When I came along, I was everything Leah would have enjoyed in another woman and wanted for her son until I married him. At first she was pleased. I was intelligent. I was a dance teacher of sorts and an artist (of sorts), and had studied art at The Cooper Union. I was a mother of a charming four-year-old daughter.

One month after Milt and I came back from our honeymoon, I caught Leah in our bedroom rummaging through our dresser. I didn't ask her what she was doing, that was obvious, I just told her that she was not to go into our bedroom without permission, and that she was never to go through any drawers or closets. She became very angry and said she only wanted to see if Milt had enough underwear. I told her that I would take care of his clothes. And while we were at it, she was never to touch anything on the desk or go through any papers or letters that might be lying around. She got out of the room, furious and complaining, and she went directly to Milt to tell him how rude I had been. So I decided a direct approach was the only one that would work for me. I spoke to him in front of her and said no way was anyone going to have the freedom to open any drawer or door in my home without my permission, and I wasn't giving in.

All this followed the battle over the key. I knew Milt's parents had the key to his apartment before we were married. The day he moved his stuff over to mine (I had the larger of our two apartments) I told him he could not give the key to his parents. He looked panicky at first, then sullen, knowing exactly what kind of flak he would get about not letting them have the key to the apartment, if not to his entire life. For a week, Leah carried on, through Will, because when she couldn't get her way with Dan or Milt she always used Will for the job. They both loved him very much and found him harder to refuse. A refusal to her was usually closing their ears and eyes and leaving town mentally. To Will, they had to make excuses.

I heard the rumblings, but I refused to be budged, and soon I heard no more about the key. I'm afraid that for Milt the whole thing was an ordeal. He hadn't counted on having to face up to Leah at every step of the way, and in truth, he tried to avoid it whenever possible.

I could go on and on about the years of weekly visits from her, some of which were mildly awful and some truly awful. There was a whole year, when I was in a depression, when Leah must have called at least once a week to tell me I was terrible, that Beth didn't like me that no one ever heard of such rudeness as I was capable of showing to undeserving relatives. During that year she almost succeeded in separating Milt and me.

On the last leg of a trip around the world in the footsteps or musical echoes of Harry Belafonte, I cornered Milt several times, the most memorable of which was in a first-class compartment en route from The Hague to Calais to catch a ferry to England. There in the grim light of a ten-watt bulb, I forced him to listen to what he didn't want to hear: that his family was not one happy lump of singing flowers; that his brother hadn't spoken to his Aunt Rose for several years after he discovered she was a lesbian; that his sister-in-law Beth hated his mother and his mother hated Beth; that his aunts and uncles disliked his mother as much as I did; and that if on our return he didn't keep her out of my hair, I would not be able to live with him.

That was the end of her tyranny, if not actually a beginning of good behavior on her part. You can't expect a woman to change at the age of sixty-eight. By that time she is what she is. However, it was the beginning of Milt handling her and a real change in his life. It was just lucky for both of us that he wanted me as much as he did.

Leah never liked me. When Andy was born, she seldom bothered to pay attention to Jenny, who then became the girl in the family, and therefore nobody. She drove me crazy.

Once I thought I would have a stroke. I became convinced that the ghastly feeling of pressure in my head must surely presage some dreadful physical condition. Our family doctor, who also knew Leah, assured me that if I would yank the phone out of the wall and throw it across the room the next time she called, my head, would feel fine.

All this and much more, but I am no longer interested in it. At the age of eighty-eight, she moved in with us. If anyone thinks that age had dimmed her energy and dislike, they are wrong. Sometimes she forgot, in her senility, that she hated me, but not for long. For the first eight months she was with us, she was not on medication, and she drove us all mad. We were in a constant state of hysteria, and it wasn't just me. She had a pattern. Every four days or thereabouts she would get up in the morning and begin to push and test, to see how far she could go in being awful. There's no kinder way to describe it. By the end of twenty-four hours she would have pinched, squeezed, or tried to strike someone, usually one of the nurses or housekeepers. Then they would call me, and I would go over and yell at her, sometimes squeeze her arm very hard, if she was having a fit of fury. I had to constantly threaten to tell Milt what she was doing. It was the only thing that seemed to work.

Will finally broke down and so did I. One day she carried on so that I began to scream and at the same time hit a cast iron fence post that she was standing next to. I struck it over and over again, wishing it were her. When I got control of myself, I told Milt she had to go somewhere else. Living with her on the property was intolerable. At that time, she still looked much as she had for all the years I knew her, and to have the burden of her madness, which seemed no more than an exaggeration and extension of her lifelong temperament, and the care and feeding of her was more than I could bear.

When he heard she was going for a visit to Dan and Beth in Chapel Hill, Will begged me not to let her come back. He was terrified of her by this time. I promised him that she would be gone for two weeks at least. However, three days later Dan and Beth called and said they couldn't keep her. She cried all the time and wanted to go home. I begged them to keep her for two weeks until we could make some other arrangement for her but they wouldn't, so Dan showed up the next day, Leah in tow. We put her in an apartment with a nurse whom she tried to push out the window. That did it. Into the hospital for observation, eventually in a straitjacket until they found the right medication to calm her down... □

AGING

The household is finally settling down to a kind of routine. The nurses come and go on time and take excellent care of Will. Milt's cousin took Leah out for three hours this afternoon. The painters have finished for the time being. Now that the terrible work is over, I have stopped playing Martha and looked at poor Will and I am very unhappy. He is so sick and he looks at us with trust that we will do our best for him. But we don't know what to do. And we don't trust the doctors. To the G.P., he's just an old man, likely on his way out—give him a bunch of pills and don't bother me. But pay the bill on the way out. It's an assembly line with the doctor popping from one office to the next, looking at the body in front of him without caring about the heart and mind and soul of the man.

Oh, Will, we don't know what to do. No more than what you could do for your parents when they were old. Just sit and smile and try to pretend that we're sure, and the doctors are wise, and you'll live forever. □

REAL MEANING

Ten years ago today we were in Menthon-Saint-Bernard in the French Alps. We stayed first in the south of France at a friend's house near Avignon, but the heat was intolerable. The house was outside a small town in the middle of hills and fields of rotting hay and vegetation, and the flies, no bother to the locals, swarmed all over us, the furniture, the food, the floor, the doorsills, and the rest of southern France as far as we could make out. The sun was so intense that none of us could go out after nine o'clock in the morning. We sat in the house until seven at night, when we ventured out to buy more food for ourselves and the flies. It was several hundred years old, a beautiful two-story stone farmhouse with walls a foot and a half deep. It had running water, an inside toilet, and a primitive shower. There were a few pieces of antique French country furniture, enough to show the simplicity and beauty of the house. Nights in the quiet of a small village were wonderful. We slept with shutters open and the moon shining through deep windows.

It was there, outside Avignon, that I realized how far Americans are from living with the rest of creation. Insects obsess us. I have always lived in houses with screens. A fly calls for a fly swatter and mosquitoes must be crushed. In the face of screenless windows, we can only think in terms of attack, poison, and retreat. And that's what we did. Armed with fly swatters, we ran around the farmhouse smacking and swatting. Then we retreated to the Alps, to Menthon-Saint-Bernard, the town below the villa of the St. Bernard who sent his dogs out with kegs of spirits to rescue people lost on the snowy mountains...I still don't like flies but they don't bother me the way they used to. In some countries, no one pays much attention to them. It's easy enough to cover food, wipe up alluring messes, and look at how interesting and beautiful a fly really is.

When I sat down this morning I was going to write about something very important that I thought about on the way to my desk. Then I ended up writing about flies. I've forgotten what it was I wanted to say. Apparently I have put off thinking about real meanings for today and will take them up at another time. □

DAYS
July 21, 1978

Today is Leah's birthday. She is eighty-six. Tomorrow, Will will be eighty-five. It's a long life, but what do they have except today? And that's not really here either. Do they know they have it, and are they aware of it passing while they have it?

I wish I understood how other cultures understand time. I don't like our way of thinking about it. When I was a little girl I thought time past was in back of me and those days were like vertical cards that my mind could turn around and pick out at will. The past was shadowy and kind of wine red like a room full of furniture in an old house. Only the last few days were illuminated by the present. I thought that the year was a kind of ellipse with me going around it, always facing forward. The seasons and months were on the ellipse with summer a bright pale gold and the smell of honeysuckle and warm air, and autumn with a big harvest moon and Halloween and the smell of burning leaves. Winter was snow and Christmas, and spring was Easter, chocolate bunnies, and black Mary Janes.

I still think of the years that way, but there are so many of them and the signposts have changed. Summer is vacation for Andy and time to see Jenny, time to travel. Autumn in California means school and missing brisk colorful days of turning leaves. Winter and spring are measured by visits to and from friends. Days are no longer clearly before or behind me. I feel surrounded by them. They are spaces with no confining edges, filled with three-dimensional happenings to be examined at will.

If I close my eyes I am in the time I wish to be in. I can smell, taste, hear, and particularly see whatever I have experienced. But I have to want it. Think of all the humans in the world who carry around in their bodies all their time past as well as their time present. Think of all that consciousness at any moment, dissolving always into other moments. Think of the new births and new deaths, creating and destroying human time. □

OCTOBER

I'm all the thoughts
I've ever had
and all the souls of all
the flesh I've ever loved
and all the life I eat,
the people I think
the colors I dream
I am the dream
dreamt and dreaming

OCTOBER DREAM

I loved seeing white smoke coming from a pile of leaves when a match was lit and a fire first took light. There was crackling as the leaves snapped and flames grew, then standing back to get away from the heat, then red embers pulsing and glowing until the fire died down, then sadness when everything was burned and the fire was out, until a few days later when enough leaves had fallen to make another fire.

If I saw people raking leaves I would offer to help if they were friends, or wait till the fire was lit before I went closer. One day, my mother and Aunt Frances, our next-door neighbor, were out raking leaves. They were both fat, and fat women in the thirties wore corsets with hooks and laces and fifteen-inch stays that made strenuous work like raking leaves difficult. Mother and Aunt Frances were laughing and gossiping, panting, collecting a huge pile of leaves to be burned, while Mary and I danced around pretending to help, waiting for the moment when the match would start the first leaf on fire.

I think it may have been the first time I was hypnotized. It's certainly the first time that I remember. There was all the excitement of lighting the fire, warnings to stay far away from it, and helping to bring small piles of leaves from in front of other houses, to be added every few minutes to keep the fire burning for as long as possible.

When my mother went into the house, leaving Aunt Frances to supervise, I drew closer and stared into the fire where shifting embers made patterns of hot beauty. Fragments drifted into the air. I saw myself in the fire, in the embers. I was in a compartment on the big Ferris wheel at Coney Island with my father and my sister, looking into the crowd below. I saw my mother with some friends. Her brown hair was curled and waved for the day's outing, and her skin looked warm in the lights of the fairway. She was at a green painted booth where a coarse man with a cold smiling face sold tickets to the rides. People were eating hot dogs and milling about in the noisy crush. Mother and her friends were laughing and talking, and she looked pretty in a printed blue-and-white dress. I called down to her but she didn't hear me.

When the last embers died, I told Aunt Frances what I'd seen, and she said, "You couldn't have seen anything like that, Rosemary." Then I went in and told my mother, and she said, "It's easy to imagine seeing things in a fire, but if I were there when you called, I would have looked up and waved to you." □

FIRE

I was fascinated by fire. From the autumn fire in which I had seen my mother to the gas stove, I loved to look at flames. There were fires at picnics, where steaks and hamburgers were grilled and potatoes charred black with moist white insides. And a visit to the Pastors, who had a fireplace in their living room where they roasted chestnuts and marshmallows and sat, watching logs turn to ashes, was a special winter occasion.

In a pinch there were always matches. I made small fires in the kitchen sink. It started one day with a match from a book left on the kitchen table. The next day I used all the matches I could find, carefully placing them in a glass ashtray in the sink. I loved the smell of the sulfur. I lit a match, blew it out quickly, then held it under my nose and sniffed the delicious odor. Then I lit the next and then the next. After a while, matches weren't enough, so I began burning bits of paper in the ashtray. Some days the flames reached halfway to the faucet.

I knew it was a terrible thing to do, but it gave me so much pleasure. Occasionally, my mother would enter the house after one of my pyromaniac bouts, sniff the air, and ask, "What is that I smell? Do you smell anything?" I tried to look as blank as possible and walked to another room admitting nothing, and Mother never discovered my secret. No one found evidence of my kitchen bonfires because I threw the ashes in the garbage pail under pieces of wet toast and ragged orange peels.

My love of fire next led me to smoking, along with Mary, Junior Heiss, and Neil Fisher. We were sitting at Junior's house trying to think of something to do, and true to form, the devil presented us with a splendid idea. Why not smoke a cigarette? So Junior stole one from his brother, Russell. Neil, the oldest and boldest, lit the cigarette, claiming he'd already smoked two whole ones. Then he passed it to Mary, who was the next bravest. When it got to me, I was frightened, but I put my lips to the cigarette and blew out and everyone laughed. Junior tried it, and coughed mightily when he accidentally inhaled.

Trial smoking was a big success, so three days later we decided to have another go at it. Junior went back into Russell's room and this time came out with two cigarettes. We were very careful not to let any of the smoke go down our throats. Then we decided that Junior's mother might walk in and smell the smoke, so we took the cigarettes to the barn in the backyard, which had long ago been converted into a garage. We climbed the wooden stairs to the loft above, where we often played. It was cluttered with faded, overstuffed chairs, old ice skates, sleds, brooms, books, and a tattered couch. The only thing we needed to complete the scene was an ashtray, which we filched the next day along with a whole pack of Russell's cigarettes. By now we each smoked our own, feeling very grown up as we lit the matches and waved them out, then dropped them into the ashtray. It was so sinful. There was plenty of smirking and coughing as we imagined what our parents would say if they caught us. The thought brought nervous smiles to our faces, but no curious adults ever came into the barn.

We sat smoking happily, averaging two a day. Once, by accident, I inhaled. I felt the smoke go down my lungs and stay there, then come streaming miraculously out of my important nostrils. My eyes crossed as I watched the smoke in front of my face. I repeated the feat for the others to admire. I was the youngest, and I never won at Monopoly or Tripoli. I was a disaster at Socco, a game that required rapid movements and excellent coordination. But my inhaling was superb.

Soon we were all inhaling and stubbing out butts, and each day Junior buried the evidence in the yard. Meanwhile, Russell was beginning to wonder why the four of us burst into gales of laughter every time we saw him. Then he noticed the missing cigarettes and asked his mother in front of us if she knew why his cigarettes were disappearing. "I don't know," she said, smiling. "I don't smoke. Do you think Kenny's smoking them?" Her face wrinkled at this disturbing thought. Kenny was the middle son, a disturbed secretive boy of sixteen who spoke only to his family and was no longer in school because of his strange behavior. He locked himself in his room, its walls covered floor to ceiling with magazine pictures of airplanes, boats, and movie stars.

One day we all agreed that the loft would be a great location for a fireplace. There were some bricks left over from building the back porch, so we made a fireplace in the corner and lit a fire with pieces of paper. The fires got bigger every day, until finally the boards under the bricks ignited. As we watched the flames creep slowly across the floor, Russell's head appeared above the stairwell. His face contorted with fear, aghast at the spreading flames, he shouted, "What are you doing?" and ran to the fire, stamping and shouting until it was out. "Get some water right away!"

That's when he saw the ashtray. "So that's where my cigarettes have gone!" He grabbed Junior and Neil and pushed them toward the stairs. "Get that water, and then get out of here, and don't ever let me catch you kids in this barn again. Don't you know there's a gasoline truck parked downstairs? You could have caused an explosion! What's the matter with you? You kids are really going to get it!"

We rushed down the stairs. Junior went into his house and Neil ran to his, while Mary and I climbed over the fence to her yard. Hearts pounding, we ran past the old sandbox, the iris beds, the dog's dish on the cement steps, and into the house. We sat down at the kitchen table, and Mary held her cheeks in her hands. "My mother won't spank me, but she's going to be very angry. Maybe she won't let me out again."

"When my mother and father find out about this, I'm really going to get into trouble. What do we do?"

"Let's not say anything about it to anybody."

I was quiet that night. Mother took my temperature. "You must be sick," she said. I sat staring into a corner, waiting to be found out.

The next day I called for Mary and we leaned over the fence to talk to Junior. "Russell told my mother, but she didn't tell my father yet." He laughed. His mother was lenient with him, and he was sure his father wouldn't find out. Mrs. Heiss still hadn't told Mary's mother, who would be the one to tell my parents. Then we heard the phone ring in the Litchhult house, certain it was the fatal call, and ran in the other direction.

At five o'clock, Mary went home, unable to postpone her doom. I spent the next hour two streets away pacing back and forth. When it was almost dinnertime, I started toward home. Halfway there, I turned around and went to stand in front of Henry's Ice Cream Parlour, looking in at the people seated at the counter eating ice cream. I felt the nickel in my pocket that my father had given me, and went in for an ice cream pop, then stood outside to eat it. I wiped the chocolate off my mouth and went across Jamaica Avenue and sat in the square.

The sun was beginning to set when I saw my father coming toward me. Even in the distance I could tell that he was smiling. He didn't seem to be mad at all. "Didn't you see me?" he asked, putting his hands out. "C'mon, dinner's ready. It's six-thirty."

"I didn't know that."

"What's the matter?"

"Nothing."

He took my hand, and we walked home, talking about nothing in particular. If my parents knew, they didn't say. I gave up smoking. I even gave up lighting small fires in the house. And I stayed as far away from gasoline trucks as possible. I didn't expect to get off so easy next time. Luck was with me, and I knew when to stop.□

IMPERFECTION

I was just taking a shower and thinking about the tiles in my bathroom. They're pretty and perky and not at all what I would choose if I had a choice. The colors are cheerful and the design is somewhat like tulips on cherry stems. Someone else, probably a decorator, chose them for the previous owners of the house. I'm enjoying the result.

It's good to live in a house that someone else has designed because while it may have been perfect for him or her, it's never perfect for you. Perfection is difficult to live with. When an architect designs a house for himself, he has a concept of perfection. He executes it to his satisfaction and then lives in it. If it's modern and functional, nothing can be out of place or it's a mess. Furniture is designed to fit certain spaces. Pots and pans hang in special directions or not at all. Beds fit into niches. Then he sells the house and the next person who comes along hangs towels where the pots were, sticks plants in the niches, and puts the baby's playpen where the couch used to be. Suddenly, a concept becomes a home where people live and do the wrong things, messy things, imperfect things.

We built a house in Connecticut a few years ago. Visitors said it was marvelous. The materials and workmanship were excellent. I made sure it was perfect. It was furnished from scratch in a most efficient way. Milt and Andy and I could clean the place in an hour on a Saturday morning, and daily work took half an hour, except for cooking and dishes. But it was boring. Everything was too comfortably simple, too beautiful. And it was all my doing. I didn't understand until we bought this house what was wrong with that one. There is a danger in household design when the designer has no limitations, when there's no one to insist on something that doesn't look good in a corner, like an overstuffed couch, or a picture window that spoils the balance of a wall.

The house we're in now has some oddball things in it. For instance, there's a lunatic soda fountain in one room that must have cost a fortune and only holds two quarts of ice cream. Milt uses that room for his stereo equipment so the soda fountain is covered with records and tapes and the freezer is turned off. His office has some leftover red and blue plaid carpet that he's very happy with, though neither of us would have dreamt of putting it in ourselves. In the living room there's an ugly stone fireplace that I really don't like but choose to see as the equivalent of the mistake that's woven into a Persian carpet to keep the weaver from creating something perfect, which is not a function of man.□

INSPIRATION

My aim in writing this journal was to sit down at the typewriter and put on paper whatever I was thinking at that moment. Sometimes I had an idea while I was doing something else and managed to retain it until I was ready to type, but usually what I wrote was on the spur of the moment. I seldom edited because I did not want the writing to become too self-conscious. I wanted these pages to sound like letters written to friends.

I was surprised when on my fiftieth birthday I wrote a mini-autobiography, reviewing my life to that day, discovering that I had more of a sense of objectivity about my life and a tolerance for my failings than I had suspected, and more pleasure at being alive.

My family included a bank president, a milkman, farmers, schoolteachers, policemen, a convicted petty thief, and the mandatory uncle who spent most of his life in a mental institution. One side of the family was practical and musical and the other was romantic and painted on china. As I read my journal, I see glimpses of them all—my cranky Uncle Gus growling, Nana was worrying, Uncle Ed being practical. My mother and father often speak through me, saying things I don't always want to say, and the child that I was is always somewhere in the pages wringing her hands because life isn't what it should be and is so much better than she expected. □

HERSHEY'S KISSES

My mother was only three when her mother died, and she was sent to live with her grandmother and her three unmarried aunts. The middle sister, Anastasia, called Nana by us kids, was the bossiest of the aunts, and she was the one who acted most like a mother to my mother when she was growing up. After my brother and sister and I were born, Nana was the only one of the aunts who held our hands crossing the street or worried about our cuts and bruises. She was the only aunt who held me on her lap, even though she may have done it just to get a good grip on me so she could deliver a sermon. "Ya know, Rosemary, Gawd doesn't like little girls who tell fibs." Nana was religious, and when she said "God," it always sounded as if she was trying to avoid saying the word, but couldn't find a suitable substitution.

We received many gifts from our aunts, but they were always chosen by Nana. She often appeared at the house with a present when it wasn't even Christmas or a birthday. Of course, she never gave a present without informing us of other children who weren't getting a gift at that moment. "Ya know, Rosemary, you're very lucky to be getting a pair of new socks. Not all little girls are as lucky as you are."

Sometimes she would take us six blocks away to the best soda parlor in town to buy us a treat. "How would you children like to go up to Meyer's for an ice cream cone? Go wash your hands and comb your hair. Meyer's doesn't want anyone who looks like a vagrant in the shop." So Jean and I washed our hands and combed our hair and walked, silent and proper, one on each side of Nana, along Jamaica Avenue to Meyer's.

When Nana bought us ice cream cones, we had to sit and eat them in the store. "Ya know, it's not polite for girls to walk in the street eating food." She drank tea with sugar and milk, while we sat licking the cones, making them last as long as we could. After I swallowed the bottom part of the cone, where it was filled with the last melted ice cream, I'd ask, "Nana, please, can we have some Hershey's Kisses?" I started planning to ask for them even before we left the house, hoping just the right pleading tone would make her give in.

Hershey's Kisses were Nana's favorite. She never bought any other candy, unless she had a sore throat and needed some Smith Brothers licorice cough drops. Any pleasure too delightful might be a sin. But how could eating a morsel of milk chocolate that could be taken from its pristine silver wrapping and popped into a mouth without soiling one's fingers be sinful? Eaten in moderation, "Gawd would understand."

"Maybe just two," she'd say, and hand the girl enough money to pay the check and cover the chocolate candy, two for each of us, including her. Maybe she'd wanted chocolate all along and that's why she invited us to go for a cone. She knew I'd ask, and that would give her an excuse to buy some.

The week before Christmas, the year I was five, Jean and I asked Nana what she was going to give us for Christmas, and she sat us down on the uncomfortable leather couch in her upstairs sitting room and told us the story of "The Little Match Girl."

"On Christmas day," Nana said, "there was a little match girl, don'cha know, who had no mother and no father and no brothers or sisters and no place to live." Nana shook her head to show that the little girl was alone with nobody to love her, and she had no one to give her presents. "Her clothes were torn and ragged, and her feet were bare, because she had no shoes and stockings to keep her warm. Nobody bought her matches that day, so she had no money to buy food. On Christmas night she walked through the streets looking in the windows at Christmas trees and people singing carols and eating dinner, and she wished that she could live in a nice warm house and eat turkey and plum pudding."

I felt how awful it was to be all alone, out in the dark, without a mother and father, and I was glad I wasn't the little match girl. "She was so tired," Nana went on, "that she fell asleep in the snow and a kind lady came along and carried her home, but it was too late. The little match girl was dead." Nana's voice was slow and solemn, and then it picked up. "It was all right though, don'cha know, because Gawd looked down and felt sorry for her, and took her up to Heaven to be with Baby Jesus and the angels, and she was never cold or hungry again."

When Nana finished the story, she pinched her lips together and turned her chin to one side to make the point that the little match girl didn't expect any presents, and didn't get any either, until she got her reward in Heaven. What was good enough for the little match girl should be good enough for Nana's nieces.

She didn't foresee the effect the story would have on us. Jean felt she was like the little match girl, missing all the fun, and I decided when I grew up I'd adopt orphans and give them chocolate candy. Because, while Nana was telling the sad story of the Little Match Girl and forgetting to count, we were dipping into the bag of Hershey's Kisses she had pulled out of her purse, the better to ease the pain. □

UNCLE GUS

My father's second oldest brother was Gus, named after Grandpa. Uncle Gus was a traffic policeman until he was hit by a car in his twenties and suffered an injury to his head that caused epilepsy and terrible headaches. For years doctors tried to give him some relief, but nothing helped. After the accident he was given a desk job by the New York City Police Department working as a clerk in supplies. He and my father were very close when they were young, and we always heard how much fun he was before the accident, loving to laugh and sing with the rest of the family. After the accident, he changed. He was awful. His sarcasm was a frightful thing, and since he pretended to smile while delivering his sallies, it was hard to stop him. I never stayed in the same room with him after I was old enough to catch his attention. I was too young to understand the severity of his problems and hated him. He married three times, outlived the first wife, divorced the second, and in turn was outlived by the third.

Gus wasn't just a difficult man. He was gross to look at, with bushy black brows and heavy-lidded dark eyes that watched with mean pleasure to see if his sarcasm hit home. He had long jowls and a thick lower lip that did more sneering than smiling. He was married to a quiet, frightened, dark-haired little woman named Jenny, and had a son, Little Gus, who looked like the son of an ugly man and a frightened woman.

Uncle Gus was my sister Jean's godfather, and she used to visit him and Aunt Jenny and Little Gus on Staten Island. One time Jean came back after a visit and told my parents that when Uncle Gus and Little Gus dried the dishes after dinner, they took turns throwing the sharp knives into the wall. That was the last time she ever went there. When Dad tried to speak to his brother about it, all Uncle Gus said was, "What are you so upset about? We were just fooling around." Mother had plenty to say. "I don't care if he's her godfather, she can't go back there. And I don't care what your mother says. It's dangerous." My mother disliked Uncle Gus, but she felt sorry for him. She remembered him as a young man and believed he couldn't help what he was.

Aunt Jenny had been dead for about a year when Uncle Gus began wooing a second wife. Martha was an attractive brunette and a Protestant divorcée, a fact that the family tried hard to hide from everyone they knew. Grandma and the aunts thought Martha married Gus for his disability pension, and they resented her for it. After Momma got to know her, she realized that Martha was too good for Gus. Martha was a secretary. She was independent, she was pleasant, and she was fun to be with.

I liked Martha. She tried to make me understand that Uncle Gus didn't mean to be cruel and harsh, that he didn't understand how he hurt people. By the time I was eight I would hide in my room when he came to our house. When I was nine I left the house and stayed about three blocks away when it was time for him to arrive. My father found me and explained that Uncle Gus couldn't help being the way he was, but I didn't believe it and refused to go home until Dad promised he wouldn't let him tease me. The moment we opened the door the teasing started. "I hear you don't like me to tease you. Can't you take a joke? Look at her, she's beginning to cry. What's that all about, crybaby?"

Dad said, "Please, Gussie, don't. She's really upset. I promised you wouldn't."

That was as much as I heard as I ran across the room and up the stairs to my bedroom. Martha came upstairs and tried to make up to me, and said Uncle Gus had promised her he wouldn't say any more. I don't remember what happened after that, but I suppose I gave in and went down. I know I didn't look at his face again that day.

After a year Martha must have begun to think he was impossible too, because she left him and he was forced to divorce her on grounds of desertion. She explained to those members of the family who still spoke to her that he had become intolerable. His temper was unbearable. She needed some sunshine in her life that Uncle Gus couldn't provide.

A year later Uncle Gus married a middle-aged blonde named Helen, a refugee (though from which country was never discussed) with a timid voice and a heavy accent. This time the family was horrified. They thought that after Martha left him, he'd give up on marriage. Not only was she a divorcee who wasn't a Catholic, but he was now divorced himself, a fact that appeared in a local paper, much to their dismay. And now he was married again, to a woman of uncertain origins. If she was a Jew, no one ever said so. Helen had appeared in 1939 with a little money and a suitcase in her hand. She got a job as a seamstress, a menial job in the estimation of the family, a step downward on the American ladder. Helen was a quiet, unimpressive woman, never presuming to know as much or more than anyone in the family. She seemed not to know that they looked down on her, despised her accent, or if she knew, she kept it to herself and remained cool and calm in their presence. She brought small gifts to Jean and me, a bit of candy, a slip, a lace handkerchief. "I never had children of my own," she told my mother, "and I hope the children will enjoy these things. It's a pleasure to give them something."

No one was very kind to her. When she wasn't around, the kids made fun of her and her different ways. The adults decided that Uncle Gus had been caught again by a conniving woman interested only in his pension. He treated her like a servant, and he never respected and admired her as he had Martha. She wasn't beautiful or independent. She needed him. She must have felt that life with Gus would be less terrible than the fate that might have befallen her in Europe.

It wasn't long before the family began to appreciate the fact that whatever it was she married him for, he married her because he needed her desperately. His headaches were becoming intolerable and more frequent, and there was no medicine that could relieve the pain. Helen took care of him during these dreadful sieges and endured his wicked tongue. She catered to his whims and tried to make him comfortable. She saw to it that he did what the doctor told him to do, even though it didn't do much good. Gradually, as Gus's condition worsened, they found he had cancer, and she became his full-time nurse, never leaving his bedside, constantly caring for him.

When Uncle Gus died in 1943, his life insurance was paid to Helen. Uncle Ed and Aunt Edith resented that the money went to Helen, and felt that Grandpa, now eighty-three and living with them, should have received the money. My mother and father said no measly insurance policy could make up for the care Helen gave Uncle Gus. "They were married for five years," Momma said. "Think of the hell it must have been for her. And who else would take care of him? Not Edith. Not Annie. Not me. They should be glad there was someone to do for him."

After he died, Helen sold their home and used Uncle Gus's pension and insurance benefits to buy a small house in the Adirondacks, which she shared with a sister who had come to America with her. Momma said, "I hope she enjoys her widowhood. She deserves some happiness. Europe must have been pretty bad if someone like Gus looked like a good catch."

A few weeks after Uncle Gus died; my parents opened the boxes that he and Helen had stored in our basement when my uncle got sick. She said they were full of stuff that Uncle Gus had saved, and Dad should do whatever he wanted with it. But instead of the pots and blankets they expected to see, Uncle Gus had ten cartons of pencils, paper, and manila envelopes all marked PROPERTY OF THE NEW YORK CITY POLICE DEPARTMENT—that, and two hundred and fifty cans of Spam in unmarked cases.

The Spam was the zinger. Dad didn't mind if his friend Joe Wagner, the butcher, slipped us a steak or an extra pound of butter without ration coupons once in a while, but hoarding food during wartime ranked close to treason in his opinion. And two hundred and fifty cans of Spam could last a family of four a year, providing they could get it down.

Dad was irresponsible about paying bills on time or mailing letters, but stealing was not one of his failings. So Dad and Uncle Arthur took the office supplies back to the Police Department, only to be told that everybody knew my uncle had been taking things; they just chalked it up to his being Gus. I don't know what happened to the Spam. We ate two cans of it under duress, and I have the feeling the rest was donated to some institution that promised not to reveal the source. □

UNCLE WILLIE

I was twenty when Uncle Willie died. The church bell tolled for him when the hearse, followed by a single limousine, stopped at the church and Dad helped Aunt Mamie and Mother out of the limousine and up the steps for the eight o'clock Mass. It was appropriate that the February snow on the ground looked gray and mottled, and the sky dark, full of snow ready to blanket the scene again. There was no open car with flowers because there were no flowers, and there had been no wake. Aunt Mamie wouldn't let us tell anyone about her Brother Willie's death. She never spoke of him, and now that her sisters Anna and Julie were dead, only a few people knew about him. The church steps were empty, with no hushed funeral bustle of seldom-seen relatives. Inside, there were only strangers dressed in everyday clothes—people who went to eight o'clock Mass every morning. Housewives with no children and nothing better to do. Old men and women, hoping that habit would stand them in good stead and leave them in a state of grace when their turn came. People passing by looked with curiosity at Aunt Mamie as my father helped her up the steps. Her face was hidden beneath the black hat with the mourning veil that she wore to funerals. Uncle Ed and Aunt Edith, dressed in black and looking suitably glum, sat in the second pew. They lived three blocks from the church, and since Uncle Ed could be trusted not to say more than, "Better this way," Aunt Mamie had permitted Mother to tell him and Aunt Edith about the funeral.

Jean and I followed the small procession down the center aisle. I had listened to the bells toll for other relatives; watched pallbearers walk toward altars with coffins; tried to imagine the people inside, but death didn't have much meaning for me. What my mind told me, my heart refused to acknowledge. Going into the pew, my arm brushed against my mother's sleeve, and I took her hand and thought, maybe she loved Uncle Willie. She knew him when she was little. Maybe he played with her like an older brother, before he went crazy and had to be put in an asylum.

I looked at the coffin and tried to see the young seminarian falling from a horse and hurting his head. I was told he was locked up because he had epilepsy from the fall, but I didn't believe that was all that was wrong with him. He was probably strange to start with and just got worse as the years went on, standing on street corners haranguing people about God and Hell. My mother told me that his sermons were gentle at first, but if people laughed, he turned violent, and threatened them with hellfire. When he tried to inflict the punishment himself, the police would bring him back to his three respectable sisters, who promised to keep him at home. But they were no match for his mission, and when he continued to go back to the old neighborhood to preach, they had to have him committed.

My mother and father were glad it was over for Willie. Forty years locked in an asylum was a terrible fate. What Aunt Mamie thought of the man in the coffin, no one knew. If she had dreaded going to see him, she never said so in my presence, and she and her sisters had visited him, the way they did everything else, quietly and consistently. For years no one had been able to communicate with him, and he never gave an indication that he knew any of them. At first Uncle Willie was in a private sanitarium on Long Island paid for by his three sisters. After the oldest sister Mamie had a serious heart attack and the youngest sister Julie died, the sanitarium was too expensive for Anna to pay for by herself, so Willie was transferred to Creedmoor, the local state asylum. When he was still in the sanitarium, my sister Jean was sometimes sent with whichever sister was visiting Willie. Jean said that in those days Uncle Willie read the newspaper every day and would tell them to the year, month, day, and hour how long he had been locked up. One day, while he and Jean were taking a walk around the grounds, he had an epileptic seizure. She had been told he might and that she should put something in his mouth to keep him from biting his tongue, but there was nothing available, so she stood and screamed as loud as she could until someone came to help.

 I only visited Uncle Willy once, one awful day when I was sixteen and my parents said I should go with them to Creedmoor. It was the day after a big storm in February, and snow was piled high along the entry drive. The sunlight at midday erased shadows on the snow and made the oblong brick buildings look cheerful. There were patients dressed in what looked like pajamas, their legs and arms hanging through floor to ceiling bars on the balconies of a three-story building. Some waved to the cars as they passed. It could have been a nursery with grownups in playpens hanging from the side of the building. We were shown into a lounge filled with patients and visitors, and there at a table, hands in his lap, sat Uncle Willie.

 Dad reached out to him. "Hi, Willie, how are you?"

 Uncle Willie didn't look up. We sat down at the table with him. The attendant prodded him lightly on the shoulder and said, "Hey, it's your family. Don't you want to say hello?" He shook Willie's shoulder a little harder. "Come on now, pal. They came all the way to see you." We lived ten minutes away from Creedmoor, but I'm sure neither Uncle Willie nor the attendant knew that.

Dad offered Uncle Willie a cigarette, saying, "Have one, Willie. You used to like this brand." The old man looked at Dad, something in his eyes, but didn't take the cigarette. My father was gentle with him, filling him in on the latest gossip. It wasn't possible to know how much he comprehended. His face—Mother's, Aunt Mamie's, and Uncle Billy's face—sat there on his shoulders, scarred by time, but unruffled by the moment. Mother leaned toward him and spoke in a kind but firm tone, "Willie, it's me, Rosemary. We didn't bring Anna this time, because she's not well and the doctor said she shouldn't come out in the cold."

"Come on, Willie, say something." The attendant looked at us apologetically over his silent charge. "Sorry. He hardly ever talks." He shrugged his shoulders. "Once in a while, he says something." Uncle Willie's watery blue eyes shifted momentarily to Mother. Did he know her? Was she anything more than an interruption in his day, like eating or washing, one more thing that had to be put up with? His eyes focused again on the table where he had been staring through most of the visit.

The attendant saw my mother frown when she noticed Willie's hair, flaked and matted with dandruff. "He won't let anyone near him to comb or wash it. It was all I could do to get a clean shirt on him today. I told him you were coming, but believe me, it wasn't easy." I wondered if the attendant tried to comb it when there were no visitors. I wondered why he stayed so close to Willie the whole hour we were there. The explanation that Willie sometimes got more excited than was good for him didn't ring true, given his apathy, and when Dad pressed ten dollars into the man's hand before leaving, the answer seemed obvious.

I turned at the door as we were leaving and saw a sunlit room filled with people, and it was hard to know who were the saddest, the ones who could leave or the ones like Uncle Willie, sitting silent and staring.

And there in the church, for a moment, I understood. It really was Uncle Willie in the coffin. That tired, resigned old man, flakes probably still in his hair. I'd only met him once, knew him for one hour of one day, had hated the meeting and wanted to run from it. And this was what death really was. A few people who cared. A few more who cared about them. And the others.

Poor Willie, sixty-eight when he died, more acceptable in his coffin than out. He spent forty years in asylums, silent, unkempt, unmourned during his lifetime, except by a few people. Hidden by his three sisters, visited by his niece and her family out of duty, and passed off by the rest of the family and by the people who took care of him as crazy, someone to forget about.

Father Kenny said the grim Mass for Willie. He anointed the coffin and said that there could be no doubt that William Godsil was in Heaven. God would reward him for a life of pain. I was still a Catholic and thought it might almost be worth being insane if you could abdicate responsibility for your actions. Sins wouldn't be sins if you couldn't reason. But I wasn't sure Uncle Willie would have taken Heaven over forty years of freedom if he'd had a choice.

The hired pallbearers lifted the coffin and we followed them out of the church. I wanted to shout at the people sitting in the pews, "Don't stare. I didn't love him, but he was Aunt Mamie's brother, so don't intrude." Dad and Uncle Ed followed the hearse to the cemetery. The limousine drove Mother and Aunt Mamie home. And I went to work with the long dread sound of bells tolling in me. □

Journal
1979
Alpine Drive, Beverly Hills

After a day without seeing Leah, I was able to go to the hospital, if not with good will, at least without being angry. They have increased her dosage of Haldol, an antidepressant, and the effect has been to make her agreeable about everything in the hospital—the food, the decorations, the nurses. She is quite placid, and there is almost a hope that if they can continue the dosage at today's level, she may be able to get along in a regular nursing home instead of requiring a mental hospital.

Milt is distraught. He has been seeing her several times a day since Dan brought her back from North Carolina. I am becoming more resentful against Dan for not sharing the misery with Milt and not helping out in this ghastly business of finding a place for her. I think she knows she is not coming back here again but I don't think she is thinking about where she will go. She doesn't even want to come back here. I think the place she longs for is Tschedrin in Russia where she was born. She has begun to write the names of her family in Yiddish, which she says she hardly knows, and she speaks often of her mother, who she says is very beautiful.

I cannot help Milt bear this because I don't know how to myself. □

ANDY

One day when Andy was six months old, he was sitting in his high chair and I was feeding him, applesauce as I recall. I was making all the usual fuss, wiping his chin, cooing before and after each mouthful, scraping the bowl to get heaping spoonfuls. As I put the spoon to his lips for the last time and he opened his mouth wide to take it, he was looking directly into my eyes and I had a thought that hit me so hard it made everything else fall away.

"This is what it's all about." All the years of running and studying, dancing, drawing, shopping, working, and even playing, only added up to one thing: that I would be there to feed the baby. So I could put food into his mouth so he could grow up and do the same thing.

Right then and there, I stopped feeling guilty about having children in a world that I thought was disgusting. All along I had been thinking that I had children because I needed them to make life endurable. It's true they have made it endurable and often pleasurable. But I know that no matter what I thought my motives were, there are things you just can't argue with. □

CRUTCHES

I'm lying in bed stewing, disgusted with myself for drinking so much wine tonight. I had more than my usual two glasses. Because it was there. Because the cardiologist to my left was a wine connoisseur. Because when there's that much wine floating around the table, I drink whatever gets into my glass.

My tongue feels dreadful and my face feels flushed and I am disgusted with myself. I will never lose weight this way and I want very much to. I also don't want to drink that much alcohol at one sitting. I wish I was like Milt and felt so comfortable that I could just relax and enjoy being out with other people without needing that crutch.

Maybe the wine will be the next batch of calories that I will let go of and that will be a way of giving it up. I don't miss coffee at all now that a decision has been made. Thank god that's off my back.

The big tree is gone out of the backyard. Poor yard looks bare and boring without it. It was really a deformed ancient thing and I felt very guilty about cutting it down. Last year I began to be nervous about it in all that rain... □

ALCOHOL

Growing up in a neighborhood of small one-and two- family houses with no more than eight feet between most of them, children learned a lot about the rougher facts of life. On summer days before air-conditioning, when windows were left open twenty-four hours a day, we heard conversations we weren't meant to hear. We heard people crying, heard women in torment giving birth, and heard domestic strife that ranged from bickering to violence. We saw houses with black wreaths on front doors when people died, and saw families driven by poverty to less comfortable places.

But the real scourge of our neighborhood was alcohol. There were the Friday night furies let loose when some man showed up having spent most or all of his pay at some corner saloon and his wife knew the family would be hungry the next week. Some men came home furious from the drink and went after anyone who got in the way. Some sang on the way home, disturbing the neighbors at two in the morning with unseemly gaiety, and seldom taking a hint from the chorus of "shut ups" and "pipe downs" that followed their progress down the street. We all knew which men might come lurching home drunk and how to steer clear of them, and which houses not to go into when the fathers were there.

My father drank moderately, but not from a need to be righteous. I don't think he needed much alcohol to enjoy himself socially. He didn't keep wine or spirits in the house because it never occurred to him to drink at home. There were neighborhood bars and a couple of beers with friends to pass time away in the evenings. But there were several exceptions to this moderate style of living that drove my mother crazy.

There were Christmas Eves when he went out to celebrate with the people from the dairy and came home cheery and bleary, to be met by my mother's anger. She came from a long line of women who detested alcohol, having seen it wreak havoc among various cousins, uncles, and brothers and to see my father drunk made her vitriolic toward him.

Every New Year's Eve there was a formal party at the American Legion, where the drinking was legendary, and being the man of excess that he was, my father kept up with the crowd and always came home happy, singing, wanting to wake us kids up to share his good cheer.

If my parents had a party at our house, my father let himself go. Maybe he thought a host should keep up with the guests, and some of them were never without a drink in hand. One night at the end of one of these parties, the bright overhead light switched on in my room and awakened me. I saw my father and two of his friends looking in at the doorway. He was saying thickly, "Look a' that. That's my little girl. My little Mickey Mouse." He lurched into the room swaying and I drew back against the wall, my hands clenched on the blankets.

There was laughter and music downstairs. Voices were raised, too noisy, too loud, too happy going up and down the stairs, back and forth from one room to the other, getting coats off the bed in my parents room, saying goodbye. The confusion was loud and it frightened me.

My father's friend, Joe Lamb, tugged at his arm and said, "Come on Walter, you're frightening her. We know she's your little girl. Let's go downstairs. You need some coffee."

Dad leaned over the bed to give me a kiss and I sat rigid, my fear evident to the other men. "My lil girl's not afrai' a me." He smiled his face loose and foolish, red from all he'd had to drink. "Goo'ni', don't let the bedbugs bi'."

They pulled him out of the room laughing, calling out ahead of them, "Hey, Mary, Walter needs some coffee," and managed to get him down the narrow stairs.

They forgot to put the light out. Passing by the door, Aunt Frances said, "You still up? Better not let your mother see that light on at this hour. Here, let me tuck you in." I looked up at her and said, "Daddy turned it on. He's drunk." My face felt stiff and my breathing was shallow.

"That didn't scare you, did it?" She gave an extra tuck of the sheet to comfort me. "You go back to sleep and forget about it. You won't even remember it by tomorrow." She kissed me and turned out the light, and I pretended to be asleep until everyone was gone. When the lights were out and the last voice in the house was silent, I turned on my side and went to sleep.

The mornings after one of these exceptions to the rule were awful. Dad would come downstairs with a terrible hangover, and my mother could never resist the urge to nag him about his lapse. He would drink cup after cup of coffee and roam heavy-footed around the house. A six-foot, two-hundred-and-fifty-pound man roaming heavy-footed in a small house is not someone to be tangled with, though it never stopped my mother. It was almost as if she had a complimentary hangover of her own, and she didn't drink.

After that, if I knew there was going to be a party in the house, I went to bed early, before anyone could down a first drink, kept my door closed, and feigned sleep until it was all over. That was the first and last time I ever saw my father drunk. There were still the Christmas and New Year's Day hangover miseries to live through. I think my father could have survived them with some sense of humor, if not for my mother's angry ill will. As it was, when he couldn't somehow cajole her into a semblance of sympathy, he'd retreat into grumbling irritation until early afternoon, when after half a dozen more cups of coffee and a good lunch, his caffeinated energy had him singing and doing an impromptu foxtrot with whomever was walking through the living room. □

PURPOSE

One day
I filled the spoon
with applesauce
and mother bird
to nestling
put it in his mouth

remembering

skipping on gray sidewalks
learning to read
typing
and all the kisses
by the front door
and knew
that was just part of the plan
to be sure
that I would be there
to feed the baby

ART

In a way, it's a terrible thing to transform your family into a work of art, to give them life and breath on a page so you can bear the pain in your spirit. Once you have them in paint or words, you can look there instead of inside yourself, be lulled by the portrait and see them as strangers. And see yourself as a stranger too, someone passing through those incidents and feelings, charmed by the dexterity that lets you distance yourself from memory.

Memory. If we were like dogs and cats and couldn't think about tomorrow or yesterday, wouldn't it be wonderful? Imagine, if you will, jealousy felt only momentarily, anger over when the barking stops, love satisfied by food and a caress, long naps in the sun a few times a day. Sounds good to me.

Instead we carry around a whole library of family albums that start somewhere near when we were born, and this library has all the most advanced technology for remembering—smells and colors, music, voices. We watch the instant replays interminably and drift, and begin to drown...But let someone get the whole thing down on paper or stone or on canvas, and it's a different story. The embarrassment of losing your underpants on the top floor of the Empire State Building becomes an amusing anecdote. The death of a favorite uncle becomes the sorrow of that woman on page 231. And the thrill of a first dance belongs to that young girl, terribly thin and gawky, back in Queens Village. □

DÉJÀ VU

Look at the girl graduate fifty-two
more cheerful than ten
more sure than eighteen
farther-sighted in today's glasses

Thinner lipped grayer haired
looking straight at the camera
as she did at three and smiling

PRETENDING

My life is pretense; I keep busy pretending and I am busy. I pretend to care. Some part of me cares about other people, but the other real part of me, the one underneath, cares for no one. Today and many days. Maybe all days. The pretender cares. She shouts and smiles and waves goodbye, following all the conventions. The real one lives inside a thick glass prison of the need to breathe, waiting to die. Death is never away from me. My death, other people's deaths, are there in us. But maybe they don't know it. Some do. Like me. And they pretend too, in order to hide from one another, to try to forget for a little while.

Why can't I give myself up to pleasure the way some people do? Or seem to do. Are they pretending too, playing the game the way they should?

I have what is called a good life, and yet it doesn't feel good to me. I want some kind of forgetting, peace, serenity. I want to stop wasting my breathing in meaningless activity.

How can I look out on this green beauty and be so depressed? I can understand why the Japanese tried to make perfect stone gardens, perfect ceremonies, and exquisite art: For serenity and peace. □

HELL

"You told a lie."

"I did not."

"Yes, you did. You told a lie." Mary balanced on the cement ledge, one arm outstretched, and finger pointing at me and nodded her head up and down. "You did too. Didn't she?"

Junior stood smiling next to Mary on the sidewalk, nodding in agreement. If Mary said I lied, then I lied, no question.

"That's a sin. Sister said so." Mary's brown eyes opened wide, and then narrowed as she looked at me.

"What's a sin?"

"That's when you do something bad and you go to Hell."

"What's that?"

"That's where the devil takes you."

It was my penny that I dropped on the ground. Mary said it was hers, and now she wanted to take it away from me. I began to cry.

"You told a lie and that's a sin." Mary smiled and Junior laughed. A year older and both in first grade, they knew more than me. Junior was a Protestant, so he wasn't learning about sin and the devil in first grade at public school, but Mary was filling him in every day on what Sister said. Mary's stories were interesting and Junior was learning all about saints, fallen angels and dire punishments.

This was my first time hearing about the dark side of religion. Up until then I thought church was fun. I liked the incense and the singing. The stained glass windows were beautiful to look at. But Mary was scaring me. I wasn't lying about the penny, but I told lots of lies. By this time I was scared, and crying hard.

My sister Jean and her friend Mildred walked by arm in arm and came over to see what was going on. Jean asked, "What are you crying for?"

"Mary says I told a lie and the devil will get me." The words were hard to say. "I didn't tell a lie. It was my penny."

"She did too, didn't she Junior? She stole my penny. That's a sin. Sister says so."

"You don't go to Hell for stealing a penny. Sister never said that."

Mary looked doubtful. She still smiled but with less assurance. "Well, she stole my penny."

"What's a sin?" I looked at Jean, hoping she would say there was no such thing.

"That's when you do something bad."

"She says I stole her penny."

"Did you?"

"It was my penny. I dropped it."

"Then it's not a sin so forget about it." Jean turned to Mary. "She didn't commit a sin. Leave her alone." Jean might attack me, but she wasn't going to let anyone else do it. Family pride required a swift defense. "What do you know about it anyway? You're only in first grade."

"Sister says if you tell a lie, that's a sin, and then you go to Hell. And she told a lie. That was my penny." Mary was defeated and her voice revealed it. Size carried the day. Mary's eyes were watering as she ran down the block with Junior, still smiling, at her side.

The argument had used up the last minutes of daylight. I stood between Jean and Mildred, frightened because Mary said I would go to Hell if I lied. Dusk began to hide the details of the neighborhood and Jean and Mildred looked at me, with eyes made mysterious by the new dark.

Mildred laughed. "Is the devil gonna get you?"

"You better not," Jean poked her friend. "If you scare her, my mother'll get mad." She turned to me. "What are you crying for, stupid? I told you, you won't go to Hell for stealing a penny. Go in the house. It's getting dark."

Mildred pointed over my shoulder. "Watch out. There he is." They laughed and I flew up the porch steps, not stopping to look back

"She's just teasing," Jean called out. "Don't be silly."

But I was worried. I'd heard about God and the devil from Nana, and now there was sin and Hell. And if telling a lie was a sin, then I was going to be in trouble a lot. □

AUNT ELVIRA'S VISIT

When Uncle Ed lost the lower half of his right leg hitching a ride on a trolley in New York City, the insurance money from the accident paid for the house on Long Island that got my father's family out of Hell's Kitchen, and bought a new wooden leg for Ed.

The house was a yellow stucco two-story shoebox with a few simple shrubs spotted near corners and doors. The only exceptions to the naked look of the house were two large lilac bushes, one white and one lavender, planted outside the dining room windows by my Aunt Elvira soon after the family moved in.

My grandparents, Gustave and Margaret Primont, had five children. The two eldest, Uncle Arthur and Uncle Gus, were policemen. Uncle Ed was the middle child and the only son to finish high school. He couldn't work at a manual job, since a wooden leg in those days was just that, a piece of wood with a carved foot hinged onto it, so he trained as a bookkeeper and worked for a textile company in Brooklyn. My father, Walter, was the youngest son. He quit school at thirteen and went to work for a wholesale milk company owned by a family friend. Dad enlisted in the army and went off to France in the First World War, to return a fervent patriot who believed there was no country in Europe to compare with the United States, and the other countries in the world counted for even less. By the time I was born, he was the sales manager of a wholesale milk company in Manhattan.

The fifth and youngest child was Elvira. At twenty-eight she became a Dominican nun and lived in a convent in Amityville, Long Island. The order that Aunt Elvira joined was freer than some, but not free enough to make her family happy. They could go to visit her at the convent twice a year, and she was allowed to visit home one Sunday a year. The whole family gathered at Grandma and Grandpa's house in Hollis for a celebration the day of the annual visit. It was Aunt Elvira's day of complete freedom. After going to early Mass, from ten a.m. to six p.m. she had no obligations—no prayers, no work. She could even have a glass of beer with dinner, if she wanted.

Her parents and brothers treated her with deference once she became a nun, but there was always affection in their voices when they spoke of her—the only girl, the baby of the family. To the rest of the world, she was Sister Mary Margaret Elvira, but to her father and her brothers, she was The Babe.

When the whole family gathered at Grandma and Grandpa's house, Aunt Annie, Aunt Edith, Aunt Jenny, and my mother made up a kind of wives' club. The four brothers, each so different, had chosen wives to suit their needs. Uncle Arthur, the eldest and gentlest, chose Aunt Annie, cheerful, self-confident, and independent. Uncle Gus, ugly-tempered and sarcastic, married Aunt Jenny, who was like a shadow in the family. Uncle Ed had

Aunt Edith, virtuous and orderly, the perfect match for a bookkeeper. My father, a man of mercurial moods, married my mother, a reader and disillusioned romantic, and she held him as steady as she could, trying to ignore his bad moods and curb his good ones. Her name, like mine, was Rosemary, but Dad always called her Mary or Maryanne unless he wanted to be serious. The wives had almost nothing more in common than that they existed for the day on the periphery of the real club—The Primonts.

When the seven of them, Grandpa, Grandma, Uncle Arthur, Uncle Gus, Uncle Ed, Dad, and Aunt Elvira were together, the bond among them made them a unit that outsiders found hard to penetrate. They spoke to each other without speaking. There were sniffs and side-glances, chuckles, belly laughs, and twitches. A lifetime of trying to keep on Grandma's good side had forced them all, including Grandpa, to develop ways to keep her happy and get around her at the same time. We grandchildren were somewhere in the middle of the two groups. If a mother was irritated with one of her children, she might say, "You sound just like The Primonts." It was the ultimate insult.

On a Sunday in January, 1932, when I was almost four, my mother told me we were going to Grandma and Grandpa's house because Aunt Elvira was coming home to visit. I didn't know who Aunt Elvira was, and didn't remember seeing her before. First my father drove my mother, my brother Mike, twelve, my sister Jean, nine, and me from our home in Queens Village to the yellow house in Hollis two towns away. Then he left to pick up Aunt Elvira at the convent out in Amityville.

We were sitting around the table waiting for them to arrive when Uncle Arthur said, "C'mon, Ma, sit down. They won't be here for another half hour." He spoke to her in a soothing voice, and patted the chair next to him.

She continued to peer through the curtains, past the snow on the lilac bush out to the icy roadway. When she turned around she grumbled, "It's eleven o'clock. They should have been here half an hour ago. I hope Elvira has an extra sweater under her cape. She might catch cold." She looked at Uncle Arthur and her voice turned plaintive, "We only have a couple of hours before she'll have to go back."

"Don't worry, Ma. I'm sure Walter's just taking it easy driving because of the snow. They'll be fine. Sit down. Take a load off your feet."

"Even Gus and Jenny may be a little late getting here Maggie," Grandpa said. "He called a little while ago and said the ferry was late leaving." Uncle Gus and Aunt Jenny lived two hours away on Staten Island with their son Little Gus, and traveling on a Sunday was a problem. With the ice and snow, if they missed one connection, it could take them three hours or even longer.

"I have to go look at the dinner," Grandma said, heading toward the kitchen.

"Let me go do that, Mom." Uncle Arthur's wife Aunt Annie started for the kitchen, but Grandma stopped her with a harsh, "I'll do it."

Aunt Annie rolled her eyes. "Okay. I just thought you might like a little help, but I'll be happy to sit here like a lady."

"The kitchen's too small for more than one person to work in," Grandma muttered.

Aunt Annie sat down again, letting her heavy body ease onto the chair with a breathless laugh. Her response to Grandma's irritation was to ignore it. It wasn't worth getting excited about. Aunt Annie was used to her mother-in-law, and she and Uncle Arthur and their family lived in the Bronx, far enough away so that she didn't have to see Grandma too often. We called them the Bronx Primonts.

Two minutes later Grandma called from the kitchen, "Artie, come and mash the potatoes." With a shrug and a smile at his wife, he went out to the kitchen to help.

"Girls," called Aunt Annie to her four daughters and my sister Jean, who were playing cards in the small enclosed sun porch. "Push the two card tables together and set nine places. You kids can eat out there."

A car pulled up to the house, and my mother hurried over to the window and pulled the curtain aside. "They're here, thank goodness. Even I was getting worried." She went to the kitchen and squeezed past Uncle Arthur. "Mom, Walter and Elvira are here. Give me that pot, and you go say hello. I'll take care of the carrots."

My father and Aunt Elvira came up the steps to the kitchen door, tramping snow off their shoes when they got to the landing. Aunt Elvira's face was red, and she was smacking her hands together. "Phew, I'm freezing." She kissed her mother and said "Hi, Ma, how are ya?" She shivered. "Boy, it's cold out there."

My mother said, "Hi, Elvira. Here, let me make you a cup of hot tea." She lit a match under the kettle and took down the tea canister.

"Ma still doesn't believe in tea bags," Elvira said. "You should use them, Ma. They're much easier. Not so much mess."

"Is that what they use in the convent?"

"Nah. The cook says you can't make good tea with tea bags, but some of us like to use them when she's not around."

"Hmm." Grandma didn't like to think of authority being thwarted, but she also didn't like someone telling her daughter what she couldn't do. Aunt Elvira and my mother smiled, and Elvira sat down at the kitchen table and warmed her hands around the cup of tea.

The house was in Uncle Ed's name, so after his three brothers married and left home and his sister joined the convent, he turned the second floor into a separate apartment and moved up there to live. They could hear his wooden leg now, sounding heavy on every other step as he came down the back stairs and into the kitchen. "Hi, Babe," he said. "You just get here?"

"Yeah." She kissed him on the cheek. "Where's Edith?"

"She's upstairs in the kitchen, icing the cake. Very important job." He winked. "She'll be down in a few minutes." Uncle Ed took Aunt Elvira's cape and pocketbook and said, "I'll stick this stuff on the bed in the back room."

"Hi, Aunt Elvira." My brother Mike stood in the doorway. "Grandpop, is there another pack of cards? We want to play a game of rummy, and the girls are playing Old Maid with the other pack."

I was leaning against my mother, staring at Aunt Elvira. She leaned over and said, "And who's this?"

My mother gave me a pat on the shoulder. "Say hello, Rosemary." When I just stared without saying anything the next pat was less gentle.

"C'mon, say hello. You know Aunt Elvira."

I shook my head no, then mumbled, "Hullo," and wandered off to the front porch where the older kids were now arguing about their favorite comics.

I leaned against Chubby. I loved Chubby. She was my oldest cousin. When the others teased me, she made them stop. And she gave me sweets to keep me happy.

"Who's that lady?" I pointed back at Aunt Elvira.

"That's Aunt Elvira. She's our daddy's sister. She's a nun."

"What's a nun?"

Chubby looked serious. "She's religious, and she lives in a convent. She plays the piano."

"Okay, everybody, dinner's ready," came the call from the dining room.

Whenever Grandma had the whole family to dinner, she always roasted a big leg of mutton, rare, with brown gravy, mashed potatoes, and lots of vegetables. For dessert there were a couple of fruit pies. It was a meal worthy of a woman who had grown up on a farm.

Aunt Edith placed her cake on the sideboard, between Grandma's apple and mince pies. The prim vanilla cake with neat chocolate icing stood in contrast to Grandma's fat pies with their thick buttery crusts, just the way Aunt Edith did, sitting ladylike at the table, surrounded by her husband's noisy family. She was tall and thin, a middle-aged Gibson Girl. She wore demure dresses with delicate lace collars. In spite of being married, her demeanor was that of a well-bred Catholic miss, modest and too sensitive. Her hair, medium brown, was set in soft waves, pulled over her ears into a bun at the nape of her neck. Her long English-Irish face, with its high cheekbones and faded blue eyes, showed shock as she tittered "Oh, Walter" at one of my father's exaggerated stories, or "goodness gracious" at one of Uncle Gus's sarcastic remarks. She was the only one who could be shocked. The rest of the family just laughed, and Uncle Ed smiled his enigmatic smile and patted her hand, muttering, "Okay, okay, that's okay, Deedee," until she recovered.

Uncle Gus, irritated and glowering, sat next to her. Since the accident that turned him from a traffic cop into a Police Department clerk, his greatest pleasure seemed to be watching people squirm under his withering sarcasm. Aunt Jenny sat next to him. She was a small dark woman with a timid voice and not much presence. If she'd ever had any, life with Gus had destroyed it.

"Pass me the potatoes please, Gussie." Elvira smiled at her brother as she took the bowl and spooned a second helping of potatoes onto her plate, then reached for the gravy. "Everything's delicious, Ma, how duya do it? The cook at the convent never puts enough milk or butter in anything. We should get you out there to give her a couple of lessons."

"I made everything just the way you like," Grandma said. There was satisfaction in her tone.

"I know, Ma. It's great. Thanks."

This was Grandma's chance to cook for her daughter. All her children were important, but Elvira was her baby girl, and a nun. Everything had to be just right. Grandma felt betrayed when Elvira went into the convent, and for all anyone knew, she was the reason Elvira did it. At least, that's what my mother said. But then, she didn't like Grandma much.

Grandma said she wanted her daughter to know something of the world she was giving up, so Aunt Elvira worked for ten years after high school. Like the rest of the family, Elvira's Catholicism was practical. She was never an outwardly spiritual kind of person, but there was no reason to doubt the sincerity of her vocation. If she was ever sorry about her choice of lifework, she never complained to any of her family.

"What time do you have to go back, Babe?"

"I'll leave by four-thirty, Walter." Aunt Elvira looked over at my father. "If it starts to snow, I'll have to leave around three-thirty."

"Wouldn't you think they'd let you stay out till eight o'clock," Dad complained. "It's not as if you were out on the town." He frowned. "It's just this one time a year. It doesn't make any sense." It began to look as if he might get into a cranky mood and upset Grandma and Grandpa.

"It's not too bad, Walter." Aunt Elvira gave him a long steady look and turned to her mother to change the subject. "Let's have that dessert now, Ma. We've all eaten too much, but it looks so delicious."

By this time the older kids were finished eating and drifted into the dining room to see what was next. "How's school? Ya havin' fun?" Aunt Elvira laughed, as if the thought that school could be fun was a big joke.

Aunt Elvira was a funny kind of nun. She never lost her Hell's Kitchen accent and said "yeah" and "wadduya know" and "no kiddin'." And, like Uncle Ed, she always looked as if she was thinking of something besides what she was saying, and it was making her smile.

As if on cue, the women got up and began to clear the table.

"Let's have some music, Babe," Dad said, cheered by the thought of music, and motioned his sister toward the living room. "Let the ladies fight it out in the kitchen." He took my hand and walked me over to the piano.

Elvira was a musician. She played the organ, piano, accordion, and several stringed instruments, and her musical talents were put to good use at the convent. She played for Mass in her parish church and gave piano lessons in schools around the diocese. Her visits home were always an occasion for making music.

Aunt Elvira came into the living room and opened up the piano. "It's too low, Walter," she said as she twirled the mahogany piano seat a few inches higher, then sat down and arranged the white folds of her habit with a rustling swoop. She leaned over toward me, our faces on the same level. "Interesting, huh?" The flesh of her face bulged around the edges of her stiff white coif and her ruddy complexion made her eyes very green behind her glasses. She had a wide smile, different from her brothers, a smile that showed long, well-shaped teeth, and she laughed at me holding on to the edge of the piano, too shy to talk.

"What would you like me to play? Yankee Doodle?" Her fingers ran over a few notes, and she turned around to my father. "What would she like me to play?" Then she played "Rockabye Baby." "C'mon," she said. "Cat got your tongue?"

I hid my face against my father's leg. The blue serge of his trousers was coarse and I pulled it around my nose, letting one eye look out at Aunt Elvira. He leaned down and asked, "Now, what song would you like Aunt Elvira to play?"

"Pmmtin n uh rokky," I mumbled into his leg.

He leaned over and said, "We couldn't hear that. Tell me again."

I bowed my head as far as it could go, "Springtime in the Rockies," my voice halfway between a whisper and a whimper. There was a singer named Mitzi Green who sang that song on my favorite radio program, and the thought that a real person could play it for me was wonderful.

"One order of 'Springtime in the Rockies,' Babe."

"Coming up."

Aunt Elvira played the melody, looking at her hands as she picked out the notes. Soon it began to have a lilt, and then she added some embellishments.

"Come on, Rosemary, you sing too." She smiled at me and sang in a clear strong voice, while I mouthed a word silently now and then.

Uncle Gus walked in, "What's that you're playing, Babe?"

"Special request from Little Rosemary." Elvira played a few chords and then ran through the first lines of half a dozen songs. The family appeared in the living room, one or two at a time, and stood around the piano.

She ran her fingers up and down the keys. "A good thing my hands have warmed up enough to play now. Hey, Pop, get your banjo."

I went over and sat in one of Grandma's carved oak rockers, hoping she wouldn't hear the noise the runners made as I rocked on the carpet. When Grandma came in and sat across from me in the other rocker, I slid off the chair, and my father picked me up.

While Grandpa tuned the banjo, Uncle Gus got his mandolin and Uncle Ed hunted for his ukulele. Dad didn't play an instrument. He could pick out chords on the piano and play by ear, but he never took any lessons. Aunt Elvira began to play old songs I'd heard my father sing—"Pack up Your Troubles in Your Old Kit Bag," "There Are Smiles," and "Whispering"—while Grandpa, Uncle Ed, and Uncle Gus played along. Uncle Arthur and the older cousins sang the melody, and Dad and Jean sang harmony. Aunt Edith stood in back of Uncle Ed and sang in her wavering elongated tremolo. My mother couldn't sing, so she sat laughing and smiling with Aunt Annie at the fun the others were having. Aunt Jenny hung back against the wall watching.

After Aunt Elvira played for an hour, she stopped and winked at Grandpa and began the chorus of "When You and I Were Young, Maggie," and Grandpa asked Grandma, "Remember when I used to sing that to you, Maggie?"

Everyone teased her and tried to get her to sing along. "C'mon, Ma. C'mon, Grandma, you sing too." She sat in her carved oak rocker, in her Sunday best dress, black with little brown and yellow flowers, not answering them, rocking harder the more they teased, muttering sour little "humphs" to show what she thought about the possibility of her singing anything.

For a long while there was a chorus of Grandpa, his grown children, and their children. Then Aunt Elvira wound up a song with a decisive ending and began to close up the piano.

Uncle Arthur said, "Don't stop, Babe, we won't get a chance to hear you play again for a while."

"I'd better get ready, Artie. I want to leave time for a game of cards with Ma. Ed and Edith said they'd take me back at four-thirty. You know them, they'll be ready on time, and I don't want to keep them waiting."

"Can she play my song again?" I asked my father

"Why don't you ask her yourself?" Father put me down and I stood in back of Aunt Elvira. I touched the tip of her veil and whispered, "Can you play it again?" But she didn't hear me. She was busy arranging her skirt and fingering the black prayer beads hanging from her waist.

Aunt Elvira walked toward the dining room. "Okay, Ma, how about a quick game of euchre." She pulled a chair out from the table and sat down. "Gee, the cake looks great, Edith. Maybe I'll have another piece. Just a small bite."

Grandma was intent upon her cards. She and Aunt Elvira were partners and Dad and Grandpa were playing against them. "Your turn, Ma," Uncle Arthur prodded. The light from the colored glass lampshade over the dining table deepened the shadows under her wrinkles and the tiniest smile turned her mouth up at the corners. "Hey, Ma, what are you smiling about? Look at how she's smiling. She must have a great hand."

"Hey, look at Grandma smile!" Even the aunts were pleased.

Twenty minutes later, Aunt Elvira got up from the table. Grandma sighed as she held her daughter's hand with its gold wedding ring, the symbol of her marriage to Christ. Aunt Elvira leaned over to kiss her mother goodbye and said, "So long, Ma, be good." Grandpa's eyes were watering. "Don't, Pa." Her voice quavered. "If you cry, you'll make me cry too. Walter says he'll bring you and Ma out in April for a visit. It's not so long till then." She straightened up and motioned to Uncle Ed over their heads that it was time to go.

"Okay, Babe, let's get moving." He held out her black winter cape.

"Yes," trilled Aunt Edith, as they were going through the door, "we don't want to be late getting there. And you know Eddie doesn't like to drive fast." Her eyes blinked back at them as she spoke, and they all kept up the pretense that it was Ed who was afraid to go fast, except my mother, who muttered to Aunt Annie, "I bet she won't let him go over five miles an hour."

Grandma looked up and said, "Eh? What'd you say?"

"I said they probably won't get there till after five o'clock."

"That's right. It takes an hour." Grandma gave my mother a cranky look. Always saying things there was no need to say.

After Aunt Elvira left, there was no more music. The rooms grew darker. Uncle Arthur and his family took off for the Bronx.

Uncle Gus and his family left for Staten Island. My mother and father began to talk of getting us home to bed. Grandpa changed his black leather shoes for his old felt slippers with the slits on the sides for his bunions, and Grandma sat at the table holding her brown rosary beads and staring at nothing. ☐

CONVENTS

My desk is empty. There's very little inside of it, and not much on top. Just the typewriter, my coffee, and the telephone, which, thank god, isn't ringing.

I love it this way. I have a drive toward simplicity, a result; I'm sure, of all those visits to convents when I was a little girl. They were so delicious. Clean, uncluttered, all waxed oak and starched linen. Nothing like home—chipped and cracked from dishes to doorways, dusty bits and pieces. Of course, there were no children, as my mother would have said with a "humph," to mess the place up.

It wasn't only the visual serenity that appealed to me, it was the sense of quiet, of people living together with a purpose and going about it with no shouting. You could take off your shoes and feel a solid waxed floor underfoot—a foundation to feel sure of.

When I grew up and stopped being a Catholic, I still missed the convents. They were the only places I'd ever been that felt like havens, a place even I might go one day when I could no longer take living outside. The stop before suicide.

Now there are fewer convents in the old sense, and everything I've done that made me not a Catholic is quite forgivable, indeed, barely noticeable, except perhaps by the oldest and most rigid members of the Church. The question is, since I did all those things when they weren't permissible, do they have to be forgiven formally or can I consider them nonexistent? The black marks, I mean. The sins. The burnable material. It would be a laugh if the only thing considered reprehensible at this point were birth control, which I've used with two husbands, neither of whom I married in Church. ☐

PARTIES

My idea of a party is six people sitting around the dining room table, leaning on their elbows, talking and talking, while the hours go by and the coffee gets cold. My idea of a crowd is ten people I don't know, either silent or talking, smiling or growling, and making chitchat. That kind of gathering has the makings of an ordeal unless someone gets on to a very interesting subject. My idea of one of the lower levels of Hell is more than twenty people laughing and talking too loud and drinking and being social. People who probably only see each other on similar occasions over the years, all looking happy and lively and beautifully dressed. Maybe what they are saying somewhere in the room is terribly interesting. It never is where I am. I have to admit that my panic doesn't raise the conversation level. I sit there tongue-tied, bored and boring, uncomfortable in my grabbed-together outfits, wishing I were home in bed where I know who and what I am.

Last night there must have been a few hundred people. Milt belonged there but I didn't. They were all people involved in opera or wanting to be involved in opera. I'm a goer not a doer where opera is concerned. I don't want to know the stars. I don't want to rub up against the bodies of the famous. I like to say thank you to people who do things that give me pleasure, but then I want to go home. I'm not a show business type. Last night when I was standing waiting for Milt, I was alone. There were people there whom I know, but I couldn't bring myself to go over and speak to them. In a crowd of two hundred my overwhelming feeling is, why would anyone want to talk to me? I don't even want to talk to me. I just want to go someplace else and feel like a person again, which I don't in a crowd. I feel I'm just eyes and ears, and no brain or smile, just a mask. That sounds crazy but I'm sure it isn't, because the minute I'm out of the crowd I feel sad but also immense relief. The sensation of insubstantiality lasts for hours and the feeling once again of failure makes me unhappy because I really want to enjoy myself, and there are people there I know I could be interested in, one or two at a time...

Every once in a while a party turns out to be terrific. Like the one in England last December in Plácido Domingo's honor at the Spanish ambassador's. When we entered the door, the ambassador's secretary showed us a diagram of the seating arrangements, me at one end of a table for fifty people and Milt at the other. When I gasped, she told me my dinner partner would be a Spanish violinist and somebody else, also with a Spanish name. Speaking of panic. I almost cried right there in the face of her smiling reassurances that they were both charming. In a panic, I turned to the maid standing to my right, handed her my coat, and sort of fell into the loo. Very fancy—I believe there was a marble washstand right in the booth. I almost decided to stay in there for the evening. Did you ever feel as if you had made a terrible mistake and if only you could hide somewhere and not look into anyone's eyes, the mistake would dissolve and be gone and you'd be someplace else and everything would be all right again? Well, that's how I felt with the door safely locked and my head leaning against the door. I may even have moaned a little, I'm not sure, but I do know that some minutes later when I came out, there was a little line of terribly chic men and women looking everything from anxious to irritated. It seems that at the Spanish ambassador's digs the loos belong to both sexes, and the first one in the line outside the booth was Sir John Tooley, the head of Covent Garden Opera House, a man Milt would probably dearly love to impress. When I emerged Milt and Sir John exchanged some amusing repartee about Milt's wife holding up the line, nothing scatological in such a churchlike atmosphere. Perhaps Sir John will remember Milt in the future.

 A heretic facing the Grand Inquisitor couldn't have been more fearful than I facing the musical Spaniard who I imagined to have sensitive hands and no English. My Spanish consists of a few words like "sí" and "mucho" and "más tarde," and it looked as if the dinner would be hard slogging. I drank two quick glasses of good white wine, talked to the middle-aged English wife of a former Spanish PR man for the embassy about the trials and sadness of having children all grown but not yet producing grandchildren without knowing what I was saying for the most part. And then the gong rang or the Ambassador signaled, something happened, and everyone started in to dinner. When I arrived at the door to the dining room the secretary shunted Milt off in one direction; and to me apologized energetically and in a consoling voice telling me that because Lord or Señor so and so couldn't make it, she was forced to rearrange things and my dinner partner would be Mr. Harold Pinter, but not to worry, he was a lovely man and I would surely find him very pleasant. Given two glasses of good white wine and Harold Pinter for a dinner partner happens to be my idea of a terrific way to dine, so just in case there was some error, I hotfooted it over in the direction she pointed and sure enough there was Harold Pinter waiting for me.

You guessed it. I had a great time. He may even have had fun. The first thing after introductions were over, I told him how much I loved the Proust screenplay he did and from there on we never stopped talking, or I never stopped talking, until his wife Antonia Fraser came over and looking bored, bored, bored, carried him away with her. She had an expression of tired, blue-gray-eyed middle age on her face that cried "get me out of this place." Anyway he was fun and it was such a pleasure to meet someone I could talk to about writers and books that I went home all glittering and glistening and couldn't stop talking even after we turned out the lights for the night.

After Antonia led Harold away while we were standing having coffee in the lounge, the young woman who was sitting on the other side of Harold (I will call him that because we were introduced and he is in show business so he probably calls everyone by first name even if he is English) accosted me, accusing me of monopolizing our celebrity all through the dinner. She was an amateur singer and she changed her tune from outraged diva to smoky crooner when she found out I was married to Milt and knew Plácido personally. Immediately, everything was darling and sweetheart and couldn't I and wouldn't I, and the answers were sorry ma'am and no way. I don't know how she got to the dinner. I guess embassies have a list of invitees and they try to match them up to get the body count right for their great oval tables.

Anyway, I had a wonderful time that night, and poor Milt got stuck between a cranky talent agent and a lady who leads a chorus in London. The result was that I tasted nothing between the wine and the coffee and Milt could describe all the food in great detail. He said it was delicious, and that was a shame. Generally the food at these things is dreadful or at best boring, and it would have been nice to have Harold on a night when the food wasn't worth eating. □

SHOPPING

"Nugatory." Another one of those words to look up. "Trifling, of no real value; of no force or effect, futile; worthless, useless. Synonyms: trifling, frivolous." I must go back and read it in the sentence. An English book not especially deep, but written with a good vocabulary.

Now where did I stop yesterday? Oh, yes, the subject was parties, specifically business parties. And most specifically, show business parties.

Each time we go to one, I walk in the door and am appalled at what I am wearing and by contrast, what the other women are wearing. After ten minutes, I swear that the very next day I will go out shopping and buy myself an entire new wardrobe, coat, shoes, dresses, scarves, jewelry, purses, hats, even handkerchiefs. The day after, of course, I will be depressed and tired from being up so late, so I won't have the energy to go shopping, and the day after that I will have forgotten my intentions until the next time I walk in the door to a party. Part of my problem is that I don't seem to have the social instinct that tells me when to wear a long dress, a cocktail dress, a suit, or dinner dress. And even when I suspect correctly, I am never suitably equipped. That is, even if I know what's needed, and I have it to hand, it's not elegant enough. I think that's because when I do decide to go shopping, I can't face paying fifteen hundred dollars for a fancy little nothing that will only look good for two or three wearing's. So there I am in my Marks and Spencer black velvet and there they are in their Dior's and Mollie

Parnises. My gold chain, their diamonds and rubies, my cracking nails, and their long, fashionable, red talons.

I don't mean to sound like a martyr. The truth is that among my friends, I don't notice what I'm wearing, though it's nice to look good, and I often feel that I do, at least in my terms. Most of my friends wear clothes like mine. None of them spend their time shopping and having their hair done. None of them wear splendid jewelry and none of them care what I wear. Most of my friends are more interested in what they are doing and thinking, and I like that and so do they. I don't have the time or patience for shopping unless I am really in the mood.

The other day when I was thinking about why I am not too well dressed, I thought of my three little old maid aunts, the ones who brought my mother up, and I had the sudden thought that even though they went shopping all the time and adored the lovely clothes they bought that were kept hanging in perfect order in their perfect closets, one died at fifty of a massive and sudden infection, one died at seventy of stomach cancer, and the last died at eighty of a third heart attack. The one who died at seventy—by all accounts, the most dedicated shopper—spent at least one day of every week of her adult life shopping. I figure she spent something like twenty years sleeping and seven years clothes shopping, and what with food shopping and worrying, which aside from teaching third grade was her true vocation, there wasn't much time left for reading and thinking. Her death was most likely in no way a result of her shopping forays to Wanamaker's and other ladylike stores. But the beautiful clothes didn't delay it any I am sure. So when I think about going out to buy clothes, I always seem to opt for reading a book or seeing a friend, or even taking a nap, because if none of these things will actually ward off the fate we all fear, they are lots more fun in the meantime. □

AUNT MAMIE

I come from a line of women who were always trying to live tomorrow today.

My mother was kind of an orphan. That is, her mother died when she was three and her father turned her over to his mother and his three sisters.

Four short ladies who wore hats and white gloves when they left the house, and who topped off the Ten Commandments with an eleventh—Thou shalt be prepared.

Their lives were governed by routines. If their custom was to have six cans of peas in the pantry, or nine cans of carrots, and one was eaten, the next day it would be replaced so that there were never less than the required number. Bars of soap arrived from Wannamaker's Department Store by the case, to be replaced when the case was half empty. Change for the collection basket was gathered on the front hall table by Tuesday, ready to be picked up on Sunday morning on the way to church. Each Thursday, before the Polish cleaning lady Helen Yarm arrived, the dishes were washed and put away, all clothes were banished from sight, and the house made to look as if no one had been in it since she cleaned and polished it the week before.

Great Aunt Mamie, born in 1870, was the oldest sister, lived the longest, and may have taken the preparedness prize. She was the only one of the three sisters who ever lived with us children, so we got to know some of her habits intimately. She was a delicate woman with white hair, fair skin, and a will of steel. Most of the time there was a faint trace of a smile at the corners of her mouth, as if life were somehow almost amusing. She survived two serious heart attacks. After the first one at age fifty, she was advised to retire from her job as manager of a Hyler's restaurant and tearoom in the financial district, and to stay at home resting. After the second heart attack at seventy, a local doctor prescribed morphine for the pain, expecting her to die in the next day or two, but she surprised him and lived for another ten years, addicted to morphine, with everyone afraid to say anything about it for fear she would have another heart attack and really die this time. The pills she took every day were called by the family "Aunt Mamie's pills," and may have prolonged her life. She spent most of the time relaxing on her chaise lounge listening to the soaps on her radio. She also spent a lot of time waiting, because while she was trying to live tomorrow today, the rest of the world was slow in catching up.

Aunt Mamie went to Mass every Sunday morning. The process always started on Saturday night. The dress she was going to wear was taken out of the closet and placed on the chaise lounge in her bedroom. Next came stockings, then shoes. Her underwear, or as she said, "undergarments," remained discretely in the dresser drawer, for what if my father should stop by her room to say something to her and see them on the chaise? She was so anxious about getting to church on time that she was up at six-thirty, dressed and downstairs before seven, where she sat in the living room facing the front door. It wasn't so bad in summertime, when she wore light summer clothes, but in winter she would sit in her heavy wool coat with her gloves and felt hat on, her warm scarf wrapped around her neck, and galoshes on her feet if it was raining or there was snow on the ground.

She would wait for Mr. George, the local taxi driver, to come take her to church. It was only five minutes away, but Aunt Mamie had Mr. George pick her up at eight o'clock, and then they'd sit in the car in front of church for forty minutes until the eight o'clock Mass was over. Then she would go in and pick out a choice seat for the nine o'clock Mass. We never figured out why she didn't leave five minutes earlier and go to the eight o'clock Mass. If any of us tried to reason with her about it, she just stared blankly, and went on, week after week, doing it her way.

Aunt Mamie was ready for whatever needed to happen next. Before she went to bed each night, she filled a bowl with Rice Krispies, sprinkled a level teaspoon of sugar over it, and put it at her place on the kitchen table, along with her cup and saucer. Then she prepared the coffee percolator, an aluminum relic from her mother's kitchen, with a round of cotton cloth from an old sheet to act as a filter for the grounds. All she had to do in the morning was to light the gas under the coffee pot, pour the milk, and breakfast would be over without any fuss.

My father asked her once why she didn't get the cereal to snap, crackle, and pop the night before, and she looked at him as if he was speaking a foreign language. Why was he laughing? She knew what she was doing. Life was neat, and there were no surprises.

She lived with us the last four years of her life. It was hard on her, because we were a family always on the edge of some unimportant abyss. And we had a dog and a cat. She ignored the dog, a Doberman who didn't like anyone but didn't like her any less than she liked him. She treated him like wallpaper, and he returned the favor. The cat was more difficult. He took a liking to her. And her chaise lounge. The first week we could hear her telling him not to come into her room, hissing ladylike shoo-shoo noises at him. After a month, he gave up. He'd look into her room when he passed by in the hall but he never went in.

Poor Aunt Mamie. When she died six months after Grandpa, her burial plot was waiting for her, next to those of her mother and two sisters, paid for in full, forty years earlier. On the day of her funeral, we came back from the cemetery and found the cat curled up on the chaise lounge. He lifted his head long enough to stare at us, stretched his front legs, and stayed where he was, while we stifled the impulse to shoo him out. If we needed any reminder that ownership is transient, or that life will fill the space we have occupied after we are gone, the cat was it. The chaise lounge was his territory from then on, and he was as strict in his routines as Aunt Mamie had been in hers. Life was neat again with no surprises. At least, not for the cat. □

PETS

Boots lived with us on 213th Street. She was the first family pet that I remember. Boots was a fat tan and white terrier, overfed and snappish. She was Mike's dog. An ugly dog, but she was his and he loved her. She would take food from anyone, but Mike was her master.

Boots was six years old when Dad brought Jack, a male terrier, home. The next year Boots was pregnant. That puppy was born dead in the middle of the night and disposed of before Jean and I got up in the morning. Somehow, I got the idea that Boots had eaten her offspring and that dog mothers were a fierce lot.

The next year Boots was pregnant again. One afternoon, I was sent to Aunt Vera's house to play with Mary, with instructions not to return until summoned. Boots sat in the yard, penned in a small wooden box with chicken wire across the front, awaiting the birth. I saw her in the box and someone told me she was going to have puppies. It all looked very mysterious. Uncle Jim Savell stayed home from work at his auto repair shop in case there was need of an old farm boy as midwife, and it was he who came down to Aunt Vera's to bring me home a few hours later.

When we got home there were six puppies in a wide cardboard carton in the garage. Boots was lying watchfully beside them.

"How did Boots have the puppies, Mommy?"

"They came out her ear." My mother shot a silencing look at Uncle Jim, who was ready to give an accurate Tennessee farmer's description of the event, while the other adults smiled at my mother's perfectly reasonable answer for a seven-year-old in 1935.

"Which ear?" I asked.

"That one."

I leaned over Boots and the little dog growled quietly. I looked at the ear. "It's not big enough. How could they come out her ear?"

Uncle Jim laughed and Mother became impatient. "They did. Don't ask questions." Then, as if the dog might give away the secret, "Come away from her. She needs a rest."

I didn't ask any more questions. Mother seemed annoyed.

I looked at Boot's ear often, sometimes lifting it up to look inside. I didn't believe that puppies came out of a dog's ear, but if not her ear, then where else? Boots was never very friendly, and now I started to dislike her instead of just ignoring her.

Two weeks later, when my mother tried to wash my hair, I began to squirm and pull away from her.

"My ears are wet. Don't let water in them."

"Of course they're wet. I can't wash your hair without getting your ears wet." She pulled me back over to the sink. "Stand still and lean over further."

I grimaced and hunched my shoulders up as high as I could. The water ran down over my face. My eyes, nose, mouth, and, dreadful thing, ears were full of water. I grabbed the towel and tried to dry myself. "I hate my ears to be wet."

"Don't be ridiculous. A little water won't hurt." Mother shook her head. "You don't usually carry on like this."

"Yes I do."

Alone in the bathroom, I looked at myself in the mirror. There were my ears. They still felt damp. What would happen if water got into them? I didn't want anything near them. Fat, sluggish Boots, the box cage, and the strong smell of puppies were tied up with ears. I scowled and pulled my wet hair down straight along my face to hide my ears. They were ugly.

Jack was handsomer than his mate, very white where he was white and a delicious chocolate brown where he was brown. He belonged to the whole family. He was a cheery dog. Now that I think of it, we had two dogs that exactly fit my father's personality. Boots, ill tempered, growling, and too ready to bite, and Jack, happy, with an enormous appetite for anything fun—chasing his tail, food, and ringing doorbells.

Mother said Jack was a good-natured slob, an expression my father shuddered to hear. In his better moods, he called the dog John. Jack was all terrier, and in a fight he had a total disregard for his own safety. His worst enemy was Rex, the large Alsatian who lived next door with the Savells. The sight of Rex or the sound of his loud bark sent Jack into a frenzy of hatred. He clawed at the living room windows through the sheer white curtains in an effort to get out and destroy his foe. For the first six months that Rex lived next door, he passed by our house ignoring the maddened dog on the other side of the window. One day Jack got out, and as a result he spent two weeks in the hospital. Jack reached Rex's throat, but he was no match for such a large dog. Poor Jack almost died, but undeterred by this minor setback, he resumed his vigil at the front window, bandages and all, on the first day of his return.

Jack loved his tail. It had a bright white spot at the tip, and any pleasant excitement set him chasing it. Sometimes he caught it, and then wandered off to find something more interesting to do.

Jack stole food whenever he could and sat close to us kids at meals to catch crumbs as they fell. He loved candy, and when he was given a piece, stuck his head under a chair to eat it in secret. His white-tipped tail wagged madly, and if it was a caramel he stayed there for a long time trying to lick it off his teeth.

When Jack was a puppy, a deliveryman wearing a cap kicked him. From then on, he was the scourge of any man wearing a cap or hat, and men were warned through the screen door to take them off before entering. It wasn't Jack's fault. He was a fast learner.

At that time we also had a cat named Mickey. Unable to bear the sight of any living thing orphaned, Dad often brought home kittens. Very few were adopted, since Mother knew that as soon as a kitten took up residence, Dad felt he'd done his duty and left her to get on with the tasks of feeding, training, and cleaning up after it. She seldom gave in, and almost as many kittens left the house as entered, adopted by other softhearted friends and neighbors.

Mickey arrived in a cake box on my sixth birthday, and in spite of Momma's grim look, he stayed. He was a skinny black and gray tiger cat who stalked slyly around the house, going his own way, treating the family indifferently. He liked to sit on top of the kitchen door, and we learned to look up before we slammed it if we didn't want the cat to land on us, claws out.

Mickey and Jack were comrades. They often rolled about on the floor together. Mickey pushed food off tables and counters, and then sat watching at the edge as Jack ate it. When Jack chased his tail, the cat tried to catch it with his paw if he could get near enough.

After Rex and Jack had their big fight, our family and the Savells agreed to use the porch lights as signals to show whether the dogs were in or out. When we decided to take Jack for a walk, we checked the Savells' porch light. If it was on, Rex was out, and Jack had to wait. If it was off, we quickly switched on our porch light and took Jack out. One night both families decided to take the dogs out at the same time, opened the doors simultaneously, reached back inside to turn the lights on, and the two dogs were nearly at each other again.

If Mickey noticed Jack going for a walk, he ran down the street and climbed up the far side of the third or fourth tree. Poor Jack always looked suspiciously at the first few trees, inspecting them at eye level, and when nothing happened, relaxed and sniffed happily. When he got to the tree the cat was on, Mickey would jump on him, preferably while he was relieving himself. Then, Mickey would scoot down the path a few trees, and repeat the performance all the way down the block.

Every time a door opened in the house, Jack tried to escape. If no door opened, a window would do. If the ground floor windows were closed, he could always manage to clamber over a windowsill upstairs and onto the small, slanting roof over the porch to jump ten feet to the ground. His goal was always the same—Trunz Butcher Shop, where Phil the butcher rewarded him with a slice of bologna or a bite of hotdog.

Someone inside the house usually heard the thud when Jack hit the ground and came running after him. The leash laws were strictly enforced, and Mike was tired of taking the bus to the pound in Jamaica to pick him out of the day's collection of dogs. In the cage at the pound Jack dropped his warrior stance and shared the limelight with the other animals, running around and falling over them, whining and barking, just another dog in the chorus.

When Jack made it to Phil's, he sat outside the shop, staying clear of the sawdust boundary on the floor, wagging his tail in anticipation and panting hopefully. Phil's red face matched the blood on his hands and apron, and he always laughed when we came into the store. "Wheresa dog? He ain't been in today. Whatsa matter? Ya feed'im for a change?"

Jack and Boots weren't allowed on the beds. Boots was pretty good about it, but Jack could never resist. When the whole family left the house, Jack went upstairs and made himself at home on my parents' bed. He'd work the covers down off the pillows and settle in for a pleasant rest. When he heard the key turn in the front door lock and the door open, he'd jump off the bed and saunter down the stairs with his tail wagging to meet us.

There was room in the house for all kinds of idiosyncrasies, and the animals added theirs. On the way to school one morning Mary and I saw a Great Dane wandering along Hempstead Avenue. He was very friendly, and stayed right with us until we turned onto the street that led to the schoolyard. When we came out at lunchtime he was still there waiting for us.

"Here, doggy, what's your name?"

"Look, he has a collar. Is his name on it?" We struggled to reach the dog's collar but his size and excitability prevented us from getting at it.

"Let's call him Pal. Here, Pal. C'mon, nice doggy."

We walked along Hempstead Avenue with the Great Dane between us. On all fours he was nearly as tall as we were, and we had to hurry to keep up with him. Like a superb dancer, he allowed us to lead him toward Jamaica Avenue and home.

"I bet he's hungry. I'll ask my mother to give him some dinner. Maybe she'll let me keep him." I looked at the huge dog. "I bet he doesn't have a home. Nice doggy." I ran my hands down his back and he turned his massive head and slavered on my coat, leaving a big wet mark on the woolen sleeve.

"Don't let your mother see that or she won't let you keep him," Mary said.

We crossed the main street carefully, trying to hold the dog back when we got to the corner. The street was his, no matter who had the right of way. Mary passed right by her house and came home with me to see what would happen when I showed him to my mother. We stood on the sidewalk and called to her. "Mother! Aunt Rosemary!"

The door opened. "What have you got there?" Mother asked in spite of the obvious answer. "Where did you get that?"

"This is Pal. Isn't he beautiful, Mommy? We found him on the way to school." I put my arm around his neck.

"Well, you can take him right back where you found him." She came outside the screen door, closing it carefully because Jack was having a fit. He threw himself at the window, barking and growling, the hair on his back in a ridge of fury at the sight of the Great Dane on his patch of sidewalk. Suddenly, the big dog decided he liked what he saw, and with one leap he was on the porch licking Mother's arm. He sat down, tail wagging.

"See, he likes us, Mommy. Can we keep him?"

"Keep him? He's too big. Besides his owner is probably looking for him right now." She looked doubtful. The dog had sores on his back. He looked uncared for. Someone probably drove him into the neighborhood and dumped him there.

"You'll have to let him go. I suppose he must be hungry. I'll get him something."

She went inside and brought out a bowl with a loaf of bread torn up in a quart of milk. She put in a few scraps of meat from yesterday's dinner. Finishing it in two gulps, Pal looked up expectantly for more.

"Rosemary, even if we had the room we couldn't keep a dog like that. He'd eat us out of house and home in twenty-four hours. That was a whole loaf of bread!"

Just then the mailman came down the street. When he saw the dog on the front porch, he crossed the street and stood on the opposite side.

"Mrs. Primont," he shouted, "don't you have Jack any more? You know the dog who always tries to bite me?" From habit he took his cap off and stuck it in his mail pouch. "Did you get a new dog?" He flinched when the dog stood up to look with interest in his direction. "That's a very big dog."

"We still have Jack. Can't you hear him in there? This is just a stray the children brought home for lunch."

"You better be careful of him. He looks pretty vicious to me. I'll leave your mail with the Rayfews and you can get it later."

Mary went home for lunch and I ignored all signs of disinterest on the part of my mother, imaging the fun Pal and I would have once the family and the mailman got used to him. He would walk me to school every day. Nobody would call me names or chase me with a big dog like Pal at my side. With him in the house I wouldn't be afraid of the dark. Jack would get used to him. He'd have to.

"Wait till Daddy sees him," I said to my mother.

"Just wait," she said, in a tone that let me know he probably never would.

When I finished lunch I went outside and took the waiting dog down the street. "C'mon, Pal, let's call for Mary." We walked back to school. The excitement on the playground reached fever pitch as children and nuns gathered around to make Pal's acquaintance. Sister Mary St. Thomas decided he was hungry and this time he got leftover stew from the good Sisters' lunch, downed in two gulps.

Pal pranced around the yard, stopping for a pat from one and giving a lick to another. Mary and I maintained ownership, racing after him, hanging possessively onto his collar. When the bell rang, the children left reluctantly for class, laughing and poking each other as the dog moved nervously between the double lines.

Several times during the afternoon, my class trooped over to the windows to look down at the dog. We saw the janitor give him a bowl of food after Father Herchenroeder looked over from the church steps and decided Pal looked hungry.

At three o'clock, I went out into the schoolyard but he was gone. I called his name and hunted all over for him. Mary and I called for him all along Hempstead Avenue but he didn't appear, and we never saw him again. Mary said that his owner probably felt so guilty about leaving him that he came back and picked him up. For months I imagined I would find him again on the walk to school and decided that someday I would have a Great Dane. □

HOMER

This has been a month of martyrdom for me in which I've had full assistance from a cast of twenty, starting with the cat. That foolish animal has begun to do something I call harking—a cross between barking, hawking, and coughing. Two weeks ago, the dog, Pokey, managed to nab a chicken bone dropped from the kitchen table and promptly began to choke on it. We got some of it out of his throat but he continued to cough for the rest of that evening. The next day he coughed whenever he barked. Each time the doorbell rang, he did his circle dance of wild barking, and when the visitor entered, he coughed for five minutes—not the behavior in a dog one wants if the visitor is a burglar.

That same day, our funny little cat, Homer, began to make weird noises, as if there was something in his throat. At first I only heard him. When I finally saw him, it seemed like a strangely random behavior. Sometimes he did it when he was playing, sometimes when walking from room to room. It began to look as if he was hallucinating, and if he'd been human I might have thought he was indulging in what our family doctor euphemistically calls "recreational drugs." Then I began to think that maybe, in my grandfather's words, the cat was just plain crazy. Maybe all those cute, far-out habits that endeared him to us were signs of incipient schizophrenia. When he crawled under the cover to go to sleep that night, he snuggled up to my foot and harked on it. I sent him downstairs to keep the dog company, and soon both were making a lot of unhealthy noise.

The next morning I called the vet and made an appointment. I put Pokey in the car and stuck Homer in his cage next to her. Homer harked on the way there. I was worried. I've heard that odd behavior in animals can sometimes be the result of rabies. But poor Homer had his rabies shot two weeks before he started harking. When I told the vet about his harking, he laughed. He said to ignore him. I asked if it was possible for a cat to start making a sound, possibly by accident, and then decide he enjoyed it. He said Homer would eventually give it up.

After the visit to the vet, it did seem for a while that Homer had given up harking. He hated the trip and the examination, and he may have known why we went there and was afraid he'd be taken back. But yesterday, he started again. Quietly, with long spaces between, but no doubt about it, he was harking. This morning he sat on my lap and he harked very sweetly up at me. He didn't look angry, and he didn't seem crazy. He was just harking.

Maybe we can learn to laugh when he does it, and show him off to friends. "Ha, ha. That's our silly cat who harks." But ordinary humans may have to go through a bit of fear and anxiety before they find his specialty amusing. We might have to keep him out of the way, like a peculiar uncle, when company comes. □

OUR CAT IS DIFFERENT

Our cat is different
Isn't that what everyone says
but it's true

We speak of cats' independence
and are piqued by their indifference
but our cat needs us

He isn't just a work of art,
viewing us as signals that
food is near

That life is adequate at the moment
and there is no need to move on
to a better situation

He follows us around all day
settling by our feet, on our laps,
in our arms
When his need is particularly great
he crawls directly up our chests
two paws encircle our necks

With snakelike undulations he rubs
his seeking pleading face against
our cheeks, our ears

Trying to be part of us
wanting to chew on earlobes
nuzzle into our beings

Such importunate desire
in a human would be intolerable
but it makes us love him

TYPEWRITER

It's a gray day in New York. Truck noises and people noises almost drown out the drone of my electric typewriter. To say "the typewriter" sounds so impersonal, and I don't feel impersonal toward my typewriter. I love it, as much as one can love any object. My typewriter is my connection...

When we moved to England in 1971, I was forced to write letters, this time in order to keep in touch with friends here at home. It was then that I understood what typewriters were to people who can't write with a pen or pencil. Years earlier I had felt that all typewriters were adversaries. They let me speak, but they flaunted my inability to be perfect. Even maturity hadn't cured me of that desire, the Palmer method intruding again on my need to prove my good character, not to the nuns, but to a machine.

Five years ago, I bought this beautiful blue typewriter with its wonderful correcting key. When I sit down to type on it, I feel I'm with a friend, and writing is a pleasure. It doesn't expect perfection. Perfection would make one of its parts unnecessary. Together we turn out page after page. I hesitate to call it writing. I can never say the words "I'm a writer" without feeling uncomfortable. Writers are always quoted as having loved to write from the time they were children. When I was a child and even a young adult, I wanted to be a painter or a modern dancer. I wanted to be a mother. And when I am so presumptuous as to label myself a writer, the ghosts of all those nuns who walked down the aisles of my life tap their feet impatiently, as if they know the real truth, that I am a non-writer.

So I think I will say that I am not a writer. What I am is a typewritist or a co-typewriter. My typewriter and I, we write together. I'm the brain and it makes the lovely shapes on the page, always the same, always perfect (thanks to that little key), exactly what Mr. Palmer would have ordered if he'd had any sense. Just think how happy those nuns would have been if they could have known it wasn't my black soul they were seeing, but the lack of my good friend, my typewriter. □

THE DECISION

Some people decide early in life what they will be. I was one of those. We were an Irish Catholic family and my father was the head of the household. I knew that. But I also knew that my mother was the important, dependable one.

One day as I pushed my straw doll carriage down the street, following my mother and Aunt Vera, I held my head in that certain way of a woman with important places to go and errands to do, and my inside voice said, "I'm gonna be a Mommy." I felt like a mother with children depending on me. I felt myself tall and fat and important. My feet moved with purpose along the rough sidewalks. I steered the carriage carefully to avoid tipping the baby. I stopped to tuck in the pink blanket around my doll and called to the women to wait for me. They turned, and my mother said, "Hurry up now, or Bohack's will be closed."

They didn't know what I decided that day, but I knew I was one of them, and I knew where I was going. □

A MOTHER'S LOVE

It was a bad day. My mother looked at us, her two daughters, with a troubled eye as we sat across the table from her. Jean's freckles stood out in contrast with her white skin and red hair. Too thin for any mother's comfort, I sat toying with the food on my plate, trying to eat as little as possible. The table was littered with bread crusts and scraps of leftover lamb.

Jean poked my arm. "What are you doing that for? You're just messing."

"I am not messing, am I, Mommy?"

Mother sighed. "Can't you two stop fighting? You're giving me a headache." She leaned her elbows on the table and glared. "I never had a sister. I should think you'd be happy to have each other instead of arguing all the time."

"It's her fault. She's not eating her crusts."

"Stop it both of you. Jean, get the pudding out of the refrigerator. Rosemary, did you wash your hands before you sat down?"

As I answered yes, my sister sang out, "No, she didn't. I was watching. She came right to the table with dirty hands."

"Rosemary, go wash your hands this minute. And you look at your own hands. It makes me sick. I spend good money on gloves for you, and you don't even wear them. Your hands are so chapped, they'll bleed any minute. Go put some hand cream on them."

Mother pushed the dishes to one side. "Nothing is right." Tears welled in her eyes. "Your father is never home, and you kids are always fighting, everything going to pieces. I'm sick of it." She sat slumped on the green kitchen chair, faded housedress matching the washed-out curtains on the windows and the chipped linoleum on the floor.

We came back and sat down. Jean poured milk on her pudding and ate large deliberate spoonfuls. I poured the milk slowly and watched it make a chocolate island. Then I made a crater with my spoon, letting the milk gush into the hole.

"Rosemary, stop messing and eat."

"Okay."

I took one mouthful of pudding and dropped the spoon on the table, wiping my mouth with the back of my hand, soiling both the table and my sleeves.

Making an effort not to scream, Mother looked down at her hands, clenched in her lap. They were strong and beautifully shaped with clear pink nails, regular moons, and white tips. "They're all I have left. I'm fat. My looks are gone. The kids are more Walter's than mine with their gangly arms and legs. No one in my family looked like that."

She looked at the two of us. "Hold up your hands. No, not that way. With the backs to me." She grunted and an unpleasant expression of triumph showed in her pursed smile. "You don't have hands like mine." She held her hands out for us to see, rotating them gracefully. "You've both got your grandmother Maggie's hands—rawboned country girl's hands." Then with added spite, "Everybody in your father's family has big hands and big knuckles."

A few minutes later Jean left the room, face red, eyes watering, chapped hands pressed to her sides. I left for school, mittened hands stuffed in my pockets. When we returned at three, Mother hurried to open the door for us. She was smiling and cheerful. "Your cheeks are so rosy, it must be cold out. Here, let me take your coats, and as soon as you change into your old clothes, come right down. I made some cookies for you."

"Thank you." Jean smiled past her, ducking her embrace.

I leaned against Mother's great warm bosom, and then walked slowly up to my room, coat over my arm, and hands still in their woolen mittens. □

MY TIME AT TIME-LIFE

When I was twenty-eight, I needed a temporary job. I had ten minutes to spare before the interview, so I stopped for a cup of coffee. Twenty minutes later, when the woman in personnel gave me a steno and typing test, she was charmed by how fast I typed with no mistakes. She said stenographers were seldom such good typists. What she didn't know and I didn't tell her was that I only had a thirty-minute stretch when brain and fingers worked that well together, thanks to the coffee.

The job was filling in for a vacationing secretary for two weeks in the office of the three top executives of Time-Life, where perfection in typing and demeanor was expected and delivered. That was back in my Greenwich Village days when I was single, had a three-year-old to support, and a wardrobe consisting of one blue dress, two skirts, two all-purpose black knit tops, jeans, thong sandals, and a pair of black leather pumps. The only things suitable for that job were the blue dress and the black pumps, and I'd worn them for the interview.

I got the job. It was a mistake. The room the secretaries and clerks were in was stratified. The secretaries (the workers) were on one side all facing in one direction, left shoulder to the wall, and the clerks (the debutantes) were two by two in a spacious alcove, facing us. I don't remember the names of the men I worked for. I only saw the back of one of them briefly once when he walked past to his inner office. There wasn't much to do, so my talents weren't really tested. You have to remember that this was in 1959, no "correct" key on the typewriter. It was just you and an eraser and half a dozen carbons, so mistakes were no joke. I drank more coffee than usual during my stay there.

It wasn't mistakes that bothered me; it was those girls sitting in the alcove that I couldn't stand. I was sure they were from Bronxville and Scarsdale. They all had little piles of paper that they shuffled when they weren't chatting about parties and sailing, or showing off engagement rings and new shoes. They were dressed perfectly in what I thought of as conventional, boring clothes, but then I'd been spoiled living in the Village for eight years. If they were snobs, so was I.

Olivia, my immediate superior, also bothered me. She was from the Midwest and prided herself on being a super secretary. She spoke of her boss as if he were a god. She was reverent. Even her voice changed when she talked about him. "Mr. Harden says" and "Mr. Harden thinks" and "Mr. Harden is." I'd worked for a lawyer off and on for seven years and I loved him. I wasn't in love with him. I didn't revere him. He was a nice man who loved his family, loved the law, and liked explaining everything to me. He was married to a woman who'd gone to the same art school I went to, so he didn't think it was unusual if I showed up for work in knee socks and read Proust when I had nothing else to do. We also shared a passion for Schrafft's ice cream sodas, and one or the other of us would rush downstairs to the basement shop before closing time for the day's treat. If I was broke, and he asked me to run down for the sodas, the treat was on him.

At Time-Life, secretaries were not allowed to read when there was nothing to do. I was told I should look busy but not how to look busy. No books. The clerks shuffled papers while they chatted in their little ghetto. I was so prejudiced I was sure they couldn't read. We secretaries pretended to work. I didn't like being a secretary, but pretending to be one was worse than the real thing. All this time I was wearing those damn black pumps, rotating my three outfits, and winding my hair up in a chignon in deference to what I knew was expected. I'd wear my sandals each morning and change to the pumps downstairs in the ladies room of the coffee shop where I got my caffeine boost in the morning. I remember scowling and muttering about it louder each day. Pumps were for going out in the evening, not for work or walking around in.

I felt like a hypocrite. There was a story in our second-grade reader back in Catholic school. It was called "The Hypocrite." The teacher said the purpose of the story was to show us that the letter "y" could be used as a vowel when it took the place of "i" in "hypocrite." But that was just a convenient excuse for piling on the guilt with another lesson. The boy in the story did something forbidden, then lied to his father and got away with it. But he was a hypocrite, and he got his before the last paragraph.

I hated feeling like a hypocrite, and I'd been feeling like one from the moment the personnel lady complimented me at the interview. I knew I wasn't a good typist unless I kept drinking coffee. By the end of the first week I was blaming my ill temper on those damn black shoes, which I knew wasn't the truth. I hated being a secretary. I hated smiling when I didn't feel like smiling. I hated having to pretend to work when there was nothing to do. Hypocrisy is hard on the facial muscles, and between that and the shoes I was uncomfortable from head to toe.

One afternoon after Olivia told me for the fourth time how lucky I was to be working in such an important office for such important people, I went into the ladies room and took a good look at myself in the mirror. There I was with my brown hair pulled back tight like a disappointed school principal. The executive ladies room, painted buff, was sterile and boring and no refuge from the office. I wished I'd gotten a job down on one of the floors where I imagined everyone was having fun designing the magazines, writing the articles, something like The Front Page in Technicolor. I was so disgusted with reality; I kicked my shoes off, then took off my stockings and stuffed them into my pocketbook. I took out my sandals and sighed. Ahh, comfort. Then out came the hairpins. Two shakes of my head and no more school principal, hair halfway down my back and a take-it-or-leave-it look on my face.

I returned to my desk and sat there without pretending to work. I didn't take out a book and read. That would have been overdoing it. The chatter across the room stopped and the girls stared. Olivia was suitably shocked and unnerved. "What if Mr. Harden walked in?" She asked the question the nuns always asked. "Rosemary, why did you do that?"

I don't think I told her that what I really felt like doing was standing on the desk and shouting obscenities, though my limited vocabulary of obscenities wouldn't have made much of an impression. I may have said my feet hurt. But that wouldn't explain the long hair. I told her that I would understand if she didn't want me to come back the next day because I wasn't going to pretend to be busy any more. The executive office of Time-Life wasn't for me. I didn't want to work in an important office for important men. I wasn't hungry enough for that. □

THERE ARE SMILES

Every time I cross the corner of Fifth Avenue and 59th Street, I think of Mr. Halaby and my evening at The Plaza, and I have to smile. In 1956, I thought that corner was the center of the sophisticated world. It wasn't my world, but now and then I had an urge to taste the good life outside of Greenwich Village.

I was sitting in a Midtown employment agency one morning, explaining that I had to have a part-time job that paid at least three dollars an hour, because I was separated from my husband and had a young child to support. The agent looked me over. "You could be in luck. This just came in this morning. It's an easy job, and if Mr. Halaby likes you; maybe he'll give you three dollars an hour." She laughed. "His secretaries are usually lucky. The last one left to get married."

"Thanks. I don't need another husband."

I took down the details and headed for the East Sixties, where Mr. Halaby had an office in his apartment. "There's even a maid," the agent said. "Her name is Mabel, and she'll make your lunch if you want her to." I figured Mabel and the easy work were the reasons the agent was smiling so much as she talked about how lucky his secretaries were. When Mabel opened the door, she eyed my cotton dress and leather sandals with disdain. She had ideas about what secretaries were supposed to wear, and my clothes didn't suit. "I'll tell Mr. Halaby you're here," she said, and left me standing in the living room, one of those perfect uptown rooms—beige, spotless, not a pillow out of place—a Manhattan version of Limbo with no angels, no saints, and nothing older than six months. Mabel came back disgruntled, probably because I wasn't an interloper and she couldn't throw me out. Without a word, she pointed me down the hall toward the office. It was a dark green room decorated with pipes and hunting prints. Behind a mahogany desk sat a man in his late sixties. He was bald with a few long hairs on the top of his head and some shreds of gray next to his ears. When he saw me, he stood up. "Have a seat." He sounded out of breath. "You're Miss—"

"Mrs." His eyes narrowed. "Mrs.? The agency said you were divorced."

"Separated. I have one child."

"And your shorthand. Is it good?"

I tried to be businesslike as I evaded his question. "I worked for a lawyer for nine years." It wasn't necessary to tell him my skills were only adequate. The lawyer had been more interested in talking about contracts than dictating them.

An expression of pleasure crossed Mr. Halaby's face. He liked the answer. "I don't have very much work, but it does have to be done properly. My business is here and in Venezuela. I'm out of the country for three months a year, so I have to have someone who can handle the paperwork while I'm gone. Can you do that?"

"Yes."

Mr. Halaby leaned forward. "My children are grown now and my wife and I are separated, more or less. She's a Catholic, so we can't get a divorce. She lives in South America. My son takes care of the business there, and he sends me duplicate invoices so I'll know what's going on. Most of the work here is filing."

I waited for him to speak about the salary. He was anxious. "Would you like some coffee?"

"No, thank you."

"Tea? Anything?"

"No, thank you."

"Mabel can get it for us." He waved his hand in the direction of the kitchen. "She's here every morning taking care of the place. I don't know what I'd do without her. She's been with me ten years. You can have her make lunch for you and bring it in here. Just tell her what you want when you arrive in the morning."

He was smiling, trying to make everything sound enticing. I figured I had the job if I wanted it. That gave me confidence enough to say, "The agent said you pay two-fifty an hour, but I'm afraid I'll need three dollars an hour or I can't take the job."

Mr. Halaby rocked back and forth in his executive chair and asked aggressively, "What's the problem? Doesn't your husband support you?"

It wasn't any of his business, but he was older than my father, so out of habit, I answered, "I get some support for my child, but I have to make at least three dollars an hour so I can pay for nursery school."

"Don't you get alimony? A beautiful girl like you shouldn't have to work. Get him to support you."

I didn't waste time explaining that it was a lost cause.

"If I can get a job that pays enough, I don't need alimony."

"How much does nursery school cost?"

"Twelve-fifty a week for half days."

"If you work ten hours a week, that's only thirty dollars a week. After taxes and carfare, and school for the kid, you won't have anything left." He frowned. "I'll tell you what I'll do. I'll make it four dollars an hour. That way you'll have something left over to spend on yourself, for new clothes or jewelry or something."

Four dollars an hour wasn't good luck. It was a miracle.

He was still muttering when I left the room. "Do you have to pay rent too? Good God, a girl like you shouldn't have to worry about these things."

By the end of the first week, Mabel made plain what she thought of me. It wasn't just my Greenwich Village outfits that annoyed her. She had no use for someone who made a living, especially four dollars an hour of living, poking at a typewriter in a dark room, where an old man was trying to talk her into going on a world tour with him. Or to Miami. Or just out to dinner.

Aside from typing two letters and filing three invoices each day, my job consisted of listening to Mr. Halaby talk of all the fantastic things we could do if only I wasn't so hardhearted. This was the part of the luck the agent hadn't mentioned. It was so ridiculous, that I tried not to hurt his feelings by pretending I thought he was joking.

He rocked in his chair, speaking persuasively. "My sister could be our chaperon. She'd love a trip. We could hire a nurse to take care of your little girl. Or maybe your mother could mind her until we come back."

I put a sheet of paper in the typewriter in an effort to appear busy, although I had nothing to type. "Please, don't be silly."

"Who's silly? Not me," he snorted. "Just think of the opportunity. I bet you've never traveled. Where have you been outside of New York?"

"Nowhere." I was annoyed, but not enough to get into the game of defending the few places I'd been. "And I'm not going anywhere."

"Why not?"

"Because I don't want to be divorced for adultery."

"Who's suggesting anything like that?" He leered at me. "I have a heart condition." He clapped his hand to his chest. "I could die in a minute. Besides we'd have my sister for a chaperon."

"I'd better finish this." I could feel him watching me, so after copying a few lines from an invoice, I pulled the paper out of the typewriter, slipped it into a drawer, and stood up to leave. "Goodbye, Mr. Halaby, I'll see you tomorrow."

The sun coming through the window, shining on his pink scalp and across his drooping cheeks, made him resemble an aged version of the basset hound in the print above his desk. "Let me know if you change your mind," he said plaintively.

I carried my dishes out to the kitchen where Mabel was cleaning the oven. I put my plate, cup, saucer, and spoon into the empty dishwasher, and smiled at Mabel's busy back. "That was delicious, Mabel, thank you."

She charged over to the dishwasher. "Three dishes! Is that what you think a dishwasher is for? You don't use a dishwasher for three dishes." She snatched the dishes out of the machine and stuck them in the sink. "I do them by hand. I don't waste Mr. Halaby's money like that." She was so busy making a scene, she missed my exit.

I shut the front door hard, annoyed that I'd been polite, and annoyed that she'd been rude. There was no placating her. She never missed an opportunity to make an unpleasant remark when Mr. Halaby was near. I knew she could hear everything that went on in the office, and I could see what it looked like to her. It even looked that way to me. There I was, sitting in that stuffy room with Mr. Halaby, getting four dollars an hour for no other reason than that I was young and pretty, while she was out running around with a mop and broom being loyal and hardworking and not making a third of that.

The next morning, Mr. Halaby was irritated. "Don't you have any clothes besides the ones you wear every day? I'm not criticizing. I just think you ought to have better clothes."

I wondered what he'd say if I told him that to me he was an expensively dressed basset hound come down off the print on his wall. However, I probably had the only four-dollar-an-hour part-time job in New York, so I said, "Do you have anything else to go out, Mr. Halaby?"

He cheered up. "You know what I'd like to do? I'd like to take you to Bendels or Bergdorf's and dress you in style." He was clucking with pleasure. "You'd be something in sable."

I leaned on the typewriter. I'd been conscientiously cool and secretarial from the moment I walked in the first day, had given no encouragement, and here he was, dressing me at Bergdorf's. And undressing me first, no doubt. I put my hand to my throat and fingered the button that held my dress collar closed.

"I can see it now," he said, "I'd walk up Fifth Avenue with you on my arm. Diamonds, furs, jewels. Every man who saw us would be green with envy. They'd go out of their minds."

That's when I started to laugh. Back in the law office, there was a client who used to bring his "secretary" Gloria along whenever he had an appointment. She would sit next to my desk in the outer office, carefully patting her midnight mink and bleached blonde hair, chewing gum in time to a mambo beat that only she could hear. I could see myself in a coat like Gloria's, snapping Doublemint, and being rushed across Fifth Avenue, Mr. Halaby clutching my arm like a policeman, his eyes darting from side to side, making sure that every man in sight knew he'd caught and dressed me.

"What are you laughing at?" He was hurt. "I'd just like to buy you some nice clothes, take you to some nice places." He held up his hand like a traffic cop, as if to ward off thoughts of impropriety. "Is there any harm in that? I mean, I wouldn't suggest anything else. I've got a heart condition. I wouldn't dare."

"Goodbye, Mr. Halaby." His face collapsed into canine sadness. "I'll see you tomorrow."

"Your problem is, you don't know how to flirt." My roommate Leila was standing in front of the mirror combing her hair. She laughed. "You're so serious."

Leila was a beautiful Greek aristocrat who had reached New York by way of Paris, Rome, and a lot of money, one of those honey-haired Greeks you see in Athens, lightly tanned and looking like silk under the sun.

"You Americans, you're so stiff. You're like children." She shook her head. "You've got to promise men something. A little touch on the arm. A special glance." She smiled and rolled her eyes.

I stood in front of the mirror to survey myself. "I can't." I was tall, thin, and very American, and I felt like a two-hundred-year-old Puritan from New England. "I don't know how."

"It's easy. You don't have to go to bed with them." Her French Italian Greek accent purred the words. "Be charming. All you have to do is make them think they're interesting." She lifted one shoulder mockingly and laughed. "And maybe they will be."

I rang the doorbell. Leila's right. Why should I be so serious? The door opened. "Good morning, Mr. Halaby." He was the first man I'd seen since talking to Leila the night before, so I gave him a big smile and walked through to the office, where I sat down and busied myself with the papers on my desk. "Would you like me to do this filing now or have you something else for me to do?"

"You're different today." He stood in front of my desk. "What's happened? You haven't changed your mind have you?"

"About what?"

"About having dinner with me."

I could hear Leila say, "Be charming," so I smiled at him again.

"You will? Wonderful." He jumped up from his desk. "I'll make a reservation for tonight. Where would you like to go? How about the Edwardian Room? Would you like that?"

"Sounds fine." Leila was right. It's easy. See how happy he is? I felt a crunch of anxiety. My God, if he's not careful, he may have that heart attack he's always talking about.

"What's the matter? You're not sorry you said you would have dinner with me, are you?"

"No, of course not." I'd heard of the Edwardian Room. It was in The Plaza. I'd never been to the restaurant, but I knew about the hotel. When a New Yorker said, "I'm meeting him at The Plaza," no one asked, "What Plaza?" At least, they didn't ask twice. The only time I had ever been in the hotel was to deliver a contract from my former boss to a client who had a suite there. The client spilled a bottle of ink on the carpet, put his foot up on the gold brocade armchair to tie his shoe, and called room service for a lunch of sandwiches and champagne, justifying my belief that The Plaza was the epitome of luxury and decadence.

And now I was meeting Mr. Halaby there for dinner. I felt very smart in Leila's black wool skirt and my all-purpose black sweater as the doorman smiled me up the steps. True, I wasn't on the arm of a handsome young man, like the models in *Vogue*, but I wasn't on Mr. Halaby's arm either, which helped the illusion.

I saw Mr. Halaby standing by a potted palm. In his expensive suit and silk tie, he fit in better here than in his beige and green bachelor quarters. Here he was just another prosperous businessman waiting in a hotel lobby.

The Edwardian Room was a revelation, white tablecloths covered with shining glasses and heavy silver, waiters constantly at attention, and a maître'd' to usher us discreetly to our table with a murmured, "This way, if you please, Mr. Halaby."

"We'll have champagne, Rudy. You'd like champagne, wouldn't you?" Mr. Halaby was in a gay mood. I spread my napkin on my lap like a well-behaved child out to dinner with an elderly relative, and said, "Yes, thank you." I'd only had champagne once, and couldn't remember either liking or disliking it, but didn't want to say so.

Mr. Halaby made a fuss about ordering dinner then didn't eat much. The food was delicious and I was hungry, so I made up for his lack of appetite. It was embarrassing to take so long to eat while he toyed with his food, but he kept encouraging me and filling my wine glass. By the end of the meal he was leaning over his barely touched plate and talking about what great fun we'd have on our trip. I kept saying I wasn't going on a trip, and he kept carrying on about the Queen Elizabeth and smart hotels in Paris and London.

Maybe it was the wine and all that food, or just sitting there and being so artificial, but suddenly I felt unhappy and tired. I noticed other couples like us, older men with younger women, the men talking, the women smiling. I felt as if everyone knew that I was wearing borrowed clothes, that I could hardly tell champagne from ginger ale, and that I didn't like the man I was with. All I wanted to do was dredge up enough smiles and good humor to be polite and keep the job.

After the doorman helped us into a cab, Mr. Halaby coughed and said, "We're closer to my place, so you can drop me off first, then go on downtown. There's no point in me taking you all the way there and having to come back up again."

At least that took care of the problem of not asking him up to my apartment. In the two weeks I'd worked for him, Mr. Halaby's face had registered everything from outraged innocence to infantile greed. When we stopped at his house it wore an expression I couldn't figure out. "I'd love to ask you in," he said, smiling an apology, "but my doctor says I have to get to bed early, and I have to follow doctor's orders, you know."

"That's fine. The babysitter has to leave by ten." I was so relieved. I felt like myself for the first time that evening. "Thank you for dinner."

"Here, take this to pay the driver." He pushed a folded twenty-dollar bill into my hand.

"It isn't necessary." I tried to hand the money back, but he was out the door so fast it wasn't possible. The driver shifted on the front seat, and gave me a know-it-all taxi driver smirk in the mirror that said, "Are you kidding? You earned it. Grab it, before he changes his mind."

Mr. Halaby leaned toward the cab window. "Don't be silly, I should have taken you home first." His smile was as false as mine had been earlier, and now I understood the expression that had puzzled me. It was the first time I'd seen him lie. He hadn't intended to take me home and he didn't want to ask me in. Whatever it was he wanted, he'd had it in the restaurant.

The ride home was unpleasant. I was used to selling my time as a secretary, a job that required office skills and a moderate amount of courtesy, nothing more. It paid the rent and fed us, and when it was over each day, real life started. Somehow, I'd let myself be beguiled by Leila into doing something I didn't understand, and I felt bought. I couldn't bear the way the driver stared at me. Silly as it seems now, I thought I deserved it. So much so, that when we reached Eighth Street, I told him to let me out, handed him the twenty, and said we might as well split the change.

"Are you kidding?" Now he smiled.

The next morning was awful. You know how it is. You look at yourself in the mirror, toothbrush in hand, a mouthful of suds, and think you're seeing the Truth. What I thought that morning was, "My God, how could you have been so stupid? You'll have to go in there and face him today. And you need that job." And after that, "What an easy way to make twenty dollars. All you have to do is sit with an old man and smile at him every once in a while."

"Good morning! Good morning!" Mr. Halaby's elation was overwhelming. "Here's something I thought you'd like." He stuck a bottle of perfume in front of me." A beautiful girl like you should always wear perfume."

"Thank you very much, but I don't wear perfume."

"Why not? It's expensive. Here, I'll open it for you. You'll see. You'll like it."

"Please don't open it. I'm allergic to perfume. I never wear it." I pulled away from my desk, but not in time. He had fumbled the seal off, then grabbed my hand and splashed some scent on it.

"Smell that. Who could resist it?"

I was furious. If I hadn't gone out to dinner with him, he would never have dared to touch me, much less pour perfume over me, one of those overpowering scents that hang in the air.

I knew I had to say something to make him understand that the night before was an aberration, a moment of bad judgment that wouldn't happen again.

"Mr. Halaby..."

"I'll have to calm down." He was hopping around his desk, dancing with pleasure. He waggled a finger at me. "It isn't good for me to be so excited. You have a bad effect on me."

"Mr. Halaby..."

"Listen, if we're going to go out together, you need some terrific clothes."

I turned my back on him. Until then, I hadn't wanted to hurt his feelings, but now I didn't care.

"Bring your book over here."

I picked up my steno pad and pencil, stalked over to his desk and sat down across from him. I knew something was about to happen. If he had been the kind of person who thought about anything but himself, he would have noticed how angry I was. I wasn't trying to hide it. I was a still-chaste ex-Catholic, ex-virgin, and the old man on the other side of the desk was waving money at me as if I were a twenty-dollar call girl.

He dictated a letter, and then stood up to go to the file in back of me for something he said he needed. As he brushed by, he leaned over, grabbed my face, and kissed me on the lips.

I shoved him away and growled, "Get on the other side of the desk or you'll be taking your own dictation."

He hurried back to his seat, frightened, as if he thought I might hit him. "It was just a kiss. I have a heart condition, you know." He huddled in his chair and whined, "I thought you liked me. Last night? The perfume?"

"This is today. I don't kiss people in the office, and I don't kiss anyone if I don't feel like it." I went back to my desk and slammed the book down. "Last night was a mistake. I shouldn't have gone out with you. It won't happen again."

That was the end of the job. He was too intimidated to fire me, so I finished out the morning, and then quit. As I gathered my things to leave, he sat under the basset hound watching me with a sad expression.

Mabel, who heard the whole thing from the hall where she had stationed herself that morning, escorted me to the door and for the first time in our acquaintance was cordial.

I never saw Mr. Halaby again. I don't remember what street his house was on, or what kind of perfume it was that he tried to give me. And I don't know whether he wanted more than just a rough kiss and some friendly smiles. Maybe he was just old and lonely and needed company, something that didn't occur to me then. Whatever it was, at some point I stopped being angry with him for trying to buy me, and with myself for following Leila's advice with so little discretion.

It was my last attempt at conscious flirtation. After that, I stuck to being tall and thin and terribly American. I never wanted to give anyone another chance to make me feel I had to split the change. □

IN THE MEANTIME

Jenny and I weren't unusual in Greenwich Village—a single mother and child, living in a small apartment decorated with baskets and posters, sitting on the floor to eat at the coffee table and using big pillows to turn beds into sofas. We lived within our means with next to nothing to spare, but sometimes, in spite of everything, when the sun came up on the right side of the bed, we splurged and ate breakfast out.

One morning, I opened my eyes and saw the sun shining on the bare branches of the tree outside our front window. The air was so clear and everything looked so new that I called out to Jenny, "It's too nice a day to eat boring old raisin bran at home. Let's go to The Bagel for breakfast."

Four years old then, she struggled into overalls and a t-shirt with a little help from me, and I made the beds and straightened up with a little hindrance from her. We piled on coats, hats, scarves, and boots and skipped over to West Fourth Street. Or rather, she skipped and I tried not to.

I was twenty-nine, and conscious of my responsibilities as a payer of rent and a client of Con Ed and Bell Telephone, as Jenny, the focus of my life, skipped next to me. The first thing I asked myself about any man I met was whether he was a likely candidate for the job of good father for her, and then, whether he would be a good husband for me. I wanted a husband and I wanted more children. In the meantime, I had to work to feed and clothe us, and that was the "in spite of everything" I mentioned earlier.

The Bagel was a small restaurant on West 4th Street with a counter and a few small tables, a simple menu, delicious fresh food, and a short-order cook who was always cheerful and greeted us like good friends. We hopped up to the counter and ordered our favorite breakfasts—bagel and lox for me, and scrambled eggs, bacon, and toast with strawberry jam for Jenny.

When I left Jenny at nursery school that morning, I made up my mind that nothing would depress me on such a beautiful day. No matter what happened at work, I would be cheerful and happy, and not let it bother me. It wouldn't be easy. I was a secretary in a real estate office on 13th Street that could have been the model for Sartre's *No Exit,* except that there were four main characters instead of three, and it wasn't as pleasant.

The office was stuffed into a dark studio apartment in the back of a faded brick building. It was almost Dickensian in its gritty depressing clutter. The desks and chairs were stained and scratched, the metal files were grimy, and the walls hadn't been painted or washed from the day the agency moved in ten years earlier. The room was so full that even the windowsill was piled high with papers, rent books, periodicals, and just plain junk. The closet that was supposed to double as storage space for coats and old banking records was always full of mops and pails, so coats were thrown over a chair in the kitchenette and banking records were filed in the cupboard under the sink. The cupboards above held office supplies, three old adding machines, and boxes of ancient stationery. Since anyone who came to clean was given instructions not to move things, housekeeping involved emptying ashtrays and stirring up dirt on the floor.

Bert looked up from the pile of messy papers he was pushing around on his desk. "Yuh late," he smirked, "one minute, huh?"

"It's a beautiful day isn't it?"

"Where did you put the receipts from 24th Street?"

"Where they belong." It was hopeless to waste pleasantries on someone whose biggest thrill of a morning was to catch you in a mistake. Bert let me know that he despised me every day we had the misfortune to work together. He was an Orthodox Jew. For him, working in the Village in the late Fifties was like wearing a hair shirt. There were single women, people with liberal ideas, painters, writers, and poets. He held me up as a prime example of what was wrong with the neighborhood. I was divorced, a mother, an artist-cum-secretary, and worst of all, a gentile dating a Jew.

I decided to ignore him, the same decision I'd been making five days a week for the last six months, and reached for the apartment listings folder. The phone on my desk rang.

"No, the apartment hasn't been rented yet."

"Can you tell me, do you rent to Negroes?" Bert had taken great pains to tell me what lies to tell in the event I was asked that question.

I took a deep breath and said, "Yes, we do."

"Because, if you don't, I don't want to waste my time or yours." The voice was friendly and practical.

"We do. Please, go ahead and look at it. May I have your name, please?"

Bert scowled. He had a well-developed bigot alarm that went off any time someone who wasn't an Orthodox Jew appeared on the horizon, and that day it was set for any black who might try to rent one of our apartments by what Bert considered insidious means, such as using the telephone to call about the ad in that day's paper. "Who wazzat?"

"Someone who saw the ad in the paper."

"A guy?" He stood up and squeezed through the narrow space between our desks and hovered over me, leaning a beefy hand on the corner of my desk. It was hard to ignore how much I disliked him. "He wasn't colored, was he?"

"Yes."

"What did you tell him to come for? Why didn't you say it was rented?"

"Because it isn't rented."

"Jeez, Mr. Kolman's gonna be real angry with you. You could lose your job that way. You know he said he didn't want any coloreds." Bert was whining. He was blamed for anything that went wrong in the office.

"I told you I wasn't going to lie."

"Yeah, but I didn't think you meant it." Saliva spluttered at the corners of his mouth. "For God's sake, don't answer the phone any more. He's gonna be furious."

He sat down at his desk and rocked back and forth in his squeaky chair. "Listen, you don't understand. He's got his reasons. He can't rent to coloreds. Look at that guy, the doctor, the one who's his best friend." Bert's lip curled. "He's colored, but Kolman wouldn't rent an apartment to him either. He'd never get another mortgage if he did."

At the thought of Kolman's business acumen Bert became almost friendly. He tipped the chair back and stopped rocking, smiling as he gave me the benefit of his ten years of experience in the quagmire of New York real estate "Look, its business. It's okay to be democratic, but if you rent to a colored, you can't get a mortgage. No bank will give you one. You gotta understand these things."

"It's the law now," I said. "You have to rent to anyone who can pay and has good references."

"Who's gonna pay attention to that law? Everybody'll get around it."

"Jim Hackett rents to Negroes."

"That Commie? He'll go broke one of these days. The bank'll find out and that'll be the end of him." Bert's eyes narrowed and he pursed his lips in pleasant expectation of the day when Jim Hackett would get his due.

In spite of swearing never to talk to him about anything more important than the weather, I was once more embroiled in trying to explain, if not morality, at least the law. Nearly every conversation we had ended exactly the same way, with Bert ranting about "the Commies." Soon he would get to the part about it being too bad Joe McCarthy didn't have time to clean up Greenwich Village before he died, and would be astounded when I said, "Like Hitler with the Jews."

"Listen, what am I going to tell Kolman?"

"Tell him anything you like."

I was more upset than I let on. Mr. Kolman might just fire me on the spot, and I needed the job. I needed it so much it wouldn't even be a relief to walk out the door and know I never had to come back. I was a legal secretary, a skill considered unusual in the Village, and I was being paid eighty-five dollars a week—five dollars above the going rate. The extra five dollars was all I had above expenses, and it wouldn't be easy to give up.

There was no more talk after that. I typed, and Bert called banks and plumbers, loving the sound of his own voice, obsequious to the bankers, patronizing to the plumbers. At noon, when I opened my lunch, he looked up from his work and asked me what kind of sandwich I had. I sighed. It was Bert's habit to lecture me on the advantages of keeping Kosher. That day I was eating a salami sandwich and drinking milk, not a gourmet combination, but no sin for an ex-Catholic.

In an effort to be persuasive, he moderated his disgust. "You shouldn't eat meat and drink milk at the same time. It's unhealthy." He put his hand up as if making an excuse. "It's not just superstition. It's for real."

My lunches may have lacked class, but they were the highlight of my working day. Sometimes I forced myself to run home at noon so I could eat without being nagged. Once I tried eating in Washington Square Park but there were so many junkies and drunks, it was hard to concentrate on the food.

"Excuse me, Bert; I'm going to read during lunch today. I have to take this book back to the library tonight."

Bert had perfected the art of smiling up to but not including his eyes, and he gave me a loud laugh and a face full of crinkles to show what he thought of my intellectual pursuits. "Maybe you could lend the book to Mr. Kolman. He reads."

At one o'clock Dan Kolman walked in, and Bert sat up so straight I thought he might salute. "Good afternoon, Mr. Kolman. There's something I need to speak to you about." Kolman was rich, educated, and the owner of several apartment buildings. He was an ardent sailor and a collector of nineteenth-century watercolors. He also had an ulcer, which may have explained the pinched, bitter expression that was always so at odds with his handsome face. He was only three years older than Bert, who both hated and admired him,

"Mr. Kolman, can I speak to you a minute?"

Kolman was good at ignoring people, usually in direct proportion to how much they wanted his attention. "Rosemary, get Dick Webster on the phone. Then have Sam come up here."

Now he turned to Bert. "He left the garbage pails out again."

The garbage men came by three times a week, and three times a week, if the super didn't catch the pails before they hit the sidewalk, Kolman hit the ceiling.

"I've told you, you've got to make him bring them in immediately."

"Honest to Pete, Mr. Kolman, the guys just came through the street." Gone was the military stance. Bert's hands were out in supplication. "There wasn't time for him to get them in."

It usually took Kolman at least twenty minutes to become enraged about something after he came in. A day when he walked in furious could only get worse.

"Mr. Webster on the phone, Mr. Kolman."

At the flip of some inner switch, Kolman's voice and eyes changed from cold to warm. "Of course, Dick, dinner first. Be there at seven forty-five. Marvelous."

He replaced the receiver and his face resumed its ordinary reptilian expression as I dialed Sam's number. I wanted to quit right then.

"Sam, Mr. Kolman would like you to come up to the office."

Sam was a favorite target for Kolman and he was a problem for me. I passionately believed in the Bill of Rights and the Gettysburg Address, and Sam was black. However, he was also drunk and stumbling, though not as drunk and stumbling as he made out when he emerged from the squalor of the hot, dirty basement where he lived with his wife, Lydia, and their three children. He was inefficient and unreliable, and nobody in his right mind would have hired him. Kolman fired him every few weeks when the alcohol fumes became too much to bear, but relented when Lydia came up from the basement laundry, where she did washing and ironing for the tenants, to beg for leniency for herself and the children.

Bert said Kolman kept Sam on because he was so cheap, but it seemed as if Kolman enjoyed having Sam around to harass. No day passed without some clear proof of negligence on Sam's part. It gave Kolman plenty of opportunity to prove his own superiority, authority, and humanity. He could berate Sam for his failures in front of us, then fire him, and then rehire him for the sake of the wife and children. Maybe Kolman's routine with Sam was a balm for his bad conscience about his renting practices.

Kolman detested Bert, but it was easy to see why he kept him on. Bert did the dirty work and knew where everything was, and he was sufficiently in awe of Kolman's wealth and position to make the remote possibility of being fired terrifying to him and gratifying to Kolman.

I wasn't sure why Kolman wanted me in the office since he didn't really need a secretary. A clerk could have done just as well. I almost quit the first week I worked for him. He didn't give me my paycheck until three-thirty on Friday, a half-hour after the bank closed. When I asked if it would be possible to have it earlier the next week so I could cash it on my lunch hour, he told me it wouldn't be convenient, that I should learn to manage my money better. I told him I would have to look for another job, since I had to pay my bills each Friday. After that, my check was handed to me each Friday morning with a remark from Bert about "some people" always getting their way. Maybe Kolman used me to get at Bert. He sometimes became friendly and confidential in front of him, hinting that he intended to make me his assistant, a promise that held no appeal for me and sent Bert into a panic. Or it may have been ego, for whenever one of Kolman's friends came to the office, he always had some dictation that couldn't wait another minute and I would have to drop what I was doing, and, steno pad in hand, play the efficient secretary. The rest of the time he was as unpleasant to me as he was to Sam and Bert, distributing ill will without regard to race, color, or creed.

The one person Kolman was powerless against was his carefully coiffed, gray-haired mother, who stopped by the office every day to drive him mad. She criticized his clothes, his eating habits, his girlfriend. If she stopped by when he wasn't in, she turned her bad temper on me. Bert escaped attack by a combination of toadying and carrying tales for her future assaults on her son.

When Sam fumbled into the room, Bert was officious. "Sam, you left the garbage pails out on the sidewalk after the men emptied them. Mr. Kolman is very angry." Sam looked at Bert through glassy brown eyes, and put his hand to his chin as if to study the problem seriously. "They come already? I din hear 'em go by. Ah'll get 'em now."

"Alright. But don't let it happen again."

Kolman twisted a manila envelope into a tight wad and threw it into the wastebasket. "It's not alright, Bert. It's up to you to see that things are done properly. You're supposed to be in charge of the building. I won't put up with this."

Sam nodded in agreement as if they were talking about someone else. "Thas right, Mr. Kolman. You right. Ah'll fix it."

The phone on my desk rang and Bert rushed over to pick it up.

"Bert, I thought I told you to let Rosemary answer the phone. You get on with that report."

"One moment, please." Bert pressed his hand over the receiver. "I think I'd better take the calls."

"Why?"

Perspiration made Bert's hair stringy where it fell across his forehead. "Uh, maybe she better tell you."

For the first time that day I looked directly at Kolman. I held my breath. I thought of my paycheck. "Because I'll show the apartment to anyone who wants to look at it."

Kolman looked as if he had crystallized. He was so icy it was surprising to see his lips move. "Can't you be discreet about it?"

"No." I felt ill. I should have walked out then, but the extra five dollars was the difference between just managing and having enough money for an occasional treat like that morning's breakfast.

We all should have quit. Sam should have told Kolman to keep his fifty dollars a month and his crummy dungeon. Bert should have stayed in Williamsburg where he could wear his yarmulke and not have to contend with the twentieth century. Kolman should have been sitting at his desk crying because he had an ulcer and a mother who didn't love him.

Instead he stared at me and I stared at him. "Take care of it, Bert."

When Kolman left at five-thirty, I covered my typewriter and cleared my desk.

Bert looked up. "Yuh leaving already?"

It was part of his cult of indispensability to be there earlier and later than I was. I put on my coat, nodded goodbye, and left, so tired and depressed I could hardly think. The job was a trap, life was a trap, and there was nothing I could do about it. I had to work, and there wasn't a better job to be had.

I held Jenny's hand on the way home from nursery school, mustering up enough strength to answer her questions with "uh huh" and "yes, dear" whenever it seemed appropriate. I think I may have groaned a few times in self-pity.

We were almost home when Jenny stopped under a lamplight and held out something for me to see. It was a pebble she'd picked up along the way. I looked down at her face, excited and glowing from the cold, her mittened hand outstretched, and I felt myself awakening. She was so beautiful. She was what mattered. The winter sky was clear, and through the branches I could see the moon and the stars. I picked her up and showed them to her. Then I kissed her and carried her close the rest of the way home.□

FIRST DATE

I met Milt at a party my roommate Maureen and I gave when I was twenty-eight. I'd been separated for a year and was busy looking for a husband for me and a father for my three-year-old daughter, Jenny. I must have been feeling festive, because two days before Christmas I invited everybody I knew, including the four young men I was dating at the time, and told them they could bring a guest along with a bottle of wine. I was busy behaving like a teenager, juggling boyfriends and having a great time, making up for my teen years when most of the young men were away at war.

My two-room apartment was on the third floor of an old nineteenth-century frame house in Greenwich Village, and on the night of the party Jenny and my mother were in my mother's apartment directly below mine. I was nervous about the consequences of one too many people on the creaky floor above them. My next-door neighbor opened her door and let the party spread to her place, but it was still a mob, so at eleven o'clock I started counting. Milt was the seventy-fifth person to come up the stairs.

When he asked for Marlene, I tried to convince him that he was at the wrong address. "There's no Marlene at the party." I held up my hand up like a policeman stopping traffic. "Try next door," I said. "I know there's a party there."

I can still see him on the stairs, looking up at me, dark hair, brown eyes, blue overcoat, hands on the railing. While I was trying to get rid of him, my roommate Maureen came out in the hall and said, "Hi, Milt. Hey, Rosemary, this is Milt Okun, the folk singer I told you about." So up he came. He was the last person we let in.

Several times during the evening, I saw him looking at me—you know, across a crowded room—and if he liked what he saw, so did I. He was leaning against a wall. He was taller than everyone else and reminded me of my favorite Uncle Arthur who was very tall and gentle. I was trying to open a stubborn window, while an actress I'd never seen before was sliding off the couch doing a writhing version of something sexy to Harry Belafonte singing "Mary's Boy Child." Everyone else was watching the performance, but Milt came over and offered to help. I think he said, "Let me do that." And I said, "Thank you." Not quite love at first sight.

Two days later he telephoned. I was out, and Maureen answered. Milt asked her if she thought I would be interested in going out with him. He didn't know she had designs on him herself. So when I came home after work, she was lying on the couch in the living room, glowering. I'm not sure she's ever forgiven me, but that's a whole other story. Anyway, when she told me what he'd said, I offered to tell him I was too busy, and she growled, "You might as well go out with him. If he's interested in you, he probably won't be interested in me."

I should describe myself in those days. Tall, thin, ex-art student, single mother, not quite grownup, a dance student, a strident daydreamer. The tall thin part was crucial to my interest in Milt, I guess. When I was growing up 5' 7" was considered an unacceptable height for a girl. The only people who didn't make comments about my height were other girls who were 5' 7" and over. We were all too busy crouching in our flat shoes trying to pretend we were short, so that boys and young men wouldn't take one look at us and decide we were undesirable. Short and curvy was the style of the day. And Milt didn't just look tall from across the room, I had to look up at him when he came over and offered to open the window. It felt good.

Anybody who knew the Village could have spotted me in a crowd. I was as typical as you could get. The clothes, the sandals, the long hair, the attitude. I was often depressed and sometimes happy. Milt happened to meet me on a crest and that was my good luck. Most leftists looked like Villagers, so folk singer that he was, he may have mistaken me for a leftist. When he called later, we made a date for dinner. I put on my black pumps, borrowed a skirt from Maureen, and we went to the Penguin, a chichi restaurant over on Ninth Street. We were only going six blocks, but Milt had driven in from Brooklyn, so we got in his Buick convertible and drove to the restaurant. The entrance was downstairs in a brownstone. It was elegant, a long narrow room with banquettes on the right wall, white tablecloths, silver, and crystal. We sat side by side at the table and went through the getting-to-know-you routine. The dinner was wonderful. I had broiled salmon and real whipped cream on a chocolate dessert. It was the best restaurant food I'd had since the days when my father, a wholesale milk dealer, used to take us to eat at his customers' restaurants in the City when I was a kid. Most of my dates took me to delicatessens and coffee shops, or to arty storefront cafes, bigger on candle wax spilled on the tables than on tablecloths.

Eating dinner didn't take long, so when we got back in the car, Milt suggested we take a drive. We turned down Eighth Street, and I was enjoying the luxury of being a passenger with nothing to do but window shop, when Milt asked, "What do you think about the Dodgers?"

The Dodgers? We were passing the Art Theater, and my best friend Mickey was sitting in the window selling tickets. She used to let me in all the time, so I saw a lot of movies, and I thought, I should be in there. What am I doing with him? He's got a car, he's wearing a tie, and now he's asking what I think of the Dodgers. I

159

could be out with my father. I tried to sound interested and asked, "What about the Dodgers?"

He turned and looked at me and said, "They moved to Los Angeles."

And I said, "Oh." He explained to me how terrible it was that the Dodgers sold out and moved to another city. They didn't care that they left their fans in shock. He asked me, "Don't you know anything about loyalty?"

We drove up the East Side talking about folk music and theater, with me thinking I'd probably never see him again. And what for? I didn't know anything about baseball, and he probably didn't know anything about art. He didn't kiss me that first night, and that was good. It gave me time to want to be kissed. A week later, I was in love, and I said goodbyes to the four young men.

It was on the second date that I really impressed him. We were driving on Forty-Second Street, past the New York Public Library, with the radio on. I listened to the woman singing, and distinguished myself when I asked, frowning, "Is that woman singing flat, Milt?" He stopped paying attention to the traffic.

"What did you say?"

"I said, is that woman singing flat?"

"She is." He was surprised—and pleased. He said her name was Maria Callas.

Fifty years later I'm still amazed that we fell in love with strangers who weren't what they appeared to be, but were exactly what we wanted. I probably looked like the life of the party. Maybe he thought I was happy all the time. And he reminded me of my Uncle Arthur, and he helped me. He is gentle, and opening a window for me was the first of the thousands of times he's helped me when I couldn't do something for myself, though mechanically inclined he's not. We still like good restaurants. I've learned a little about music and he's learned something about art. I'm still not interested in sports, and even though we've lived in Los Angeles for the last thirty years, he still won't root for the Dodgers. We've both learned a lot about loyalty.

And as for being a good father, in Jenny's own words at the age of ten when she was explaining to a friend that Milt had adopted her, she asked, "Mommy, how old was I when we married Milt?" □

HAPPY ANNIVERSARY

A year ago we spent our anniversary, May 11, working together, sitting apart, and then dining with Steve and Mickey Randolph at Christ Cella.

The work consisted of taking Lee Holdridge up to visit Cherry Lane and introducing him to all the staff. I believe he must have been impressed. I am, each time we go up there.

The sitting apart was at the Hilton Harbor Inn where Milt and Lee and the Cherry Lane executives ate lunch and where Rose Reitter and I sat at a table not far from them but out of sight, reading her poetry and my essay on my typewriter. I am so easily distracted that when Corrine said she couldn't make it this week, I almost gave up and joined Milt. Then I decided that it was more important for me to keep on working with Rose, being listened to and read, than being part of the Cherry Lane "team." Time for that tomorrow.

The reading was great. Rose's poetry is wonderful. She makes me know how much I love her when I read what she has written. Or should I say, why I love her. Her thinking is so gemlike. The words follow one another like the links and small and delicate jewels in fine antique jewelry.

God. I never knew it would be so hard to write about words. It's more than words with Rose. It's the images and a quality of words dancing, and making points with great precision. I love what she writes.

I suggested to her that maybe sometime in the future we could do a small book together and call it FRIENDS. That sounds like a funny title, because we don't write about ourselves as friends, but I had the feeling that it would be appropriate in a way. If people read what we write, in a sense, side by side, maybe it would be apparent why and how we are friends.

And the anniversary dinner with the Randolphs was fun. We always enjoy being with them. Mickey and I grow to understand each other better and better over the years, and Milt and Steve have a very comfortable friendship. It's funny; I always think that Steve and I are alike, much less accommodating to other people than Milt and Mickey. Steve and I are very mechanical. We love the plumbing. We're conservative in our approaches and conclusions. We have rigid standards for our own behavior and everyone else's. Mickey and Milt are more amenable to bending with necessity. Necessity that Steve and I don't see as necessity. They are much more practical about business and a lot less idealistic. It makes for a pleasant and easy friendship.

But what's an anniversary all about if not thinking about the big day in the past when you joined hands and said this is it. I suppose the first thing one considers is, where did all that time go? After the feeling of being a new bride wore off, I always expected it to come back again, and never ceased to be surprised that it didn't. Even now I sometimes catch myself longing for that feeling of wonder. Of course, I have a feeling of wonder: I was ever so lucky to meet Milt. I don't think any other person would have been the right one for me.

And the wedding. Thirty-five people gathered at Leah and Will's apartment on Livingston Street in Brooklyn Heights. All Milt's and his parents' friends and relatives, and no one from my side of the family. His family thought it was strange but had to accept my explanation that my family were Catholics and, therefore, couldn't attend the marriage of a Catholic, even a lapsed, excommunicated, divorced, unbelieving one like me, to someone in a ceremony, religious or nonreligious, outside the Catholic Church.

Jenny and I dressed ourselves up in our wedding dresses—hers a sweet pink organdy with white lace trim purchased by Leah and Will at Saks the day Milt and I told them we were getting married, and mine a brown and oatmeal cotton size ten (the only size ten dress I ever fit into, and never wore more than five times at that). I must have been exceptionally thin for me.

I think Milt stayed at my apartment the night before and we arrived by taxi, Milt, Jenny, and me. I remember walking up the stairway to the apartment, and seeing Milt's brother Dan and his daughter, Tema, standing there. Jenny and I had met the two of them already. Then Dan called to Beth, his wife, to come and meet me, and she popped around into the doorway and said, prophetically as it turned out, "I'm so sorry you and Milton are getting married. It's been so wonderful having him all to ourselves." Or did she say "myself"? Beth's a strange bird who certainly says what she thinks, and it was a fitting beginning to the end of Milt's relationship with her and the start of her no relationship with me.

I was happy my family wasn't there. If the Catholic Church hadn't had such a rule, I would have made one up. I was sorry about my mother, but I knew she was glad I was going to be married and not "living in sin." My father was probably glad too. I didn't ask. My sister was probably glad. It was her ghastly husband I really didn't want at the wedding. Jimmy was a chip-on-the-shoulder, sentimental, sodden, third-generation, professional Irishman. I could imagine Jimmy or my father hearing just one remark from one of the guests or from Milt's parents, all of them ardent or semi-ardent leftists or at least tolerant middle-of-the-roaders, that possibly union members weren't a bunch of thieving bums, and then, wedding or no wedding, the patriotic side of the gathering might have begun a brouhaha in earnest.

Bob and Louise De Cormier were our attendants. They were friends of Milt's and had become sort of friends of mine, though I knew in my heart I could never meet their standards of leftist perfection. I'm not a joiner. I follow my own way. Or think I do. To them, I was not a good influence on Milt. I persisted in sticking my two cents in and asking "why?" about everything he said, and too many "whys" make Jack a doubter, maybe even a nonbeliever.

There were all Milt's aunts and uncles, and probably some cousins. Everyone seemed to be very happy for us. They were all happy, except for Beth that Milton was finally settling down and they were one and all delighted with Jenny. Will endeared himself to me when, on hearing of our plans to marry, he started to carry Jenny's picture in his wallet to show to everyone, saying how clever his son was to bring him such a beautiful granddaughter as well as a daughter-in-law.

The food was homey and delicious, and I am sure that we had champagne, meatballs, and chopped liver. Jenny and Tema played and giggled. I know I chatted with people, but I don't remember anything I said. The cantor who married us wanted to sing professionally. I think it influenced the little talk he gave before he pronounced us man and wife. He informed everybody that he really didn't know me well, but Milt was a terrific (my word) person and I would really have to be something to match up to him (the cantor's words). Sounds reminiscent of Leah's little speech to Beth on her wedding day about her "being inferior to Dan and needing to try hard to be his equal."

Well, we left the reception about four o'clock, and with nothing else to do, we went to see *Around the World in Eighty Days*. Milt says it was at the Rivoli on Broadway. We were suddenly very shy with each other. In love, but shy. I was thirty and Milt was thirty-four. We were unsure of what we'd done and why we'd done it. I think getting married is some sort of compulsion, not necessarily a cultural one. Maybe human animals, especially females, have the need to secure for themselves and their children someone to make a haven for them. Children are dependent for so long, so many years, that it's hard to take care of them alone. It's also terribly hard to convince most men that marriage can be a pleasure as well as difficult, and that a wife, and the joy of seeing your own children grow, is a good thing.

I had a hard time convincing Milt. When I did, and he succumbed to my persuasions, I didn't know what to do with him, except to go to a movie. I mean, sleeping together was not a novelty by that time, and if we had gone home and gone to bed at four in the afternoon, on top of all that food and champagne, we probably would have had to get up and go out to a movie anyway because it certainly felt as if we didn't have a single word to say to each other. There I was in my skinny oatmeal dress, and Milt in a nice blue suit and a white shirt, and all we could do was hold hands and sit in a movie being bored to death. It was a terrifying feeling. God, its a hundred years ago.

Will and Leah took care of Jenny when we went off on our honeymoon. It's hard to believe that we were ever so young and silly. And we were silly. I was as ill equipped at thirty to be married as I had been at twenty when I married for the first time. And Milt, well, he was even more of a baby than I was and even less experienced. The only area where I could have been said to be an adult was in relation to Jennifer. Compared to many other single mothers I was very mature. I took my responsibility to her seriously and believed with old Mother Nature that I was alive for the sole purpose of helping her survive to adulthood (where no doubt both old mother and I figured she would follow in my footsteps).

Milt thought I was wonderful, and I thought he was wonderful. Like the mirrors in an old-fashioned barbershop, I think I may have thought he was wonderful because he thought I was. Did he think I was wonderful because I thought he was? We had that, and we still have it. I admire Milt and love him today more than I did then, and I think he feels the same way about me. That quality may be the most important ingredient in long-term happy marriages. They have to be better, have more admiration, more pleasure in the other person, than in the beginning, because being in love doesn't last, not in any consistent way, or only comes and goes in short bursts over the years. You can only be a bride for just so long, but if someone thinks you're wonderful, you can live in a quiet glow for a long time.

So twenty-six years and a day later, I can look at Milt and say, "There is no one I have ever met who I would prefer to you." And Milt will say, "whom," and I will know that there are other reasons for loving him. I'm used to his jokes and he keeps me on my toes with my grammar. And it is absolutely necessary for me to respect my husband for his intelligence.□

L'AUBERGE DU PÈRE BISE

At ease beside the lake
coffee, books, a touch
all gifts, under plane trees
pruned for summer shade

A royal armada, the swans,
sailing toward the mountains
untroubled by thoughts of winter
or yesterday

And we smile understanding
the parting of leaves
and passing of birds
the silver sound of a spoon

And by the lake
in sunset joined
drinking from cups
with painted violets

We remember
all the years of August roses
heavy with petty angers
and share amused despair

Seeing life that might have been
had we known of September
and being still by the lake
with the swans and violets

1984 OLYMPICS

Well we've won eighty-four gold medals in the Olympics. A fitting number. I just watched the closing ceremonies, or at least, the last presentation of medals, to the competitors in the equestrian events, two of them Americans and one woman, a Swiss. While they played "Star Spangled Banner" and ran up the American flag, I wondered about people. Is there a country that doesn't inspire its citizens with love and a sense of belonging?

Even for the Jews, it wasn't the lands they came from that they didn't love, it was the governments, the stupidity of the people who ruled and tried to destroy them. I've been through all phases of knowing I was an American. From my childhood in a suburb of New York City—old-time America, old-time American patriotism, and my family on all sides here from the mid-1800s, one hundred percent flag-waving Americans.

One of my early memories that this Olympics has awakened is of the ceremony each Decoration Day, during the silence to commemorate the dead soldiers in the wars. To me, "the War" was the First World War, the one my father fought in. That made it real. As young as five or six, I was sad each time I heard the bugler play taps. It could have been my father, or his friends, who were dead, for whom people would listen silently to that sad call. That's what it was, a long sad call and the faraway mysterious answer from the dead.

I knew they died for me and for everyone else around me. That's what I believed. Then World War II and more dead. But for a reason— a madman's unreason. I understood that, and as much as a teenage girl responding to her own unreality can believe, I believed it was right. As an adult, I can say that today, if that war were to be fought again, I would fight it. I would do what I could to help.

Then Korea, which I couldn't understand. No one understood it. Who was the enemy? Where was he hiding? Was it worth dying for? I don't think so. I thought it was crazy. There was no Hitler, no reason that I could see. And I felt no patriotism. Then Vietnam. We didn't belong there. They sent thousands of young men to die and kill for reasons no one understood. Who could be convinced it was right, except those who believed "my country, no matter what." Conscience, intelligence, nothing mattered. So I became an expatriate. An anti-patriot, a non-patriot convinced that there was no country on this planet worth paying allegiance to. I was a sunshine patriot. A summer soldier. I still think I was right. I felt so full of shame for the dead and maimed and disinherited that I left America. When asked where I would like to be, I couldn't answer. There was no place on earth that I wanted to be. I didn't like human beings, and there was no country without them.

I had my first inkling that America wasn't the worst place in the world during the impeachment proceedings against Nixon. I watched congressmen and women threshing out the pros and cons of impeachment with intelligence and restraint. Particularly restraint. And suddenly I understood what I was seeing. It wasn't perfect, but it was awfully good. Like my parents, whom I had long since forgiven for their human imperfections, my country had a lot of faults, but when it wanted to get rid of its leader, it impeached him, it didn't kill him. Reasonable men and women discussed the rights and wrongs of the matter, and decided to do without him. Not to do away with him. I think it was the first time in my adult life that I was proud of my country, proud of its Constitution, and glad to be a part of it.

Probably all countries have good and bad things in them. Characteristics that are unpleasant and characteristics that show what the human spirit can aspire to. Any new immigrant can understand the stupidity of a third- or fourth-generation American who doesn't understand how good this country can be.

The Olympic competition has caught me up in a wave of pleasure that my country has done so well. And I feel pleasure when a competitor from another country, big or small, looks to his flag and listens to his national anthem. The women and some of the men cry, and I cry with them because I understand how they love their patch of earth, their families, and their people.

One of the things that gave me the most hope for America during this Olympics was the number of black Americans who won medals for themselves and their families and their country. And the tears of pride and joy that some of them shed. Maybe now in 1984 they can feel what I felt when I was a little girl and I knew that men had died so that I could be happy in my country. The Constitution is for them. The government is for them. The applause is for them. The people who saw their accomplishments and clapped were proud of them as Americans. This patch of earth is theirs, just the way Queens Village in the City of New York, in the State of New York, in the United States of America, was mine.

I am a patriot. And today I am proud to be an American.□

AFTERLIFE

November 11 passed the other day with just the faintest touch of nostalgia about my father's birthday. I didn't allow myself to be very sad, but I did think about the bugler on Decoration Day playing taps. And I came across a poem and a page that I wrote about what taps meant to me when I heard it played as a child. And funny, but now I almost always think of my father as a soldier. Maybe because of that letter he wrote to his parents on Armistice Day when he was in France with the AEF in the First World War. Maybe that picture of him is more appealing to me, the young, handsome boy with brown hair and green eyes, seeing a new world, learning a new language, raw, not unruly, I think, still able to like strangers, if not the Bosch. What did he call them—krauts?

Did I dream that I thought of his and my mother's graves? Her birthday is the 27th of this month, this sad month of November. Was it their deaths I was always mourning in the autumn?

Autumn. The letters that make up the word autumn, the "a" and "u," the sound of "tumn," spelled orange and gold, pumpkins, candy, the beautiful smell of burning leaves. But after childhood, after my father's death, not in the month of November, but in May, November has always been a sad time.

I thought I didn't love him, but I mourned for three years. The day of his funeral I cried harder than I ever had before. The night of his funeral, Milt's mother Leah and I had the only moment of closeness in the twenty years of our knowing one another. I was stricken by the knowledge that his body was under the earth. The horror of knowing that was almost intolerable. I was standing in Leah's kitchen on Livingston Street, and she saw the look on my face and knew what I was feeling. She didn't touch me in sympathy. I don't even know if she felt any sympathy. What she felt was empathy. She'd had the experience so many times herself, and she knew it would pass, and she knew I'd feel it again for other people. It was enough for me, just to know someone else understood without explanation what was so terrifying.

Years later, when Andy was six years old, and in the same kind of terror at the thought of death, his own and everyone else's, that I had felt about my father, in trying to help him, I helped myself. I told him that I believe that after life is over for us, we go back to being part of the earth, and maybe some part of us would be a part of rivers or rain, or part of the grass and trees, and that made me happy. It satisfied him then, and it comforted me, and has ever since.

I think that was the turning-around time in my life when I finally got rid of the Catholic hell I was tortured with as a child. In my world of hereafter, there were rivers and streams and lightning storms; and trees and people and dogs and cats. There were awful things and good things, but there were no devils or angels, no hell, no fiery torments. No gloating evil spirits. There is evil enough around us without imagining for little children an unknown and worse evil.

I would like to be buried near, or under, some beautiful hemlocks, maybe in a forest, maybe a part of it someday. In death, I would like to rest in stillness where small sounds of insects and growing things can be heard. I would like to be warmed by the sun, frozen by the mythical Jack Frost I believed in as a child. I would like to lie under great mounds of snow. I don't mind the thought of worms and rotting flesh. No one will notice the ultimate corruption. And in time, all the happiness and the pain purged, I can be part of everything without the limits of skin and bones. I will be the great Earth, the great Earth Mother, and I'll be part of my parents again, and they will be part of me.□

ONE DAY

One day
I shook hands with the president
(who didn't know he shook hands
with me) and I thought
how my father would have been impressed
It was the first time in three years
of mourning
that I wished him alive

The next time
was after my mother died
I saw a couple
walking on a London street
The man was tall and stooped
and wore a gray raincoat
He was holding the arm
of a short plump woman
I didn't see their faces
but something in the way they walked
made me think for a moment
it was my father and mother
and I cried
there in the street
I must have loved him sometime

NOTES TO A NEW WORD PROCESSOR

Good morning, my dear word processor. Or are you spelled "er," I wonder? Since my daily bread no longer depends on knowing how to spell, I no longer know how to spell. So word processor or word processer, it's all the same to me...

Will I find you as interesting tomorrow morning as I find you now? Will I be as anxious to get up just to turn on your switch?

Ah hah! I've done just what I wasn't going to do. I edited three mistakes out as I was typing. I intended to type "heads on" (I must learn the jargon) until I could amass a huge pile of letters and paragraphs, and then print, then edit, then print again, like a real writer. But how deliciously tempting this magic machine is, and how difficult to resist its possibilities for instant perfection, for proving how clever one can be.

By one I mean me, Rosemary Primont, Rosemary Klix, Rosemary Okun, the three names I have used on various occasions in my life. Rosemary Primont, that Smith Corona incompetent, the only girl in the class typing minus three words a minute by graduation. And Rosemary Klix. She took that temporary job for a Russian immigrant shoe manufacturer on Forty-Second Street and proved that she could type letter-perfect dialect. He begged her to stay on, but then he couldn't tell a typo if it jumped off the page and kissed him. And Rosemary Okun. Well, to date, she has blundered through thousands of pages of type, supported, sustained, and sheltered by IBM's other stupendous invention, the correcting Selectric, always knowing her limitations, always expecting at any moment to be found out.

But this wonderful new invention, the word processor! To paraphrase whichever one of the Brownings said it, "How do I love you"—let me count your disk drive, your little red and green lights, your everlasting hum! I will treasure you always, and with luck, you and I will combine to say interesting things and boring things, but things we will say, with all mistakes deleted, and only we will know.☐

November 27, 1984
New York, NY

Dear Jenny and Andy,
I think I'll write this letter to both of you because it's about our family. When I turned on the computer it told me that today is November 27. You probably don't remember, but the twenty-seventh was Nana's birthday. We all know about me and numbers,

but since she was born in 1895, I guess that would be something like eighty-nine years ago. It's funny, but each year I picture her growing older and older, and I'm sad that she isn't here for us to love her. She died before any of the terrible things that happened to Leah and Will could happen to her, and I picture her as smaller, with fine white hair and her skin soft and pretty. I don't think a long life would have treated her as kindly as my imagination, so I don't let myself be too unhappy that she isn't with us.

Some months ago, one of you suggested that I write down the names of the people from Queens Village on their pictures so you could tell who was who if you ever wanted to match them to the stories I wrote about them. That inspired me to get some photo albums when we were in L.A., and I carried them here to New York where all the pictures were. I got out the boxes of pictures and sorted them. I was surprised to find that my senior year and graduation day from high school were the easiest. I started with the absolutely most self-centered time of my life, and worked back year by year then upward and onward.

Once I reached Jenny's arrival, the number of pictures of me took a sharp drop, and I was on the other side of the camera most of the time. However, during the time between your birth, Jenny, and yours, Andy, I still seemed ready to have my picture taken. I was togged and coiffed and fit to be caught on film a lot of the time. After your birth, Andy, that seems to have changed. From then on, the sheer number of people and complications in my life, and, I think, the fact that every spare minute was spent doing things I enjoy, like drawing and reading and being with people I liked, took the place of looking in the mirror.

I noticed, during my ordeal by photograph, that the only other people whose pictures I took or kept were my mother and father, my sister and brother, Michael, Peter and Irene, and a few friends. Mickey Henrion and Rose Reitter are there, and Mickey's children. And, of course, the two of you, and in a casual way, some of your friends. I have inherited pictures of Leah and Will and Dan and Beth and their kids, and I have pictures of Sniffy, Lucy and Charlie, Pokey and Little Bear. I also have a lot of pictures that Jenny took when she was in high school. It's funny, my eyes gave out and I couldn't focus anymore, and about a year later, Jenny took up photography, so there's not too much of a lapse in continuity.

I have some beautiful pictures that I took of you, Jenny, in a rage of love the year you started to have difficulty in PS41 with that disgusting teacher. The pictures were my way of telling her that you were perfect. And they still say it.

Andy, I notice that the year between five and six is almost uncharted. That was the year of the nightmares and misery, and I guess we didn't take many photos...

I used to think that before I had a family of my own, my mind must have been completely empty. I couldn't remember what I thought about. But this weekend, reliving my life while I did the albums, I remembered again what I was like, the things I did, and the things I thought about. It's as if I was able to connect the two parts of my life, as if it all happened to one person. Oops.

Well, I've run out of albums, and I still have Milt's early life and his family to do. And I have a lot of work pictures of Milt's to insert throughout the years of our life. I was going to make a separate album for your wedding, Jen, but I decided to keep that day right in with all the others because then we can just browse along and see those pictures in their time and place...

I'm reading a silly romantic novel about King Arthur's court, and there was an incredibly gory scene where Lancelot slays a dragon. I wonder what color it was.

Love,
Mother

LOVE HAPPENS

It's 1953. I'm twenty-five, lying on the floor in Montclair, New Jersey. I've got a backache and I've tried lying on the bed, sitting on a chair, rotating, standing, and walking. I've tried it all. Only the floor was left. The pain eases for a moment. An awful thought goes through my head. There's no other way out of this. I'm going to have to go through labor and have the baby. There's no other way. It's the end of July, hot, humid. The scratchy rug under me has the smell of twenty years of dust and wear. This is my first pregnancy, and I'm scared. Terrified. I stare up at the ceiling and moan without sound, "I can't do this." I'm afraid of giving birth. I know I want a child. I want the child that's kicking and squirming inside of me. I know I'll take good care of it. What I don't know is that my life will change in a way that has nothing to do with the details.

I'm still young enough to believe that there is a right and wrong way to do everything. Natural childbirth is right. Anesthesia is wrong. Dr. Murphy, my obstetrician, is a nice man, but he doesn't believe in natural childbirth. So every time I tell him I don't want anesthesia, he smiles and tells me there's nothing to worry about. "I won't give you anything, if you don't need it, and I promise you, the baby will be all right." I can't admit to myself, or to him, that my real fear is not of pain, but of being smothered if someone puts a mask over my face.

When I was six and had my tonsils out, I was so afraid of being smothered and fought so hard to avoid the ether mask that they had to put me out with ether on a piece of cloth. The operating room was white and cold and I was strapped onto a table. Half a dozen nurses and interns were moving around, chatting and laughing, ignoring me, until it was time for the surgeon to arrive. One of them said, "He'll be really mad if she's still awake when he gets here." That didn't seem important compared to being smothered by a black rubber mask that made a hissing noise, and the more I struggled and refused to inhale, the more excited they got. One of the nurses told them all to back off. She put her arms around me, and while reassuring me, put me to sleep with a cloth and a smile.

So now, reassured by Dr. Murphy that everything would go well, and having no idea what childbirth was really like, when the first contraction happened I was up and out the door, on my way to the hospital. After eight hours of labor, I was grateful when I was offered a pill to help me relax between contractions. Five hours later, when someone put a mask over my face and said, "Count backwards from five while you inhale," I said obediently, "I'll be a good girl." I just wanted my obstetrician to know that he wouldn't have to put me out with an ether-soaked cloth. I was ready for anything they could give me.

The next thing I knew, two nurses were wheeling me through a bright white hallway back to my room. They smiled and told me I had a little girl. I was smiling and telling everyone we passed, "I have a little girl, and her name is Jennifer," but I was still groggy from the anesthesia, so my words were slurred and I sounded drunk. Everyone seemed to be laughing and saying, "Congratulations," and whenever we passed a window, I could see autumn leaves glowing in the sunshine.

The nurses brought Jenny to me in the ward a few minutes later, and when I saw her, I forgot the nine months of discomfort, the labor, the past, and fell in love with my child. Up to that moment I had lived my separate life in the company of others, and in a second everything changed. I was a mother.

In 1962, when I became pregnant a second time, I still felt it would be better to go through labor without anesthesia, so I found an obstetrician who used the Lamaze method. Breathing exercises, husbands in delivery rooms, assistants during the labor. My expectation was that I would get through the labor with a minimum of discomfort. I had already given birth once, and there were exercises to perform before and during the labor. Milt and a Lamaze assistant would be with me, and Dr. Segal would be at the hospital when I arrived.

Andy was born at Beth Israel Hospital in Manhattan. It's in a bleak part of the city. No trees to look at from the sixth floor. I was going to be induced. I had been so dilated since the sixth month that they were afraid I might not make it to the hospital in time if they waited for labor to start naturally. On the due date, very businesslike, I picked up my small bag, said goodbye to my mother and Jenny, and Milt, and I headed across town to Beth Israel.

It was a short hard labor. A shock. I was one of those exceptions for whom things didn't proceed as planned, and when it became apparent that mine was not going to be a great example of the huff-huff, grin- and-bear-it school, but more of an oh-my-god-do-something routine, I felt I'd made a big mistake. But I refused to have any painkillers. I didn't want to "fail Lamaze." It was Dr. Segal who insisted, in the fourth hour, that they give me Demerol. After the Demerol, all I could hear was his voice, panicked, pleading as he leaned over me, "Rosemary, why are you doing that? Stop rolling your eyes back in your head like that."

I'd seen a painting of Saint Sebastian in the National Gallery in Washington, D.C. He's pierced by arrows, his sickly white eyeballs turned all the way up into his head in despair. I must have been saving that image for the right moment, and, according to the doctor, was doing my best imitation of the saint each time I had a contraction. The Demerol allowed me to relax between contractions but did nothing to help me through the pain of labor. Some primitive part of me took over and acted out the only thing that made sense at the moment. I lost sight of the labor and believed I was besieged.

Then I was being wheeled on a gurney through a dark corridor. I saw Milt looking scared, dressed in a coverall and a funny paper hat, hurrying along next to Dr. Segal. When we got into the delivery room, the doctor said, "Okay. Now, Rosemary, push very hard on the next contraction." I pushed with all my might and nothing happened. St. Sebastian was gone, and I was a big Mack truck pushing up against one of those huge concrete walls that kids play ball against in city schoolyards. And nothing was moving. There was only pain. A few more contractions like that, and the doctor said, "Rosemary, we have a problem. I'm going to have to give you something." The doctor waved Milt out of the room. I was between contractions and thought, "Thank god it's not 1862."

And this is where memory stops, until two hours later in the recovery room. Milt was there gazing at Andy in a bassinet with the same look I must have had when I first saw Jenny nine years before—glowing, rapturous, adoring. I was exhausted, hardly able to turn my head to look at my son. Andy was nine pounds at birth, a large baby with a very large head. He looked three months old.

Maybe love happens in different ways at different times of your life. At twenty-five it was sudden, superb, and illuminated my life. At thirty- four, I'd survived divorce, relative poverty, the death of my father, and for the second time in my life, a major depression.

I'd given up the tooth fairy and the rest of the pie-in-the-sky stories, and knew that living happily ever after was going to require good luck and a lot of hard work.

For a week, every time I looked at Andy and saw how his head had molded to get through the birth canal, I felt the pain all over again. I didn't want to feel that way. I hadn't expected to, and I've always been sad that the labor was so painful and exhausting that I missed those first moments that could have been so good. So I held him next to me, nursed him, carried him from room to room, keeping him near so I could talk to him, make him mine, and I grew to love him imperceptibly, minute by minute, hour by hour, day by day. I saw his beautiful intelligent eyes, I held his sweet child's body next to mine, and relished loving someone who would let me love him. It must have been enough, because on his 37th birthday, when, half joking, I asked him, "Where is that little boy I loved so much?" He patted his chest and said, "Don't worry, Mom, he's still in there."□

November 30, 1984
New York, NY

Dear Wendy and Peter,
When I was fourteen, I made a resolution that someday I would be organized and put all the family pictures into an album. Jenny and Richard will celebrate their first anniversary in a few days, and it's fitting that I have spent the last half hour putting their wedding pictures in an album. Those were the very last pictures out of the thousands I've collected in my lifetime and which I have also just finished placing in albums. So far I have four albums filled, and the wedding pictures are the beginning of the fifth. It seems amazing that something I put off doing for—how many years is it, forty-two?—could be done so easily in one weekend.

Jenny called the other day to say that she and Richard may be here in New York for a few days next week. We're looking forward to seeing them, and will celebrate Christmas early...

We are leaving for California on the twenty-second of December and will be there off and on for a few months. Winter in Los Angeles can be rainy and often quite unpleasant with flooding, mudslides, and other natural catastrophes. But spring and fall are both pleasant seasons, and I hope that you will come and visit us, perhaps, the next time that the children visit. We still have that owl that hoots for us at night, and our garden is sometimes filled with hummingbirds. I'm sure that you would enjoy some of the sights along the West Coast, especially the redwoods, and while the birds of Beverly Hills wear Gucci shoes and gold chains, they might be fun to watch for a few minutes also.

Please excuse the fact that I am typing this letter rather than writing by hand. My handwriting is so poor that even I can't read it. Also, I have a new word processor and I am finding it irresistible. It doesn't make my letters more interesting, but it convinces me that I am a wonderful typist, and one should accept such innocent flattery whenever possible.

      Love,
      Rosemary and Milt

EVELYN

As the stage rose from the pit at the Paramount Theater on Broadway, Evelyn Brendel jumped out of her seat and screamed, "Bennny, Bennny! It's me! It's me, Evelyn. Hey, Benny, over here. Evelyn."

Benny Goodman, looking just like his picture, smiled and played his clarinet while the kids in the audience howled, but none so loud as Evelyn. That was why she insisted on sitting in the second row right of center. She'd seen the show six times, and knew where Benny Goodman always stood when the platform full of musicians was transported from the depths of the theater up to stage level. In fact it was Evelyn who was transported. Her eyes shone with maniacal love. "Benny, Benny, it's me," she shouted, "Over here. Evelyn."

She was so loud he heard her above the din and turned to nod as she collapsed, wild with pleasure, into the velour folding seat.

"He saw me. He saw me." She grabbed my arm and squeezed it ecstatically. "He knows me. I told you he knows who I am."

I peeled her fingers off my arm and tried to act as if I knew what was going on, but I felt as if I was in a foreign country. Why was she so crazy about Benny Goodman? I hesitated to call him Benny, even in my thoughts. He looked so old to me, his face creased and cheeks red, as he huffed on his clarinet. The closest I had come to hero worship so far was a romantic certainty that Tyrone Power was smiling at me in the local movie house. I wasn't interested in reality, and Benny Goodman looked terribly real to me.

Sitting next to Evelyn was hard work. Every time the band finished a number, she started screaming "Benny, Benny" again. And each time she turned her happy face in my direction I was afraid my lack of enthusiasm might dampen her pleasure and she would know I didn't get being a fan. So I gave a few thin shouts, worrying that Benny might shift his attention from Evelyn and berate me for only pretending. I felt I was failing at something and at the same time discovering that though we'd been classmates for two and a half years, I didn't really know Evelyn. She was easily the best-liked girl in the school and could always be counted on to make us laugh. When something worried her, her eyes would show confusion, as if she was puzzling at the unfairness of being unhappy, and a few moments would pass before she shrugged her shoulders and her normal good cheer brought the thought of something amusing.

Dominican Commercial was a strict Catholic school, dedicated to turning out docile, Church-abiding young women slated for motherhood or the convent. Rumor had it that out of every graduating class of one hundred and two, at least six would enter the convent. By November of the freshman year, it was apparent which six girls were going to be nuns. If they didn't announce their intentions openly, their behavior did. They seemed to have few doubts. Some had brothers or sisters who were priests or nuns, and some came from families in distress over their decision, but nothing seemed to shake their purpose. They were adamant that they would enter immediately after graduation.

The other ninety-six of us looked at them in wonder. How could they give up the world—trade families, smart clothes, and freedom for black-and-white habits and total obedience? The rest of us wore the uniforms. We said the prayers. But we broke the rules whenever we could, and Evelyn was the happiest rule breaker in our class.

Discipline was consistent but not corporal. The nuns gave out demerits as a punishment for misbehavior. Ten demerits in a semester meant a trip to the principal's office. That was one statistic I understood. The principal, Sister Rose Gertrude, terrified everyone in the school, from the handyman to the holiest of nuns. A nun would think hard before she handed out the tenth demerit. The tenth demerit could mean that the nun who imposed it might have to accompany the sinner to the office to witness the punishment and that was dangerous. Sister Rose Gertrude never had any difficulty finding fault with anyone who entered her office, and the nun might come out crying harder than the student.

The procedure for giving demerits was simple. The teacher looked sadly at the student, wrote a note in nun-perfect penmanship explaining the misdeed to the secretary in the office, and had the girl take herself and the note down to watch the demerit listed on her school record.

If it was a first offense, the secretary, another nun, looked shocked and surprised. If the student was familiar from past offenses, the secretarial face wore a "not you again" expression. She hauled out the demerit book, sighing as if it contained a list of all the sins in the world, too many of them committed by the girl in front of her.

Student expressions ranged from denial and indignation to tears and remorse. This gave me some difficulty on my first trip to the office with a demerit slip. I was caught, barehanded as it were, leaving school without my hat. I was barehanded because the mitten I should have had on my right hand was sitting on the top of my head, thumb down, and fell, thumb up, as I bent over to pick up a book that Sister Mary Charity dropped. Sister Mary

Charity, one of the cheeriest nuns and much loved by the girls, only gave me the demerit because my indiscretion was witnessed by two other nuns, and none of them could allow themselves to be seen conspiring to help the girls flout the rules. However, she advised me that if I was going to be so polite in the future, I should find some bobby pins.

With her laughter in my ears, it was hard to take the secretary's solemnity seriously. Denial and indignation were out of the question. Tears and remorse would have been excessive. It was only a first offense. Two girls came into the office and responded correctly, right down to a promise never to do wrong again. How can you apologize for wearing a mitten on your head without sounding like an idiot?

The dress code at Dominican was severe. No girl was allowed to attend school in anything but the school uniform. The warm weather uniform, tan blouse and brown skirt was, by accident, not ugly, but the winter dress, a coarse dull brown, was poorhouse plain. Orphans in the nineteenth century were given dresses like that to ensure humility and gratitude. Sister Rose Gertrude informed us on opening day of school, in a talk larded with demands for gratitude and patriotism that we were lucky to have such attractive uniforms. In spite of wartime shortages and competition from the army, she had located a few hundred bolts of the wretched fabric, thereby depriving the army, as well as the orphanages of the world, from making use of it.

I took revenge on my uniform by hanging it on my bedroom doorknob for four years, ignoring all requests, suggestions, and entreaties from my mother to wash or iron it. I told her that some of the girls washed theirs and they fell apart. It was such a dirty color brown, no one ever knew the difference.

All year long we were forced to wear hats to cover our potentially attractive teenage curls and braids. Sister Rose Gertrude would have preferred to dress us in sackcloth and ashes. Lacking that possibility, she insisted that we wear medium-heeled brown oxford shoes with ties, the kind worn by nuns and middle-aged ladies with foot problems. However, shoe rationing proved stronger than the principal, and it was a measure of our childishness and teenage vanity that we felt that if there had to be a war, it was lucky it happened during the four years we passed through the school. Our parents probably didn't mind sending us off to school looking like premature old ladies. Possibly they thought it would keep us out of the arms of stray men we might meet during the day, but even the most loving parents weren't keen on being seen with us in dowdy brown shoes on a Sunday morning coming out of church.

I figured the nuns in the office didn't know how to smile, until one day I was sent down with Evelyn and the secretary burst out laughing as Evelyn slapped her demerit slip on the counter and said in a happy voice, "Zounds! Foiled again." The mousy assistant secretary, who usually spoke just above a whisper, and whose rosary beads were the noisiest thing about her, said in a perfectly normal voice, "Now, Evelyn, you know you have seven demerits already."

"I know. It's awful." Evelyn danced on the tips of her toes. "Hey, take care of my friend, will you. She wants her name in the book too."

"Stay away from this young lady." The secretary glanced at me sympathetically, and then slammed the book shut with a smile. "A bad influence."

Evelyn collected more demerits than any other girl in the school, but no one stayed away from her. She was too much fun. That's why I agreed when she pulled me aside the day before our trip to the Paramount and said, "Hey, let's play hooky tomorrow and go see Benny Goodman." I'd never cut classes before and I was nervous. I'd have to forge a note from my parents to get back in the next day, but that wasn't what bothered me. What I feared most was my inability to do anything out of line without being caught. It would be just my luck that the first time I played hooky, Sister Rose Gertrude would decide she had to see Benny Goodman to find out why "her girls," as she liked to call us, thought he was so great. Or the truant officer would raid the theater, and we'd be collected with the five hundred other truants at the show that day. Okay for Evelyn, short and cute and good-natured, but not okay for me, taller by three inches than the nearest nun. Tall girls soon discover that there may be advantages to being tall, such as being assigned a seat at the back of the class where no one can see you, but no teacher will think you're cute.

When Evelyn and I met in the local bus station that morning, we changed out of our uniforms, which would have pegged us immediately as truant, and stashed them in a locker. Then we ate our lunches so we wouldn't have to carry them and took the subway for New York. Somewhere between Jamaica and Manhattan I sat on a piece of chocolate, so I gave Evelyn my sweater and borrowed her raincoat. The sweater, too short to cover the chocolate on the seat of my dress, drooped over Evelyn's shoulders and covered her fingers. My arms hung six inches out of the sleeves of her size eight coat, and every time I made a sudden movement I could feel the seams crackling ominously. After trying so hard to appear sophisticated and inconspicuous, we looked like a pair of cartoon characters. We decided that if anyone asked questions, we would say a sorority was hazing us.

On the trip into the City we talked about what would happen if we were caught by a truant officer. Even Evelyn quailed at that. It meant instant dismissal. Aside from the prospect of facing Sister Rose Gertrude and the anger of my parents, there was something to be said for being expelled. I had wanted to go to a public high school that specialized in art, but my parents believed that artists were temperamental and lived in attics and secretaries were respectable and got married, so I was trapped for four years in Dominican Commercial, learning the finer points of filing, typing minus five words a minute, and studying the plant life outside the classroom windows.

It wasn't all bad. I liked most of the students, and some of the nuns were exceptionally kind and good. Some were good teachers. Sister Grace Florian encouraged us to make our way through Dickens, Austen, and Eliot. She also came into class the last week of school and dictated a list of periodicals young Catholic married women should read in order to keep up with their husbands' intellectual superiority. After browsing through *Reader's Digest* we were advised that we might go a little deeper into life and politics with *The Ladies' Home Journal* or *Liberty Magazine*.

One of my favorite teachers was a sister none of the other girls liked very much. She taught business law and gave me almost the only sensible information I took away at the end of my four years. Hers was the only class where I chose to sit up front. That's how I can swear that one day, in answer to the question, "Sister, what's a pawnbroker?" I heard her mutter, "The only man in the world with three balls." Her name was Sister Mary St. Louis, but no one, including the nuns when they thought the girls weren't listening, ever called her anything but Louie.

Catholic Schools followed the same curriculum as public schools but our textbooks were different. Our biology book, approved of by Sister Rose Gertrude and the Diocese, began its chapter on human reproduction with the sentence, "Like all living things, human beings must reproduce." Then it meandered on about plants, love, Heaven, and the state of grace. And where earlier chapters dealt bravely with reproduction in cells, this one avoided the subject altogether. Naturally, it was the only chapter without diagrams.

Sister Jeanne d'Arc, our biology teacher, started a new chapter each Monday. On that Monday, as we sat snickering at our desks, she walked in and said, "Girls, you are to take your books home and read the next chapter quietly to yourselves in the privacy of your room. You are not to speak about it with anyone else. Now, turn to Chapter Ten and begin."

Sister Anne Regina, my art teacher, with crossed eyes and a loving heart, encouraged me to go on to art school in spite of my parents' fears. She listened with patience as I complained about regimentation and school rules. But she almost lost my respect one day when she caught me whistling in the corridor and told me the Blessed Virgin cried in heaven whenever she heard a girl whistle. I almost lost hers when I told her that if the Blessed Virgin had nothing better to cry about, that was her problem. Sister twitched her nose and chose to ignore my remark. We couldn't afford to lose each other. I was her best student that year, and she needed me to do the school posters. She taught my favorite subject, and I needed her encouragement. I also needed her kindness and support to help me bear four years of animosity from Sister Cecilia Marie.

Sister Cecilia Marie was a five-foot termagant who detested any student more than two inches taller than she. Her ideal class would have been thirty-two dwarfs. I had the misfortune to be in her homeroom class all four years I was at Dominican. The only comfort I could gather was that the smartest girl in the class and the most determinedly sweet girl in the class, both taller than I, were treated like enemies too. They were good students, so Sister had to be satisfied with meting out simple rudeness and ugly looks in their direction. I was a different story. My handwriting was unreadable. The only date I was sure of was 1492. And my excessively long legs, with which I was forced to maneuver carefully between the narrow rows of desks from my seat at the back of the room, made me look so slow and deliberate that Sister was driven to admonish me to hurry each time she called me to the blackboard. I did hurry. I got there as fast as the next girl. But awkward growing tall people tend to knock over everything in sight. Impossible to explain because it would have been necessary to use the word "short." We quickly learned never to use that word in front of Sister Cecilia Marie.

As if having grown seven and a half inches taller than Sister wasn't crime enough, I gave her all the proof she needed that my height was intentional by teaming up with Evelyn in a harmless prank. It was Evelyn's idea, and Sister might have thought it was a good joke if Evelyn had only chosen a different partner-a shorter partner.

Life in an all girls' school didn't provide much excitement, and anything that broke up the monotony of classes and prayers was welcome, including the silly pageants we put on each year for our parents. It was during one in my senior year, where my class tottered around the gym to *Waltz of the Flowers*, that I inadvertently put an end to Sister's harassment of me.

As the vine made its appearance, the audience gave an involuntary gasp of nervous laughter. I say nervous because Sister Rose Gertrude had been known to get up and harangue a pageant full of parents if they irritated her. That day she came close to it, her face turning an unhealthy red and her mouth getting meaner by the minute as she caught sight of our predicament.

Her orders had been to keep us decorous and over-covered, but throughout the fifteen-minute routine the vine was in a constant undulating motion as each girl tried to re-button the girl in front and be re-buttoned by the girl in back at the same time. With me, they gave up trying to re-button and concentrated on keeping the dress on. By this time, the entire audience, with the exception of Sister Rose Gertrude and the nuns sitting nearest her, was tittering and laughing.

We stumbled up the stairs to our homeroom, barely able to talk from laughing so hard, and settled in to wait until all the grades had performed and we could go back out and mingle with the guests. While we were waiting for Sister to return to the class, Evelyn said she had a great idea.

It was the job of each homeroom teacher to keep her class entertained during these soirées so that the girls wouldn't become too boisterous. Each nun had her own method. Some played word games. Some let the girls read to themselves. Some played board games. Sister Cecilia Marie always held amateur hour. Girls who liked to perform went to the front of the room and did whatever they wanted. When there were no more volunteers, she would coerce some of the girls with good memories to recite poems. Evelyn and Joan used to get up and tell jokes. After that, Sister would say she knew a song she could teach us, and every year she taught us the same song. It was a song out of kindergarten about a man who had a goat who ate three shirts off the clothesline. First she sang a line. Then we repeated it after her. She always smiled her narrowed-eyed smile as we followed her lead. We never knew whether she remembered having taught it to us before or if she took a perverse pleasure in making us pretend this was the first time we'd heard it.

Evelyn suggested that she and I get up last and say we had a special song, then sing Sister's favorite so she wouldn't be able to conduct us. We made it through the first line, with Sister smiling at the sound of a familiar tune. By the middle of the second line, her face was contorted with rage as she came toward us, blackboard pointer in hand. We ran to the ladies room and stayed there until Sister Mary Charity came to fetch us. We were cruel, she said, and shouldn't have teased Sister even though we only meant it as a joke. She allowed herself a glimmering smile. We must go back to class and apologize.

Sister refused to look at us, so we apologized to the top of her head. Up to that point, Evelyn, only five foot two, had been exempt from homeroom mistreatment. Now she had to endure weeks of pouting and complaints about ingratitude until she was forgiven. Sister never spoke to me again. If she wanted me for something, she made a motion with her head, as if to say, "Hey, you." It was wonderful.

In our last year at school I missed the first three months because of illness. My books were sent home with lists of assignments in each course. Several of my friends took notes in class and sent me copies. I was very enthusiastic about working at home for one day, and then lapsed back into my regular habits. When you have gone through school for eleven years without doing homework, six weeks in bed isn't enough to change the habit of ignoring academic demands. There was some talk of me going to school an extra six months to make up the time. I was adamant. There were only three subjects I needed to get a diploma— Social Studies, English, and Gym. And Sister Rose Gertrude insisted on Religion. So I doubled up on those classes in my last term, and had the best time of my school life. For lack of time I was excused from a second year of Filing, a third year of Typing and Shorthand, and what would have been a horrendous introduction to Bookkeeping. In that five-month period, I learned to write legibly for the first time. And I took some notes in class. I never looked at them, but I took them down occasionally. Up to that time I'd been taking notes in shorthand, intending to transcribe them later but never doing it.

When I came back to school in December, I went to regular classes for five weeks before final test time. I was told to take the tests but not to expect to be marked on them. The morning of the first test, I happened to be the second one in the classroom. I found Kathleen Smith there, first to arrive as always, but red-eyed and shaking. I figured something terrible must have happened. In between sobbing and twisting her hands she managed to pant out that she was sure she wouldn't do well on the test because she hadn't been able to stay awake all night studying. It was ludicrous—me sailing into class unprepared, figuring I could do a ten-minute cram before Sister arrived, and Kathleen, stuffed with knowledge and facts, hysterical because she hadn't been able to cram for one night out of a whole term. It was hard to get her to see the humor of it, but she finally smiled and asked me how I could not be worried about tests I might very well fail. I gave her the old "you can't always be perfect" lecture and had her in a better mood by the time class started. The irony of being cheered up by feeling superior to me escaped her entirely. After that, when I thought of it, I was nicer to her, but I didn't think about her much and neither did anyone else.

We all knew that Kathleen meant to be a nun. She talked about it often. But we didn't understand why the nuns were less enthusiastic about the idea than she was. Most of the girls who felt they had vocations were encouraged to go to work for a while first. Some of the girls were adamant about entering immediately. I suppose they were the ones who had made up their minds in the first grade. Some were bright and some were holy. Some were beautiful and some were homely. One girl had three brothers who were priests. There didn't seem to be any one thing they shared except that they were all sincere and all determined to be nuns.

It must have been a measure of a girl's dedication and conviction that she could go through four years at Dominican Commercial, watching the nuns and students cower as Sister Rose Gertrude's footsteps clumped through the marble passageways. We were like animals that had developed a sixth sense for impending danger. No matter what was going on in a classroom, absolute silence or total chaos, there would be a sudden tension, a lifting then ducking of heads, a quick shifting of papers and bodies, as teachers and students prepared themselves for whatever might happen. We all held our breath, as the ripple of silence and order that surrounded her passed, like the eye of a storm, down the hallway. No teacher ever knew when the steps might stop at her door.

Her furies, triggered by who knows what, and blamed always on the people around her, were a blight on our lives and on the lives of the nuns who served under her. They were committed to absolute obedience and abdication of the right to complain. I never heard a nun say a word of criticism about the principal, and she was as cruel to them in public as she was to the girls. Each Monday morning we had Assembly in the auditorium. The program consisted of someone singing or reciting, then a small talk by Sister Rose Gertrude meant to be inspirational but which usually turned into a harangue about our bad behavior. We were exhorted to do her credit in public and private, to be silent and ladylike, saintly and dedicated, uniformed and humble, before God, the Blessed Virgin and Sister Rose Gertrude. That she gave the list in that order never fooled anyone.

On alternate Mondays we were shown a movie. Before the movie, she always stood up and exhorted us not to laugh or snicker, and to behave like young Catholic ladies. Now and then her little pep talk fired her up to a full-scale blast and instead of a movie we had to watch her stomp back and forth bellowing and gesticulating until she was tired and ran out of inspiration, at which point she sometimes decided that we were so terrible we didn't deserve to see a movie.

Sometimes she would rant about tuition, the five or ten dollars a month we were supposed to pay. Some girls were late with payments. Some thought they could have an education for nothing. And the uniforms. Where were the hats? Why did some girls not wear their hats? They were not ladies. They were disgusting. They would be caught. And punished. And makeup. Painted faces. Her girls didn't wear makeup. Leave that to the unfortunate creatures who went to public schools. Our parents were struggling to send us to a wonderful school and we were so ungrateful that we didn't wear our hats. We disobeyed orders. We were ungrateful to the nuns who worked so hard to teach us how to be educated young Catholic women. We were ungrateful to her. We would reap the punishment we deserved.

Sitting there listening to her was all the punishment anyone needed. Not a nun or a girl dared to move. No one shifted in her seat. No one coughed. To do so might attract attention and the shifter or cougher might be called to the foot of the stage to explain.

She was crazy—a demented general in an army of Catholic administrators. She had absolute power over the terrified nuns and nearly absolute power over us. Any girl who defied her openly was expelled. I knew of two in my freshman class who were called to the office to be screamed at, escorted back to class to pick up their possessions, then put out the front door. We were then subjected to a tirade on how fast it would happen to us if we had the temerity to talk back, and were saved only by the bell that sent us to our next class.

Sister Rose Gertrude obeyed the bells as promptly as we did, and a good long ring could stop her in mid-shout and turn her attention to the next matter at hand. Sister Rose Gertrude wanted no excuses. Nothing less than a uniform lost in a five-alarm fire was considered sufficient reason to wear something else to school. Nothing less than appendicitis or a raging toothache allowed a girl to call her parents and leave school early. Routine dental check-ups and medical appointments short of surgery had to take place after school hours. She viewed excuse notes from our parents with distaste and suspicion.

I hated school and took every opportunity to stay away, but I never played hooky until that day with Evelyn and the trip to the Paramount. It was impossible to fool my mother, who took my temperature and looked me over carefully before allowing me to stay home. She was also apt to prescribe something unpleasant if she thought I was really ill, so I would get up, dress for school, and wait until she left for work. Then if my father was still home, I would go to him, my face wan and drawn, my walk listless, an act I had perfected over the years to wring the most sympathy from him. If I were lucky, he would suggest that maybe I should stay home. If he wanted me to stay home, who was I to argue, so I would limp off to bed, throw myself groaning and still dressed under the covers until five minutes after he left, when I could be sure he was on the bus on his way to work. Then out of bed, off with the uniform and into real clothes, downstairs to the refrigerator and some chocolate cake or pie and milk and a good book, and I was set for the morning. It was necessary to stay in the house until afternoon, when I could miraculously recover good health, lest a neighbor see me looking too cheerful early in the day and report it to my mother. That night, I would ask my father for an excuse note, and of course, he gave it to me. Mother was always annoyed, but since she hadn't made a routine check in the morning she couldn't be sure that I was lying. I don't think she wanted to know.

On the day of our big jaunt to the City, what worried me most was the forgery of the note. I didn't mind faking consumption to convince my father I needed a day off, then writing a note for him to sign that read, "My daughter said she didn't feel well yesterday." If the principal didn't like that one, she would have to call him and argue the point. But to write the note and sign it myself seemed awful. My father had only been angry with me a few times in my life, and I knew playing hooky and lying to cover up would let me in for some heavy lectures and constant future surveillance. So that night I approached him, frightened and remorseful, and told him I'd done something terrible. I wasn't that keen on Benny Goodman, I'd ruined my dress, and I could be thrown out of school if I was caught.

When I finally stopped repeating that I'd done something terrible, and got the courage to tell him what I'd done, he just laughed. He was so relieved to find out that I hadn't quit school or gotten pregnant that he wrote the note without argument, though for a few days he kept looking at me and shaking his head, saying, "Benny Goodman? Why would anybody want to go see Benny Goodman?"

How could I explain Evelyn to him? It was easier to let him think I was just a crazy teenager with a crush on a bandleader than to tell him I went along to accompany Evelyn on her seventh trip to see Benny. My ears were still ringing with "Benny, Benny, it's me, Evelyn!"

I guess Evelyn wrote her own note. Her mother and father were divorced, a fact we learned during our freshman year. "Yeah, they're divorced," she informed us, shrugging her shoulders, her face rueful and serious. "What can you do? It's not so bad."

Evelyn mentioned her mother as much as any of us. But she spoke differently about her, aware that her mother might come in for criticism because she was divorced. Divorce between Catholics wasn't spoken of. Her mother had a boyfriend who wanted to marry her, but while it was possible for a Catholic to divorce, it was not possible for one to remarry. So Mrs. Brendel remained unmarried and Evelyn remained without a father. Evelyn spoke well of the boyfriend and told us about presents he had given her, but she seemed wary when she spoke of him, as if even she couldn't quite accept the idea of a mother who had a boyfriend who gave out presents.

Evelyn gave the impression that she and her mother were good friends, a relationship that wasn't common in those days, and that her mother didn't take her misdeeds too seriously. Still, I doubt whether she asked her mother for notes to cover the days missed in pursuit of Benny Goodman.□

December 4, 1984
New York, NY

Dear Fran and Irv,
If this letter turns out a little strange, it's because I'm trying to comprehend all the intricacies of our new computer, which I plan to use only for its word-processing program. The rest of its possibilities are beyond me because they deal with numbers, and for a lady who can't remember her own telephone number or birthday, numbers will never be the pathway to either greater information or the Kingdom of Heaven...

We are here in New York until December 22nd, and then we will be in California off and on for about three months. After that, I hope we will divide our time between New York and France, where we have bought some land in our favorite town of Talloires, and where we expect to build a house commencing this spring. We have an architect who I presume is working on the plans but we haven't seen them yet. I don't know about Milt, but I am in no hurry to begin all the fuss and bother. I just like owning the land and feeling that I am a part of something I love so much. We've made a number of good friends and acquaintances there, rather easy to do, since it is really 99 percent vacation town and everyone is anxious to make friends, no matter what the nationality. It seems we are the first Americans to actually buy property with the intention of building. We really should keep in touch, and when you are at all near, if we're there, you must come and visit with us. And that, as you know, is not just a polite formula cordial invitation but the real thing.

Jenny is celebrating her first anniversary, and she and Richard will be coming here for a few days, so we will celebrate the anniversary and Christmas at the same time. She is having a very big show in London in March and another here in Manhattan in June. Maybe you will be somewhere nearby and get to see one of them. She's becoming incredibly good, and is better known in England than here.

Andy got his Physics degree from London University last June and is now taking a one-year course in economics and history (or something) at the London School of Economics. I don't think he knows what he will do after he finishes this year. Perhaps he will take a year off and go to work, then return to school again for an advanced degree. We will see how well he does this year, and he will see if he likes the switch from science to liberal arts. I think he is the kind who could happily take courses for another ten years in fifteen different disciplines, never making up his mind just what he would like to do. I see Andy as the perfect nineteenth-century gentleman's son, not too rich, not too poor, not too ambitious, not too lazy, puttering about, sometimes in his library, sometimes in your library, and sometimes in a museum in Florence or in northern who-knows-where, always surrounded by papers that he will someday sit down to organize, but not today. Perhaps today he will learn to play the violin.

He has a wonderful mind, and he and it are quite happy to walk around the mountains instead of tunneling through them the way the rest of us do. If I draw you a picture of a happy young man, I think it's pretty accurate. So far, life is good to Andy and he is good to it in return.

Milt is still working with Domingo, listening to opera, and running Cherry Lane with great enthusiasm. We love being here in New York together and have lots of fun walking and going out to dinner, to the opera, and sometimes to the theater. I like New York. Milt really prefers Los Angeles, so we're splitting up our time. New York is now officially our residence. It's where most of the underwear is, and also the family photographs, and that's what makes it official. I wonder if the tax department will agree.

Be well. Write soon to let us know where you are these days, and to catch us up on all the news.

    Love,
    Rosemary and Milt

               December 5, 1984
               New York, NY

Dear Elinor,

I haven't written or called since we returned to the States, because the moment we stepped into the apartment in New York, we decided that we had to repaint it. Then while we were doing that, I decided we might as well do something about decorating it and replacing two of the bathroom sinks that were cracked. Then I decided to put in some overhead lighting in the living room and dining room, and from then on until a week from tomorrow, when the double windows to insulate against the sound and dirt will be installed, my life will have been a long double and sometimes triple file of workmen messing things up faster than I can clean up. So any visit we might have made this fall is impossible from all points of view. When do you plan your next visit to Europe? If it is on a tour and you can get away, or if it's free form and you are on your own, maybe you will think of visiting us, if we are there at the same time. That's an awful lot of "ifs" but maybe we can work something out. We would be so happy to see you and Phil again. I'm really sad that our lives have gone in such different directions, and we have so little expectation of seeing each other.

    Joan and Bill were here for dinner last week, and we had a wonderful time with them. Bill seemed very relaxed, and in spite of the fact, or maybe because of the fact, that he had some kind of health problem recently, he was nicer and pleasanter than I have ever known him to be. Maybe we were too. Maybe we're all getting mellower in our late middle age, and the things we used to be so passionate about are taking their places in the parade of events and time where we can see them with more perspective. Also, I felt as if he has accepted completely Joan's work and her interests. And that she has accepted them as well, without any real feeling of guilt toward him. For the first time, she made no apologies about how foolish it is for her to be working, and how unimportant it all is compared to what everyone else is doing. She just spoke briefly about what her particular field of research is about, and when appropriate in the conversation, added information, probably more accurate than anything the rest of us were saying. Isn't it too bad it takes us all so long to grow up?

    I hope that everyone will have a wonderful holiday. Jenny and Richard are going to be here for a week or ten days. Our apartment is really too small for two extra guests for that length of time, but we will manage as best we can. I wouldn't be surprised, however, to see them take off and stay with friends for part of the time just for some breathing space. Now I wish I had an extra room big enough for two people to be comfortable in instead of a not very glorified New York City maid's room. After they leave, Andy will come for one day, then leave to visit his girlfriend in Massachusetts, and some friends from France will be here a few days, and then follow us out to L.A. for two weeks. We expect to be in California until about March, then back to New York, so maybe we can make it to Cape Cod in the spring.

    I have been feeling very nostalgic lately about the days when we all lived in Chappaqua and our children were still young. I wonder if I wish for the energy I had then as well as the pleasure of being with old friends and seeing my children's young faces. I miss the hemlocks, and buying plants at the nursery and watching them grow. As always, I can never remember what I thought about years back, and feel that I must have been empty headed and foolish and wasted my time on nothing, then I realize that the things I remember and miss, like the trees and the seasons, and the good friends and the sunsets, and how beautiful our children were, sound like a pretty good life, and so what if I wasn't thinking spectacular thoughts. Who was I going to impress anyhow?

Be well, and write soon, and let's see if somehow we can plan something for the spring.

      Love,
      Rosemary

             October 20, 1985
             New York, NY

Dear Michael,
The doorman delivered your letter before I could get to the computer to start this, but I must have known it was coming, because this morning I had a strong urge to sit down and write to you....

I hesitate to respond to what you implied in your letter, but, knowing me, I will. I can't suggest any particular course of action, because I don't know what you want, but I will say that I believe there's not much point in expecting the pain, whatever it is, to subside, because the more you mature the more you realize that the pain never goes away. The most one can hope for are distractions.

So now for distractions. If your heart is careening, Michael, don't stop it. Do what you want. If you want to stay more than you want to follow it, then stay. But if you want to leave, then leave. Whatever it is you want to do will probably harm no one, and in the long run, if you do what you want, you will be more content, not without pain, just more content and a better person for yourself and the world.

When older people talk about the pain subsiding, what they're saying is, "After a while you'll settle down like me and give up your dreams. The pain will become a dull ache for most of the time and at least you won't have fallen off the edge."

But the edge is where life is most interesting. Maybe when you first went to Taizé, it was the farthest edge you could find. A new country, a new language and culture, an acknowledgement of your own dedication to do something meaningful, idealism put to use. A place where the gifts you had to offer were accepted.

I'm not a person with many illusions. I'm not sure I have any. I don't usually tell people that, but I can tell you. I often hide my feelings, even from good friends, because knowing the truth, even someone else's truth, is like facing the Medusa, and they'll leave me in order to save themselves—and their illusions.

I was very pleased and happy for you, Michael, when you found Taizé. I could understand some of the reasons why you were there. I would have given a lot to be there myself, because without illusions, there wasn't much outside to give me comfort. But if you decide to do something else, I will be glad if it is what you want. I'm sure you know that.

I'm sure you won't allow anyone else's opinion to influence you in your decision. Jean might not be the only one disconcerted by your taking another direction. You may find that even people with no religious inclinations feel put out by any change in you—people who would use you as a symbol of what they would like to be themselves. You know, Plácido sings our pain and joy for us. Great writers and philosophers speak the things we think and can't express. And those who are formally and identifiably religious perform the good deeds we feel incapable of doing for whatever reasons. It would be wrong for you to continue at Taizé for the sake of what other people want without regard to what you yourself need.

A long time ago, when Milt and I offered to help you through school, you thought we wouldn't want to do so because you were interested in Divinity School and we weren't formally religious. It wasn't true then, and it isn't true now. Whatever you want to do, if you need or want our help, we're here for you. Our love, you have.

Nothing is irrevocable, Michael. Change your mind today. Change your mind again tomorrow. It's all like one long vacation anyway, and the only way to keep growing is to accept the changes. Think of the people who don't accept change. Do you want to be exactly what you are today, twenty years from now? If the answer is yes, then be it, and if it's no, do what you have to do not to be it.

You haven't said what you are being pulled to do. My suspicion is that it may be to write, and on that score, your letter of today is so well-written and so far beyond anything I've seen of yours before this, that I'm ready to say, go for it. You certainly have a lot to say. The gift for discerning the spirit can be put in writing as well as spoken.

I wish I could help you because I love you, and I will help you if I can, and I know that I'll approve of whatever you do, even if I don't approve of it, because I love you. So, take that from your old Aunt Mitzi.

October 21

(continued)

Dear Michael,

Another day, another letter.

I'm glad I called you today. It's better to know that you want to hear what I am thinking than to think it aloud and fear I'm speaking out of turn. And I hope my call was a comfort to you if only to tell you that we're thinking of you and want to understand.

Today I'll tell you what I hope. I hope that you choose with no desire to please anyone else. Tell me what you want, Michael, and I'll tell you truthfully if I think it's attainable. I promise not to lie and say what I think you want to hear or what I think I should say.

I think you're right when you say you have a talent for understanding people, but I don't think because someone has a talent and a power that he owes the use of them to the world. I think that "owe" and "must" and "should" are words men created in order to control themselves and often, other men, and I think we have to weigh those words carefully. I don't believe in souls, but I know I have one. I care about it and I have an image of myself that's consistent with doing a certain amount of good, not for the good of my soul, but because I have one. More than that I believe in telling the truth. And because I also have the gift of seeing, probably with less compassion and generosity than you, it's very painful. There's a lot of truth that I don't like, but I almost always like it better than a lie. We all live little lies, but it's best not to live big ones. Look at the life you are living and decide whether, if you stay, you will be living a lie.

I've met other people who live in religious communities and somehow I have a feeling about you that isn't consistent with their lives and the life you live...I'm not being negative about Taizé. I know the community has great value and they do good work, but I think that the sum of your intelligence and ability is greater than the sum of all the people there. I believe that as much as a man can be unique, you are. I would never have said this, except that you've asked me to say what I think. The good work that the community performs will continue with or without you. Some people gain most pleasure from working in unison with others and some prefer to work alone. One intelligent man living in the maelstrom behaving decently serves the same end. You're a good human being and whatever you do will be done well. It's true you serve a purpose at Taizé, but forcing yourself to the point of physical and spiritual exhaustion won't save the world, and maybe not even a small corner of it if the end result is that you lose your own soul, whatever a soul is.

Is this too desolate a picture of life? I don't think so. There are still the mountains and the sunsets and a smile from someone, human faces, new life, a flower, a good feeling now and then. You can probably tell me all the reasons why I'm wrong in my estimate of you and of Taizé and maybe you will be right. But I would be right in saying that there will always be Taizés, and always be young men and women who must make the choice.

Maybe you can give other people the same gifts that you give the wanderers and seekers at Taizé, only in a different form and in a different place, just by being where you want to be and doing what you want to do.

       Love,
       Rosemary

INDEPENDENCE

I was three years old and just out of the crib in my parents' room. We had returned from the summer in Honesdale, Pennsylvania, and they bought or inherited a new bed for their room, so they put their old double bed in my sister Jean's room and she inherited me. They may have kept me in the crib that long to protect us from one another, or maybe it was just economics. They had the crib, and as long as I wasn't doubled up in it from being too big, it could do.

That first night in the double bed was awful for Jean and me. I wrapped myself around her primate style and thought I loved the new arrangement. I loved her. She was my big sister. She hated it. I was her little sister. The interloper. Poor Jean. Poor me. Not only had I taken her place in the family, now I was taking part of her bedroom. And hanging on to her. The next six months were like trench warfare. A little blanket here. Eight inches there. A lot of noise. Win a little. Lose a little. And a lot of pain. The first pair of twin beds someone wanted to give away, we were separated and a sort of peace reigned. The next six years were spent ignoring, fighting, and crying.

Then Hitler and Mussolini intervened. My brother Mike enlisted and I was given his room. I was thrilled. There was a bed, where I spent most of my time reading, and on the wall right next to the bed there was a reproduction of a painting of a locomotive that fascinated me. There were only two pictures hanging in our house, both by the same painter: one, in my parents' room, of sailing ships, probably the Niña, Pinta, and Santa María, and the rushing locomotive. Years later, I saw the painting of the locomotive in a book of nineteenth-century paintings. I don't know the name of the painter but he must have been important to make it into an art book.

I used to try to see how many faces I could find in the painting. There were clouds of steam billowing from the smokestack and clouds in the sky, and all the mechanical parts of the train, and weeds and flowers by the side of the tracks, so it was easy to imagine faces. When I wasn't reading, often I'd reach up with my foot and swing the painting from side to side to see how far I could go without making it fall down. Sometimes I'd read and swing at the same time. My right foot remembers the swing of the painting along the wall, and I can still hear the sound it made brushing against the pale green enamel.

Maybe studying the painting was the beginning of wanting to be an artist. Every Friday afternoon in school, we were handed a piece of seven-by-ten cream-colored drawing paper and given a subject—a house, a dog, a flower. I don't have any of the drawings I made, but they were usually the best in the class. If my handwriting was awful and I couldn't do math, I could draw. Sometimes the teacher would be pleased enough to give me a second sheet of paper. Those were the banner days, the only happy times I had in grammar school.

There were no letter writers in my family. They weren't even list makers, so there was no paper in the house. There was certainly no blank paper. The only blank paper I could find was the front and last pages of the books that I received for my birthdays and Christmas. I drew on them all. I drew in the margins of all my school notebooks and on the insides of the covers. I wish I could say my drawings were interesting and showed great promise, but they weren't and didn't. I was only interested in faces. And the faces I drew weren't interesting until I grew old enough to start shading them in and understanding how to show differences.

I went to a Catholic girl's high school where only students who were failing important subjects were made to take art. Since I wasn't failing, I had to talk my way into the class in my junior year. The level of the art class was as minimal as you would expect in a school dedicated to turning good Catholic girls into good secretaries while they waited to get married and produce the next generation of good Catholics, but at least I could sit for two hours once a week and draw without being accused of wasting time.

My parents were secretly proud and openly appalled. An artist. Was I going to be temperamental? Maybe I would become a bohemian and live in sin. Unthinkable. Even I didn't think of it until I heard about The Cooper Union, a free art school down in Greenwich Village. Cooper changed my life. I walked into the building and found people who never looked puzzled and asked me, "Why did you say that?" It was the first time I ever felt I belonged in the place where I was.

It didn't take more than the first two years for me to realize that while I had talent, I didn't have the dedication or determination to be an artist. I didn't have the drive. I married, had a child, stopped drawing, read a lot, studied modern dance, divorced, dated, remarried, and after ten years started drawing and painting again. A group of suburban friends and I hired a model and worked for three hours each week. It was as if in the years of not drawing, I'd reached another plateau in skill, just by living and watching.

Then we moved to Europe and that was the end of drawing again. I began to write letters to friends and finally to my nephew Michael, who wanted to know about our family. That was the open sesame to writing for me. I've always needed some way to speak—drawing, dancing—and writing stories and anecdotes for Michael, beginning to explain the older members of our family and the town and times they lived in, was a thrill for me. I found writing the most satisfying art to do. Writing was exhilarating. It was nothing like drawing. Drawing is mesmerizing, calming. There's something interesting to look at when you're done. I'm always surprised when things turn out. I'm not very creative when I draw, but I save the happy accidents and feel mildly hypocritical when someone praises one of them. My real talent in art is knowing what to put on the wall and what to throw out.

So after thirty years of writing, I'm drawing again and teaching myself to do watercolor. I'm copying my grandchildren—I leave all my stuff on the table, no clean up. Every time I pass by, I look at what I'm doing, and when I feel like it I stop and do more. The kids don't worry about how much paper they're using or where it comes from. I pretend that I have a fairy grandmother, just like them, with an endless supply of materials, and all I have to do is use the stuff and maybe something happens.

Maybe that's my real talent in life. All the years of starting this and stopping that, picking things up and putting them down. Learning what to get rid of, what to pick up, and how not to be embarrassed about the changes. Not to think you have to be one thing all your life, a daughter, a Catholic, a painter, a dancer, a writer, a mother, a sister, and definitely not a secretary.□

October 27, 1985
New York, NY

Dear Michael,

Yet another letter. A good friend of mine showed me a poem yesterday in the hope that I could help her with it. It seems she was trying to say something negative about someone without saying it; and trying to say something important without quite saying it; and trying to say something unpleasant about people who see terrible things without seeing them, something I think we all do at times. There was one line in the poem, unexplained but understandable: "What good is goodness?"

It seems that a friend of a friend of hers who is a sculptor went to Chile or Argentina, came home devastated by the terrible things he saw, and proceeded to purge himself of his misery by sculpting four hundred heads, the heads of the "disappeared," which he hung all over the walls of his home and his garage. He was a good person who saw something terrible and did the only thing he knew how to do to make a statement about it. He's not famous so probably no one but his friends will ever see the heads and hear his personal cry of despair. Rose's point in the poem, which she didn't quite say, was, "What good does his goodness do if he doesn't get out there and do something about it?"

But that's not what she wrote, and not being a Freudian, I see it as a lack in her ability to get everything down on paper rather than a desire not to look at the darker question. It's the despair about goodness that causes me more pain than anything else. All "good people" seem to want to end all the pain and terror in the world. We want to feed all the hungry children, put blankets over the shoulders of all the cold and homeless, and stop the senseless slaughter of one man by another. I don't know how old we are before we understand we can't make it all happen by our passionate desire or our efforts. At some point we change to hoping that someday there will be no more hungry children, no more cold and homeless people, and no more murders. Then comes the time when we look at life and the history of man and we say, "I can try, but it's hopeless." We try to do what we can, given what we are. With luck, we make our own miniscule contributions.

As lives go, I have an easy one. I'm not hungry or alone. I've lived through wars, though at a distance. I have no diseases beyond those to be expected at my age, and fewer than some of my friends. But I'm a loner. Six people working together on a project can drive me out of my mind. I want to work with other people but I'm overwhelmed by the enormity and savageness of life. I try to do what I can for the people I meet and the people I love, and I try not to think about the world and human life beyond that because when I do, I wish I had never been born. And what good does that do? What good is goodness?

Last night at about seven o'clock, Milt and I decided to take a walk before dinner. We thought we might find a pleasant place along Third Avenue and drop in for dinner. If not, we'd get some pleasant exercise and come back and have a salad at home. Everything was almost gay, lots of chatter and some silliness and laughing. We walked up to Seventy-Ninth Street and started east. Halfway between Park and Lexington, an old man, shuffling along just ahead of us, peered around and asked us where Lenox Hill Hospital was. Milt told him, and we were about to move on when the man said, "You see, I'm blind." It was dark out, he seemed to be in his mid-eighties, and he didn't have a white cane. I could see that he was sort of looking at us, so I knew he wasn't completely blind, but he did look kind of helpless. So I said, "Follow us, we'll show you where it is."

When you're eighty-six and shuffling in the dark and you can't see very well, maybe because of cataracts, you don't go very fast, so by the time we got to the corner he had us hooked. He was obviously dazed and didn't belong out by himself. His clothes were clean and he had on a crazy sort of fashionable wool fedora with the brim turned up in the front and down in the back, and his white hair was a bit long but not uncared for. He had a kind of lost, rakish, man-about-town look. I figured we'd walk him to the hospital and that would be the end of it until I heard him tell Milt, in the middle of the Seventy-Ninth Street traffic, that he was the Prime Minister until Maggie Thatcher got in. Halfway down the next street, we stopped and asked him where he lived, and he told us he lived at Lenox Hill Hospital. Said they'd know him there. Now hospitals like Lenox Hill don't have wards for mental patients, especially ones who are really benign and sweet, even though they think they're ex-prime ministers.

He said he'd been living at Lenox Hill since the Tories got in. At that point Milt and I couldn't look at each other, but we also couldn't leave him, so we turtled our way on down toward Seventy-Sixth Street. With every agonizingly slow step the certainty was growing that we weren't going to get out of it by just dropping him off at a big city hospital where they wouldn't know him and certainly wouldn't want him. At Seventy-Seventh Street he pulled out a folded-up paper and rattled on about being a patient at the hospital. He let me read it, and lo and behold, his name was Harold Wilson, no kidding, and it was a letter from the hospital to his insurance company about some appointments he had there last May. He said his name was Mr. Wilson and he complained about something that happened to his eyesight in Miami, the exorbitant rents on Lexington Avenue, how the Nineteenth Police Precinct was forced to move from Seventy-Sixth Street to Ninety-Something Street by apartment developers, and the Maggie Thatcher problem. He said they'd know him at Lenox Hill.

Well, the three armed guards at Lenox Hill were kind and nice, maybe because we were with him, and naturally they'd never seen him before. With a little help from them, we discovered his address was 819 Madison Avenue, and got the Nineteenth Precinct number in case 819 turned out to be a recently developed major hole in the ground. He talked every now and then about his son, who had provided him with a cheap chrome identification bracelet with his social security number engraved on the back. He also said his telephone was out of order, and anyway he lived alone, and no longer claimed that the hospital was home.

Fortunately, number 819 actually existed. However, it was on Sixty-Seventh Street and we had started at Seventy-Sixth Street, and there wasn't a taxi to be had, so we could only shuffle our way down very slowly. With my terrible feet, the worst thing I can do besides standing still is walk very slowly. So Milt held Mr. Wilson's arm and I skittered around on one foot and the other back and forth diagonally and in circles all the way downtown, suffering all the impatience of the hyperactive, coming back to them every minute and a half and at the crossings to help, catching snatches of the most beautiful and charming lucidity and delusion imaginable. He was as nice and smiley and intelligently sharp and crazy as could be. I wondered at one point if he wasn't an ancient actor, and this was his way of capturing an audience for the evening.

At the corner of Seventy-Fourth and Madison an incredibly neat and intelligent-looking black man carrying a beautiful little girl in his arms stopped and asked me if I could give him some money for food. Well, there was Milt twenty shuffling feet in back of me, being beautifully patient, urging Mr. Wilson on, so I opened my purse, something I wouldn't have done in the dark on a public street if I had been all alone. It was the child on his shoulder I suppose. I had fifty dollars in my purse, so I gave him ten. He said thank you, and made his way down the street, stopping people as he went, and as I watched them give him money, I wondered, cynically, if he had rented the child the way beggars sometimes do in Hong Kong when they go begging. I realized that at the rate he was going he could make more than Marian, our secretary, in a lot less time, and I knew that guilt was rampant on Madison Avenue and I even felt that it should be.

When we got to Mr. Wilson's door, for which he had a key but couldn't quite make it work, he very firmly said goodbye and thanked us, having enough sense not to let two strangers into the building with him, though he was so frail even Tinker Bell could have pushed him aside. A woman in her forties with a teenage boy was coming out the door as he was going in, and when we asked her if she knew him, she said that she had lived in the building many years but had never seen him before. So we checked the mailboxes. It seems she lived on the sixth floor and he lived on the third. It was a small building with a self-service elevator, which he insisted he could manage, and our last view of him was in the elevator as the doors closed.

All the way on that prolonged walk home, I was between tears and laughter. For him, at him, at myself and Milt, and for us someday, thinking about Milt's parents and the tragedy of their later lives, which lacked the pleasures of Harold Wilson's, even if most of his were delusions.

We were doing a good deed, more or less under self-applied duress, but why? I thought of my mother during the Depression when I was a little girl and an old man who was hungry and worn-out came to the door asking for food. We were eating our lunch in the kitchen. She couldn't let him in because there were no men in the house and he was a stranger, so she scooped out a big bowl of something hot and gave him some slices of bread and milk, and he ate it out on the front porch. She looked so sad and I asked her why. I was very little, but I never forgot her answer. "Because maybe someday your father will be hungry and I hope that someone will be able to give him something to eat."

I think that people who were brought up as Catholics in those days found it very easy to think in terms of spiritual insurance, which probably led them quite naturally to physical insurance. But it was her thought of my father as she tried to do something for this poor man that I remember, and it made me love her.

Is goodness good in itself? What is it anyway? Is it intentions or is it results? When I was a teenager there was a great debate in the Archdiocese of Brooklyn. In every order of nuns there was one or two who felt that their mission in life was begging. Outside of the Little Sisters of the Poor, who kept a kind of adult orphanage on Springfield Boulevard, it was very embarrassing for the orders and for the archdiocese because most came from orders far richer than any of the people they were begging from. No matter how many commands not to beg came down from the Cardinal and the Bishop, no matter how firmly they locked the convent doors, or how hard they tried to convince the nuns that everyone in the order was well fed and well shod, somehow they always got out, and you could see the same little old nuns nearly every day on their favorite corners, ragged round baskets slowly filling up with pennies and nickels. I guess, for some people, happiness is doing what you think you're supposed to do, and both the beggars and the givers felt a glow of grace. And grace is what came into question round about 1945 when it was discovered that a few of the regular beggars were hiring their habits from a theatrical costume company in Brooklyn. Catholics spent a lot of time trying to figure out whether the givers of charity to the charlatans were getting as much, or indeed any, grace when the results were two dollars down on Lickety Split in the third at Belmont instead of hot soup for the poor, though one couldn't be sure if the money collected by the real nuns got any closer to the poor. The rich orders didn't have a great deal to do with the poor either, or if they did, their second-hand charity was doled out with a lot less grace than when it had been handed to the little old nuns.

So what am I saying, Michael? I don't know. I don't have any answers for good people. I think we do what we do, sometimes out of guilt, sometimes because we want to, sometimes because we think we should, sometimes for future good luck insurance, and sometimes, I guess, for no reason at all. Do I believe in grace? Probably. Do I believe we'll be rewarded for it? Probably not. Do I get a glow from doing what I think is good? Not always. Do I think that matters? Only to me. Do I want to be liked for it? No. Or maybe only by those I love.

And what does this have to do with your problem? I don't know. It's just what happened yesterday.

      Love,
      Rosemary

                November 28, 1985
                New York, NY

Dear Michael,
It's fitting somehow that I should write to you on Thanksgiving, because you're part of my gift of life. And because you're part of my shared family Thanksgiving past, though you don't remember those days the way I do.

I was eighteen when you were born, and winter days were crisp and crackling. Colors were mauve and so subtle it was like looking into paradise. November twenty-seventh was my mother's birthday, and the twenty-fifth was Aunt Mamie's. Papa's was Armistice Day, which seemed fitting for a man who was always right. So it didn't surprise me at all that Thanksgiving was a November day too.

I'm not sentimental about Thanksgiving, not like Christmas, probably because I wasn't a big eater. I loved having time off from school and loved the mashed potatoes and turkey skin, but the rest was unimportant.

When I was little, children used to dress up like ragamuffins and darken their faces with coal, then go out with bags and baskets and beg from house to house, but my father never let us. He would wince and frown when he saw them and tell my mother over our heads that it wasn't right, not a nice thing to do. I thought then that he meant it made the children look dirty and not respectable, but I understand now that he was thinking of the really poor children who had nothing but what they could beg in those Depression days and that it was wrong for people to let their children pretend to be beggars.

He was very patriotic, so he told us about how lucky we were to be here in America. But I think it was the expression on his face, the grimace when he thought about people who weren't as lucky as us that meant more to me than all the stories about Pilgrims and Indians that I heard in school. Because he was generous, our Thanksgiving dinner was usually shared with other people.

I only really began to like Thanksgiving when my family was growing up. I cooked the turkey and cranberry sauce, and I fed them, and sometimes some friends. I don't know if I succeeded with my children in helping them to understand other people's hunger. It was a different time. An affluent time. And maybe I busied myself so with cooking and managing, that I had no energy after all to wince and think of anyone else. I don't remember.

Today Milt is in Barcelona. Andy and Jenny are in London, where Richard will cook a grand turkey dinner that won't mean anything to him except that he loves to cook. Someone will make a joke about Indians and Pilgrims. Richard will have good friends there, and giving them food will make him happy. And maybe just sitting down and sharing food is what Thanksgiving is about...

My friends the Randolphs have invited me up to Chappaqua for dinner, where I will be the guest. That will be fun in a way. I'm not sorry not to do all that cooking. It means that I can sit here this morning in unhurried peace and write a letter to you, my family from the past, my friend present, the love I feel the satisfying meal at my private Thanksgiving table that I want to share with you.

               Love,
                Rosemary

ANYONE FOR SECONDS

Why do I cook cranberries
every year
and turkey and turnips

Now that I know
how tired my mother was
when she came smiling to the table

Where are they now
voluptuous mounds
of food and flesh

Artie likes the drumstick
give grandpa the wing
more, more potatoes

And, when the red berries boil
I will act the part as if
the feast will never end

THANKSGIVING

Family holidays are like a relay race. Sometimes parents relinquish the right to host the celebrations to their grown children with grace and even open relief. After all, a twenty-five-pound turkey begins to feel like a fifty-pound dead weight after you reach a certain age. Other parents find it difficult to give up a family ritual. They know it will never be quite the same again. Old traditions make way for a combination of new ones—his family always has candied sweet potatoes and hers likes strained cranberry sauce. His family filled stockings hung over the fireplace mantle, and hers opened the presents on Christmas Eve.

By the time I was born, both Christmas and Thanksgiving were celebrated at our house on 213th Street. Dad picked up my three aunts and my grandparents before noon. Uncle Ed and Aunt Edith were always there, and sometimes Uncle Arthur and Aunt Annie, with all or some of their five children. There was the hustle and bustle of preparing the feast, which always dissipated my mother's bad mood from the night before when my father came home late, too cheery from celebrating. The five of us were in charge of the vegetables, though Dad did most of the work, attacking them the way he attacked everything he did. Mother was the boss on those days. She loved to cook and to heap food in bowls and listen to the praise of satisfied family and guests. Both she and Dad loved to eat delicious food.

It was a far cry from the decorous doings at the home of my three Aunts—all gentility and polished silver—where Thanksgiving dinner was held in former years, or from the gloomy atmosphere in my grandmother's dark apartment at Christmas, where a mountain of simple delicious food was put on the table more in the spirit of Bah! Humbug! than Merry Christmas. In our house, there was hardly room to sit around the dining room table, and not enough space in the living room for all the adults to sit at the same time. The cat found a warm spot on top of the refrigerator, eyeing the movement of food and waiting for the right moment to steal a forbidden bite. Even the dog had to go outside if he wanted to chase his tail.

In the morning, Mom and Dad set us kids to making the stuffing, she up to her elbows in the pleasures of cooking for twenty people, and he moving his great weight lightly about the kitchen shouting orders, drinking coffee, making phone calls, and wishing the world Happy Thanksgiving. While I broke up the bread, Jean added the melted butter and thyme. Mike peeled the garlic, holding it out for all of us to smell. Dad broke the eggs and Mother cried as she peeled the onions. Dad's friends stopped by to wish us a Happy Thanksgiving, as relatives began to arrive for the coming dinner.

In our house, great respect was given to the oldest family members. Children never contradicted them, and they were given the best chairs. My father and mother, who would gladly have given up the most delicious bits of meat or candy, made their children do the same for their grandparents and three elderly aunts.

The dining table with its several extensions stretched into the living room. Grandma and Grandpa sat in a place of honor at the opposite end of the table from Mother and Dad. Nana, Aunt Mamie, and Aunt Julie sat in a row at Mother's right, silently watching the boisterous side of the family—my father's—at the other side of the table laughing and talking their way through the meal, the aunts answering politely when asked a direct question. The rest of us sat in no particular order, except for me, placed next to my father in the early years to see if he could cajole me into eating more than a small mound of mashed potatoes with gravy and a bite of turkey.

Thanksgiving and Christmas were the only days on which the family drank wine—a glass each of sherry before the meal began. Everyone ate with huge appetites, except for the three aunts, who sat picking daintily at their food. Every few minutes somebody asked them if they wouldn't like more of this or that, amazed at their restraint in the face of such a feast. When first helpings were finished, seconds were passed around, and thirds appeared for the heartiest. Seconds and thirds never diminished in size from firsts, and it was understood that if anyone took the plunge and let the plate get into my father's serving hands, the water would be deep and the swimmer would need strength. Ice cream, whipped cream, pies, coffee, candy, nuts, apples, and stuffed dates rounded out the meal. The family sat at the table for hours, only moving as the afternoon grew dim and lights had to be turned on. Women and children dried and put away, while Dad washed so energetically that they couldn't keep up. He gave orders, teased, joked and laughed as he raced through the dishes. No one knew what to expect next, and it was with great relief when, bored with their slowness, he left the kitchen to smoke a cigar in the living room with one of his brothers.

Thanksgiving dinners always smelled marvelous in the cooking, but none was so satisfying as the year my father gave my mother a four-pound box of chocolates the day before. Thinking to save some for the next day, she hid the box in the drawer below the oven. When the turkey began to cook, the beautiful fumes of melting chocolate and browning bird combined to make an odor that drove the family mad. They hunted for the source, until Mother suddenly remembered the chocolates. All that remained was a purple box of gooey mess. Jean and Mike and I stirred it, hoping to find something we could pick out and eat, but no luck.

Mother hid many things and forgot them. There were colored eggs hidden for the Easter morning hunt that turned up a week later in Dad's sock at the back of his dresser drawer or in the coal bin. March or April was sure to bring a Christmas gift hidden from prying eyes in November to someone who needed it in the wet spring. We always knew what to do with the gifts, but the eggs were a problem. To eat or not to eat. Fear won out, and after sitting like a joke on the dining room table for a few days, the egg would be thrown away. I learned that the price was too high for such questionable consumption when I ate a candy hidden in a perfume box for six months, my mother's favorite—Evening in Paris. The result was that I swore off jellybeans for the rest of the year, and that perfume forever.

I wasn't there the year my mother decided that the holidays would be spent at our house, but my brother Mike told me about that day, and this is how I imagine it happened.

A light snow was beginning to fall. Mother pushed the carriage in the direction of Hollis. I can hear her saying to herself, "This is the last time I'm going to make this trip on Thanksgiving. Let them come to me from now on." She looked with irritation at the two pies wobbling on top of Jean's knees, hoping the wax paper would keep the pies in and Jean's hands out.

"Don't touch that, dear, that's for dinner."

Six-year-old Mike, dawdling along next to her, stopped to scoop up handfuls of snow.

"It doesn't make good snowballs, Mommy."

"Thank God. That's all I need. Hurry up or we'll never get there."

Dad was working at the dairy that morning, and the thought of getting two children, two pies, a bowl of candied sweet potatoes, and herself onto the trolley was overwhelming, so she decided to walk the two miles to Hollis. That way she could pile everything into the carriage. She had tried to insist that her aunts come to her for Thanksgiving, but tradition was strong and their quiet persistence at how "nice it would be in Hollis" forced her to accede to their wishes.

When they arrived an hour later at the imposing brown frame house, they were covered with snow, and Mother was red and puffing from the exertion.

At ten o'clock the phone rang. "Mamie, will you tell Mary that I'm just leaving the dairy now? I'll go home, wash up and change, and be there about noon."

"That's nice, Walter," Mamie murmured politely. "You'll be here at noon. I'll tell her."

"And tell him not to be late," my mother added. "We're eating at one."

Nana, Mamie, and Julie fussed about the kitchen and dining room like small, round birds.

"Mamie, did you slice the cranberry sauce?"

"No, Julie did. Didn't you, Julie?"

"Who did the celery? Mamie, did you put the sage in the stuffing? Remember you forgot it once."

Large lower lip in a pout, Mamie said, "That was six years ago."

"Where is that blue dish for the dates, the one with the pink daisies? I saw it at Easter. Did it get broken?"

The three sisters gathered together on the impeccable green and white linoleum to worry over the fate of the blue dish with the pink daisies.

"Oh, put the dates in another dish. No one will notice," Mother said.

The house filled with the smell of roasting turkey. The table was set with good silver and crystal. Candles waited to be lit and appetites sharpened. Twelve-thirty, and no Walter. One o'clock. Still the doorbell didn't ring. At one-fifteen, Rosemary began to be irritated. "Dinner's almost ready. Where's Walter?" She picked up the phone in the butler's pantry and called home. No answer. "He must be on his way. He'll be here shortly." She looked out anxiously at the snow. "I hope he put his heavy sweater on. He'll get pneumonia."

An hour passed, and still no sign of Walter. She called home again.

"Maybe he had a heart attack walking through the snow, or maybe he slipped and he's lying at the bottom of the stairs helpless and can't get to the phone. Oh, answer it, answer the phone!"

At three o'clock she dialed Uncle Ed. "Ed, Walter should have been here hours ago and he hasn't arrived. I haven't heard from him and I'm worried."

"Where was he, Mary?"

"He had to work this morning and said he was going home after to get cleaned up. I'm afraid there might have been an accident. I'm here at my aunts' with the children and I don't know what to do. Could you go down to our house and see if he's there?"

"I'll stop by for the key. Be there in ten minutes."

Mother put down the phone, only mildly relieved. By this time the snow was so deep that the trolleys had stopped running. In any case, she'd never make it home with the children that day.

As Ed left with the key in his pocket, she called out after him, "Be careful in the snow," conscious suddenly that she was sending a one-legged man out in a near blizzard. Ed was apprehensive about what he might find when he got to the house. He might be hurt, but it was just as likely that unreliable Walter had too much holiday cheer in some bar on the way home, or got caught up in a conversation with some barfly.

Ed put the key in the door and opened it. The dog growled. He ignored her so she slunk out to the kitchen, circled twice, and curled up on her blanket near the refrigerator.

The fire was out and the house was cold. There were no open windows or doors. He didn't like the feel of it.

"Walter?" he called out. "Walter, are you there?"

Ed walked to the kitchen, opened the cellar door, and peered down into the dark, calling out again, "Whoo-oo! Are you there, Walter?" Then he went back to the living room and climbed the stairs.

Loud snores could be heard from behind the closed bathroom door. He knocked and opened it to the sight of his older brother sleeping, cradled in the small tub, wet newspaper draped over his chest, and a dead cigar in the ashtray on the floor next to him.

"Hey, Walter, wake up! Everybody's looking for you. C'mon, wake up. Mary's worried to death. What the heck are you doing in the tub?"

My father roused himself enough to give his brother a smart Hell's Kitchen answer: "Cutting my toenails, what do you think?" Then he sat up suddenly, feeling the icy chill of the water.

"What time is it? I must have fallen asleep."

"Four o'clock."

"Holy mackerel, Mary'll be furious! I'll be with you in a minute. Have some tea. And make some for me. I'm freezing."

On the shivering walk to Hollis, he planned his defense. "Be a sport, Mary. I fell asleep. Anybody could fall asleep."

"For four hours? In a tub full of cold water? Anybody, Walter? Not in November."

It was too funny to be angry over for long, and a good joke on him. That day Dad ate reheated turkey, and from then on Thanksgiving was celebrated in Queens Village.□

FIRST LOVE

Second grade was held in the basement of St. Joachim and Anne Catholic School in a room sandwiched between the auditorium and the cafeteria and out of the normal flow of traffic through the rest of the school. It was somewhat like a dungeon, and our warden underground was Miss McCartney. She probably had a first name. I seem to remember "Adelaide," but if that wasn't it, it would have suited perfectly. Why spend time on Miss McCartney? What part could she play in a story about first love? Well, she was there, a witness to it, inextricably bound in my memory to that experience, and in some way a part of all the love I have felt since.

All the other classes were taught by nuns, which may have been the reason second grade was in the basement. How would it have looked for a visitor to open the door to the class and find a skinny stick of a woman in clothes that were often too bright and always ill fitting? Not that she wasn't respectable or quiet enough. She was quiet to a point of fault. When she spoke, her thin voice was pitched high, her vocal chords covered with the gravel of age. She was sixty-eight. Her hair was dyed an unpleasant blonde-brown, and showed a generous portion of white at the roots. Her furrowed skin was dry with powder and rouge meant to make her look young but instead made her look like a corpse.

Miss McCartney was neither kind nor unkind, just nor unjust. She existed as a caretaker whose duty it was to drill us in the arithmetic tables, spelling, and geography, and she did it with all the enthusiasm of a machine. Once a week she passed out one sheet of drawing paper to each child and told us what to draw, admonishing us not to mess up the paper. She saw to it that we hung up our coats and hats when we entered class and put them on before we left.

Morality was simple in Miss McCartney's class. Very Smart Good Girls were good, and all boys and the rest of the girls were bad. Children who spoke without being spoken to were bad. Children who laughed in class were bad. Miss McCartney never told a joke, so there was no occasion to laugh. Sometimes, but not often, she smiled.

I was in the schoolyard playing tag when my sister Jean, then in seventh grade, grabbed my arm and pulled me over to one of her friends. Jean said her friend's name was Pat Brady, and Pat Brady said she had a brother in my class. "He says you're his girlfriend." They were standing there laughing at me, so I started shouting I wasn't anybody's girlfriend. And then they began chanting, "We know your boyfriend" and "Ha, ha, Mrs. Brady," and pointing to a brown-haired, brown-eyed boy over near the fence who was grinning and blushing. Before I could do more than shout one last time that I didn't know Jerry Brady and I wasn't his girlfriend, the bell rang for school to start and we all scrambled to our places for the march into class.

I could see Jerry ahead of me in the line, and when we marched down the stairs to our room I saw his head bobbing up and down, and then he turned around and grinned at me. I made my angriest face at him in spite of my intense pleasure that someone, a boy, was interested in me. I felt that strange mixture of joy and rage at succumbing and being seen to succumb, at desiring to maintain dignity and at the same time to throw it away. By the time I reached the classroom door where Miss McCartney waited to usher us in, I was as excited as it was possible for me to be.

Miss McCartney didn't smile or say good morning, and didn't expect us to either. All she said in her dried-up desert voice was, "Put your raincoats in the closet and your umbrellas in the wastebasket." It was a cool October day, with a light rain falling, and I was carrying an old red plaid umbrella of my mother's. As I made my way to the front of the room, there was Jerry blocking the aisle. No combination of words—no adjectives, verbs, or adverbs—comes close to telling that incredible moment of first love. If I say he looked beautiful, it doesn't describe the electrifying radiance that surrounded him like a huge halo as he laughed and danced in front of me, teasing me without words to deny that I loved him.

So I did the only thing I could. I hit him over the head with my umbrella. It may have been the most perfect act of my life, spontaneous and without thought of consequences, an act of pure love. He understood. He ducked and yowled, pretending to be hurt, but still beaming appreciation and victory.

The problem was, Miss McCartney didn't understand. She came up behind me and grabbed the umbrella I was waving in the air. "Why did you do that?" She rasped at me. "Why did you do a thing like that?"

I was terrified. I looked up at her and said, "I don't know." And it was the truth. I didn't know. Why had I hit someone who looked so beautiful? Why did it feel so good to do something so wild and exuberant? I didn't know then that I was in love. That it had only taken five minutes from hearing Jerry's name to sealing our pact with my umbrella. I sat down in my seat, my stomach quivering with fear that I would be sent to the principal's office, or worse still, be reprimanded by Father Herchenroeder.

"You go stand behind the supply closet," Miss McCartney said to Jerry, and pointed to the oak cabinet at the front of the room, her favorite place of exile for boys who misbehaved. I was treated like a pariah all day, and she ignored Jerry, which was wise, since he wasn't in the least crushed by being kept out of his seat for the day. Instead he wriggled and jiggled on one foot then the other, sat on the floor, crawled under the tall legs of the cabinet, all the while winking and blinking at me, trying to make me laugh, and pretending to cry when I wouldn't. I was mesmerized. And still in love. I stayed in love with Jerry Brady until I graduated from grammar school. And I still love him, the way we love people who have given us moments of perfect happiness.

And somehow, for me, love has always been mixed up with Miss McCartney. She's that skinny stick of a woman at the back of my mind who rasps in her pained frigid voice, "Why did you do that?" When I let myself sink into the pleasure of being loved. It's Miss McCartney who stops me from crashing about in ecstasy at a smile from a stranger, Miss McCartney who sends me shivering into myself counting consequences. But it's also the specter of Miss McCartney, with her dull, distant eyes and wrinkled, unloving arms that forces me back out to take another chance to love again. □

THE MOVIES

"An instrument of the devil," growled Grandma, her eyebrows arched in a frown across her forehead. "Walter, don't take us again, and don't you go again."

"Okay, Ma." Dad smiled tolerantly at his mother. Dad and Mother had taken Grandma and Grandpa to a movie the night before.

"Movies are bad for you," Grandma grumbled, "It's unhealthy to sit there in the dark with all those people breathing germs. You never know who sat there before you. People eating candy and throwing papers on the floor. There might even be mice in the place." Her loose false teeth made a rhythmic backbeat to the syllables in her words.

"What about vaudeville, Ma?" Dad asked. "Remember, we used to go all the time." His whole family had loved vaudeville and had gone as often as they could.

"Vaudeville's different." Her face brightened.

"Okay, Ma."

She scowled again. "Don't let the children go to the movies. It's a sin to watch things like that." She turned her hazel eyes on him, with their drooping lids, the whites showing under the irises.

Mother was furious. She had told Dad it wasn't a good idea to take his parents to a movie, but he insisted that it would be good for them to do something different. Now she knew that the next time she wanted to go to the movies, Dad would use Grandma as an excuse for not going. He didn't care much for movies. "All that love stuff," he'd say. "And you know what Ma said."

The next night at dinner, Jean looked at him, her eyes bright with pleasure. "We saw a good movie today, Daddy. It had elephants in it."

Dad put down his knife and fork and looked across the table at Mother. "You heard what Ma said, Maryanne. Maybe we shouldn't let them go so much."

"Your mother says a lot more than her prayers." Mother turned away from him and passed the butter to Jean. "What do you say, Jean?"

"Thank you, Mom."

"Well, don't take the kids. It's not good for them to see all that stuff. A bunch of phonies running around." He frowned. "Ma's probably right. Forget the movies."

"Forget the movies? If she had her way, we'd all be up on the farm in Syracuse planting turnips."

"Now, don't be that way, Maryanne, it's not nice."

"Not nice? Don't you not nice me! You don't have to go if you don't want to, Walter, but I like the movies, and so do the kids."

Queens Village had two movie theaters. The larger one, the Queens Theater, had more red velvet and gold-painted curlicues in it. There was a good-sized front lobby, four sections in the orchestra, and a small balcony. The six front rows of the balcony were called The Loge, and no one sat in those seats unless the cheaper seats above were taken. New movies came to the Queens Theater and stayed three days, then moved on to the smaller Community Theater four blocks away for the rest of the week. The price at the Queens was fifteen cents and ten cents at the Community, so when families felt rich, they went to the Queens. Kids usually went to the Community. As long as it had a candy counter, what more did they need?

Movies were a problem for me. In those days people believed that what they saw on the screen was real. It all began for me with Walt Disney's *Three Little Pigs*. I was five. It was my first movie, and it started out fun. We stopped at the candy counter on the way in and I got some Raisinets. The pigs were cute. I liked their houses. I liked the little pig's tail that curled and uncurled in time to the music. But I didn't like the movie theater. It was dark, the screen was big, and scary things began to happen. I didn't like the wolf. My mother must have gotten tired of me squeezing her arm and yelping in terror, because she finally took me out to the lobby and bought me some more candy. We stayed out there for a few minutes while I picked out what I wanted from the young girl in an usher's uniform behind the counter. When my mother tried to take me back inside, I dug my feet into the thick red carpet and whined, "I don't wanna." She tried coaxing, but that didn't work, so we waited on a red velour couch next to the candy counter, where my mother could see into the theater and I could play near her. When it was over, Aunt Vera, Jean, and Mary came out to where we were sitting, and someone said, "See, Mary didn't cry, did you, Mary?" And Mary smiled, happy to be a year older than me, and braver than I would ever be.

What happened next happened every time I went to the movies for the next few years. In my family we were all blue-eyed and very sensitive to light and had to learn how to ease from dark to bright light. At five I hadn't figured that out yet, so when I stepped out into the brilliant afternoon sunshine, I got a fierce headache and for a couple of years thought that getting a headache was part of going to the movies.

At least once a year I ran out of the Community Theater, breathless and in a fright. I don't know if my mother ever checked what we were going to see when she sent Jean and me off on a Saturday with ten cents for admission and a nickel each for candy. I bought my candy if there was a serial on, even though Jean told me nothing bad would happen. I didn't want to see some girl tied to the railroad tracks and a big train heading toward her.

The day I ran out on *King Kong*, Jean was furious. She was supposed to be taking care of me and had to run out of the theater after me. One look at the ape and I was out of there. And *Frankenstein*. That was another bad day. I held my breath and groaned as I stumbled past Jean to get to the aisle.

"Where are you going?" she hissed.

"Home."

She hung onto my arm. "What's the matter? You scared?" She laughed.

"Leave me alone. I'm going home." My heart was beating hard. I peeked around the red curtain behind the last row to get one final look, and drew back in a hurry. The monster was up now, walking like a dead puppet around the room. I passed the ticket taker and went out into the blinding sunshine, hand over my eyes, trying to forget what I'd seen on the screen. My nickel for candy was still in my pocket, so I went next door to Sam's for an ice cream cone.

"Hi, Sam."

"Hullo. Whatsa matter? You don' like the movie?"

I tried not to see the monster in my mind, stood in front of the counter with as much dignity as I could muster, and mumbled, "Ummm."

"Too scary, huh? Here, have an ice cream cone. It'll make you feel bedda." He took a sugar cone off the stack. "What kine you like today?"

"Peach, please."

Sam busied himself with grabbing the scoop and leaning deep into the freezer to get the peach ice cream for the cone. When he straightened up and handed it to me, it was a double, piled extra high. I drew my breath, worried. "But I only have a nickel, Sam. I don't have eight cents for a double. Can I owe you?"

"Neva'mine. It's a treat."

"My father says I have to pay, Sam."

"Okay. I tell you fadda. He's a rich man. He can pay the rest later." Sam wiped the cover on the freezer top with a clean wet rag and smiled.

Sam was a happy man. A year ago, Dad, Jean, and I, hoping to escape the boredom of a Sunday afternoon at the three aunts' house in Hollis, went for a walk and happened into Sam's tiny ice cream shop next to the Hollis movie house. It was strawberry season, and Dad, always the milk salesman, saw the hand-lettered sign "fresh strawberry ice cream" and asked with an amused smile, "Did you make the ice cream yourself? Are the strawberries really fresh?"

Sam looked with scorn at the stranger questioning his integrity. He threw his head back in a sharp movement, and said, "Shoor. Only fresh. I make myself. No junk in it."

That quieted Dad long enough for him to taste his cone. The strawberries were red and delicious. There was no fake pink coloring in the cream. The sugar cones were crisp and perfect.

Sam stood behind the counter, vindicated. "Ha, you like?"

An hour later we were back, this time with my mother and the aunts. Everyone had strawberry ice cream except Aunt Mamie, who said in her soft way, "I'll have vanilla, please, Walter."

"Try the strawberry, Mamie. It's delicious."

"No, thank you. I'd like vanilla."

"But strawberries are in season, Mamie." Nothing but unanimous approval of Dad's new ice cream discovery would satisfy. "C'mon. You can have vanilla any time. Take the strawberry."

"No, thank you." An expression close to a frown passed over her forehead and she smiled cordially at Dad, the closest she ever came to a confrontation with anyone in her older years, and said again, "I'll have vanilla, please."

Dad took the family to Sam's three times that week. We began to branch out to other flavors, chocolate, coffee, pistachio. The rest of the ice cream was just as good as the strawberry. After the Legion meeting the next weekend, Dad brought a car full of friends to sample the strawberry. The next week there were several more cars following. An idea began to hatch in my father's mind.

"Sam"—by this time they were Sam and Walla—"what are you doing in this little shop? You need to move to a bigger place, in a better location."

"Walla, I'm doin' pretty good here. I'm only two yeahs in the country an I got my own shop. Dat's pretty good for a Greek like me. I'm doin' awright." Sam smiled, dark eyes bright under long thick black brows, his teeth stained yellow from the cigarettes always found hanging from his lips. His mouth turned down at the corners even when he smiled, making him look like a happy lemon, and there were deep creases from his nose to his mouth. A smile was his usual expression.

"Sam, Queens Village could use a good ice cream store. You'd have no competition there. Hollis is too small." Dad used his most persuasive voice. "There's not enough business in a small town like this."

Six months later Sam opened his new shop next to the Community Theater. It was four times the size of the old one, with half a dozen tables where people could sit and relax while they ate their ice cream. Opening day was a smash. My father rounded up his friends and acquaintances, his children and relatives, and we piled into the shop, cleaning out the ice cream barrels in a couple of hours. Sam worked like a demon, and Dad went behind the counter to help him, the two of them sweating as they turned out sodas, cokes, cones, and banana splits. Sam's reputation was made in a week. Customers waited for tables and stools at the counter. Jean, Mike, and I were warned by our parents that we had to pay, but what could we do if Sam put a little extra on the cones before he passed them over the counter?

"Maybe they let you go back in, now the ice cream make you feel bedda."

"I don't think so." The ice cream made me feel better, but looking at a real person, smiling and being nice to me, was what I needed. Sitting in Sam's shiny white store, I knew the movie wasn't real, but...

In time I learned how to leave the movie theater with my head averted so there were no more headaches, but I still had trouble with reality even when I went to see happy movies. I was Vivien Leigh and Maureen O'Hara, and I was in love with Tyrone Power and Leslie Howard. It was okay to feel wonderful being Ginger Rogers dancing with Fred Astaire, or Sonja Henie, skating on black ice, waiting for John Payne to propose. It wasn't okay to be Boy as he was chased by a giant spider in a Tarzan movie, struggling in a ropelike cobweb, with jungle vines hanging overhead and a monkey screeching hysterically as he danced on the branch of a tree.

Writhing in the movie seat, I clutched my sister's arm. "What's gonna happen?"

"How do I know?" She shoved me away and turned to the screen. "Be quiet."

"Eeeeeyaaahh!" Putting both fists to my mouth to silence myself, I watched the progress of a huge spider. It was as big as the Boy, fat and hairy, ready to devour him, head first, then one limb at a time.

"Don't worry. He won't die." Jean didn't take her eyes off the screen. She disentangled herself and stuck the remains of her candy bar in my hand. "Here, eat this and be quiet."

Boy was still struggling, almost as scared as I was. The spider moved around in front of him, preparing for the feast. The jungle was in an uproar with monkeys, birds, bugs, and elephants going mad. I put my head down so I couldn't see. As I looked into the blackness of the floor, I heard the familiar yell. Tarzan! Maybe I should look. I did, and caught a glimpse of the spider, oblivious to the yell, hairy legs moving with purpose, two feet from Boy. This time, taking no chances, I crouched on the floor and held my hands over my ears. Tarzan wouldn't get there in time. Nobody could.

Jean was laughing. She leaned over and poked me on the shoulder. "I told you he'd be okay. You can look now."

In a daze, I stood up and faced the screen. I blinked. There was Tarzan, swinging from tree to tree, home to Jane. In his arms he carried Boy. The jungle was in an uproar again, only this time all the animals were happy and it sounded like singing. Tarzan's biceps rippled as he put down his son and saluted Jane. The spider was dead, and Boy was still there for another movie.

"Gee whiz, I'm not gonna take you to the movies anymore." Jean got up and hurried me toward the exit. "What a pest."

That night I sat up. The house was dark. A noise. Under the bed. It must be a spider with large hairy legs and a big chomping mouth. It was crawling around. If I looked at it, it would come up and get me.

"MOMMYY!" I yelled.

"What is it?" I heard my mother jump out of bed and come running toward my room.

"There's a spider under the bed."

She turned on the overhead light. She bent down and looked under the bed. "What are you talking about? I don't see a spider. Was it big?"

"I think so." I began to realize that there wasn't a spider under the bed, not like the one in the movie.

"Where is it?"

This was not the time to say there wasn't one under the bed, so I pointed and said, "It went down there, in the corner."

Mother pulled the bed out. "Get up. I'll shake out the covers. Are you sure you saw one?" I stood with my back against the wall, and she tucked the covers in. "How could you see in the dark?" She gave me a quick skeptical look. "Well, it's disappeared by now, so you go to sleep."

I got back in bed, and she leaned over and kissed me on the forehead. I lay there in the dark for a while, then sat up, hands gripping the blanket. A noise. A creak on the stairway. I sat like a stone. There was a spider. I could picture it. A spider with long, hairy legs coming up the stairs to my room. I stared into the black space that was the doorway, waiting for the spider to come in and get me. If I didn't move, it wouldn't know I was there. Maybe I could fool it.

"Mommy, I'm afraid." I was rigid in the dark room, eyes staring, only my lips moving to call out the words.

"What is it now?"

"The spider. I'm afraid. It's on the stairway."

"It's just your imagination. Now, be quiet and go to sleep."

So I took up my watch in the spider-infested house, but I didn't cry out. I don't remember going to sleep, but I must have, because I woke up the next morning in sunlight.

At breakfast, Dad teased me about spiders, and I gave him a cool look. I knew what was in the house. He didn't. He was asleep. Overhearing the conversation, Jean told them about the movie, describing me on the floor, and how she gave me her candy bar.

"Is that what it was all about?" My mother laughed. "Why didn't you tell me? I was ready to start vacuuming at two o'clock in the morning."

I read myself to sleep that night and awoke at three-thirty. The spider was there again. This time I didn't wait. "Mommy!"

The bed springs creaked across the hall. "What do you want?"

"I'm afraid."

Three months later, Mother washed me and dressed me in my Sunday best, and we went by bus and subway to the doctor. Doctor Mundell, who lived around the corner, took care of broken arms and chest colds, but this doctor was a specialist. He was a children's doctor, recommended by Uncle Gus's special doctor, who operated on people's broken heads.

The children's doctor would know what was the matter with a child who woke up every night afraid of spiders that weren't there and kept the whole family, especially her mother, awake for two hours by the clock.

My mother was worried. Imagination was one thing, but this had gone on too long. Even Dad, who managed to ignore much of what happened at home by not being there, couldn't avoid my nightly vigils. The lights were never put out until Dad came home and went to bed, and the spiders never arrived before complete darkness engulfed the house, magnifying the sound of their creeping toward my room.

The doctor's nurse took our names, and we were ushered into his office. He sat at a polished wooden desk playing with a silver fountain pen as he listened to my mother's story. By this time, she was so undone by lack of sleep and worry, she couldn't keep complaint out of her voice.

The doctor called me around to his side of the desk. I looked at my mother for instruction, and she nodded me over. He held me by one arm and listened to my chest with his stethoscope. He looked in my eyes and ears and gave me a pat. "Would you like to write on some paper with my pen?"

I shook my head from side to side.

"No? Well, go back and sit down while I talk to your mother." He noticed me looking at a picture of a little girl on his desk and smiled. "That's my little girl." The girl had on a perfect dress and her socks were brilliant white. Just from looking at her, I could tell that she didn't stay awake at night worrying about spiders.

I sat on the green leather chair, dangling my skinny legs back and forth and catching them on the cross bar, until a flick of a look from my mother stopped me. I clasped my hands in my lap, then moved them, still clasped, to the arm of the chair. I studied the room. There was none of the clutter visible in Dr. Mundell's office, no shiny instruments, no cotton, no tongue depressors, not even a thermometer. There were plants and sets of beautiful matching books lining the walls, some easy chairs, and maroon drapes framing windows that overlooked the city street. The doctor didn't wear a white coat like Doctor Mundell. He just sat there in his brown suit, blending into the room. Only the stethoscope around his neck made him look like a doctor.

I heard my mother's voice repeating the last line of the family litany, "never eats a thing."

The doctor looked stern. "She's anemic, that's all. I'm going to give her something for her appetite. Picking up the silver pen, he wrote on a piece of paper and handed it to Mother, then turned to me. "Your mother says you don't eat enough to keep a bird alive, so I'm going to give you some medicine that will make you want to eat. It's delicious. My little girl takes it every day and she loves it. You'll like it too." He turned to my mother. "She'll be all right in a few months."

I sat there feeling strange. I was anemic. When the doctor looked in my direction, I pointed to the picture and asked, "Is your little girl anemic?"

"No."

"Why does she take that medicine?"

"Because she likes it." He shuffled some papers on his desk. "In the meantime, don't wake your mother up in the middle of the night anymore. She needs her sleep and so do you." I stared at him, and he went on, "If you do wake up, I want you to remember what I'm telling you. There aren't any spiders big enough to eat you, so there's nothing to be afraid of." He smiled in dismissal.

Mother buttoned my coat. "She'll remember."

At the table that night, conversation hummed with talk about the Children's Specialist. The words "she's anemic" were repeated, and the family looked at me and at the bottle of thick, brown tonic that the doctor's daughter loved and I already loathed. If spiders were liquid, they would taste like that tonic. The idea may have been to poison me before the spider could get me. After losing the first two spoonfuls to the sink, I swallowed the third with much gagging and tears.

My father grimaced as I tried to get it down. "Wouldn't CuFe-tone do just as well?" CuFe-tone was the tonic I took when I was three years old. It was bright red and tasted like a sweet white wine. The only appetite it encouraged in me was for more CuFe-tone. I loved it. I used to get the small pink cordial glass they measured it in and stand in front of the refrigerator asking anyone who passed by to give me some.

"I paid a dollar for this medicine and she's going to take it, Walter. Besides, the doctor says she's anemic. She has to eat."

I still woke every night and sat up in bed, ready to protect myself. If I called out to my mother, she would say, "Go back to sleep and remember what the doctor said." I could see him sitting behind his desk, playing with the silver fountain pen, and hear him saying, "There are no spiders big enough to eat you in this country." The spider shrank to a regular size, only now other bugs and worms accompanied it, so I sat up waiting for them all to go away. I was careful not to look at the floor, convinced they would get me if they saw me looking at them.

CuFe-tone would have worked just as well, meaning not at all, for there was no change in my eating habits. Magic pounds and round, rosy cheeks didn't appear. At some point, the tonic was forgotten. So were the spiders. After six months, Mother mentioned one morning that I was sleeping better, something I hadn't noticed.

It was embarrassing to be afraid of spiders in the night and then to forget about them. So I said, "It's not that I'm not afraid of spiders any more. I just haven't been awake, so I don't have to worry about them."

One night I awoke, sat up in the bed, and tried to imagine a spider coming up the stairs, but my mind wandered to something else and I fell back on the pillow and went to sleep.

I'm surprised they ever let me go to the movies again after the spider episode. The only movies I remember refusing to see as a child were *Dracula* and a couple of Laurel and Hardy films. I may have looked at the *Dracula* poster in front of the theater and decided it would be better to turn around and spend my fifteen cents on something else. And Laurel and Hardy were supposed to be funny, but to me the fat cranky one reminded me too much of my father in his bad moods.

In 1936 the Legion of Decency banned a film called *Blockade*. Sermons were delivered from the pulpit in every parish telling parishioners that it was a pro-Communist film, against everything the Catholic Legion of Decency stood for, and no Catholic should endanger his faith by watching it. Solemn pledges, with hands over hearts, were taken to boycott any theater that showed the film.

Dad didn't belong to the Legion of Decency, but he was all for upholding their judgments about whatever they believed to be obscene or sinful. Since he had no idea what the movie was about and found most movies boring, he was quite strong in his condemnation of Alden Theater, three towns away, which held out against the pressure and showed the film.

"It's wrong to show something like that. Why can't they show good movies?" He was asked to lead the movement to boycott the theater and delivered the ultimatum to the owner himself, heavy on sarcasm and hints of impending financial disaster. Jean and Mike and I were told that we were never to go to the Alden Theater again.

Six years later, there was a resurgence of interest in vaudeville. Dad loved vaudeville. The night he met my mother he was singing on stage at a church social. She was sitting in the second row, and he sang all his songs to her. By the time he finished they were convinced they were in love. That may have been the most time he ever spent making a decision about anything. When advertising began to appear in the Long Island Daily Press for Friday night vaudeville after the double feature at the Alden, we knew he couldn't resist. For a whole week we teased him, and he acted as if he wouldn't consider going to a theater that hadn't knuckled under to the ban on *Blockade*. By this time, Russia was our ally in the war, so he could excuse himself when he shouted for all of us to hurry up and hop in the car if we didn't want to miss the movie.

Each week he piled everyone into the car, including any friends who happened to be in the house at the time, and we went to the Alden. He watched countless movies that bored him, just to be able to sit back at ten o'clock with happy eyes and a smile on his face, as he enjoyed the dancing and singing and forgot for a while that he was a grown up.

When we teased him about backsliding, after taking an oath in church with the rest of the congregation, he gave us his "things change" smile, and said, "That doesn't count anymore." We went there for as long as they showed vaudeville on Friday nights, and Dad got so friendly with the manager that he brought him sodas or coffee when he went out to get food for us at intermission.

I don't remember the last movie I saw at the Alden Theater, but I remember the newsreel that came on at the end of the double feature. I was seventeen and too old to run out of the theater in horror. But a part of me recoiled from what I saw and I've never recovered. The newsreel included a film made by the army after the liberation of Buchenwald. It showed the open doors of the ovens with skulls and skeletons still visible among the ashes. There were people starved to near death. Bodies heaped like so much rubbish. In 1945, people weren't used to seeing photos or films showing human evil on such a mass scale.

Every once in a while I still flee the movies, but for different reasons. I remember leaving the Paris Theater on 58th Street in Manhattan when Jenny was sixteen and in love. The movie was *Romeo and Juliet* and when it got to the scene where Romeo returns and finds Juliet, still as death, I left the theater crying so hard I didn't think I would be able to stop. It was too painful.

I never go to scary movies. By this time, I know myself. I don't want to be terrified. I don't want to pay to panic over earthquakes, exploding ships, and psychotic human disasters. I'd rather use the money for a dish of ice cream and maybe a little candy for comfort.□

February 15, 1986
New York, NY

Dear Elinor,
I have wanted to write to you since I received your last letter, something like six or eight months ago, however, every time I headed toward the typewriter, I was waylaid by the feeling that much as I wanted to write to you, I had nothing to say.

Well, I have no more to say today than any other day, but I am here in New York alone for two weeks, so I have no one to interrupt or distract me. Milt is in California on business. And I am here in New York on business. Believe it or not, I now work full-time up at our office in Portchester, running the office, more or less, with a lot of help from our employees. I find it hard to believe and at the same time completely natural that I am running a business that employs thirty-five people.

To the bossiest kid in the first grade, running a business full of people is a cinch. Making money at it may be something else. The reason I'm there is that we had someone running it who didn't understand profit and loss and getting work done. All he understood was the business jargon and long liquid lunches. It's a big mess, and yes, I'm having fun.

When I was five years old a neighbor gave me a pink and white wool handkerchief case. Not having any handkerchiefs, I used it for a baby bunting for my Didy Doll. One day, when I was about seven and bored out of my head, my mother suggested that I wash the handkerchief case, which was by that time very gray and dirty. So I went into the bathroom and under the running water, I washed it clean with Ivory soap. I've never enjoyed anything more than watching the filthy gray water run down the drain and smelling the wet wool as it turned back to sparkling pink and white again. I was so pleased that the next day I tried to wash it again. I've never been more disillusioned. Some things just don't get any pinker or whiter. I suppose that will happen with the company too. Once I get it straightened out, I will leave it for something more interesting.

For the moment, it's fun. Meantime, I come home from work every day exhausted, plop down and watch a tape of "One Life to Live" on the VCR, eat dinner, and try to get enough sleep to go back to the office the next day and get on with the wash...

I think of you whenever I see the weather map on television, or when I think of Chappaqua and our younger days. We have winter and snow now, but I miss those winters and that snow, and our young children, mittens and all. It's hard to believe that we will never be there again, never feel quite so brisk and energetic, that nature is done with us feeding and nourishing the next generation of child bearers. Funny that living it we didn't know why we were there really, and that we thought it was all by choice.

Strange, I just realized that the years of my early childhood, the ones I remember most vividly, are the years my mother was putting my mittens on, so they must have held the same nostalgia for her that my Chappaqua time does for me.

You never know what you will write when you sit down and finally get to it.

Please give my love to your family and keep a lot of it for yourself.

              Love,
                Rosemary

THE PIANO

When Uncle Gus's poor dark wife Jenny died, he broke up house on Staten Island, giving all sorts of wanted and unwanted things to members of the family. To our small house on 213th Street came many items, probably because Dad didn't have the heart to refuse them. I was seven, so I only remember the two biggest ones. The larger and more exciting was a tinny sounding upright piano, not an antique, just an old oak piano, nicked, spotted, and uncared for from life spent with Uncle Gus. Next came an overstuffed chair almost as big as the piano.

The chair jutted out into the living room, blocking the narrow path to the dining room. It was covered in dark brown leather, dried and rough in spots, and had an air cushion that went whoosh when someone sat on it. Mary and I called it the ghost chair; the exhaling whooosh and the inhaling hooosh each time we sat down or got up seemed to come from some creature deep inside it. Then we began to call it Aunt Jenny's ghost and would only sit up and down on it, snickering and squealing, in the daytime with adults in the next room. When my mother and Aunt Vera discovered why we were laughing and carrying on so much, we were lightly reprimanded, as if our behavior was a form of speaking ill of the dead.

From the day the chair and the piano showed up, my mother made a face every time she walked past them. Our living room was not much more than a passage from the front door to the stairs to the second floor or to the dining room and kitchen. It was the Depression, and the few pleasant things we owned in the living room were overwhelmed by the two unwanted gifts.

The chair lasted longer than the old piano. It took the Second World War, the Draft, and the start of prosperity to give my mother, untrained to be anything but a housewife, the chance to go to work. The first thing she bought with her money was a leather chair and ottoman, and the ghost chair was gone.

When the piano arrived, the family was ecstatic, though even tuning didn't improve the sound. We sat around it every night singing, as Dad, who could play by ear, picked his way through the songs he knew with lots of oompahpahs with the left hand and a bit of light tapping of the melody with the right. Jean begged to take lessons, and even I learned to play "Chopsticks" from a girl down the street. We played and sang for a few weeks, but soon the novelty wore off. Dad lost interest and begged off from the nightly sessions. He just wanted to put his feet up and read his paper after dinner. And my mother, not very musical, saw the piano looming ever larger in the small living room. First of all, she didn't especially like her brother-in-law Gus, giver of the gift. Second, the piano lessons were a failure because Jean didn't practice. Mother nagged Dad to take a stand with Jean about the lessons, and she nagged Jean about practicing, and when her nagging got no results she made her own decision. The piano had to go.

Dad promised he'd think of something, but week after week went by, then a few months, and the piano was still there. Mother tried to give it away, but no one wanted it. No one would even take it away. Dad couldn't face Mother's ire, but he feared hurting Uncle Gus's feelings even more. And he knew Grandma would be furious if he got rid of the piano.

One day as his back was disappearing down the street on its way to work, Mother ordered Mike to go to the basement and get the axe. Eyes bright with pleasure, he complied. All morning they hacked at the piano, putting both large and small splinters of wood, screws, and wires into bushel baskets for the garbage men to haul away. By noon, there was a collection of debris piled in the baskets against the tree in front of the house, as well as a collection of neighbors, all anxious to get in on the act, applauding Mother's courage in vanquishing an unwanted enemy on her territory.

The entire frame was gone except for some pieces they couldn't detach from the sounding board. It's hard to chop up a piano of well-seasoned oak but it's impossible to chop up a sounding board with an old boy scout axe, two screwdrivers, and a hammer with a broken claw. Mother and Mike sat there in the mess on the living room floor, covered with dust and perspiration trying to figure out what to do with the remains, for while it was all right to solve the problem in this violent way, it would not be a good idea to have the corpus delicti, or its skeleton, where the butler left it when Dad returned after a hard day at work.

Mike's friend Billy suggested that they put it on skates and roll it out the door to the street. It was a good idea except that the porch was four feet above street level, making it necessary to navigate the sounding board down six cement steps. With the help of one of the older boys they hoisted it onto the skates, and Mother shouted, "Watch out," as the awful thing took off on its own. It went rolling through the door, across the porch, and like a harp thrown out of Heaven, flew down the stone steps into the street.

The noise was breathtaking. Open mouthed children lined its path on each side. There were loud hurrahs and congratulations for Mother, heroine of the day, for having demonstrated her ingenuity and strength.

Ten minutes later, when the garbage men came through the street picking up the week's accumulation of trash, George Hauser called out from the top of the truck, "Hey, Mrs. Primont, what happened to the piano?"

"I didn't like it so I chopped it up." Mother put her hands on her hips and looked at him with a sour expression, defying him to argue about taking it on the truck. He pushed his hat back on his head, eyebrows up and eyes wide, and called down to his partner in the driver's seat, "Hey, Charlie, she didn't like it, so she chopped it up." He laughed. "You better get out of the truck and help me up with this thing."

It was little wonder that children showed Mother great respect and her neighbors didn't argue with her. Even my father was impressed. In one day she accomplished what he couldn't bring himself to do in six months. And what did they tell Uncle Gus? It must have been something reasonable, like they gave it to someone who really wanted a piano, even an old pockmarked, bad-sounding one. Either that, or Uncle Gus, famous in the family for his raging headaches and cutting sarcasm, may have thought that chopping up a piano sounded like a good day's fun.☐

CHRISTMAS DECLARATIONS

Dear Andy and Jenny,
Well, the ball has dropped in Times Square, the Rose Bowl Parade has subsided into normal football madness, the dishes are washed, and there remains only the Christmas tree to be planted in the yard so we can get on with it—whatever it is.

Ever since I left home, back in my early twenties, Christmas has been a melancholy time for me. The older relatives, the ones I cared about, were dead by the time I was a young adult. My parents no longer had a home. And I always wished it could be the way it was when I was little, a big holiday with family and friends and neighbors dropping in, and us visiting them in turn. It was the most important holiday of the year for us back in Queens Village. We may not have been happy, but we were a family, and it couldn't help but be exciting to us in those lean years to buy and wrap presents, to have the luxury of the tree and a feast of food and sweets, and to wish everyone a Merry Christmas.

Then I married Dick, who sneered but "let" me have a tree. It was the first time that I remember being embarrassed about Christmas. After I left him, and not because he was sticky about Christmas, which I think he enjoyed as much as I did, it was just Jenny and me. We had our own apartment and a pretty little tree, so Christmas was pleasant even though it was much quieter than the Christmases of my childhood.

We were living on West Fourth Street in the apartment over Nana and Poppa. A friend and I decided to have a party the week before Christmas. Like most parties it got pretty big before it faded out, and Milt showed up, guest number seventy-five, looking for our roommate Maureen. Fortunately, he was persistent and didn't let me discourage him from coming up the stairs. I was worried about the weight load. That building had a real cardboard feeling to it and you and Nana were downstairs under the festivities. It was lucky we were all thinner back then. The house didn't collapse. Milt had mistaken Maureen's name and was asking for Marlene and when that was cleared up, he stayed, and we fell in love.

The year before Milt and I were married, I invited friends over on Christmas Eve and we had a great time. Milt was on tour someplace with Harry Belafonte, so I was unaware of his feelings about Christmas festivities. I guess he had forgotten that we met at what was really an undecorated Christmas party. Inexperienced as I was with partying and drinking punch (the only thing I could afford), I drank so much that I woke up with a horrendous headache and a quivering stomach. Unfortunately, I hadn't washed up after the party, or emptied the punch bowl, which was still a quarter full with dreadful banana slices floating in it, and the apartment looked as if it had been visited by more than St.Nick in the wee hours.

Jenny, that was the year you were four and we were living on Commerce Street. On Christmas morning, carefully ignoring the punch bowl sitting on our one and only table, we opened the presents my mother and father had brought over to us and the things I was able to buy for you, then went next door to give Sean his present. Both Kim and Bob came from big families, and since Kim was famous at the time, presents had come from people all over the country. There was a tree right up to the ceiling and probably a hundred beautifully wrapped boxes, which they were in the process of opening. It was overwhelming, and I was depressed as well as hungover, because I was sure you would compare their

Christmas with ours. I know I did. I was embarrassed for myself and reassured for you when we walked back into our apartment and you saw our tree and your new toys and whatever else we had piled around it and said you wished everyone could have such a beautiful tree as ours. Sounds like Tiny Tim, doesn't it, but then that's what Dickens was writing about.

Then, I married Milt, for whom Christmas meant little more than the season for pogroms and wreaths on front doors to show crazed peasants and raging Cossacks which houses they shouldn't burn down. He was horrified at the idea of a Christmas tree in his home, so the first year we were married I put the Christmas tree in your room, Jen. The next year it was perched more or less in the doorway halfway between your bedroom and the living room. Each year I attempted to explain to Milt how Christmas trees and mistletoe were just a continuation of long ago pagan rites and didn't have anything to do with contemporary religious fanaticism. And each year, in order to soften his anger and irritation, I invited friends, his, mine, and ours, over on Christmas Eve. But never made punch again. Those parties were the only things he liked about those first few Christmases together.

The first year we lived on Eleventh Street, Jenny, you were seven. Milt was very grumpy but said maybe he wouldn't mind the tree so much if it was all blue, so we had a blue tree—in a corner in the dining room. It was beautiful. But not very Christmasy. And whereas, before I had tried not to be too visibly enthusiastic about the tree, that year I had to show more than I felt for what looked to me like a corner of the north pole.

The next year we went back to colored lights, and you gave us all wonderful presents. Milt's was a special wooden-handled soup spoon because his favorite food was soup. He loved it and used it for years to eat cereal with chocolate in the morning, as well as for eating soup. I think you gave Rose Reitter something pink and flowery. I don't remember Leah's gift but I think it was something to use when she had company. Maybe it was a salt shaker. Whatever you gave Will, he showed it to everyone he met for the next three weeks and talked about how clever his granddaughter was. I think it was a letter opener. I can still see how excited he was, beaming and showing it around to us and talking about how wonderful it was that you got us all things that we really wanted and liked. My gift was something for the kitchen. My memories are all mixed up with ribbons and white wrapping paper and the pleasure that you gave us. The best idea for a gift that you had, even though we didn't let you give it, was a bag of dirty laundry for Sniffy so she could roll around and snuffle in it anytime she pleased.

The week before Christmas, the year you were ten, Jenny, you told me you didn't care whether we had a Christmas tree. We were on the Fifth Avenue bus on our way down to Charlton Street and I remember looking at the lights on the tree in Washington Square, trying not to believe you meant it. I figured that was one way you could identify with Milt, who still sulked each year when we brought the tree into the house, and that you'd change your mind by the next day, but you didn't. So that year I didn't get a tree. It seemed so childish for me to care when no one else did. I don't know if it pleased Milt. We gave each other gifts, but as usual I had the impression that for Milt, a trip to the dentist was probably more pleasant.

You know how you feel when you've been ice skating and you take off the skates and walk on boring flat ground again? That's what that Christmas felt like to me. Each year, I invited friends over on Christmas Eve and that year, some of our friends who were Jews were as let down as I was. Several of them said it was like being children again—the only kids on the block with no tree. We sat around in the gloom on Charlton Street like little match girls wishing we were someplace else where (we were convinced) people were having fun among the tinsel.

The next year we were living in Chappaqua, and the week before Christmas Milt volunteered that if I wanted, I should get a tree. He said he realized how much it meant to me, and that it was silly not to have one because he didn't mind anymore and he could see how much I wanted one. He was smiling and so nice and I hadn't asked. Somewhere along the way he had started to enjoy the holiday and catch some of the pleasure in it. I had resigned myself to next to no Christmas if that was how it had to be. I didn't put up a wreath on the front door, not after Milt's Polish peasant Cossack explanation, but I ran out and got a tree. I still had the old decorations from our funny little trees, but this tree was large, so I chose some more. Jenny, you assured me you didn't care if you never had a tree. However, that was the year you made the tree decoration in the shape of a menorah as a gift to Milt. Maybe you wanted to placate him, I don't know. Andy, it was your first tree. And while I don't remember it as fact, I am sure we spent the entire season trying to keep you from eating everything on it. Eating inanimate objects was one of your specialties at that point in your life.

Every Christmas Nana went to stay with Jean. She took her presents with her, and left us ours to open on Christmas morning. I missed having her with us. Milt and I had our ups and downs, with him happy some years and grumpy others. We still had friends over around the holiday, and most years Leah and Will were with us. Sometimes I asked you to help me trim the tree, Jenny, and if you did, you complained and said that Christmas meant nothing to you except for the presents.

As you were growing up, Andy, you helped me buy and trim most of our trees. We had all kinds—big ones, small ones, live ones, dead ones, English ones and American ones, some on the East Coast and some on the West Coast. We left a record of our Christmases planted in Chappaqua and Greenwich and here in the yard in Los Angeles. One year, we arrived in L.A. from England so late that we said we weren't going to bother, but then on Christmas morning we dug out the decorations and trimmed the little monkey tree and stuck it in the living room.

When you were a teenager, sometimes we opened our presents on Christmas Eve. I liked getting presents and giving them, but I always felt uncomfortable, as if something were missing. I didn't know what it was. Most of the time you weren't with us, Jenny, and I thought it was that. Christmas, unless we were in England, was a phone call. Then we began to build a kind of family again. You weren't there last year, but Leonard and Dorothy and Barbara joined in. This year Michael was with us, along with the Strauses and George. So now I have a Christmas family, and maybe each year I'll add some more to it.

We decided to have a big New Year's party in addition to a feast at Christmas. I worked for days planning menus, getting the house ready. I bought a beautiful live tree this year—and lots of new decorations. Many of the old ones are battered and broken, and what I could use, I did. I have some ornaments that Louise De Cormier gave us back on Commerce Street, and some of the glass balls must be from then too. The silly paper angel with the yellow mop hair that we used to put on the top of the tree each year since back in the Chappaqua days didn't look as if she'd make it to New Year's Eve so she was replaced by a sculptured gold ribbon. And I finally threw out the last of the tarnished tinsel funny stars that we used to stick in the center of the tree to catch the reflections of the colored lights. They were from Eleventh Street. The menorah decoration and a beribboned bagel—I'm not sure where that came from—sat in a nest of evergreens on the coffee table.

We had evergreens all over the house, and ribbons, and baskets filled with things. Michael and Milt and I exchanged presents Christmas morning and laughed a lot, and I wondered why we weren't more self-conscious. While we were cooking and waiting for people to arrive, we listened to magnificent Christmas music played by James Galway. We had candles and champagne and goose stuffed with prunes and pâtè. And lots of company.

I did some thinking afterward, Andy. Why was this Christmas so pleasant, even though I was sad when I had time to think about you're not being here? Then I realized that this is the first time since you were little that there's been someone else here, Michael— he loves the tree and says so—who thinks Christmas is a great excuse to decorate the house and have friends in to share special food, and who doesn't seem embarrassed to enjoy something that's just gay for its own sake. All that embarrassment and guilt seems to have started when I lived with Dick. It's as if I always had to have some excuse to have Christmas.

For years I've imposed Christmas on all of you. Left to your own desires, maybe we would have given gifts, but that would be all. Maybe not even that. It sounds so dull. Or maybe without me, you would have evolved some kind of Christmas ritual that meant something to you. Maybe you have and I just don't recognize it.

It's funny; this year when Milt saw the tree decorated, he said it looked pretty. I believe he liked having it and was pleased that everyone else liked it. It was more beautiful than that first tree in Chappaqua and as beautiful as the trees we had when I was a child and believed in magic. We had a wonderful Christmas with lots of good food, good friends, wonderful music, and lots of laughter.

I think all these years I've been lying, as much to myself as to anyone else. Part of the continuity of Christmas, to me, is the religious celebration of the Christmas story. When I was a child, we had a crèche under the tree, and the story of the poor family in need of shelter meant something to me. Unfortunately, in my adamant atheism, I deliberately pushed away one of the few parts of my religious upbringing that I liked. I'm not sure if I ever told either of you anything about Christmas that could have had any meaning to you at all. Whatever you know about it, you learned elsewhere, and I regret that.

We had all the food and shelter we could want, more luxuries than we ever expected. What material things are there left to really want? Not that I'd like to return to a time when we didn't have as much, but to me, the gifts themselves are pleasant but almost meaningless. I like knowing someone cared about me and wanted to please me. It's the giving and receiving that I like, knowing that someone cared enough to think of something I would like.

I suppose Christmas is a lot like Thanksgiving, only more so. Growing up, the best part of Christmas for me was everyone around a big dining table, satisfied and laughing and enjoying themselves. It's the opulence that I love—the exaggeration of the tree and wrapping of gifts, special treats and too much to eat. I love the continuity that ties one year to the next and to all the ones before. I have a Christmas tree inside of me, decorated with all the year's Christmases, happy and unhappy. Tree lights, mistletoe, carols, people saying, "Merry Christmas."

But I have figured out how to enjoy it more. Surround myself with people who want to enjoy the day, and who, even if they don't share my background, can be charmed by the tree and evergreens, satiated by the food, softened by the Christmas music, and pleased by my hospitality.

This letter is my Christmas Declaration of Independence. Andy, I made you promise that next year you would be with us. Forget the promise. We want you here, but not because you feel obliged. And, Jenny, we would love to have you and Richard come for the holidays next year if you feel like it, but it isn't necessary any more. You and Andy aren't children and neither am I.

    Love,
    Mother

ANOTHER CHRISTMAS

This time there's no tinsel
no treelit crèche
no plaster Christ child
It's the time between children

Breasts and beards
and hurrying hands turning pages
And we wait for new hands
to string the popcorn

    October 7, 1987
    Alpine Drive, Beverly Hills

Dear Jenny,
The announcement for your show arrived and the photographs are wonderful. If I were a painter and you photographed my work, I would be miserably unhappy, because you take the work of the painter and make it so much more interesting and exciting. Unfortunately, there is no possibility of going to New York in the next three months, so we won't be able to see the show. I hope that you will bring your portfolio so we can see them here.

October 12

When you come, please bring pictures of you and Richard. If there are some very nice ones, bring the negatives so I can have enlargements made. This time Pepper, or whoever it was chewed them up, will not get at them.

Remember the owl? Owls, it turned out to be. In the last year the piece of property just south of the Straus house was sold and some large trees were cut down. This must have disturbed their resting place, and suddenly, at odd times, we would see them take off from tree to tree. Last month I caught sight of one of them on a bare branch of a big pine just up from our driveway. The other morning, I happened to look up, and two of them were perched up there. One flew off and the other just sat ruffling his feathers, and from that angle he looked more like a cat than an owl. Ten minutes later I looked up and he was gone too. I notice that they can be seen round about dusk in the evening and up until the sun comes out in the early morning. That is, they can be seen, if I happen to be up and thinking about owls at that moment. There's something very satisfying about having finally gotten to see them.

Please give my best to Richard's parents and to Mrs. Wheeler.
      Love,
      Mom

Journal
November 18, 1987
Alpine Drive, Beverly Hills

Driving across Sunset and Alpine, I asked myself what I'd do if I knew for sure I had just a few years to live, and the answer was that I would go home and write. I'd write first to Milt to tell him how I love him, how I have loved him, how I will love him however long I have left. But how do you tell someone something so mundane and what do the words mean? Could I tell him about how nice it is when he puts out his hand and touches me?

It's good to be sixty. I like today's gentle warmth and trust, the lack of selfishness. I love you, Milt, and I love living with you. In fact, life has never seemed more worth living than it does today, with you, here in this place, close enough to check out your smile or frown, and close enough to know that you love me, more now than ever before because we know we're the best friends we always were.□

SOME PEOPLE SATISFY

Like Milt
saving tears for the times
when only tears will help
arms that hold in a gentle way
the ones who promise
then give more

THE GODSILS

Today was my mother's birthday. The twenty-seventh sounds right. It's the date I've most often thought was her day. Ninety-two years ago, on November 27, 1895, a baby girl, christened Rosemary Elizabeth, was born to William and Elizabeth Burns Godsil in the Borough of Brooklyn, City and State of New York.

There was a photograph of Elizabeth Burns that I remember seeing as a child. Her face was long and thin, unsmiling, her forehead covered by a hat placed far forward. Perhaps she knew how young she would die and couldn't smile for thinking of leaving her three young children to be cared for by someone else. That was what I thought when I was a child.

In my mother's case, that someone else turned out to be four people—her father's mother and his three sisters, Mary, Anastasia, and Julia. My mother was always jealous of her brothers, Percy and Bill, who were taken into the family of her father's brother John and raised together. Why her father gave his children to his brother and sisters, she never knew and never forgave. And when in her teens he met and married a young woman a few years older than herself, her brittle bitterness formed a core of rejection that left her feeling unloved.

If this was her résumé it would tell which public grammar school she attended, then go on to say that she graduated from Brooklyn's famous Erasmus High, where she studied whatever girls studied in the early nineteen hundreds. For some reason, she didn't go to work after her schooling was completed, possibly because her three aunts, themselves prematurely liberated, in the sense that all had responsible jobs that carried with them some authority and financial independence, felt that their niece should remain at home, ladylike and passive, as much a flowering of their hard won success as the large suburban home they were soon to become owners of.

Who were they, these ancestors of mine, these contributors to what I am, these animals past from some common giver of life to us, to me, to my children and their children. My wishes mean nothing, but I wish them anyway. Certain characteristics I wish would end with me and my generation. We weren't an admirable lot. Not the worst, but not much to emulate. I have always believed that heredity is the most important factor, given a reasonable environment, so what I see in myself and in my family past and present makes me feel that we only have a few traits the human race really needs, and I'm not sure the human race really deserves the rest.□

UNCLE PERCY GODSIL

Leap year. Was it Uncle Percy who was born on February 29? Or my mother's Uncle Dave? No, I think it was Percy, whose only other distinction, besides looking so much like my mother, was having a daughter who had two or three illegitimate children by the man who had been her employer.

The reason I'm vague about the number of children my cousin had is that at the time, her name, and certainly her situation, was never mentioned in our house. In those days I didn't think of her as my cousin. Uncle Percy had several children, so I had several cousins, but I never met any of them. For some reason my parents didn't think much of his wife, so though they lived six or eight blocks away from us, we never saw any of them except Percy himself. He used to come visit my mother now and again during the day, when no one else was around.

He and Mother would sit in the kitchen drinking tea, saucers clinking, not saying much, and just talking quietly. They were both pretty quiet people, and both had the capacity to look very sad sometimes. Frequently when they were speaking, my mother's face would take on a sardonic expression and her voice would grow harsh, while Percy would be smiling tentatively in a detached kind of way. When I was a teenager, I remember my mother telling me that Percy had a hard life. I think his wife drank. Maybe that was why we never saw her. Then there was the daughter and her children. Percy had to support all of them, as well as his own children. This was during the Depression, and he worked on the railroad, so he was rather poor.

My mother had two brothers, Percy and Bill, neither of whom she was especially close to, but Bill she saw only once a year and only in a formal family setting. She had always resented the fact that at the age of three, when her mother died, she was sent to live with her grandmother and three aunts and Percy and Bill went to live with their Uncle John and his family. She lived under strict Victorian female supervision, while Percy and Bill, being boys and in a more ordinary family setting, were allowed greater freedom to do as they pleased.

Bill was the success in the family—a bank president who hobnobbed with the local politicos, a father of three beautiful daughters, and husband of a beautiful woman. My mother, emerging from her cocoon-like childhood, was ill-prepared for making sensible choices, and went from ladylike Victorian religious stability to marriage with an adamantly raucous, intelligent, undereducated, over-opinionated salesman, who had only loyalty and a white collar to recommend him to her family. His sense of humor, which he had in abundance and dispensed without discretion, was a mystery no one in her family ever appreciated.

Poor Percy of the sad and gradually reddening face—he may have shared his wife's hinted at problem—was the quintessential middle child. He looked and acted as if it were his fate to be always less than the others, living in the shadow of his older brother's success and in fear of his brother-in-law's noisy opinions. He had a low-paying, low-status job, punching tickets or cleaning freight cars (long before unions and society demanded good pay and, consequently, respect for ordinary workers). During the Depression, of course, just having a job was a kind of miracle to be thankful for, but Percy didn't seem inspired by it. And on top of being at the bottom of the family heap, there were the wife and the proliferating daughter, who in those days were seen as helpless dependents doing their helpless thing, not two independent women fulfilling themselves, the way we might look at them today. Today Percy could shrug his shoulders and say, "Listen, welfare gives them a check each month. What can I do? It's none of my business." Back then, all he could do was face down the shame and stretch his salary to cover the lot of them so they didn't die of neglect.

One day when I was about eight years old, he brought his oldest grandchild, a pretty little boy of four with brown hair and big dark eyes, dressed neatly for the occasion, as if navy blue pants and impeccably clean hands could make up to the world for his mother's mistakes. He was a shy child, afraid of our dog, not sure enough to play with me, and needed coaxing to climb up on one of the kitchen chairs to have some milk and cookies. I can still remember seeing this small boy in the background of quiet conversation and unlit November kitchen noonday gloom, looking to his grandfather for affirmation that it was all right to accept an offering of food from a stranger. (Though how anyone could think of my round warm mother as a stranger, I couldn't understand.)

I think his name was Robert. I may be making that up, because Robert seems such a substantial name, and he was a very solid three- dimensional little boy. After Uncle Percy and Robert left, I began to ask my mother all about him. The sound of her voice, and finally her words, let me know that there was something unusual about Robert. I'd already caught that from a few sentences that passed between the adults earlier.

In answer to a question or statement from my mother, Uncle Percy had sighed, and nodding his head toward Robert said, "True. But how can anybody blame the child? It's not his fault." When they left, after my mother tucked Robert into his coat and Uncle Percy put on his mittens, he walked off down the street holding Robert's hand just like any other grandfather.

Later, quite naturally, I asked her what wasn't Robert's fault. Her face pinched up in disapproval, and she said she supposed he was a nice little boy, but his mother was no better than she should be, which didn't explain much except that my mother didn't like his mother. She made a few more cryptic remarks about being good and poor Percy, and what could you expect with a wife like that...

Although I saw Uncle Percy every now and then if I happened to be around when he paid a visit, I never saw Robert again that I know of, though we probably passed in the street. I didn't see any of the other children either. When Uncle Percy died, in his late sixties, one of his children contacted my mother, and I think my brother talked with one of the grandchildren—maybe Robert.

Uncle Percy held his grandson's hand and spoke to him gently. When he spoke of not blaming Robert, there was compassion in his voice, and a plea for understanding for an innocent. I wonder if he was always as kind to his children as he was to Robert.

After that day, I always liked Uncle Percy, despite his obvious depressed detachment, and felt that there was something mysterious and forbidden about his life. I didn't understand how painful and tedious it must have been to have a family that didn't conform in a small-town atmosphere where neighbors knew everything that happened outside—and an awful lot that went on inside—those tiny houses and apartments, and where relatives avoided one another out of shame and to escape social stigma.

The last time I saw Uncle Percy was at my parents' ice cream parlor. He was sitting at the counter, his ruddy complexion in deep contrast with his rusty blue suit. He looked much older than my mother, but by then I knew it was more a result of attitude than of years. We tried to look interested in each other, but his vague "ums" and "you don't says" couldn't penetrate my young adult concerns. This time he made a pretense of admiring my four-year-old, his sister's grandchild, but he had already given up whatever momentary liveliness he'd been able to conjure in earlier days, and he sat there with his aging family face and fading eyes looking into the past and perhaps the future, not seeing the present at all.☐

OF RELATIVE CLEANLINESS AND GODLINESS

"Rosemary, it's time to get up. Come on, you'll be late for school. Get your clothes on."

My eyes opened at that. I had half my clothes on already. I wiggled down inside my pajamas, enjoying the warm friendly feeling of clothes worn several days. Grandma Primont—my father's mother—had brought her children up to believe that windows must be open, top and bottom, no matter what the temperature outside. I hated the cold, and on a lot of nights I probably hated Grandma and her edicts as well.

It was too cold these nights to take off all my clothes before going to bed. I knew that my mother didn't like me to wear my underwear through the night because then it was too cold to take them off in the morning and put on clean ones. They'd be worn yet another day, and at the end of the week when the laundry went out, my underwear count would be low, and Mother would scold, "You must take off your underwear every night. You'll smell like that horrible old man we saw in Jamaica the other day. Would you like that? Would you like to have people laughing at you and turning their faces in the other direction? What would Nana say if she heard?" Her look told me, if I had any doubts, what Nana would say, and I resolved each time to take off my underwear that night.

My resolution was never strong enough if the weather was below sixty degrees, and the only time the lovely clothes were removed was when some larger person came along and forced me to take them off. That person was usually Jean, who was much more concerned with cleanliness and beauty. She curled and combed her hair and wore lipstick, and above all, she bathed. In our house, where the bathroom was small and had a tub and a water heater to match, long hot baths were more apt to give a backache than get rid of one. Since Dad was six-foot-two and weighed 250 pounds, and Mother, while much shorter, was 180 pounds, the bathtub didn't present an appetizing invitation to them for relaxation. It was crammed into a nook, and the only way into it was to slide in feet first toward the drain.

Mike usually found it impossible to get into the water. He was an active boy, and sometimes at the table when Mother looked at him, horrified at the day's grime so close to the food, demands were made that he bathe immediately after dinner. "I don't want to see you until you're spotless," Mother would say, her voice firm and implacable, "I want you so clean, I won't see a speck of dirt on you." And off he went with much groaning, the sound of running water in the tub coming down to us minutes later.

One time, he left the table quite willingly, ran the water as usual, and remained in the bathroom for half an hour. "He must have reformed," Mother said. "My goodness, he'll be so clean we won't recognize him."

"Maybe he has a girlfriend." Jean's mind turned to romance for any reason.

When he returned, in the same clothes, with one arm clean and the rest of him his usual gritty color, it was obvious that he'd been sitting next to the tub all that time, waggling his arm in the water to create the sounds of someone bathing enthusiastically. That was when Jean started calling him Big Chief Dirty Neck of the Never Wash Tribe. His surprise at being caught, when he thought he was so clever, showed how little he understood the difference between clean and dirty.

I loved to be in the tub until I was six years old. Aunt Vera gave me a set of wooden boats on my fourth birthday. I played with them whenever I took a bath. The boats bobbled up and down in small undulating waves when I moved an arm or a leg. I draped the washcloth over the ferryboat, my favorite, and gave it a push to sail it toward the faucet, the washcloth drifting in its wake. I tried to sink the ferry but it was hard. I put my finger on the smokestack and pressed down, and the boat rolled to one side then plopped upright again. It was painted green, yellow and red with a black smokestack. I pretended I was on it, leaning against the chain at the back, as the ferrymen closed the gate when it was full, my hand in my father's as the ferry churned out from Manhattan past the Statue of Liberty. I could smell the river and the dank wood of the boat and see millions of bubbles in the wake as the boat plowed through the water. I felt the rumbling of the engines. I heard boat horns, whistles, bells ringing, the grinding and creaking of the wooden pilings as the ferry sidled into the slip when it reached Staten Island.

I took turns playing with the other boats, sometimes the dinghy, sometimes the ocean liner, a sleek black-and-white ship with a red smokestack. I didn't know what to do with the tanker and wasn't fond of the tugboat. I would have liked a red fireboat that spouted real water, but the set given to me by Aunt Vera didn't include one. The paint began to peel on the boats, and when the water went swirling down the drain at the end of the bath, I sat in the empty tub looking at small flecks of paint, pushing them around, trying to put them back on the boats they came from. Then I set the boats on the crack between the wall and the tub to wait for the next bath.

The family member who spent the most time in the tub was the cat. Mickey loved to sit near the faucet, his head flicking up and down as he watched the drips gather and fall into the drain. Sometimes they came fast, sometimes slow or not at all. The bathroom door was in line with the hallway, and Mickey had a habit of starting a headlong flight from whatever part of the house he was in, up the stairs, around the bend, through the hall and into the tub, coming to a halt inches from the faucet.

Every once in a while, when the bathroom door was closed, whoever was in there would hear a thud as Mickey, zooming up and unable to put the brakes on in time, hit the door. Sometimes, when the tub was filling and the door was open, we heard a squawk as the cat came flying out, drenched, and raced back down the stairs to hide and dry off. One steamy summer day, Dad—no great lover of cats, in spite of trying to adopt so many—left the bathroom door open to cool off while he bathed and read his newspaper only to hear the familiar sound of Mickey bounding up the stairs, the bell on his collar sounding the alarm. We heard Dad shout, then the sound of splashing water and crumpling newsprint as he tried to heave his heavy frame out of the water, followed by a screech from man and cat as they met someplace about a foot above the tub. It was the end of the tub that day for my father. But not for the cat. He was back watching the tap a few hours later as if nothing unusual had happened.

One afternoon Nana came for tea. She was getting ready to leave when I passed through the kitchen on my way up to my room to find my skates.

"It's almost dinnertime," Mother called after me as I ran up the stairs. "While you're there you'd better take a bath. Wait for me. I'll come up and fill the tub."

"Can she manage by herself?" Nana asked. "Doesn't she need someone to scrub her elbows and knees?" She worried with her forehead. "I'll go up."

I heard my aunt's light step coming up the stairs and flushed the toilet in a hurry so I could get out of sight and maybe out of a bath with Nana in charge.

Nana advanced down the hallway. "Rosemary, take off your shoes and socks. Mother says you must take a bath now." She leaned over the far end of the tub and began to run the water, then stood back by the sink surveying the situation. "Get a clean towel and wash cloth."

I pulled off my sunsuit and underpants and then tugged at my shoes and socks, my bottom cold on the tile floor. I stood up and leaned across the tub to pull the wooden boats into the rising water.

"What are you doing?" Nana's voice sounded harsh.

"I have to get my boats in the water so I can play."

"You mustn't play in the water."

"Mommy lets me play with my boats."

"You mustn't play in the water."

"Why?"

255

"Because you don't have any clothes on. Gawd doesn't like to see little girls with no clothes on."

"Why?"

"Because."

"Why because? Doesn't God like little girls?"

"Of course Gawd likes little girls. But he doesn't like to see them without their clothes on. You should get in and out of the tub as fast as you can. Just stay long enough to get washed and that's all."

"But my Mommy always lets me play with the boats."

Nana's hazel eyes narrowed disapprovingly. Her lips drew together, small lines like rays coming in from all directions. I got into the tub and was rapidly washed with particular attention to elbows, knees, ears, and neck. I couldn't keep my eyes off the boats now back up in their resting place. I forgot Nana for a minute and took the ferryboat and tried to sink it. It wouldn't stay under the water. It bobbled out from under and surfaced with a glup. I put it back up with the other boats.

Nana's voice was cool and businesslike. "Now get out and get dressed right away." She rubbed my back with the towel and told me to hurry and dry off.

Later I asked my mother why God didn't like little girls who didn't have their clothes on and she asked, "Did Nana tell you that? Don't pay any attention."

"But why did she say that?"

"Because she's a silly old maid, that's why. If she ever tells you a thing like that, you tell her that I said it's not true. If she had her way, we'd all take baths with our raincoats and galoshes on."

But Nana had the last word. I never played with the boats again. I tried, but it didn't work. Maybe Nana was right about God. She was much holier than my mother with no visible chinks in her religious armor. She prayed a lot. She carried her rosary in her purse. There were holy pictures on the walls in her house in Hollis. And she was always saying things like "Holy Mary, Mother of Gawd" if something got her excited.

After that, I dressed and undressed in great haste, not only for my bath, but all the time, trying to make myself invisible to Nana's invisible Gawd. I began to leave my underwear on as permanently as possible, without telling anyone why, and only changed them when my mother or Jean came into my room and forced me to.□

FAITH

The first seed of my atheism was planted in second grade. I was seven when Sister Thomas Marie told us that we must go home and tell our parents to go to Confession and Communion during Lent or it would be a mortal sin. If they died without doing this, they would go to Hell.

I hurried home at lunchtime to tell my mother that there was only one week left for her to make her Easter Duty or she wouldn't go to Heaven.

"Who told you that?" my mother huffed.

"Sister Thomas Marie said so, Mommy."

"Sister says more than her prayers! That's a lot of nonsense." She looked very uncomfortable as she said this. "It's nobody's business what I do. They shouldn't put silly ideas into your head like that." Her face was grim, lips pressed together.

"But why don't you go, Mommy?"

"I don't want to. Now don't ask any questions." She turned away and continued preparing the food. "Here, eat your lunch now and forget it."

"Will Daddy go?"

"Probably not."

I started to feel anxious. I saw myself all alone in Heaven looking down to see if I could find my parents below. I wanted to cry but managed to mumble my way through lunch, fidgeting with my sandwich. "If you and Daddy don't go to Heaven, then I don't want to go either."

My mother laughed a little and smiled at me. "Don't worry about it. It's a long way off and we'll all go to Heaven. I wouldn't tell the Sister you don't want to go to Heaven. If she asks you if I'm going to confession you just tell her to speak to me. I'll tell her a thing or two. Now eat your lunch."

I walked the long way back to school with Mary but didn't tell her anything. When the teacher asked the children several days later if we had told our parents I said "yes" with the rest of them and kept my decision to myself. Catholic children learn early the things that must not be spoken. There are secrets, and then there are the secret secrets.□

DEAR MILT

I love you. After all the sleep I had yesterday, I'm awake and thinking clearly at four in the morning. It's so quiet in the house, and there are no demands being made by the house or other people in it, or people who are to be in it, or met outside of it, and I can think about you and how much I love you. It would be sad to let this moment go by without telling you.

You haven't been sleeping well the last few nights and I don't know how to help you rest better. I wish I could. The way that I always do want to make your life better, but so many unimportant as well as important things get in the way and I wonder if you know how much I care.

When I woke up earlier and knew I was slept out, I sat on the edge of the bed for a few moments thinking, and what I thought was I've had a good life. It's not possible to fill every moment in a lifetime with good things, and mine has had an abundance: books, music and art as well as love. If not everyone I've loved has felt the same about me, well, that's about how it is for each of us.

I once wrote a poem that said that I loved you not because you loved me, but because you made love possible, and I still feel that way.□

                                        Journal
                                        January 21, 1988
                                        Alpine Drive, Beverly Hills

This is the first time in a very long while that I've gotten up at four in the morning. Usually if I'm awake at this hour, I force myself to stay in bed resting, listening to tapes, because I know that if I get up so early, the day will not go well. But today, this morning, I am rested. I'm fully awake, and the peace and quiet of the house is a pleasure.

It's as if, after many years, it's safe to be up and alone in the sleeping nighttime world. Milt, for the last few nights, has been dreaming and waking fitfully. Strange to think of all the different lives happening in the same house at the same time, neighbors nearby, some quietly, some like Milt uneasily, dreaming their dream lives, some like me, awake thinking middle-of-the-night thoughts.

Thoughts that seem clear and true, like the terrible thoughts one has looking into a mirror after drinking alcohol, only not so bitter and despairing. In the middle of the night, when you give in and get up, colors sparkle and all physical things seem to be waiting while you sit and contemplate them. Your mind is free to see your life.

I've had a life of seeing and understanding, not filled with, but certainly occupied often with, art and music and books. In spite of early disappointments, I've had lots of love and moments of joy. There has been lots of laughter, and there has been intelligence.

I wish I could hold Milt and comfort him and help him to dream peacefully in this night, but it isn't possible.

Nighttime is for being alone and thinking and dreaming only your own thoughts, whatever they may be, happy or sad or merely pedestrian.☐

MILT

My world has many colors
   taken from leaf and cave
      and the soft hissing of fear

I am Eve and the apple
   and the serpent
      and you are the garden

WILL'S FUNERAL

February 13, 1988
Alpine Drive, Beverly Hills

Dear Jenny,

Will was buried yesterday. Dan, Michael, Melva and Tema and her husband Tom came here for the funeral. The only other people besides Milt, Andy, and myself were Ellie and George, Marian, Dan Rudin, Mickey Rudin, and four of the nurses. I am sorry that you weren't with us, because knowing that Will, or the shell of Will, wasn't still living in some indifferent, unthinking limbo, made it possible for all of us to think of him as he was when he was the head of the family and a person to turn to for advice and stability. The difference between Will's funeral and Leah's, when only two people, Milt and Tema, thought of her with love, was also sad. The setting was the same, but this time no one was uncomfortable, and it was hard to leave the cemetery.

Dan spoke about how Will came by himself to America at the age of twelve, speaking no English, with just his name and the address where he was going pinned to his coat, and how when he arrived at Ellis Island, through some error or mistiming—I think maybe the boat arrived a day early—there was no one to meet him. A cousin picked him up the next day and took him to Brooklyn to the address where his father lived. Dan said it was hard to get Will to talk about himself and his early years, but he remembers Will saying that his father lived in a railroad flat, and when Will entered the apartment and saw his father down through the long corridor of rooms, it was one of the warmest and best feelings of his life.

Mickey Rudin, Michael, and even Yolanda spoke about things they remembered of Will. I wanted to talk about the very first thing that endeared him to me, but I couldn't speak. On the day Milt told Leah and Will we were getting married, Will started carrying a picture of you in his wallet so he could show everyone his new granddaughter. I heard from several people later that he was so happy; he kept telling everyone how clever his son was to find a wife and a wonderful daughter at the same time. While he was going around showing your picture, Leah went to Saks and bought you the beautiful pink organdy dress that you wore to our wedding. I was always grateful for what they gave us. It wasn't just acceptance. They really welcomed us into their family so spontaneously that I could never forget it.

I have a lot of good memories of Will, but there was another early one that meant a lot to me. He didn't often seem very affectionate or emotional, but he told me that when Milt and I were on that long trip around the world, the two of you were driving down from the country one day and you started to cry because you missed us and wanted us to come home. So he told you he missed us too, and he cried with you and then you both felt better.

I didn't have any real problems with Leah until Milt and I were married a year. There were several skirmishes—when I refused to let Milt give his parents a key to our apartment; when Leah rummaged through our bedroom to see whether Milt had clean clothes; when she started reading the papers on Milt's desk; and when she took it upon herself to inspect the refrigerator to be sure I had enough of his favorite foods. These struggles were easy because Milt moved into our apartment when I married him and because I was thirty by the time they happened.

But, unknown to me, Leah was using both you and me as weapons against Beth. She would tell Beth how much cuter, sweeter, and more generous you were than Tema, and how loved you were by everyone who met you, and then go on to say how beautiful, talented, clever, well dressed, and marvelous I was. When Beth had had her fill and expressed her inevitable revulsion at hearing any more about us, Leah started telling me how much Beth didn't like me. She kept that up for the next twenty years, practically assuring that Beth and I would never get along.

I don't think Tema has ever acknowledged how unkind Leah was to her, but Beth knew. Tema came after Michael so she never had a lot of attention from Leah and loved her no matter what she did. With you it was different. Living in New York you saw Leah and Will all the time and you had four years of being the center of attention before Andy was born. If he'd been a girl, you'd have gone right on being the most important. A boy, especially a first son, is a king to a woman like Leah. You were immediately replaced, unimportant by comparison, and took your place with the other females in the family as far as she was concerned.

I tried to protect you from her as much as I could. When talking to Will and Leah didn't improve things, I had to insist that Milt intervene. They weren't allowed to bring presents to Andy every time they came, or even without permission. If they brought things without asking, I put them away in a closet until the next Christmas. If they had brought gifts for the two of you, I suppose I wouldn't have been so strict.

After Andy was born Leah did some awfully unpleasant things to you, the kind of things she'd been doing to Tema, Beth, and me over the years, giving the boy a marvelous present and the girl some old thing she found around the house. I don't know all the things that happened in North Carolina but I can imagine them. Similar to the time she made you go shopping with her for a grand toy for Andy and gave you an old straw hat or something that she'd been using for years.

If it's any comfort to you, one year she gave Milt a very expensive hi-fi, and I was handed (handed is too polite a word, the box was shoved at me in the doorway as she entered the apartment) a shabby cloth and brass belt that I'd seen her wearing for a couple of years. Not only that, the box was a soiled Macy's box with no tissue inside or wrapping outside to soften the blow. That was right after she started telling me how much Beth disliked me.

Being a parent I always felt somehow I'd failed because I couldn't make her be fair to you, and I couldn't prevent you from noticing her unkindness. That was stupid because, with her exaggerated shtetl mentality, I could no more make her be different than I could stop a hurricane. However, I hated her for hurting you and never forgave her. I was often angry with Will because he did nothing to stop her. Now I wonder if even he could have.

And if I couldn't control what Leah did, I had even less control over how you and Milt felt about each other during the first years of our marriage. The moment you understood my feelings for him, or that I even felt something toward him, you disliked him. You were just three and a half but you let him know how you felt. I guess I hadn't had three dates with him when you walked over to him, pointed to his face, and said, "you have a big nose," and you didn't mean it as a compliment. You liked everyone else that you knew, but you didn't like Milt. It's hard to like a child who doesn't like you, so Milt wasn't crazy about you either. And that's how it was until you were eight years old.

You tolerated each other. You, because you wanted a father and you were stuck with him. And Milt, because he wanted me for a wife, so he was stuck with you. It wasn't a lot of fun being in the middle for years, trying to placate the two of you.

It was easy to see why you were jealous, less easy for me to understand Milt's feelings toward you. I don't think he understood them. He thought I catered to you too much. He couldn't understand why you made so much noise early in the morning and why you weren't a grownup. I think men who marry women with children are attracted by the very maternal qualities they resent the women showing toward the children after the marriage. Maybe they want all that attention lavished on them. Whatever the reasons, it was difficult.

You two had passed the outright battling stage and were carrying on a kind of mutually suspicious armed truce by the time you were six and a half when Milt adopted you. The adoption probably wouldn't have taken place then if Dick hadn't precipitated it. I don't think Milt was ready for it, but once the process started, he accepted responsibility completely. The adoption took place in the general atmosphere of grumpiness that existed when the two of you were together.

Then, when you were about eight years old, we went to see *West Side Story*. It was very sad and the three of us sat there, you in the middle, sniffling and passing the candy back and forth. When we left the movie, you took Milt's hand instead of mine crossing Seventh Avenue, and that was the beginning, at least from what I could see, of your liking Milt. And when you started to like Milt, he started to like you. The next year Andy was born, and then, if Milt thought about it, he understood how I felt about you.

But he didn't understand how difficult it had been for me until one day when Andy was about five years old. He was asking you something and you were ignoring him. Milt and I were upstairs in our bedroom reading and you two were in the living room, so we could hear what was happening. Andy kept trying to get your attention and you just didn't answer. Milt finally turned to me looking really hurt and said, "Why does she just ignore him? Can't she hear him asking over and over for attention?" I told him that now he could understand how I felt all those early years when sometimes you used to talk to him and he just ignored you. He couldn't believe that he'd done the same thing. I would be a liar if I said I wasn't pleased to see how much pain it gave him to think that he'd ignored you in just the same way and never thought a thing of it. I also pointed out to him that he'd been almost forty at the time and you were about fourteen. It was the first time Milt and I were able to communicate about his early feelings toward you, because now he could understand from a different perspective. It was the first time we were able to talk about the tug of war the two of you had over me, and the probability that he was as jealous of my attention to you as you were of my attention to him.

I could see from the moment I looked at Milt's face after Andy was born that Milt loved him. I recognized it because that was how I felt when you were born. For some people it may be the strongest emotion they will ever experience.

I know that Milt loves you, but I don't know when it began. From the day we married, he was your father and you were his daughter. Neither of you doubted that, as far as I could see, but you both acted as if love was for other people. I was the buffer between you. I tried to keep you from infringing on his territory and to soften the edges of his indifference and your dislike.

After the first time you took his hand, you two became friends very quickly. You went from friends to affection and by the time Andy was born, Milt was so fond of you that I don't think you felt left out of his attention, though you certainly resented my caring for Andy. You didn't believe that I loved you. You said so. And no assurances meant anything to you. I don't know if you ever believed me again. I don't know when you stopped believing me or if you ever did.

The mistake I made was to think that I had to go on being a buffer between you and Milt to make up to you for what you hadn't had and to him for all he had done for us. A woman with a child from a former marriage and a new husband spends a lot of time dissembling, so I did a lot of pretending that I wasn't troubled by things that happened between you and me, out of loyalty to you, and I tried hard to create a climate of generosity on Milt's part that he didn't always feel, out of loyalty to him. I wanted you both to love each other someday as if he had been your parent at birth and had loved you from the first moment he saw you. I didn't understand then what I understand now, which is that I should have let the two of you slug it out over the years. My intentions were good, but it just wasn't my responsibility after a point.

If asked today, I'm sure we'd all say what a good and understandable thing it was that I left Dick, found and married Milt, and had another child. In spite of all the difficulties, each of us has benefited by it. And if Leah came with the package, what could we do? She was Milt's mother.

But how would a child look at it? A mother picks a man to love, brings him into the home, and treats him with deference as if he is as important as the child. She locks her bedroom door, leaves the child at home, and takes a long trip with the man, makes the child obey new rules set down to make life easier for the usurper. The child can only declare war, sometimes outright, other times guerrilla, and can only lose, even when it seems to win.

And in a child's eyes, if the mother were a good mother would she have another child? If the mother were a good mother would she allow a grandmother to treat the child unfairly? To a child, a mother can do anything she wants, or so the child thinks. And the mother thinks she should be able to do everything, and tries to, to make the child's life happier and better. The mother's fantasy is as foolish and unattainable as the child's and so she loses the battle too.□

FIRST THINGS FIRST

Soon Othello will kill Desdemona and repent—too late. Isn't that always the way? It's always too late when we learn. Nature has it all wrong. We should spend our first nine months learning the things we learn at the ends of our lives, omitting only our deaths. Then we'd be prepared properly for living. And if we knew our deaths, that might be just as well too. If I knew how and when I would die, what would I be doing at this minute? Something frivolous or something important?

 A week before my mother died, when I knew she would die, and she knew she was dying, I told her I loved her. I wanted her to know—in words—that I loved her. I wanted to have said it to her, to have finally made her know how much she meant to me for all my life for being herself. I must have told her before then. I know I held her and was held by her thousands of times before that, but that moment was for holding her hand and telling her that one fact of my life—and hers. She wasn't a woman who could say the word, "love," so I don't know if she ever told me except by caress, by loving looks, by food, or by tenderness in her touch what her feelings were, but not for a second did I doubt that she loved me. Being the part-puritan that she was, she found it hard to take an emotionally personal compliment, but that last time she accepted my words and said, "I know."

 I wonder what words I would say and to whom if I knew I was dying. There are people whom I would never see again. Things I wouldn't bother with. Places I wouldn't go. Even though they pass the time pleasantly.

 If I had known when I would die, would I have spent the month writing? Would I have felt it didn't matter any more? That my life full of mistakes was nearly over and what could have been so precious wasn't and wouldn't be? Others would remember what they remembered of me, and I would remember nothing.

 Did I write what I wrote for them or for myself? Oh, nature, you've got it all wrong, start to finish. Why do some of us chase after what we can't have, spend years crying to have things that can only hurt us? Well, we are what we are. But even at that, it would be better to start at the end, and end at the beginning. ☐

I HAVE BEEN TOUCHED BY MY DEATH

I have been touched by my death
into thinking of moments
when love breathed

The fragility of green gold
mountains in sunshine
days of summer, winter snows

Imperfect keeper wakening
to perfection
where love happened
in this second before eternity

MOM AND DAD

My parents' wedding anniversary was March 17th. I'm not sure what year they were married, but it must have been about 1917.

I have to reach that date by strange subtractions. Mother was born in November 1895 and died at the age of almost seventy-seven in October 1972. The First World War ended in November 1918, and I believe my father must have been in the Army for at least a year before. He was in France on Armistice Day, and had arrived there about four months before the end. Now that I think about it, I remember Mother saying that they eloped one weekend and he took off (back to camp, or was it to France?) the next day and left her to face the music her three aunts and new mother-in-law were going to make.

How long was one in the Army before going overseas? They were either married March 17, 1917, or March 17, 1916, depending on how long men trained before they were sent overseas. In 1916, my mother would have been twenty-one and my father twenty. In those days a woman had to be twenty-one to marry without her parents' consent, and men had to be eighteen. They were Catholics, so once married they were married forever till death did them part. And that was the way it was. If their marriage had taken place in 1946, it would have been among the one in four that ended in divorce. As it was, they stuck it out. Or rather my mother stuck it out. That may have been why my father married her. He needed someone who would stick it out, someone to keep him from flying off into some incredible follow-your-nose craziness. And she needed someone a little crazy, someone to open the door and give her a home where she could swear and shout and use her strength to climb a few mountains.

Momma and I talked a lot in the years we lived together, the ten years after Dad died. I was in my late thirties and early forties, and we could speak as adults. Once she said, "You all thought I should have left him. Where could I have gone? He had his faults, but he was a good man. And I loved him. None of you understood that. He was a good father. Maybe he could have done things better, but he was a good man."

She was right. Sadly, I understood it then, but I hadn't understood it until I was twenty-eight or nine, and making a mess of my own life. Then I knew. He did the best he could. He was what he was. She had picked him in a time when unpicking was nearly unthinkable, so she didn't think of it. He was lucky. She loved him, and she thought she had to stick by him. She didn't have an easy life with him. Lots of times it was awful. But in the end she could say that he was good and he loved us, and she was right.

There were three of us kids. I was the lucky one. Somehow I got my mother's determination and my father's intelligence, her love of children and home and his irreverent skepticism, her strength and his crazy courage, her practicality and his aspirations. If I got some of the worst physical traits, like her chronic depression and his manic depression, I was still lucky, because I was the one who came closest to being a good fifty-fifty mix of the two breeds. Poor Mike. He inherited her silences and pettiness and his erratic arbitrariness. And Jean, she skipped a generation and took on the narrow righteousness and rigid religious views of his parents and her three aunts, and from some Irish uncle, a weakness for alcohol.

All the while, growing up, I raged inwardly whenever someone said I was like my father. I couldn't believe it. How could I be like someone who was such a problem in the house, who was depressed one minute and too happy the next, who had a hundred friends and a hundred enemies who didn't know which category they'd be in from minute to minute? How could I be like someone who had the neighbors intimidated, bossing them around, telling everybody how to live, and when and where? I spent my conscious years from fourteen to twenty-eight trying not to be who I was. I even married someone who would be sure to prevent me from being that person, and consequently, I see now, I became even more strongly what I was. And thanks to all those lucky genes, the very things I was trying not to be were the things that helped me to escape.

So, this morning, I'm celebrating my parents' anniversary, a few weeks and many years too late. I think of them with the love of all the years—my father, the man with the giant strides, the great storyteller, and my mother, the warm, loving woman who gave me life, long love, and strength to survive. I am the body they gave me, the continuation, the giver. In nature, they served their purpose, as I've served mine, but that isn't how I think of it. What I think of is the love.□

IN ABSENTIA

In Queens Village, one of the things that distinguished good friends from enemies, acquaintances, or just neighbors, was that kids called their parents' grownup friends "Aunt This" and "Uncle That." These aunts and uncles were usually better loved than the real thing. They laughed more often and seldom criticized. When we visited them, we were given cake and candy without the lectures that usually accompanied such things from real relatives.

Uncle Andrew was different. His wife was my mother's best friend, so I called her Aunt Vera and him Uncle Andrew, but he was a mystery to me. He was there and he wasn't there. His body was there, but he was more like a shell than a living person. While he was a soldier in the Army during the First World War, he caught sleeping sickness during an epidemic and was sent home to sleep out the rest of his life in a small house down the street from us. He and Aunt Vera were married before he enlisted, so he had a home to return to and a wife to take care of him. The honorable discharge from the Army made him eligible for service benefits and membership in the American Legion. And the American Legion gave him a semblance of a social life and provided his wife a group of friends to turn to for friendship and consolation.

He was handsome, with grizzled hair and heavy-lidded brown eyes in a smooth untroubled face. On days when he felt well enough, Aunt Vera would send him shuffling to Bohack's grocery store on the corner with their daughter Mary for a loaf of bread or a container of milk, but most of the time he sat in his easy chair in the dining room, wearing an old brown sweater, turning the pages of a *National Geographic*, sunlight shining through the fish tank on the table next to him. Whether walking to the store or sitting in his chair, his dog, Blackie, an old unclipped poodle, stayed by his side.

Mary was a year older than me. My mother used to claim that she was partly responsible for Mary's birth, because when Aunt Vera, who assumed she'd never have a child, took Andrew away for a week's vacation, my mother bought her a beautiful black nightgown and Vera came back pregnant. So Mary was my playmate. One time when we were playing at her house, we stopped by Uncle Andrew's chair and he patted her head. He pointed to a picture in one of the magazines and smiled at her, but he didn't say anything. Aunt Vera came into the room and told us to leave him alone, he needed his rest. Someone was always warning us to stay away from him. I never knew whether they meant he had to sleep, or that he would be angry if we woke him up. The only time he spoke to me directly, his voice was soft and distant. "Mary's outside," he said, as he lifted his hand a few inches from his lap and motioned toward the back door.

The day Uncle Andrew died Mary was in school, and a friend of the family came to take her home. I was seven and I knew it was special to leave school in the middle of the day. It made Mary important in the children's eyes. When I saw her later in the day, I felt strange, because she was crying and I wasn't. I didn't wonder about death. It was hard for me to understand that Uncle Andrew was Mary's father. He was so quiet. He never laughed or yelled. He didn't go to work. It didn't occur to me that someone could be so unhappy that he died.

That night, while the undertakers were laying Uncle Andrew out in the Litchhults' living room, Mary stayed with the Kudleys across the street. Aunt Vera came to our house, and I sat next to her in the kitchen while she peeled carrots for the pot roast my mother cooked on the stove.

Aunt Vera's eyes were red from crying and my mother tried to comfort her. "He's better off now, Vera, you know that. It's not pleasant to hear, but it's true."

Aunt Vera said to my mother, "Oh, Rosemary, I'm a widow now."

She started to cry again, and I leaned against her and asked, "What's a widow, Aunt Vera?"

Mother said, "Hush now. You go in the other room and leave Aunt Vera alone."

Aunt Vera tried to smile. "A widow is a lady whose husband is dead, and now that Uncle Andrew's dead, I'm a widow." She held me close and said to my mother, "Let her stay, Rosemary, it's a comfort to have her here." Aunt Vera was warm and soft and I put my hand up to her face and spread her tears over her cheeks. I patted her throat and told her not to cry. But she did cry, and my mother too.

The next morning, I heard my father telling my mother how the undertaker found out about the life insurance and the amount of Vera's pension and sold her a funeral that would take every penny—coaches and a fancy coffin, all for the benefit of the undertaker. Dad called him back to the house and tore into him in front of half a dozen people for taking advantage of a grieving widow with a child to support, and the result was a funeral that cost half as much, which would leave a sufficient amount until Vera found work.

I could imagine how the undertaker must have felt to be yelled at by such a large man as my father. I pictured him cringing in the Liddells' living room, hat in hand, backing out the door, then making an ugly face when he knew my father couldn't see him.

When the undertakers left that night, Blackie crawled behind the cloth draped over the bier and took up guard under Uncle Andrew in his coffin. For two days the men from the Legion and some of the neighbors took turns trying to get the dog out to feed him. My father put a plate of roast beef scraps down near Blackie's nose, and someone else brought a piece of raw steak, but nothing worked. He lay huddled against the wall, unmoving except for his upper lip, raised in a silent snarl when anyone lifted the cloth to look at him. There was talk of calling the ASPCA. Everyone was afraid the dog might bite someone when they moved the coffin, but on the morning of the funeral, when they looked under the coffin, they found Blackie dead. Fourteen was too old for a hunger fast. Aunt Vera couldn't stand the thought of sending his body to the pound, so that night he was wrapped in an old overcoat of Uncle Andrew's and buried across the street in the Kudleys' backyard.

After Uncle Andrew died, a funny useless thing happened. There was a small triangular park at the end of our street that served as a kind of traffic circle. It was an insignificant patch of concrete with nothing on it but three wooden benches and an undernourished maple tree. My father decided it needed a name, and what better name than Uncle Andrew's, so he pressured the American Legion members to pressure the Town to pressure the County to name the park Andrew G. Liddell Square, in spite of its triangular shape. Some Legion members argued that Andrew had never done anything important enough to rate a park being named after him. This incensed my father. After all, Andrew was a veteran. He couldn't help it if he got sick before he saw action. His intentions were good. According to my father, it was almost an act of treason to doubt that Andrew would have been a hero, given the chance, and so the park was named after him. My father was irritated for years because after the first flowers and small trees were planted for the dedication ceremony, nobody did any weeding or picked up the papers that settled under the benches. He used to go down to the park now and then with a broom and sweep it clean himself. He said it was a crying shame that people could name a park after someone who wasn't there and then not bother to keep it clean.□

NAMES

Standing on my bed in the half-light of a winter morning, I pulled up my flannel pajama top and looked at my smooth chest. I wondered if my name was wrapped around me on the outside like my skin—or did it go all the way through me? If someone cut me straight across like a sausage, would they find it inside me with all those other things like your heart and stomach they said were in there?□

WHERE IS

Sixty, and where is the child with soft flesh that I can still feel and see, in pink, printed pajamas, toys piled on the floor, shoes jumbled, books and broken dolls, the old iron radiator under the window, stars shining in blue, dark skies, November clouds tearing past three-quarter moons?

　　Where is Anne and where is Mary, where are the brownies and milk, tangerines and tinsel, corner stores and life in three dimensions? Where are the maples and weeping willows, and the roller skates that wore out on the gray sidewalks? Where is that little rise in the cement before the corner store, and the ledge to jump off of in front of the house, and Jack and the Boots and the little back kitchen? Where are Mother, Jean, Daddy, Nana, Mamie, Julie, and Grandma and Grandpa? Where are clean things and order, school and arithmetic, Sister and Father? Where are they all? Where are they? And where am I? Where is the I that I was when the sky was blue and my body was small? For one moment to be so young and unknowing, so young and open, the child of my past— what I was when I was me.☐

OF TUTUS AND SPLINTS

Culture came to Queens Village in the shape of Annamae Drinkwater, a very blonde Indian. She had swarthy skin and black eyebrows, and she charmed the little girls in her dancing classes with her purple nail polish. "Come, girls," she'd say with a flick of her graceful fingers, "plié, up, plié, up." Her studio, a long room with a few mirrors along one side, was one flight above Murphy's Bar and Grill, and her students straggled up the worn wooden stairs each week on their way to fame and fortune. Jean studied acrobatics and tap dancing. Mary and I studied ballet. While Jean did backbends and energetic leaps with the other ten-year olds, Mary and I pretended to be flowers and birds, waving our arms in time to music played by the pianist, a colorless woman who never impressed her name on any of us because she wasn't the star.

Annamae was the star. Annamae with her daring blonde hair and vivid makeup smacked of show business and Hollywood, and many a mother saw in her swaying daughter an undiscovered Shirley Temple, a future partner of Fred Astaire. Perhaps mothers pictured themselves walking down the street with their children and being stopped by a producer, who would say, "What a charming child. If only she could dance." The mother would smile and the child would sail into a Pavlovian leap. Then after suitable notice to the neighbors, mother and child would leave Queens Village forever in a chauffeur-driven limousine to make fame and fortune on the great screen.

Annamae staged pageants and dances for local organizations during her stay in the neighborhood. We were in one at the American Legion. Jean and her group did cartwheels and jumps in blue gym suits and then the obligatory tap dance in top hats to "East Side, West Side," makeup smearing on their tense faces as they counted and grunted their way through the number. Mary and I, the youngest members of the ballet class, were given a small dance to do, which we performed well until the last moment, when I was so pleased with being graceful and flowerlike that I carried my stage bow to its ultimate end and kissed the floor.

One evening when acrobatics and ballet were being taught at the same time, Annamae went out to get some coffee and the assistant sat at the piano, a musical baby sitter, making weak suggestions. "Louise, don't run up and down the room like that, you'll hurt yourself," and "Catherine, you mustn't hit your little sister. It's not nice."

I wandered over to where the big girls were practicing backbends off a chair, and asked Joyce Rayfews, one of Jean's friends, "Can I try too?"

"Sure," she said, "just get up on the chair, turn around, and put your hands over your head. Go over backwards and I'll catch you." She caught me, but not before I broke my left arm, ending the lessons for everyone that evening, and for Jean and Mary and me for good. If a child could break an arm doing acrobatics, what might not happen doing ballet? My father and mother were called, and Annamae was given a hard lecture by Dad on not leaving young children unattended.

My show business career was ended but a new one got underway. Every other year until I was eleven, I walked around with a plaster cast holding some broken bone in place. I seemed to know all the wrong ways of falling, and every time I stumbled, my parents held their breath. I got used to X-ray machines, plaster of Paris, whirlpool baths, and slings. I got used to Doctor Mundell telling me stories about all the trees his daughter fell out of and fences she fell off of and what a good girl she was when he had to set an arm or leg for her.

There were advantages. In school, kids crowded around to look at the casts. They were warned to be careful and not to be rough with me. Teachers who always complained about my handwriting smiled and forgot to remind me that changeable handwriting was a sign of a bad character. It must have been a lucky coincidence that it was always my right arm I broke once I got into grade school. It turned out I was ambidextrous, and out of boredom I learned to write with my left hand. It was foolish of me to let anyone know, because after that, whenever I broke my arm, someone would remember and say, "Use your left hand." No teacher ever complained about the quality of my left-handed writing. Maybe they didn't think that would be fair. And if they noticed that it wasn't any worse than my normal handwriting, they never mentioned it. I guess left-handed writing didn't count.□

November 17, 1988
Alpine Drive, Beverly Hills

Dear Mary,
I almost want to say "Dear Marylitchhult" because that's the way I always thought of you when we were children. I was Rosemaryprimont and you were Marylitchhult. Or I feel as if I should be like Junior hanging on the back fence calling for you the way he used to— MAAARY, MARY LIIIITCHHULLLLT.

    Every once in a while, Jean gives me news about you and your family. My two kids are grown now, Jenny is a photographer, married, and living in London, and Andy is temporarily here in Los Angeles trying to dredge up a career as a journalist. Very poor to nonexistent pay, so he's staying with us for the moment.

    Christmas is almost here, and it's the time of year that always makes me think most of Queens Village, especially of 213th Street. I think I loved the months leading up to Christmas better than any other time of the year. I loved walking home from your house in the gray dark. I loved being cold and going into a warm house. I loved sitting in the dark in front of the radio, watching the lit dial and wondering how the people who were talking could get inside the tubes, always sure if I snuck around back quietly enough, I'd get to see them in there.

    I'm glad our mothers were fat and soft and liked to feed us. I'm glad they gossiped and liked to read and had kitchens that smelled wonderful. I think of all the times I stopped by your house on the way home from school just to be hugged by your mother and given a honey bun or a glass of milk. I know it was the Depression and she probably couldn't afford it, but I don't ever remember her not offering me something.

And I'm glad our mothers had each other. Each in her way had a difficult life, as much by temperament as by situation. I guess you and I always played together because they brought us up to play together, and they wanted us to be friends. I'm sure they thought there weren't any other children on the block (though we both played with other kids), except Junior for you, and you and I, who were up to some standard they set. I wonder if it was more than mildly irritating to them that we didn't duplicate their close friendship as we grew up, but people have to, and do, go their own ways.

But this letter isn't about the things we didn't do together. It's about what we did do and enjoyed doing together. It's about the thousand times we walked back and forth to school together. About playing cops and robbers in the empty lots along Hempstead Avenue with the O'Hare kids. Do you remember how Irene O'Hare, the oldest one, the one who was pale and skinny, a little older than us, wanted to be an artist and her favorite movie actress was Danielle Darrieux? How did any kid in Queens Village, especially the daughter of fiddle-playing Neil O'Hare, get to know about a French movie actress with a name like that? That's been one of the unsolved mysteries of my life.

Do you remember our trips up Jamaica Avenue to the Green Shop before Christmas and birthdays to pick out the books we wanted? All the hinting and muffled laughs and pretenses that we wouldn't buy each other the books we asked for? And then reading them before wrapping them up to give to one another? The only title I remember is *The Blue Junk*, but I don't recall who bought it—you to give to me or me to give you. I only remember standing in the entryway to the Green Shop, the two of us in paroxysms of laughter over the title, and Miss Whatever her name was coming to the door, very pink-cheeked, faintly, or was it nervously, smiling, to see what we were up to, and why we weren't either inside buying or else getting ourselves out of her doorway. I always had the feeling she thought we were slightly dangerous if our mothers weren't with us. She was so much nicer when they were.

And your Christmas tree, with beautiful delicate ornaments from Europe, treasures to love. I can see it now and smell it, and I see you next to it, showing me your gifts and smiling. And our tree —more ornaments broken than not, fraying light wires, tinsel thrown on, always overdone, always too tall for the living room. Your crèche neat and whole, ours—oversized, but looking as if it had been through a siege—plaster noses, hands, and heads (animal and human) missing. Not that I didn't love our tree. I did. To me it had magic, and in my memory I sit on a chair near the radio by our front window in the early dark, drenching myself in its silent colors, believing in everything good to believe in. Believing in God and the child in the manger and paradise.

Do you remember Henry Tiedemann's terrible, round, vanilla ice cream pops, and how my father always got into fights with him, and my sister and I couldn't go in his store for months at a time until the two of them cooled off? And the fresh rye bread and sugar buns from Hajak's bakery? And Wilson's Department Store around the corner? I can still see Mr. Wilson bustling around, very short and too light on his feet. And the Creos and Aunt Frances and Uncle Jim? And Erna Lanza and her parents, the Guerins, the Kudleys, and the iceman who had a blonde wife and two blonde children and lived a few doors down from you?

Do you remember how we used to go wait in the park on the corner for Uncle Charlie to come home after work? And how large and wonderful the moon above the railroad overpass was? And how he would hold your hand walking home, and sometimes try to juggle his lunch pail so he could hold my hand for a few steps too?

Two years ago, I wrote a couple of stories about people on the block—some of what I remember, or think I remember, and some of it made up. I don't know where the line is drawn. I've enclosed them and maybe you would like to read them. I'm sure you will remember things differently than I, but perhaps it will mean something to you to know that you live in my past; in my Queens Village, and that you and your mother and father and Uncle Charlie are part of the good memories that bless my life.

I now look exactly like what anyone but myself could have expected me to look like at sixty. I've got a crazy combination of my mother's and father's faces, so that when I come across myself in a department store mirror, I'm always startled by how much that lady looks like somebody I know from the distant past.

I wear a size sixteen, still several sizes less than either of them, but a lot of sizes more than I ever expected to wear. My skin is pale, my feet hurt, and I wear repulsive tie shoes. I have my grandfather's bunion and liver spots on my hands like my Great Aunts. My life is a constant rejection of mess and disorder and a longing to let go and not bother with anything. I am still bossy, opinionated, and love to dance like my father, and maternal, a good cook, and like to read like my mother. I've spent my adult life taking care of my husband, home, and family. Over the years I've painted, danced, gone back to school, and done some writing. That's the messy side. The neat side made sure I didn't do it more than a little. I am more like my three aunts than I would like to admit.

I've wanted to say hello to you for years. I started a letter to you about two years ago, then decided you'd think I was crazy. I'm sure we could both remember times from those years and the ones before our twenties and thirties that were painful, but that's not why I'm writing. This is to remember the good times. Popsicles, watermelon, brownies, Christmas stockings, hollyhocks, honeysuckle, fireflies, let's Pretend. Do you remember Ovaltine and the blue Orphan Annie mug that you had? I'm sure it was Orphan Annie, but maybe it wasn't.

I hope all is well with you and yours, and I hope that life is good to you.

Rosemary Primont

WILSON'S

Wilson's Department Store was the largest store on the block. At first it sold work clothes and underwear, but as the Depression eased and more people had work, Mr. Wilson began to include less utilitarian items such as ladies' dresses, pocketbooks, gentlemen's scarves, and even suits. The merchandise was displayed on counters, five-and-ten style, with boxes of stock underneath. The twenty-five watt bulb hanging from the ceiling never shed enough light on a purchase, so if it was determined that a person who walked in was a customer, not just a browser, Mr. Wilson turned on a seventy-five watt bulb, possibly two.

"You need more light in this place," Dad complained. "It's like a cave."

Mr. Wilson, short and round, was determined to be firm in the face of such tall impertinence. He looked up at my father, knew his enemy, and smiled, teeth together. "Surely, Mr. Primont, you can see it clearly. Take it to the window. It's a sunny day. You'll see its very good quality, one hundred percent cotton."

"Turn on the light. Customers shouldn't have to stand in the middle of Jamaica Avenue to buy a handkerchief." Dad snorted as he smiled and then dropped his bantering tone. "You lose more money by being cheap than you save. I hate to come in here it's so dark." It became a matter of principle to him to get the shopkeeper to turn on the light. "For heaven's sakes, put a light on."

Mr. Wilson reached back and flipped the switch. "There, can you see it now?" His pale-lashed eyes blinked. It may have been suppressed contempt or just the bright light. Resting his hands on the counters palms down in a conciliatory pose, he looked as if he had swallowed something unpleasant. "I think you'll find them satisfactory, Mr. Primont." The door opened at the back of the shop. "School must be out," the shopkeeper said, and turning to the fourteen-year-old boy who entered, addressed him formally: "Mr. Wilson, will you go to the basement and get another box of TC113 white cotton handkerchiefs, please?"

My father, with his customary tactlessness, asked, "Do you always call your son Mr. Wilson?"

"Yes." Mr. Wilson's face remained bland. He was speaking to a customer who often purchased things on a whim, spending more than a prudent customer might.

"That's not a very friendly way to talk to your own son," my father said sarcastically. He had forgotten how unfriendly he often was to his own son.

"This is business, Mr. Primont." Mr. Wilson took the handkerchief away and began to fold it, the diamond in his finger ring catching the light.

Dad, noticing the ring, said, "Humph." Then, realizing that the handkerchief was being put away said, "What are you doing? Don't be in such a hurry. I'll take a dozen of them."

"Very good." Mr. Wilson reached for a paper bag under the counter. "That will be...wait a minute." He turned to his son. "Mr. Wilson, go into the office and find out how much those handkerchiefs are by the dozen." The boy carefully put down the boxes he was carrying and hurried into the back room.

"Will that be all, Mr. Primont?" Mr. Wilson's unctuous tone was intended not so much to sell as to convince Dad that it had been a pleasure to serve him. If it hadn't, only Mr. Wilson knew. Dad felt the little man should be pleased that someone had patronized his store despite the lighting. If Mr. Wilson had any sense, he'd take advice from those who knew better, and make something out of the place.

The owner took the gold watch hanging from the thick chain across his stomach and checked the time. He was anxious to turn out the light before another customer came in and he had to leave it on. He moved about deftly refolding socks. "Come again, Mr. Primont," he crooned.

Mr. Wilson turned out the light. "Mr. Wilson, go upstairs and ask Mother to come down. I have to go out for a few minutes."

Putting on a trim overcoat and gray fedora, he left the store. When he felt the cold air, he took out his black leather gloves, and noticed with satisfaction the ring with its beautiful diamond. Successful, with a gold watch, diamond ring, quiet wife, and two obedient sons, he was a cut above the neighborhood.

As he walked along, his quick steps seemed to say, "Drink up your money in saloons. Waste electricity. Not me. I know how to run my business."

He smiled and tipped his hat at a passing woman. "Good afternoon, Mrs. Kane. I have some very nice aprons in today. I think you might like them. Stop by. Mrs. Wilson is in the store right now."□

THANKSGIVING FOR ALL

Thanksgiving must seem like a funny kind of national holiday to people from other countries. It's our most important holiday, with aspects of the pagan side of Christmas but without the drinking and decorations. There's a huge dinner and everyone cooks too much and eats too much, almost as if it's an obligation to do so. The leftover food from the feast is as much of a tradition as the original meal, and people eat it all week long.

The Fourth of July is a patriotic holiday, good for political speeches, flag waving, and parades. Most adults don't pay a lot of attention to it. It's just a holiday. Thanksgiving, on the other hand, is a happy positive holiday, one that says "how lucky we are to have so much." We stay in our homes with family and friends and eat our traditional New England, harvest-time meal. We don't necessarily spend the day thinking about how great it is to live here, but we are all, or most of our ancestors were, refugees from something—politics, poverty, lack of opportunity, boredom. We call ourselves Irish Americans, German Americans, Mexican Americans, Japanese Americans. We value our differences, but the one day we celebrate as a nation seems to be Thanksgiving.

It's also the one holiday that most new Americans celebrate with enthusiasm. Immigrants who can hardly speak English yet will tell you about the turkey they are going to have on Thanksgiving Day (it may be in chocolate sauce or stuffed with hot peppers), but they have an even better sense than the rest of us of why they are celebrating.

The other night, at a formal dinner, we sat next to a Hungarian who had survived a Nazi labor camp where he was taken at the age of thirteen. His mother, father, sister, and many of his other relatives died in the camps. His wife, also Hungarian, was in

Auschwitz and is the sole survivor of her family. They met at the end of the war in Hungary where each had returned to start life over. His family had been wealthy industrialists, and since he knew the business, he rebuilt the family factory only to be pushed out by the Russians. Because he was a capitalist, he and his wife were refused permission to work. They had no income and no prospects for a future in Hungary, and in 1959 they immigrated to the United States. I asked him when was the first time they celebrated Thanksgiving after their arrival here, and he said, "Right away. And we celebrate every day of our lives that we live here." If you think about all the immigrants who feel like that man, and who tell their American-born children and grandchildren the stories of why they came here and how lucky they are to be Americans, you can understand why Americans think they come from the best country in the world.

Milt's father traveled from Russia by himself at the age of twelve because as a Jew he wasn't permitted to go to high school. When he came here he went to high school and then to a free college in New York, one of the best in the country, and became an engineer. My grandfather's parents, originally from Alsace Lorraine, came here when that territory fell into German hands. I don't know what kind of work my great-grandfather did in Europe, but in the United States he became a tinker and peddler. My father's mother's family came from Ireland around the time of the potato famine. They were farmers and settled in upstate New York in lush dairy country.

We grow up believing that we are lucky ourselves, that America, even with its obvious faults, offers more to its citizens than any other country. That sounds like arrogance, but perhaps there's more of a naive gratitude than arrogance in the sentiment. After all, we're a young country. I wish we were perfect in the application of our Constitution. I wish no one were poor; I wish everyone were educated; I wish there were no prejudice; I wish everyone were honest and well intentioned. I wish a lot of things. But given our short history and the fact that until after the Second World War we were isolated by two very expensive-to-cross oceans, and given our chastening experience in Vietnam and the disillusion that followed it, we may finally be coming of age as a nation. I suppose all that means is that we'll scrape along, making as much of a mess as every other country does, but perhaps with a greater sense of perspective than we've had previously.□

I GAVE MY BIG RUG TO ANDY AND JULIA

After two men took the carpet to Mar Vista
from the room where it was
to the room where it is
I can breathe again

I hope the kids like it
or sell it
or give it away
and know that I love them
and I love their children

And by Thanksgiving
when we sit to eat turkey
if the rug is under their table
I'll know they will have forgiven me
for giving them that rug
because I'm too old
and tired to cope
with such a big possession

COUSIN SUE

I remember the first time I met Sue. It was a few months after Milt and I were married in 1958. Milt is her husband Richard's first cousin on his mother's side, also his second cousin on his mother's side, but Richard could explain that to anyone who was interested.

I see the four of us standing in front of the building on Commerce Street in Greenwich Village where we had an apartment over the Cherry Lane Theater. Were they coming to visit us and we were late coming home from somewhere? Did they just take a chance that we might be in and dropped by unexpectedly? I don't remember, but there's sunshine and daylight, and I am being introduced to cousins in this complicated new family of mine.

Richard and Milt were part of a family. Richard and Sue were a family. Milt and I and Jenny were a family. But what were Sue and I? We were strangers, looking at each other and wondering. There should be a word that describes the women who are married to the men of a family.

I remember what I wondered about that day. Sue looked as if she was expecting something—maybe wonderful, possibly interesting, and probably amusing. I've never forgotten the image of Sue, young, pretty, eyes shining, dark hair curling, with an air of hoping to hear something to be happy about.

I didn't know then that we would grow up in different ways and different places and after all become cousins. What are cousins anyway? We've both been through so many stages and phases, not at the same time or to the same degree, but they bear a likeness. We've been wives, mothers, artists, writers, and questioners. We've had times of contentment and sad times and everything in between.

I was born last in a long line of cousins, way too late to be anything but a nuisance to them. I like having a cousin who is my contemporary. Especially one like Sue who asks questions with her arms wide open. She learns as she goes along and she doesn't flinch at a new idea. And I never see her without somehow seeing still that young woman, tentative, searching, expecting something new and interesting.□

February 2, 1989
Alpine Drive, Beverly Hills

Dear Elinor,

The picture of your house in Florida fascinated me. From Chappaqua to Cape Cod to Boca Raton. Trips to Europe and offshore islands. If you had asked me twenty years ago which of my friends would be least likely to travel or move to a totally different climate and way of life, I must certainly have said it would be my good friend Elinor...I think that good changes are great for the soul. Not too many, and not daily, just enough to keep us learning new things and thinking about things in new ways...

I'm reading the new Robertson Davies book, *The Lyre of Orpheus*, and loving it. He's more fun than any writer I've read in years. After reading *What's Bred in the Bone*, as you had recommended, I read *The Deptford Trilogy*. It made my summer. There are so few books I feel like reading these days. At first it made me feel guilty. It may be that I've gone past the point of caring about romance, politics, intrigue, fantasy, psychological misfits, and tragedies. Those same old five or is it ten basic plots that writers have to choose from seem so old and worn out and not worth holding a book upright for.

I don't even read in the same way anymore. I used to read a book straight through in as short a time as possible. Now I read a few pages, perhaps a chapter, and then go on to something else. Sometimes it takes me a few weeks to read a book. If it's good, I'm not anxious to finish it. If it's only moderately good, I probably won't finish it at all. I no longer feel committed to finishing what someone else has chosen to write.

It's time in my life to do the things I want to do without guilt. Without pushing myself about, trying to conform to some image I have of earned sainthood in reader's heaven.

                Be well, and give my best to Phil,
                Rosemary

LETTER TO MYSELF

This should be in the "letters" category because in a way it's a letter to myself. I'm almost sixty-one. That sounds much better than sixty. It's Sunday morning, and I'm a little depressed. Sixty-one, and still unable to manage comfortably. I should stay home by myself, hidden in my closet among the shoes and old toys, away from social chaos, and, as the psychologists call it, interaction or interfacing.

What's it like to be Michael—to make friends all around, to ignore people who you think aren't worth bothering with, to judge without hurting yourself in the judging, to be easy and open, almost shallow, but not really. Maybe you need to be hurt so horribly as a child by the hatred of a parent that you can never feel too deeply about friends, so that if someone disappoints you, you can dismiss him without pain, or with much less than that original pain. He turns off or sheds disappointment at the actions of others so easily. I envy him. If someone doesn't behave well, he forgets them and concentrates on all the other people in the world who are wonderful and want to like him.

I'm glad I wrote about Michael, because now I know what I have to do. I have to turn my head away from people who don't like me or dismiss me, and know that none of us, including myself, can like everyone, or care what they think...□

AND WHAT OF TODAY

>Early morning visit from the cat
>kneading, caressing
>Away animal
>let me dream
>of time not time
>and world not world
>through chambers
>and fields
>of my own making

Journal
May 16, 1989
Alpine Drive, Beverly Hills

Last night at dinner at a friend's we met a man who said that he was impressed with my eloquence and the way I formulated my thoughts. He said I should write because I expressed myself so well. It was the first time in months that I spoke from my heart, maybe years, without peering out from behind myself in an effort to protect myself from ridicule.

I don't understand anything. I don't understand anybody. I am alone in this godless world of space, without parents, without roots—not without company, but without understanding, primarily my own.☐

DEPRESSION

She felt depressed. She tried to fight it, telling herself that today was no different than yesterday, that she was getting her period. It was only hormones that gave her this misery to carry around for the day. She pulled the blankets over her head. Yesterday was the mirage. Her feelings today were accurate. This is what *I am. Nothing. I don't care about anything.* She wanted to sleep, *forget it all. I won't go in today. I'll call and tell him I'm sick. I am sick. Sick of being alive. I wish I were dead. I wish I'd never been born.* It was cold in the apartment. Or was she cold from lying there? *I wish I were dead.* The phone rang. She listened to it several times, then got out of the bed and walked lethargically toward it. The gray fog was still there filling her body, slowing her movements. She had nothing to be sorry for, but she was.

"Hello, yes, I'm sorry. I was going to call. I won't be able to come in today. I have an upset stomach."

She got back into the bed and looked up at the ceiling.

Why couldn't I tell him I'm depressed? Because he wouldn't want to hear it. Nobody wants to know. I don't want to know either. Lead. Heavy. Oh, God, I wish I didn't know anything. If I could just be a dog or a cat and sleep in the sun...☐

JUNE NIGHT

Pale lights
glowing cool
in the hands of children

Fill the jar
to the brim
It will not show the way

But here and there
and there in the honeysuckle
the great dark softens

></p>

July 5, 1989
Talloires, France

Dear Marian,

Thank you for my birthday card. I loved getting it. Sixty-one wasn't half as bad as sixty. That was harder to take psychologically—don't ask me why—some birthdays just are.

How was your holiday weekend? I thought about you at the lake. We put up a satellite dish so we were able to watch the Santa Monica fireworks display on TV, and that was enough of a Fourth for the moment.

Actually, we're not feeling very holidayish. Assunta's sister Paula was diagnosed the week before we arrived as having breast cancer. They operated immediately and found that she had three tumors and that it had metastasized to three of the lymph nodes. They started chemotherapy the day after they operated, and I haven't heard what the prognosis is, but it can't be very good. She is a lovely young woman—thirty-eight— with two young children. She's the one married to Shad Moarif. Assunta is overwhelmed, but managing. Paula, Shad, and their two girls are with the Chatelains for the month of July, and Paula will remain for six months of treatment.

This has made the time somber and all are rearranging their ideas for daily work. I've done the only thing I can think of, which is to make soup and run errands. After Shad and the girls leave, I'll ask Paula if she would like to give me some French lessons the way she did last year. That way she can earn some money, and it will occupy her mind and help me at the same time. Also, it will get her out of the house, where she will be alone while Assunta works in the boutique. Or if she doesn't feel up to coming out, I can spend time with her at the Chatelains.

It really is upsetting, but "upsetting" is such an inadequate word. Paula is a really good, kind, generous woman. We all know life isn't fair, but it doesn't help to know it. I guess we just have to try to remember to live life well while we have it.

Now for something less sad. The sunsets are spectacular. The bread is great. Milt is sticking to his resolve to lose weight. No desserts. Unfortunately, he is eating margarine on the bread, which slows down the process quite a bit. However, he's sleeping wonderfully well, and that's terrific. He hasn't started playing tennis yet, but he walks a little every day...

I spend most of the time cooking and washing the dishes, but the food is so good, and it all seems worth it. The property has a fence around it now, so we don't have daily patrols by all the local German shepherds. Pierre Chatelain, Jacques' brother, who put up the fence, said that for the first couple of weeks, the dogs paced back and forth like lions in a zoo, trying to figure out what was what, then finally gave up. It makes me feel that this time the good guys won.

I miss Pepper terribly, but I just read another article about air travel for dogs, and decided that unless the Sultan of Dubai, whoever he is, lets us travel in his private 747 and keep Pepper in the cabin, he'll never travel by air. Sometimes dogs go deaf from the noise, and that's about the least of the awful things that can happen.

I hope and am sure that he's doing well with all the company he has. I'm sure when we come back he'll ignore us completely, preferring to stay with Mavis. I hope she's strong enough with him so that we don't find her on the wrong end of the leash. Maybe, without me there, she asserts herself more with him and let's him know who's boss...

Well, it's time to go make lunch. Thanks for the magazine. If I thought that exercise and living "right" would make me twenty-six again, *American Health* would be more interesting. However, there were one or two recipes and the article on Lyme disease that were good. I hope you read it before you sent it.

Be well, pet Pepper for me, and give my best to Jim and Mavis.
    Love,
      Rosemary

            Journal
            July 7, 1989
            Talloires, France

I can sit here on the balcony with my little computer, my friend, *mon cher ami,* and watch the waning of the day. Today *sombre* and *gris, un petit trou dans le nuage pour que le soleil puisse se glisser sur le lac.* Above the merest sliver of sunlight on *un très haut nuage,* small birds swooping and fluttering in its brilliance. Above and in the distance the thunder makes the sky ominous, and a passing plane *fait avec lui en mélangé de brouillard. Un autre petite coin rose de nuage se glisse sur* the lowering clouds and the bells of the village church sound the hour of nine o'clock. And I am here, in the land I believe to be of my ancestors, swathed in the gray beauty of a hidden sunset.□

            July 8, 1989
            Talloires, France

Dear Valerie,
After days of steaming and cursing at the Supreme Court for their stupid ugliness, I wanted to write and say that it will work out somehow. If the people who believe that abortion should be legal and available to rich and poor stand up and are counted, it will work out soon; and if they don't stand up for themselves and

others who don't know how to stand up, it will take a very long time, and you and I can't change everything by ourselves.

If you want to make it your exclusive life's work, do it, but if not, do what you can and get on with what you must do.

I know that probably sounds stodgy. I've seen so many unfair, unjust, disgusting things in my sixty years, things that somehow improved over time, but I have a confidence I didn't have before. It's not that everything gets better, but that a lot of things get better. I think this will be one of them because so many people, men and women, will suffer because of the whittling away of rights.

I'll write again.

Rosemary

July 14, 1989
Talloires, France

Dear Andy,

How are you, my good son? Are the Federal Courts more fun than lonely all-night vigils on Sunset and Vine? I hope so.

Things have settled down here somewhat. The Chatelains have made a kind of peace with Paula's illness, at least publicly. The shock of discovery has worn off and all are determined to take the best view possible until and if anything worse presents itself. I keep making propitiatory pots of soup, really to the Gods, and taking them to Ramponnet to take some of the burden off Assunta's shoulders. It's particularly hard for her during the tourist season, and some days she is beyond exhaustion. Shad and the two children will leave at the end of the month for Pakistan, though I don't know how they will bear the separation from Paula under the circumstances. At that point I'll take some French lessons if Paula has the energy to work at all. I think the next course of treatment will be very, very fatiguing for her, though I hope not...

I spoke to Jenny the other day and told her that we will go to England in mid-September and stay about two weeks. She says she is going to put a door across the stairway on the first floor of sixty-two so that there will be a separate apartment upstairs. She asked again that we stay there in September and we may...

I realize not much happens here in never-never land (except to the French) because we are only reading, watching, eating, and digesting as usual. Of course, there were all the Bicentennial carryings on, but except for the fireworks down at the plage, seen from a distance, we hardly knew it was happening.

This year Dad installed a satellite dish for the TV, so we get about sixteen channels, including two Italian and several German. The only American station is CNN, so we're up on all the murder, mayhem, and political scandal we can accommodate.

       Love,
       Mom

                                             July 22, 1989
                                           Talloires, France

Dear Julia,
All winter long, at Gelson's, I looked for Lavazza coffee for espresso, which Andy assured me he had bought there, and I finally found it last week at the supermarket in Annecy. So I bought six packages to bring back with me in the fall.

We're really enjoying the house this summer. Everything is much easier now that it's all furnished. Last year we spent more time in hardware stores and bath shops than we did in Talloires, and I guess I thought it would always be that way. We are sorry that you and Andy won't be able to spend time with us this summer.

Thank you so much for my birthday card. It was fun and very cute. I know it really came from you much more than from Andy and that makes it special in a different kind of way. Thank you.

Marian tells me that Morgan (the cat) has been living in the extension and liking it, and that she and Mavis visit several times a day. I hope Pepper and Morgan decide to like one another.

Milt has lost about fifteen pounds so far and hopes to lose another ten before we return. It's getting a little harder now, and he will have to cut back on more than dessert—start giving butter and salad dressings a pass too. He was doing that in the States, and decided, when we came here, to eat a little margarine with his bread and more than a little dressing. We've eaten at Père Bise a few times, but it just isn't as much fun without the ice cream and berries. He really has been awfully good.

I, on the other hand, have been eating awful things, like potato chips and pain au chocolat. Today I have started a new regime. No more pain au chocolat for breakfast. No milk (in my coffee) or cheese, and very little salad dressing. I haven't gained weight, but I was at my highest weight ever when we arrived, and the things I've been eating here are all the things the doctor has told me not to eat...

  Love,
   Rosemary

            Journal
            July 27, 1989
            Talloires, France

I don't seem to have the urge to write these days, only letters to friends—letters that don't even sound like me at all. I'm not able to let myself go and say anything important. They are letters from an old friend who has forgotten intimacy and substitutes formal nothings for ideas and feelings.

Maybe it's the afternoon storm outside that has helped me to loosen up. I haven't even turned on the light for fear of inhibiting myself from putting my thoughts on paper. Faverges is hidden by clouds and rain and the lake is magnificent. The wind for the moment is rocking trees, tossing the rain about. There's lightning and moderate thunder happening. I hope it stays that way.

Oops, the lightning is getting closer and fiercer and I think I'll go sit with Milt till it's over. I'm not so independent. I'm used to storms here, but I'm still a little chicken when they happen in the backyard...

Well, the storm is over and the mountains beyond Faverges have reappeared, but not without a lot of lowering clouds and harrumphing—nature reminding us that into each life and behind every cloud, etc.

We decided not to drive up to Denis's new restaurant, La Folie, but to eat in Menthon at Au Bon Vieux Temps. It has just as heavy a menu, noisier, not nearly so beautiful, but close by, and not a cliff in sight. God, the sun is putting on a show. It's incredibly beautiful out there. I can believe in anything when I look at those mountains to the south. When I look across the lake, to the southwest, at Duingt, I believe in the eighteenth and nineteenth centuries, and when I look at the Roc de Chère, I believe in 1969 and the Palace Hotel, on the other side, where we stayed with the children on our first real trip to Europe. Memories are such funny things. Each direction is a memory, and now this house has this happy time in it to be remembered.

I feel myself being another person this year, more relaxed, easier in myself, less driven than before.□

July 30, 1989
Talloires, France

Dear Jenny,
I'm trying to get myself going by writing a little each day, so today will be letter day...I keep passing by stores that sell baby clothes but I don't know what you need or want. It might be nice to start a daughter out with a French wardrobe—some chic diapers, perhaps, called something like Mademoiselle Bébé. I would like to have the fun of bringing a few things when we come, so tell me what you think would be nice to have.

Dad and I saw the funniest thing the other day. There were three women with little girls in tow, three young mothers all dressed sort of punk with short skirts, scrawny tee shirts, and funky shoes, and their three daughters were in little organdy pastel dresses with lace-trimmed collars, white anklet socks trimmed in lace, and Mary Jane shoes. So much for childhood dreams. The kids will probably grow up wearing lace dresses and dressing their own daughters in scrawny tee shirts, etc.

The first time I put a dress on you, you spent a lot of time patting yourself on the stomach with both hands and gurgling your pleasure. It was hard for me to believe. My generation had struggled so hard to be rid of ribbons and bows and get into jeans that I couldn't understand why any female, even a child, would want to be dressed up. Up to then you wore little overalls and tee shirts. I started enjoying getting dresses for you, because you liked them so much. When you went into first grade, I bought you five dresses, a ridiculous luxury at the time, so you would have a clean one for each day at school, and as I recall you made quite a fuss about which one to wear and what socks to wear with them.

I hope you received the sash to the blue dress intact (Dad sent it off this morning) and that it serves some purpose. Not the most glamorous outfit, but then this isn't the most glamorous moment in your life. You'll be so happy to get into regular clothes again, you'll probably forget about these months very quickly.

Love,
Mom

ELIZABETH ROSE SPARKS

I heard the baby's tiny mumblings and squeaking and suddenly I had a new relative. Funny how hearing her cry made me know her presence in the world. Just to know she existed would have meant very little, but now, even if I never see her, I know her in her three dimensions as a human being living somewhere in the world... Jenny had a terrible, long, and arduous labor. I wonder if she'll ever have another child. She might not, even if it had been easy, since she didn't seem to want children, but after that kind of ordeal, I think the chances are slim. Who knows how any person will react to suffering. Having been there for the whole process, Richard may be less inclined to want another child and be happy just to have one.

It is a relief to have it all over with and Jenny and the baby safe. I hope all goes well from now on.□

August 14, 1989
Talloires, France

Dear Rose,

Your summer seems to have been one long trial. I hope things are going better now and that all the invalids have recuperated. It doesn't seem fair. You've had your share and more of health problems in your family.

As to being unwound, I am. This has been a bath in soothing waters for me. Alone with Milt except for one side trip to Salzburg with friends. Then silence and mountains, sunsets, good food, six kinds of mustard, and more friends. I feel pretty good after my winter of tension and last summer's depression.

Now we have a granddaughter, Elizabeth Rose, born August 11, six pounds, thirteen ounces, and have heard her cry and squeak over the phone so we know she's real. Jenny had a miserable forty-hour labor, flirting with toxemia, high blood pressure, temperature, etc., and has since mumbled on day one that she didn't think she'd have another child, and on the second day, that she didn't see how the human race got this far if that was the way they had to do it. I spoke to her today and she was talking about the house and housekeepers, nannies and the nursery, so maybe it's fading a little.

I remember crossing Sixth Avenue and Charlton Street to catch a bus with you and Milt when Andy was about a month old, and moaning to Milt that we should be careful because I didn't want to be hit by a car and die after having spent my last year in such a miserable condition. Milt gave me a hard look and said, "If I didn't know you were nursing, I'd think you were getting your period," which I did the very next day. So much for nature's method of contraception.

We'll go to England for the September 24th Christening.

I think we will be a week in New York when we return, so I'll call then. Be well, and say hello to all.

            Love,
               Rosemary

August 16, 1989
Talloires, France

Dear Molinda,

Votre français est parfait. And that's about all I can put in writing without recourse to dictionaries and husband help. It was so nice to get your letter and be reminded of last year's fun and games here in Talloires. This summer's highlight was three days in Salzburg at the music festival with the Randolphs and the Chatelains. I know that opera is not your cup of tea, but the tenor part in one of the operas, *The Masked Ball*, was sung by Plácido, and, of course, in the end he died a very noisy, satisfying, musical death, surrounded by people weeping and moaning *"adieu."*

You might not have enjoyed the music, but you would have enjoyed the scene. Most of the women in Salzburg go all out with luxurious evening gowns, and the men are almost all beautifully dressed in tuxedos or white dinner jackets. At each interval everyone pours out into the wide street in front of the opera and parades back and forth. It's like one of those aquatints from the nineteenth century, where High Society parades in Kensington Gardens or the Bois de Bologne.

All of this was superseded in importance, to say nothing of relief, by the birth of Jenny's daughter, Elizabeth Rose, on August 11. She wasn't due for another week or two, but the doctor decided to induce labor when Jenny showed signs of toxemia. She had a pretty bad time of it, a long labor, with her blood pressure going up and down and a temperature that lasted twenty-four hours after the delivery. Richard stayed with her the whole time and is deliriously happy with the baby and impressed with how wonderful his wife is. We'll go to London in September for the christening, and then on to New York to catch *Aida* at the Met.

Tell Harold that Milt has lost eighteen pounds. He's feeling so well and the air is so good that we're thinking to spend five or six months here next year. We're eating at Père Bise tonight. We'll drink a toast to absent friends in your honor. See you in October.

Love to all the Karpmans, canine as well as human,
Rosemary

Journal
October 18, 1989
Alpine Drive, Beverly Hills

The London house is falling apart, the New York apartment is filthy, and Los Angeles has its share of malfunctioning faucets and a complaining dishwasher. The last two months have prepared me for a career as a house mover/cleaner/restorer, as I went from country to country and coast to coast straightening out my world. I could probably get a doctorate in reconstruction, renovation, and rubbish removal. Jackie Onassis with her well-trained staff I'm not, so I need a month-long vacation. I want nothing more than a few days staring at the lake and the luxury of three full days of meals at the Auberge.

The baby is beautiful, like all babies, and then some. She has the most doll-like sweet face of any baby I've ever seen. We chose the right moment to appear in London. Jenny was almost recovered and the baby was beginning to sleep less and notice more. The change from five to seven weeks was incredible. She seemed to grow and become more solid before our eyes. Or, perhaps, our eyes and hands just became more used to her fragility. □

December 7, 1989
Alpine Drive, Beverly Hills

Dear Michael,
If I didn't have you, I know I'd live, but having you makes living better. You're my connection with myself. My relative. My family past. The good genes. After I speak to you, I can believe I was once eighteen and wore jeans and a red and black checked wool shirt. That's who I was when I loved you unquestioningly. When you were "Michael, dear" and I was your old "Aunt Mitzi."

And if I was eighteen when we met and forty-two when we met again and you twenty-two, the love I once felt for you has been accepted with pleasure and a like amount and more given back to

me, as great a gift as I can remember. We have a chance for love between related friends, without parental, marital strains and tensions. Our love is like the love of grandparents for their grandchildren only we both feel like grandparents looking into a mirror of almost likeness. We're like fraternal near-maternal twins born twenty years apart with just enough differences to give us balance. Let's enjoy it.
    Rosemary

          December 8, 1989
          Alpine Drive, Beverly Hills

Dear Jean,
It's almost Christmas again. I think this year has gone faster than any other of my life. I find this season a happy and unnerving one. I keep wishing Mother were alive. She would have been so happy to see us both situated as we are. My reasons for wishing her alive though are less altruistic than that. I just miss her. Crazy to be sixty-one and wishing you could be welcomed home each day by your mother.

  Andy and Julia found an apartment and moved last week. And Jenny and Richard and the baby are due here on the twenty-second to spend Christmas with us. I'm trying to gird the house for a baby visit. Trying to get myself in mental shape for crying during the night, picking up a baby and maintaining some kind of back serenity, etc.

  California is so hot this year it's disgusting. The air is foul from the Santa Ana winds and the temperature is up in the high eighties. That probably sounds good to a Connecticutite, but sixty-five would feel more like the ideal. At least it would be possible to think of mistletoe and holly leaves without feeling silly. I keep wanting to send out Christmas cards with New England snow scenes but that's ridiculous. Are you going to Florida for the holiday? Enjoy it wherever you are, and if possible don't do the cooking.
    Love,
      Rosemary

Journal
February 15, 1990
Alpine Drive, Beverly Hills

Life is strange. Here it is February 15, 1990. I was married to my first husband in 1950, and his birthday was February 14th. Every year when the date passes, I think how lucky I was to be unmarried to him after seven years and then married to Milt. It's almost as if I want to celebrate every February 14th that he's having his birthday somewhere out of my life.

I hardly ever think of him, except fleetingly, and seldom with any animosity. He hasn't mattered for so long in my life that it's hard to think of him even existing. And right here in Venice or wherever. We were both so young and so inexperienced, and we had no business being married...

It's too bad that having children becomes harder to do at exactly the point when you're old enough to appreciate them and deal with all the difficulties they bring. Having them young may be healthier and what nature intended, but having them later works better. At least in the beginning. I don't know if that holds true for when they're in their early twenties and thirties and still may need help...□

THE GIFTS THEY GAVE

I woke up this morning thinking about the nudist camp in New Jersey that held such fascination for my first husband. I was thinking that being a good sport would have made married life pleasanter in those days, but then, when I was born a few of the Good Fairies didn't make it to the christening, and Good Sport wasn't among the gifts I received.

He and I were married for seven years. Sometime in year five he extracted a promise from me that if I would go with him to a nudist camp for a weekend, he would go with me to my friend Peggy's house for dinner. It was a hard bargain, but we did more buying and selling in our marriage than giving and taking. He was a painter, interested only in art and other artists. I don't remember all the jobs he had, but it was understood that they were beneath him, meant to keep things going so he could do his real work. Peggy and her husband Ben weren't artists, which made them non-people in his eyes, equal in pain for him to be with for an evening as a weekend at a nudist camp would be for me. Or I guess that's how he saw it.

We lived in New Jersey at the time, and they lived on Long Island. The trip to their house was an hour and a half by car, or an arduous three hours by two buses, train, and taxi. Since my daughter Jenny was a year old and I didn't drive and he did, he had a lot of leverage. This was before marriage contracts and Pampers. He didn't babysit. I didn't throw the diapers out. So a visit to Peggy on public transportation was like emigrating to a foreign country, if you counted all the diapers and applesauce packed in shopping bags, to say nothing of the baby and the stroller. So I agreed to go with him to the nudist camp as long as I didn't have to take my clothes off.

When he and I met we were both going to art school, and I was used to seeing people posing nude in life classes. But nudist camps were something else. They were often shabby places with a furtive air about them, not like the beautiful open sandy beaches where people sunbathe nude today. Also, public nudity had a kind of religious fervor to it. There was a self-sacrificial quality about taking off your clothes and presenting yourself to the public to be scorned, and sometimes arrested. Nudists were Joiners with a Cause (another missing fairy gift) who tried to talk other people into marching into the arena with them. I was an ex-Catholic. Despite reading Thomas Paine's *Rights of Man,* I hadn't rid myself of a lifetime's strictures about modesty and found the thought of a nudist camp appalling. And as a fourth-generation New Yorker, I found the thought of a nudist camp in South Jersey particularly horrendous. Yet there I was, being driven to the South Jersey shore, the visit to Peggy and Ben a thing of the past. There's nothing so over and done with as a visit to old friends when it's time to pay for it with a weekend at a nudist camp.

The drive past the faded green-and-white sign at the entrance to the camp was the beginning of our divorce proceedings. All the way there, I was convinced that he would relent, but the sign finished off that hope. The welcoming green sign, which I think had the word "sun" in it, should have included a few other words, starting with "party of the first part." It would have given us a better idea of our future. It's probably hard now to understand the enormity of that weekend. In those days there was no nudity on television and none in magazines, except the kind you had to know the candy store man to buy. In the movies, married couples slept in separate beds, and bare feet may have been the closest thing to nudity in any first-run movie house.

In spite of life classes and art school, I wasn't prepared for Camp Sunny. I found myself standing next to my husband in the manager's cabin, waiting to register for the weekend. The manager was middle-aged and wore nothing but a crumpled hat and a wristwatch. He smiled as he told us the rules. Camp Sunny was strictly two-by-two, no singles, a Noah's Ark club, with the exception that couples could bring their children. As for keeping my clothes on, there was another rule: one half of a couple could wear clothes one time only; after that, it was everything off. I said that since I wasn't coming back again it didn't matter, and he said most reluctant guests quickly relented, his smile implying that I would be a relenter. I still don't know whether it was the looking-glass ordinariness of the scene, the hat, the coffee pot, the peeling pink paint, or the complacent assumption that fifty bare bodies like the manager's would tempt me to follow suitless in the sun, but the more he chattered on about being healthy and natural, the more irritated I became. He was obviously a poor judge of people. He was looking at a fair-skinned former child who couldn't be talked into smiling at a nonexistent birdie by a nice photographer. Along with the Ten Commandments, I had two more: "Stay out of the sun" and "Don't give in."

When we left the little cabin, my husband was smiling, and my face felt like hardening cement. The first thing I did was re-tie the ribbon on Jenny's bonnet in such a way as to show any nudist who might be watching that nothing was coming off the female side of the family. The first thing he did was pitch the tent, take off everything but his smile, and head for the volleyball court, where he became friendly with an engineer and a middle-aged couple wearing straw hats with little straw figures jiggling on top, the kind of hats people buy when they stop for an hour's shopping at a port of call on a Caribbean cruise. He was delighted to make their acquaintance, whoever they were, though a week later, in a library or a bar, genitals covered, he would have said they were bores.

I busied myself unpacking, folding and unfolding clothes, fussing with Jenny, and trying not to see my tent neighbors, a foot away, gathered around their Coleman stove preparing lunch. I couldn't help wincing each time the cook put more bacon in the frying pan, and I heard it sizzle and spit, causing him to jump back and shout "Ouch!" as the hot fat hit his bare skin.

The volleyball court wasn't far from our tent, and my husband, who was laughing and trotting around with his new friends, kept calling to me to come over. After half an hour of stalling, I decided I couldn't stay in the tent all weekend, partly because it was too hot, and partly because it wasn't tall enough for me to stand up in. I added a ruffled sunsuit to the diapers, rubber pants, and hat that Jenny was already wearing—more clothes than she'd had on all summer—picked her up and headed for the action. Imagine an animated volleyball game played on one side of the net by two naked people in straw hats with things bobbing on them, and on the other by a grinning husband and an engineer dressed in nothing but green socks and hiking shoes. Thoughts of mad dogs at noonday mingled with my loathing for the camp and everyone in it except Jenny.

I spent the weekend trying to hide my discomfort, and trying to muster enough savoir faire to match what I thought was the correct point of view. I did not succeed. So much for the Grace Fairy. I'm not talking about Catholic grace that lets you get to Heaven, but the kind of grace that lets you put yourself and other people at ease. We were awful. He made fun of me all weekend, and I didn't talk to him. I tried to be pleasant to other people, but my smile hurt so much it couldn't have fooled anyone.

I stuck pretty close to the tent, taking care of Jenny and reading a large red book by Henry James, *The Wings of the Dove*. It was hard to keep my mind on it, in part because it was the least likely thing to hold one's attention in a nudist camp, but also because every fifteen minutes someone with no clothes on would stop by to see why I wasn't out doing one of the activities. Maybe nudist camps schedule activities to keep things from taking their natural course, but I'd given up on the Activities Fairy by the time I was six years old and refused to go to a birthday party where I knew they were going to play musical chairs. Not engaging in any of the activities was the one thing I didn't feel uncomfortable about that weekend. I watched my husband play a game of checkers with our neighbors, the ones I tried not to see earlier in the day, and I remember sitting in a boat with a healthy, happy nude family of five, all laughing as they lectured me on the disadvantages of wearing clothes. I left when the conversation turned to the marriage of the fifteen-year-old daughter and her eighteen-year-old boyfriend who had joined us in the boat, and with whom she was giggling and holding hands under the indulgent eyes of her parents.

That was Saturday afternoon. In the evening there was a picnic. Everyone brought their food to the volleyball court and sat around at rough wooden tables. There was a small portable radio playing staticky music. I stayed long enough to eat, then, using the excuse that I had to put Jenny to sleep, went back to the tent. Now and again, I'd glance over at the group, which in the dim light of a hundred-watt bulb strung up on a post looked like something in an avant-garde movie. Picture fifty nude people at a party pretending nothing unusual is happening as they wriggle around and swat themselves in a swarm of thrilled mosquitoes. The nudists weren't the only ones having a picnic.

I was almost asleep when I turned my head and saw a man's face near the ground at the door of our tent. By this time, I was so bemused by the bizarre quality of the weekend that I wasn't surprised when he hissed at me, "Are you one of them?" and then crawled on his hands and knees toward the next tent. I noticed that he was carrying his clothes and a whiskey bottle in one arm, making it difficult to crawl, but he still had on his shoes and socks and a tie. I figured that like a lot of the other nudists, he didn't mind sitting or leaning on uncomfortable things, but he couldn't stand feeling them on his feet. The tie was more of a mystery. Five minutes later he returned still on hands and knees to hiss in at me, "Look at them. They're disgusting." By this time, I was awake enough to ask him who he was. "It doesn't matter," he said and crawled off again.

The man from the next tent arrived, dressed in pajamas. I wondered why it was okay to go to bed in pajamas but not to wear them outside to keep from getting sunburned or bitten by mosquitoes. "Who was that?" he whispered. "He seemed a little odd." I whispered back, "I don't know," without adding that I didn't think the crawler was much odder than anyone else in the place. He hurried over to the volleyball court, where there were still some stragglers. After a few words, they fanned out in the direction the crawler had taken, and suddenly there were shouts and sounds of shrubs being trampled near our tent. In the near dark, I saw what could have been a typical hairy prehistoric human battle except for the shoes, socks, and tie on the victim, and the crazy straw hat on one of the captors. They dragged him gasping and dazed over to the hundred-watt bulb, where they could keep an eye on him while they waited for the police. The outraged couple in the straw hats started yelling things like "sorry sight" and "nothing more than a Peeping Tom."

When the police arrived, lights flashing on the squad car parked next to the volleyball net, the man collapsed into a chair, sobbing about his glasses, broken in the scuffle. By this time the manager had on a pair of pants as well as his hat, and the others had melted into their tents. The lawyer from Newark, for that's what the crawler turned out to be, wasn't the first peeper in that part of the woods, and after a few laughs, the police prodded him into his clothes and took him away to sleep it off in the local jail.

That weekend was high on my list of reasons for leaving the marriage, and it was many years before I could see how funny it all was. Everything was funny, except the divorce, but that didn't come until later.

The lawyer came voluntarily and took off most of his clothes, so why didn't he come through the front gate? Maybe his wife wasn't a good sport, or maybe he wasn't married, so it was the Noah's Ark rule that stopped him. I pictured him in jail the next day, hungover, wondering why his glasses were broken and how come his tie was under his half- buttoned shirt instead of on top of it.

Are there still nudist camps today? How would I act if I went to one? I don't think it would hurt my face so much to smile. And in spite of the sexual revolution, I still wouldn't take my clothes off, because the passing years have really brought a lot more with them than just the gifts of Maturity and Perspective.□

FROZEN

Impossible. I used to think the twenty-first century was so far in the future and now it's only ten years away. Will I reach it? Unless men do something incredibly manlike, the world—meaning men and women—will reach it.

The 1890s were my grandfather and grandmother's years. Bustles and leg-of-mutton sleeves, daguerreotypes, unicycles, Diamond Jim Brady, and fifty-five oysters at a sitting. Now we have the 1990s. If I live another ten years, I'll be seventy-two.

On television this morning, there was a doctor who invented a machine that rewarms the blood of victims whose body temperature has dropped rapidly, say by being immersed in icy water. That's what happened a month ago to the patient sitting next to him in the studio. His car was swept into a river and he was under water for a half an hour. He is the first patient the machine was ever used on, and clearly it was a success. He seemed rather dazed, almost as if he were still under water, but made sense when he spoke. Who knows what he was like before. Maybe he was always dazed. He was just happy to be alive.

I wonder if I would feel that way if I were resuscitated under those circumstances. My first thought when I looked at him was that perhaps they didn't do him a favor. He wasn't in pain, and for him, essentially, it was all over. Thoughts of a bonafide depressive, those.

As I write, I remember that when I am depressed I don't care whether I live or die, though I'm not always suicidal. I just don't care. Nothing seems important. But then when I am no longer depressed, I'm glad to be alive and I feel good.

This man looked depressed, but he obviously felt good. Maybe it takes time to thaw out completely after being near frozen for half an hour. When it's depression, the changes seem to happen from one moment to another. One day, getting out of bed, even putting your feet on the floor, seems a monumental effort; speaking to people, even the most mundane social contact, seems an impossibility; sunsets seem reasons for melancholy. And the next day, you don't remember putting your feet on the floor. Colors are brighter; lines sharper; feet move quickly as if life were a party; smiles are genuine; people, even strangers, seem worth talking to.

I don't want to be depressed again. Ever. I probably will be someday. But—I must be talking to the God I used to talk to when I was a believing Catholic schoolgirl—please, not for too long.□

ONLY FOR THE TRYING

>Does it matter how we die
>if dead is dead
>Only to the dying
>
>Does it matter how we lived
>when we are not
>Only to the living
>
>Why hope
>if it is false
>Only for the trying

JEWELRY

I am wearing silver earrings and a pin. The earrings, I know, look good on me. They're fairly large and in my late, late middle age, large earrings are a lot more flattering than the tiny gold ones I usually wear.

But the pin—a beautiful silver butterfly from Tiffany's that a friend gave me—is making me uncomfortable. It's funny what an effect jewelry has on my spirit. I want to wear it. I see other women wearing jewelry, and I admire it on them and them in it. But when I put it on myself, I feel like a swan out of water. A rabbit with a duck's bill. An elephant with a giraffe's neck. Or a fish on piano legs—three piano legs.

All my resolutions about being chic, like other women I see, fade before my image in the mirror. I hate my clumsiness. I feel just the way I do when I try to count out the change here in France when I buy something in a store. Incoherently clumsy!

So I tell myself that I'm good at something, just not at wearing jewelry and counting change. Oh, well. From out of somewhere today I knew that the word "deuce" was probably of German derivation. Don't ask me how I knew. It's just one of the things I'm good at...◻

THE SILVER RING

The Depression years were difficult for almost everyone. We were lucky. My father had a job, so we never went hungry. Some weeks the owner of the milk company where he worked just split whatever money came in among all the men, including himself, so no one went home empty handed. It might be no more than five dollars each, but it was something. There was nothing extra for luxuries.

Every birthday meant an argument. Dad had no sense about money, and most of what he did, he did on impulse, without much regard for what we needed or wanted. So, in the early years of the Depression he was told off in angry tones by Mother because of the money he spent on presents and the unsuitability of what he chose to buy for us.

My fourth birthday opened with the usual scene of complaint and indignation. "A ring. Why did you get her a ring?" Momma looked as if she might cry. "That's a ridiculous present for a four-year-old. She'll lose it by tomorrow. How much was it?" It was my father's job to earn money and my mother's job to get it away from him to buy food and pay the bills. Knowing him, she could believe the ring cost anything from twenty-five cents to twenty-five dollars, depending on what jewelry store he was passing by when he decided a ring would be just the thing I'd like.

"For heaven's sake, Rosemary, what's the matter with you? It only cost a couple of dollars." His face became gloomy. "It's just a little ring. Don't carry on about it. You'd think it was emeralds or rubies or something."

"Ridiculous. Buying a thing like that for a child. Why don't you spend the money on something she can get some use out of?" She stomped around the kitchen, slamming dishes on the table. I sat silent, afraid to talk or move. I didn't know why my mother was so angry. I liked the ring and every once in a while I peeked at it on my finger, held low in my lap. I rubbed left forefinger and thumb around the ring, twisting it up and down on my ring finger, over the knuckle and back.

"Can I have some milk, Mommy? I'm hungry."

"In a minute," she said, not finished yet with being annoyed at my father. "Next time you get her a present, ask me and I'll tell you what to get for her. I don't know where you leave your sense sometimes."

Dad gulped his hot coffee, lifted his big frame off the green painted chair, and left the room. Mother brought a dish of steaming oatmeal and a glass of milk. "I want you to eat every bit of this today. Don't leave a mouthful on that plate, and don't drink the milk first."

I put the spoon in the sugar bowl and sprinkled heaping spoonfuls on the gray mess in front of me. The sugar turned to a semi-transparent granular syrup across the top of the cereal and I used my spoon to scrape along the surface trying to get as much sugar and as little oatmeal as possible for each mouthful. Three swipes and the sugar was gone, in my mouth or mixed into the cereal. I swallowed the milk rapidly to get rid of the tainted sweet taste, put down the glass, got off the chair and said, "I'm finished, Mommy."

"You didn't eat anything. I don't know what I'm going to do with you."

"Can I wear my ring?"

"You might as well. Your father gave it to you. Now don't lose it. Or put it in your mouth. And when you wash your hands, don't take it off."

"Don't you like it, Mommy?"

"It's pretty. It's just not the right present for a little girl."

I was careful with the ring. It was silver and had my initial on it. I showed it to everyone I met. I waved my hand, always conscious of it. When I lifted food to my mouth, my eyes watched the ring instead of the fork. I looked at it in the mirror and under the bath water. Its silvery surface made me somebody else, fancy and interesting. Jean hated it. She said it wasn't much of a ring. She had plenty of better ones. Anyway, who wanted a dumb ring with no stone in it? "I do," I said, and we both felt cheated.

The ring lasted six months, not bad considering the age of the wearer and the abuse that it took. I got around the command never to put it in my mouth by only putting it in my mouth while it was on my finger. It meant sticking the whole finger up to the palm of my hand in my mouth which I stretched large enough to accommodate it. I chewed on it like a puppy, taking great pleasure in the taste of the metal and my finger was often wet and pink around the ring. Gradually it became dented as I put more pressure on the fragile silver. Mother made sure that the ring could still be removed and that it didn't stop the circulation in my finger.

The ring appeared in the picture taken of me as a gift for Dad on his birthday that year. Mother dressed me in my good, blue velvet dress, clean white socks with blue borders, and Mary Jane shoes, and with Aunt Vera for company, we set off for Jamaica on the trolley car to have my picture taken.

"We'll have a nice picture taken for Daddy's birthday. You can smile for the photographer and then in two weeks we'll get the picture and have it framed."

I smiled up at Momma and leaned against Aunt Vera. I was very happy to be doing something important. "What's a photographer?"

"That's the man who takes your picture."

We got off the trolley in Jamaica and walked beneath the dirty frame structure of the El to a building with a green door. Aunt Vera made a face and said, "This must be it."

"It doesn't look like much, does it? I hope the pictures are better than the building." Momma opened the door and she and Aunt Vera, with me in between them, began to huff up the steep wooden stairs to the hallway above lit by a small overhead light bulb. The hallway was dark and musty smelling. It looked as if it had been painted years before in brown gravy.

"I don't like it." My voice began to go up and my breathing became a pant. "I wanna go home."

"Don't be silly. It won't be like this inside. You'll enjoy it." We walked in the door and were greeted by wires, lamps, a big box camera on a tripod, a young lady, and a very cheerful man who said,

"Good afternoon."

"I'm Mrs. Primont. I made an appointment to have my daughter's picture taken."

"Is this the little lady? Hello, little girl." He leaned over and smiled a big professional smile. "Comb her hair and then put her over there."

Mother fussed over my hair and dress and walked with me to the piano bench against the wall that the photographer had indicated. She bent down and coaxed, "You smile when the man takes the picture and then we'll have a nice present for Daddy." She went back to Aunt Vera and the two of them looked benevolently at me sitting on the bench.

"And after, we can go and have an ice cream cone."

I stared at the photographer and the young woman. She came over and smiled at me. "Now, let's fix your dress a little."

"Turn her to the side, please. That's it."

"Here let me fix your hair. No, don't pull away."

I pulled away from the hands with their bright red polish to look at them. "You have long nails." The girl held them up so I could inspect them. "I like them that way. Now let's get you back in the right spot."

"Look this way." The photographer ducked his head under a black cloth, shifted his weight from one foot to the other. "Don't move. Okay, smile. See the birdie?"

"Where?"

"In here." He waggled his hand around the front of the camera.

"Why is he doing that?" I turned my head to the girl.

"Just turn around where you were and smile when he tells you to, so you can have a nice picture for your daddy's birthday. Don't you want a nice picture for your daddy?"

I nodded, corners of my mouth turning down. I wanted a picture for my father but I couldn't smile.

"Be a good girl, Rosemary, and smile at the camera. We don't want to be here all day, do we?" Momma wasn't smiling any more. She looked irritated and embarrassed. I sat on the bench dangling my legs, face muscles frozen.

"If you don't smile I'm going to go home without you."

She walked out the door and I shouted. She'd never threatened me like that before. I cried out loud, tears running down my face, dripping on my dress. I got off the bench and ran after her.

Aunt Vera picked me up. "Momma's just outside. She wouldn't go home without you. She just wants you to smile at the man." Aunt Vera held me close to her. "Don't cry. Here she is."

Momma came back inside. "We don't have all day," she said. "I want you to sit over there and do what the man says."

"I don't like him. He says there's a birdie and there isn't."

The photographer was trying to keep his professional smile, but he looked displeased. There were other people coming up the stairs, and this was taking too long. "Wash her face and let's try again. Why don't you ladies step outside? Maybe that will help."

I sat miserably on the bench, fingers twisting the silver ring while the girl pushed me into the right shape. "Where did you get that pretty ring?" she asked, lifting my hand with her red-tipped fingers.

"My daddy." For the first time I felt friendly and liked the girl. I looked up at the carefully curled brown hair and saw the red, smiling lips. Even the girl's nose looked friendly. She moved slowly back to the photographer.

"Don't mention the you know what. Let me do the talking."

"Why does he put that black thing on his head?"

"That's so he can see better. After you have your picture taken, he'll show you what it looks like. You be a good girl now." The young woman's voice was syrupy and smooth. "When did your daddy give you that pretty ring?"

"On my birthday."

"When's your birthday?"

"June twenty-ninth." The corners of my mouth moved up in a faint smile, the camera clicked. The photographer threw the black cloth forward and stood up. "That's done." He turned his back and smiled at the next customer.

I was hustled into my coat and down the stairs before I could ask to see where the birdie was. Mother was still annoyed, and when I asked for the promised ice cream cone, she looked more inclined to punish than reward me. It took a few minutes for Aunt Vera to convince her that we all needed some ice cream after our ordeal, and the day ended pleasantly.

Nothing more was said about the picture until it came, and my mother looked with dissatisfaction at the hint of a smile on my face, hands in my lap caught in the act of twisting the dented silver ring. Dad said he loved the picture, and it was soon relegated to the drawer in the dining room cabinet that passed for a photo album.

Two weeks after his birthday the ring was no more. I chewed it into such a shape that it could no longer be removed from my finger, so Dad and I were sent to the jeweler to have the ring sawed off. Dad's face was contorted as he winced when the jeweler used the little round-toothed instrument to sever the ring.

"You know," Dad said to Momma when we got home. "A ring probably wasn't such a good idea. Maybe I should have gotten her something else." □

>
> July 8, 1990
> Talloires, France

Dear Eda,

I'm sorry not to have answered your letter long before this, but I don't think I wrote any letters in the last few months before we came to Talloires this year. Somehow, it was all so hectic, and I seem to have lost my capacity for marching coolly through the hectic times in life. I get as fussy and fidgety as my mother's three old-maid aunts ever did, so I figure the genes must have skipped a generation—but did I have to get them from all three?

We decided to come for six months this year instead of three or four, and since the man who worked for us for the last ten years died of flu last December, essentially, it meant closing up the house (except for the office), turning off the gas, and covering everything with sheets. Marian, our secretary, will have a cleaning crew in every three weeks to do the downstairs, and Andy and Julia will be there on the weekends to do their laundry. I tried dialing the house this morning, California time 11 p.m., and caught them in the middle of folding their sheets and watching *The Dead Poet's Society* on tape. They don't have a TV, so they use the laundry night as a weekly treat...

I passed through New York on the way here, but only for one night. I was so frazzled by the time I got there, it's a wonder I even made it. After making all kinds of plans to bring our dog—packing all his stuff, getting medical certificates, food, getting the travel crate ready, making plans for New York and Geneva—we had to put him to sleep. It's hard to even write about it.

A year ago, he bit a woman who came to stay at the house. It was inexcusable, but, in a way, her fault. She didn't understand dogs and tried to take some food he'd stolen from the counter out of his mouth. I could have done it, and so could Andy, but not a stranger. I punished him severely and figured that would be the end of it. When we came back in the fall, I noticed a change in him, particularly in relation to his food—the kind of a growl a dog gives when it hears something outside that it can't see but doesn't like. Over the winter, three or four times, he growled at me if I lingered too long near him as I gave him his food. I tried a number of things, like feeding him whole meals from my hand, giving him treats during the day, always from my hand, and each time figured that everything was going well, until he'd growl again. I figured that somehow while I was away he'd gotten used to being the boss and was trying to keep it that way.

I wasn't especially worried until I started to get him ready for the trip, about the beginning of April. He'd been leash trained, and by and large was pretty obedient. I mean, he knew a lot of commands and, like most Labradors, enjoyed performing—most of the time. When he didn't want to do something, he had a slinking, sidling kind of walk that made me unhappy. And he also had a way of holding his ears straight back when you went to pet him. These two things always bothered me about him from the time they showed up at about six or eight months, but I figured what the heck, that's what he is, we've adopted him, he's ours, and we love him. You can't get rid of your kids if they turn out like your Aunt Millie, and you don't get rid of your dog because his ears go back.

Well, it seems I was wrong. With the pressure to be walked on the leash ten or fifteen minutes a day, to begin to use the crate and have the door shut for five or ten minutes at a time, and changes in household arrangements, everything I'd noticed last winter became intensified. We had a trainer, a nice, kind, gentle man, who came to the house to work with Milt (who'd never been on the other end of a leash), and he told me some things that convey dominance to a dog, like putting the hand on the upper back by the shoulder blades, and that it would be good if I added a few of them to my repertoire. As I did, the dog became increasingly irritated and hostile. The final moment came when he got up on my bed and I told him to get down and reached out my hand to pull him off. He took one hard look at me and commenced to growl long and ominously. He was between the door and me, and it took a lifetime of dog ownership and one-upmanship to walk around the bed while ignoring him and call cheerfully over my shoulder, "Come on, Pepper, downstairs." He followed, and I locked him in the laundry room.

I was actually afraid to go in there in the morning and feed him. An angry dog and a frightened owner do not make a comfortable combination. And when the dog is a sixty-five-pound animal with large jaws, it gives one pause.

So I called the vet and described what was happening. His first question was, "Has he bitten you yet?" When I said no, but that he had bitten another woman a year ago, he said, "Well, he's going to. It's only a matter of time. He's going to bite somebody. If you're lucky, it won't be a child."

He went on to tell me that the slinking and the ears pulled back were in the breeding, that I was lucky to recognize them as bad signs, and lucky that the dog was giving me plenty of warning. He said he was surprised that he'd lasted as long as he did without biting more than one person. Probably having him neutered had helped. He said categorically that we could not give him away, couldn't take him to the pound to be put down because they might let someone adopt him, and that left us no way out except to have him destroyed.

It was a terrible decision to have to make. He was really a companion. If a dog is old and sick or in pain, you can feel you're doing something you should do when you have to put it down. If a dog is a healthy three-year-old, even though it is in its nature to be an outlaw, it's hard to face destroying something so alive.

But we did it—that morning. It's about a twenty-minute ride to the vet, and the traffic was crazier than usual. Milt and I had to be pleasant, positive, and not permit ourselves to think about where we were going, because the dog was roaming around in the back of the car, being very serious. When we got to the vet, I realized he wasn't joking about the dog being ready to explode. I used to joke that Pepper was the only dog I knew who loved going to the vet. He never minded anything they did to him, always wagged his tail, and loved all the other dogs. This time he was very—perhaps cold is the word, or hard. When the vet, who has seen him many times before, took him out of the examining room, he held him on the leash a good two feet away. The dog went with him, and that was the end.

But it wasn't the end. I still miss him. And at the same time, I can't forget the bottomless look he gave me that last night. Afterward I heard every horrible story about dogs that turned on their owners, including one the very day after, which killed a child here in France.

So why have I decided to tell you all this? I guess because you've had dogs, one of which I was very afraid of, and as I remember, she had dysplasia and you kept her, in the way I kept Pepper, ears back and slinking, even though I sensed that they weren't good signs. There's more to having a dog than just taking on a responsibility. There's the image one has of oneself as a decent human being.

I think it's also the first time I've been able to write it all down and look at it objectively. I know what I did was correct—from my human point of view—but it hurt to do it, and I feel poorer for it.... It seemed terrible to have the power of life and death over another creature. I keep telling myself that he was like a loaded gun in the house. But still, it's not as if I killed him in a violent temper or in an accident. It was just plain cold-blooded practical sense, like an execution. It was an execution only the dog hadn't done anything—yet.

Enough of unhappiness. What's done is done and all that stuff. The sun rises and sets in all its wonder and beauty, and French food is still a pleasure. If you're going to be in Europe before October 15, I hope you will come and stay with us and share our life here for a few days. If not, until next winter when I hope to see you again in California. Lots of love to you and Lennie.

    Our Best,
    Rosemary

July 22, 1990
Talloires, France

Dear Marian,
I can't believe we've been away for two and a half months. We've gone from weeks of cold, rainy weather to hot, hot summer, the way in New York we used to go from winter to summer with no spring in between. I was embarrassed when we built this house and Milt insisted on air conditioning. "But, Milt," I said, "no one in France has air conditioning." And he said, "No air conditioning, no house." Now each summer, during the three or four weeks of heavy, humid, ninety-five-degree weather, I tell him how wonderfully smart he is and how foolish I am to care whether anyone thinks we're ugly Americans, as long as we're cool Americans. I heard one carpenter telling another (in French) that it wasn't all so rare any more, and more and more people are having central air conditioning put in their homes.
      Rosemary

TALLOIRES 1

    Mist over the lake
    hovering
    like thoughts of beginning

    Trout, curious and clever
    darting from the hook
    nudge amber rocks

    Underwater visions
    reflect deepening dawn
    in the country scent
    of waning August
    and fading hill

LIFE IS A BABKA

That's what Milt and I used to call a muddle, a mystery: Life's a babka, we'd say to each other, with our hands opening out, shoulders raised—who can say?

Michael's birthday was November 17th. I was talking to him and he reminded me that I could wish him a Happy Birthday. Just last night I understood why I feel so close to him. He's the only one I know in my Queens Village family—the Primonts—who seems like me to have emerged, not unscathed, but thinking.

His family was like my family, with long-term misunderstandings and open hostility. My brother's family life was a continuation of my early family life—the same complaining pettiness and dislike—in the same way that my sister Jean continued her version of our early family life

Michael's brother Peter deserted the family emotionally by the age of twelve or thirteen, and made a nest for himself in his future wife Sheila's family. Perhaps he didn't think about it, to judge by his way of relating to things today. He just did it.

And my sister's children are continuing their own family disabilities in their adulthood, so I don't feel connected to them. I have always watched Jean's family from the outside, because early on I realized that nothing I said would ever help her to change. You have to have ears to listen with and a belief that you can change. You have to look outside yourself for ways to be different to even imagine the possibilities.

But Michael is different. I don't think he suffered from his environment more than Jean's kids, but he did it with understanding. He did it with character. He really took responsibility for being different—for trying to be different, even if he didn't always succeed.

Peter has character, too. He needs his wife, his daughter, success, material pleasures. He's practical, honest, and responsive to other people. Only his way was to walk out. Not on his mother, but on my brother and the way his family lived. I've walked out on impossible situations myself. So has Michael. The difference seems to be that after Michael and I walked, we thought about it, weighed ourselves in the situation, tried to change things where possible, to accept them where not, to forgive the others, and see the whole. Peter just said, this is impossible, so I'm gone. Peter doesn't have the need to think about possibilities and probabilities if they're not practicalities. Michael I understand. Peter I envy. Michael I love like a twin. Peter I love like an aunt. Michael is my relative/friend. Peter is my nephew. And both wouldn't have it any other way. Interesting.

To change the subject: If I accept the idea that the problems I've been having with my heart are caused by nothing more than stress, then I must ask myself what is so stressful about my life. I've come up with some answers. What happened in the last six months that overwhelmed me?

First, there was Ellie. I've written about that at length, but I'll state it briefly for my own benefit again. Ellie was a big public rejection. Public being the Manuses, the Bergmans, George and Milt, and anyone else who knew that George and Milt and I have been longtime friends. Ellie feels like a failure. I feel as if she is one of a long line of failures, one of those brick walls I've come up against in my life. No one should feel like a failure because they can't float through what to them is a brick wall, but I don't seem to handle it too well...

Would I have cared if someone else had had her reaction to me, someone I barely knew, a man possibly? Not at all. But she's George's wife, and I tried very hard to get along with her. I'm sure that was a mistake. Some people see that kind of behavior as weakness and have to strike out.

Perhaps my problem is with being accepted by women. There must be something about me that isn't very likably feminine. I don't know how to join the club, except by lying or pretending, and that always rings false. I seem to be friends only with people who can accept me as I am.

So for almost a year now, I've been grinding my heart teeth over Ellie. Sometimes I forget a little, but it's almost always there. We have to invite her and George to Andy's wedding. Andy wants George to be there, and with him will come Ellie, whom I don't want. I probably want to hear that she and George are splitting up, but I don't want George to be unhappy. I'd like to have him in my life, but not her. Then that makes me feel guilty. What does it have to do with me anyway? And why does just thinking about it make me feel guilty? Shit.

The second thing that happened: My dog Pepper turned on me. That was an awful rejection. So what if the vet and the trainer say that nothing could be changed, that it was in the breeding? It hurt. I loved him and took care of him, took responsibility for his being alive. Then I had to take responsibility for his being killed. I know I had to do it. I saw the way he looked at me. I was the enemy. I saw how the vet handled him so delicately and cautiously when I brought him in to be destroyed.

If you have a dog that is vicious toward other people, outsiders, you can face the fact that it has to be killed. But when the dog turns on its master, how do you explain that? Perhaps it's in the breeding. More likely, you feel it's in the master. That's how I felt. What made the dog dislike me? What made Ellie dislike me? What made my sister dislike me?

I know the sensible answers to those questions. Breeding. An egocentric twelve-year-old mentality. The fact that I was born as I was.

So why can't I accept these reasonable answers? If Ellie is stuck at twelve, I must be even younger. I need someone else to approve of me. When they don't, I go into my corner and cry. I know it's stupid...

Somewhere in that childhood back in Queens Village, I must have failed so many times to be what was expected that there's not much of me left intact. "Nobody loves you, Rosemary. I'm prettier than you are. Who cares what you think. You're just a baby. You get everything. You're such a spoiled brat. You never do anything. You're dumb. You're selfish. Nobody likes you." That was Jean.

It's a sign of a bad character to have changeable handwriting. "You must have cheated. Your parents will not go to Heaven if they don't make their Easter Duty. The Devil will catch you. God doesn't like girls who lie, or who never do homework. Why did you fail? Why did you succeed? Why did you do so much? Why did you do so little? Why aren't you perfect? Why did you make it red instead of green? Blue instead of purple?"

Well, with whatever is left of me, I must get into the ring again, accept what exists, and go on to other things. I've got to take life and its vagaries with a more casual attitude. Good luck me.□

NOVEMBER AGAIN

Where are they
they were here a moment ago
whispering, sighing
"Sing the music
  of our lives
  let your blood be ours
  give us tomorrow
  and red apples
  and burning leaves"

Journal
November 21, 1990
Alpine Drive, Beverly Hills

I haven't written in my journal more than a few times in the last six months. I wrote letters to friends, but I didn't have a lot to say to myself.

I don't want my journal to be just a long meow about my life, so I must have thought that not writing was preferable to seeing it all out in front of me. I don't understand psychological terminology too well, but if I understand it at all, I think I could say I don't have an ego. Not that there isn't an "I" who feels things and wants things and wants to be noticed. It's just that the "I" can be demolished—can become the negative instead of the positive—by any systematic, repetitive attack, usually by a woman. Perhaps there was an attempt by a man, but I don't think that other than my first young adult love, any male has made me suffer.

I can't say the same about women. It's crazy, because I like women. I find them more fun to be with generally. I understand them. I don't understand men too well. I like them, but most of the time in the past, there was an element of sex involved—and still is in an inactive way— and I like that too. But only Milt, of all men, could hurt me, and he never does, and I don't believe he ever will, not intentionally. But women—I have been hurt by them. And I'm sure I've done some hurting. Am I always looking for the sister who will love me? For the nuns who will find me satisfactory? I'm not a rebellious person, so I didn't glory in dislike and provocation. I never even meant to provoke. I wanted to be liked. Maybe I provoke by being vulnerable, and that brings out the bully in some women. Most men can't bully me because I suppose I'd tell them to shove it. But I do find myself being bullied by women, and very often I feel defensive before a kind of onslaught. Do I do that to other women? Is that something we do to one another and I just can't take it when it's being done to me?

I think back to grammar school and I wonder what happened to the other kids like me. Are they sitting around whining about not feeling loved? There were so many of them. And so few of the sure ones. What makes us all tick and what makes us stop ticking? Interesting analogy, since it's my heart's ticking and tocking that's been a problem lately.

Maybe I can write this now because I'm out of my late summer slump and into my winter upturn. The cool weather is here and I feel invigorated. Also, the pills that Harold gave me seem to be working and my heart is marching like a good little soldier, somewhere between seventy and eighty beats a minute. I don't feel as if I have an enemy in my chest. Has a regular heartbeat made me feel better, or is my heart beating regularly because I feel better?

Do I believe that all this introspection is going to help me the next time I run up against an aggressive woman who needs somebody's chest to stand on? I hope so. Will it solve my current obsession? The fact is, I know I'll get over that eventually. But I'd like to get over it now. Yesterday. Last week.□

THANKSGIVING AGAIN

Thanksgiving again... No matter how depressed I become, I am always aware of the truly awful things that could be happening in life, the things that do happen to people. It doesn't help the depression usually, because I don't think that's where little depressions come from. They come from some spot within, having nothing at all to do with external reality. Maybe they're the ghosts of miseries past, or an imbalance in human ingredients, a mix-up in the recipe—too much flour, or too much leavening.

But today is Thanksgiving, and today I'm not depressed. Like everything else that I am or do, I don't know why. This morning for some reason I lolled in bed until nine-thirty. Again, I don't know why. I just did. I awoke at six and again at seven-thirty, and each time made a conscious decision to go back to sleep. I got up rested and in a good mood. Maybe I need more sleep.

No one in the house because of the holiday. Heaven. Just Milt and me. Great. No cooking. We eat at the Strauses. Turkey and all the rest. I love it.

I miss my mother, but today I don't miss Queens Village, and certainly not all the tension of those days. My life has been so much better than hers, so much calmer and more rewarding. I have my ups and downs, but I also have a husband who loves and cares about me, who is quiet and gentle, selfish and generous in the best ways. Who lets me be selfish and generous in turn.

After my mother lived with us for some years, Milt used to joke that if we ever got a divorce, I could have the house and the kids. He wanted custody of my mother. After my brother and Irene were divorced, it was Irene who still loved and saw my mother, not Mike. She did something right and I will too, if I can figure out what it was. □

PHYSICS

When people describe the 1920s and 1930s as the Golden Age of Physics, they are usually thinking of Einstein and Schrödinger and the subtle mysteries of quantum mechanics. But for some of us growing up then it was the twilight of a darker age of physics. Castor oil was one of the favorites. Parents believed physics would keep their children hale and healthy if they could just choke them down somehow.

Every month Jean and Mike were given a physic, usually Citric Magnesia or Milk of Magnesia. They preferred the Citric Magnesia, since there was a deposit on the bottles and they could take them back and collect the money after the medicine had taken effect. I was too young yet for the routine.

Nana, my mother's aunt who was like a grandmother to us, was also Mike's godmother, and she doted on him. That was fine with Jean and me. One of the ways she showed her devotion was to call every evening at dinnertime to find out whether his bowels had moved that day. She was the Aunt who kept a stock of Ex-Lax in the medicine cabinet, and it may have been her daily calls that inspired Mike to buy some Ex-Lax around the corner at the drugstore when he was twelve years old and feed it to half a dozen unsuspecting kids in the neighborhood.

Monthly purges were one of Grandma Primont's edicts. She could look to her own five children, all of whom had survived the regimen and showed every sign of a healthy, hearty adulthood. Grandma also encouraged an annual physic, akin to spring or fall cleaning, which involved a dose of castor oil. I only witnessed the ritual once, though I understand that in previous years only Jean, with her capacity for wanting to please, could get it down.

One October morning after I turned eight, Dad walked Mike, Jean, and me to the drugstore for a "chocolate soda." He gave the order to the druggist with a wink, and we were handed frothy chocolate sodas with a quarter-inch layer of castor oil floating just below the bubbles. I watched as Jean drank hers dutifully, eyes watering and face contorting when she got to the clear part. Mike gulped his down, and then ran out the front door almost spewing chocolate-colored castor oil over an astonished woman entering to buy a tin of tooth powder. I cried and refused to even touch the glass my father tried to hand me.

Embarrassed, Dad collected me, Jean, his change, and Mike

retching at the curb, and led us grim and bedraggled back to 213th Street to inform my mother that hereafter, spring or fall cleaning of insides was as much her province as the cleaning of closets. And that was the end of castor oil for us in our house.

I was the only one who escaped the dreaded purges since I couldn't get anything down my throat that I didn't like the taste of. Once they weaned me off CuFe-tone, that delicious ruby-red first tonic that was supposed to give me an enormous appetite and make me fat like the rest of the family, nothing that anyone said would be good for me was anything I would swallow.

The last day that an attempt was made to give me a physic, I retched unhappily over the kitchen sink as my mother tried to force a tablespoon of Milk of Magnesia down my throat. To show me how easy it was, she took one. Then Dad took one. I kept shaking my head "no" when asked if I wouldn't just try, just to please them. At this point, my father, his authority challenged, became impatient. "I've got to get to work. Give it to me and I'll give it to her upstairs." He took me by the hand, and not understanding the situation, said, "It'll be good for you. You'll like it."

We went into the bathroom and he opened the bottle top, poured the liquid into the tablespoon and moved it toward my mouth. I closed my lips tight, looking at his fat belly, near the second button on his vest. My head wagged no from side to side.

"Now come on," he said, for once irritated with me, "I haven't got all day."

From inside my closed mouth I made a "no" sound then groaned. I wasn't used to him frowning at me, so I opened my mouth a crack

"Open up." He pushed the spoon into my mouth. "It's good for you." And with an upward movement that tilted my head so that all the medicine slid in, he said, "See, Mother and I took some, and it wasn't so bad."

I tried to swallow, but it didn't work. With my eyes squeezed shut, my lips closed and my cheeks puffed out, I gagged, and with more force than one might expect from an eight-year-old, turned it into a jet spray of Milk of Magnesia. Dad tried to duck out of the way, but the bathroom was so small that even though he swung me away from him, his three-piece navy blue suit and maroon tie were covered with a fine spray of white droplets. The brown bathroom door was sprinkled white and the walls and floor were spotted.

"That wasn't nice." His voice was fierce, but he didn't open the bottle again. "You mustn't do things like that." He stomped downstairs and I heard him complaining in a bitter voice to my mother that he'd have to change his clothes and he'd be late for work.

The incident had a dampening effect on the frequency of physics for us kids. Bowels were talked about, but not often meddled with. Dad was a neat man who hated any kind of mess, and Mother was never enthusiastic about following his mother's advice about anything, so they let the matter drop.

Fortunately, the concept of purging for health began to go out of style. Years later, when Jean began to complain about pains in her left side, Mother, convinced that it was nothing more than constipation, first suggested a physic. But when Jean cried that she was too sick to take anything, Mother sent her to the doctor. On Monday evenings the doctor had office hours from six to eight, and since Monday was also the night of the weekly American Legion bingo game, Mother and Dad left me with a babysitter, and sent Jean and Mike off to Doctor Shanno's office.

Maybe Dad was the one who suggested that the Legion run bingo games as a way to make money, and that was why he got to sit up on the stage and call out the numbers, or maybe, bossy as he was, he just chose himself as the one to sit at the microphone every Monday reading the numbers pulled out of the rolling basket by some lesser light.

After a few friendly comments to the players out front, Dad started the games that evening. The aim of the Legion was to build a new clubhouse, something worthy of a patriotic organization, and Dad was ready to whip the town into shape with his bingo calling. Cooperative women played four cards at once to further this aim, and the building was getting closer each month.

The third game was nearing the end when a young man hurried to the stage signaling for Dad's attention. "Later, Joe, I'm almost finished."

"But, Walter."

"Not now, Joe."

People in the audience were restless. Only a few more numbers to go. The interruption was annoying. It was a big prize—twenty-five dollars— and they were concentrating on making their numbers come up.

The young man hopped up on the stage and whispered in Dad's ear, "The doctor called. Jean has to go to the hospital to have her appendix out."

Dad jumped up from the table and ran off the stage without an explanation. That was upsetting enough to the audience, but they shouted and groaned with dismay when the table got up with him. It turned on its side with a crash, dumping the basket of balls and the master card with the record of the numbers already called. There was mutiny in the audience.

People were yelling. "I had everything but G4...I2...B3..."

"Where did he go?"

"What's the matter? Did somebody die?"

"Why the hell did he throw the table over?"

"He should be more careful."

"It's a swindle."

Many of them stood, the better to yell at Jim Savell on the stage, who now knew what a lynch mob looked like. All the greed and competition of gamblers, the hope of something for nothing, came out in ugliness on a lot of those faces. Paranoia bloomed in those who felt cheated by the people in power. It was a direct insult and affront to everyone who was sure he would have won that game.

Jim tried to quiet them down with his soft Southern voice. He'd have done better to sing a song. Music, rather than reason, might have soothed them more quickly. "Now folks, you know Walter Primont wouldn't leave a bingo game like that if he didn't have to."

"Yeah, well, if that's so, why did he dump everything?" screamed a fishwife in the second row.

"Well," Jim said, embroidering a little, "he just heard that his daughter, Jean, is in the hospital. She has to have her appendix out."

"No kidding."

"That's still no excuse."

"Now we don't know who won."

"How can we figure out what numbers were called?"

Jim carried on bravely, voice quivering slightly, for he was a tender-hearted man and he was thinking of Jean. "She's only fawteen folks and ah guess he got extra excited about it."

Five other Legionnaires were trying to thrust the balls recovered from the floor and front rows back into the basket. One of them grabbed the mike and in a loud, upbeat voice tried to coax the audience back into a semblance of docility. "It's alright now everybody, as soon as we check to see if all the balls are here, we're going to continue. We'll start a new game and the prize this time will be fifty dollars instead of twenty-five. How's that? I'll call the numbers. I won't do as good a job as Walter" —there were a few boos from the back— "but I promise I won't dump the table."

"Hurry up."

"Get on with the game."

"Is the kid alright?"

"If we hear anything, we'll let you know."

"Get on with the game."

"Okay, first number—B5."

Meanwhile, Walter, in a state of empathic misery, was being driven by Vic Chavoushian to the doctor's office to pick up Jean and take her to the hospital. When Dad walked in and she saw his ashen face, she became frightened. She and Vic helped him out to the car, where he leaned his head limply against the window. He refused to acknowledge his own aches and pains—wouldn't have a cold, got out of bed the third day of a bout with pneumonia to go to work—but when someone else in the family was sick or in pain, he collapsed into helpless infancy.

My mother, who'd gone directly to the hospital to start organizing things, met them in the admitting office. She immediately took charge of the situation, answering the clerk's questions, reassuring Jean, and ordering Vic to get coffee for Dad while she propped him up in a chair in the waiting room.

His eyes were filled with tears for Jean. The thought of someone using a knife on her made him weak and sick. They told Jean it wouldn't hurt at all, assuring her that her only problem would be trying not to laugh at the jokes her visitors would tell after the operation was over, so she went into surgery blithely, worrying only about whether she would get into trouble for not having completed her homework. The next day she lay in bed, raging with anger at the pain, furious with them all for lying to her.

She had lots of visitors. A good number of the Legion membership seemed determined to make at least one visit if not two. Kids brought candy and flowers, and then presents began to arrive from bingo players, possibly sorry now for their lack of consideration for her health. The woman who won the fifty-dollar game sent Jean a box of candy with a note saying that her appendix brought the donor great good luck and she felt a need to express her thanks.

It gave Jean pleasure to relate to people that her mother might have killed her with a physic if she hadn't felt so sick she couldn't take it. The doctor had said so. The doctor also convinced Mother and Dad that physics were a thing of the past and not necessarily good for health, no matter what Grandma Primont or the advertisements said. So there were no more ritual purges. Citric Magnesia was a bad memory and the company that made Phillips' Milk of Magnesia had to survive without our support. A gentle, natural laxative called Serutan (natures spelled backwards the ads said) became the solution, almost guaranteed not to burst an appendix, possibly not even to work. Nana called every evening right up to the time Mike enlisted in the Navy to go fight in World War II and still kept a supply of Ex-Lax in the medicine cabinet, because one never knew when one might want a bit of chocolate, and taking it in medicine form seemed so much less sinful.□

MY DEAREST MILT

It seems strange to be addressing a letter to you when you're just downstairs and I'm up here in my office.... I want you to know that I have loved you from almost the first night that we met, certainly from the first night that we kissed. No one else has ever interested me from that time to this. Your love and goodness to me has made my life worth living. Our child, whom we gave life to, and my child, whom you adopted, my mother, whom you took to your heart, and your parents, whom we both cared for, these are the people we have shared. All the music, the ideas, the hopes and dreams, laughs and pain, they were all part of our life together.

My life with you was more than I could ever have thought possible to have. When I think of you, I think of you coming toward me, with love in your eyes, the way you did all those years ago, crossing Eighth Street and Sixth Avenue, in your beautiful new clothes from Bloomingdale's, daffodils in your hand, and a smile just for me. That's the image of you that I have inside me, always ready to comfort and warm me.

All the wonderful moments of bliss, moments of tragedy, the plain ordinariness of all the everydays we had together. I wouldn't give up any of them. Think of love, sex, ice cream, conquering the subjunctive, kissing, baked potatoes, lurid mysteries, Puccini, Verdi, and even me learning finally to like some Wagner.

We've been so lucky, Milt, to have each other. I wrote a poem once that went

> I think of him not
> because he has given
> me pleasure
> He makes pleasure
> possible

I could have better used the word love instead of pleasure. You have made love possible for me when possibly no one else could.□

GROWING UP

I was thinking, first, about how I appear to Andy. Then, how I wish I could speak to the Andy who was sixteen. We could say so many things to each other back then. And I questioned how I appear to myself. What am I? Am I a noticer, an information gatherer, a collator of disparate facts? I think I'm more than that. But do we know what we are, ever? I think what I am, at my best, is a good connector of experienced information. I think I have the spirit of an academic, without the position, dedication, or qualifications. I love to talk and think about subjects I'm interested in, but I don't always have someone around who's interested in the same things.

I wonder what I would have been if I'd grown up in a family and in a milieu that believed a woman could do anything she wanted? Maybe I'd be just what I am. When I was a little girl, I wanted to be a mother. I remember being no more than about three, walking down 213th Street behind my mother and her friend Vera, pushing my straw doll carriage and knowing that's what I'd do when I grew up. I'd be like my mother.

When I was five, on the annual trip to Macy's toy department at Christmas, I picked out a red fire engine big enough to ride around in and asked Santa to bring me that. My mother and father pointed out dolls and other toys, but I kept on insisting I wanted the fire engine. I found it in a box in the garage two days before the holiday, assembled it, and horrified my mother by showing up in the street with it. She wasn't impressed with my mechanical ability. She was mechanically inclined. But my father was impressed. He couldn't put the simplest mechanical thing together, and I'd saved him from certain defeat on Christmas Eve.

When I was nine I wanted to be a pilot. I asked my parents to buy me a red-and-white metal airplane in the window of the candy store around the corner, but they laughed. And their friends laughed. My sister and brother made fun of me. "What do you want that for? Girls don't play with airplanes." Finally, a boy named Frank who my sister was dating bought the plane for me for Christmas. I loved it.

Then I wanted to be a painter. An artist. They really laughed at that. The only blank papers I had at home to draw on were the blank sheets at the beginning and the end of books, so all my books started and ended with drawings—always of people. Each Friday in school, we were given a sheet of paper to draw on. Anyone who finished quickly and did a good drawing was given a second sheet. Friday was the only good day in school for me, the only day I succeeded in pleasing my teachers. I think I was once given a third sheet—in eight years—but I don't remember that I did three "good" drawings that day. My teachers moaned about my handwriting and complained that if I could draw so well, I should be able to apply myself and write legibly.

My family called me "temperamental" with a sneer. I don't think they knew what the word meant. I think they thought it meant different. And different meant somehow bad.

At ten, inspired by the film credits of the Westmores, I decided I wanted to be a makeup artist. I would paint the faces of movie stars someday, and to get started, I spent whatever money I had left over from candy dots and Milk Duds on lipstick, rouge, and eyebrow pencils at Woolworth's, and painted the kids on the block who would stand still long enough. Periodically, my mother received inflamed telephone complaints from mothers who felt I was corrupting their children.

At fourteen, I entered high school, a girls' Catholic school dedicated to turning out secretaries, bookkeepers, file clerks, and obedient errand-running kowtowers to male bosses. No teacher ever suggested that a woman might be a boss. I still couldn't write legibly. I graduated typing less than five words per minute. I could add, subtract, multiply but not divide, and couldn't manipulate numbers that included sevens and eights. It took three years to convince the nuns to let me take an art class because, in spite of my obvious flaws secretarially, medically, and clerically, I was considered too smart to waste my time fiddling around in the art room.

At eighteen, I graduated, an incompetent office, shall I say, worker, destined to displease, with no idea that I could do anything but mark time until I became a wife and mother.

I may not have been able to type at first, but gradually I got better. My favorite boss was a lawyer who somewhere in the third or fourth week of my employment carried my typewriter back into his room to finish something I was making a mess of. I stayed with him off and on for nine years. I'm sure the reason he kept me in his employ was because he liked to teach me about the law, and when he made mistakes dictating contracts, I understood enough of what he was saying to catch them for him. Between us, we made a good team. Neither of us liked to work too hard, and we were both addicted to Shrafft's chocolate ice cream sodas.

The only thing I did well, really well, was read. The first long book I read was one of my sister's, *The Message in the Hollow Oak*. I was eight years old. It was a Nancy Drew mystery and the beginning of my love for books. When my mother saw how much I enjoyed it, she gave me all of her books from her childhood by L.M. Montgomery. I read them over and over again, taking time in between to read all the Judy Boltons, Nancy Drews, and other girls' series. I had my own library by the time I was eleven, and had exhausted my collection, but it didn't stop me. In seventh grade, I upset my nice teacher, my favorite in all of grammar school, Sister Theresa Julie, by switching from girls' to boys' books, finishing *Bomba, the Jungle Boy* series and starting on Edgar Rice Burroughs.

I had a hard time at the public library. There were inflexible rules in Queens Village in those days, and children of twelve were not allowed in the adult section. At twelve, I read a Zane Grey book, and that was the end of the children's section for me. The romance of the great western skies was what I had to have. My mother took them out for me, with the librarian giving us dirty looks. At thirteen I was allowed to take out books from the adult section, if the librarian thought they were not too daring.

At fourteen, I discovered romance. Romance discovered me. I read *Gone with the Wind* from cover to cover for a whole year, and then the next year it was *The Sun Is My Undoing*. My mother was a Book-of-the-Month Club member, so there were other things around to read, but whatever they were, they didn't make much of an impression until at fifteen I read something pretty raunchy (for those days) by Faulkner, and mother started keeping her books out of sight.

My reading was undirected, often erratic, until I went to The Cooper Union, where for the first time I heard names like Proust and Joyce and Henry James. I just read whatever fell into my hands.□

June 25, 1991
Talloires, France

Dear Dorothy and Leonard,
Here goes my annual letter. How are you? How is the baby? She must be getting cuter and cuter every minute.

We had Elizabeth with us for the first two and a half weeks that we were here. She was in her parrot stage and repeated anything we said, so she charmed the socks off of everyone in town by saying, "Bonjour monsieur, merci, s'il vous plait, croissant, garçon." You name it, she'd say it. She calls me Nana and Milt, Grandaddyo! Naturally it sounds great to us, but in the abstract, a little silly, I guess.

Since then I've talked to her on the phone and she's learned to say NO very emphatically to everything she's asked except, "Are you a big girl?"

The house is very comfortable this year. Thank heavens we brought Alicia with us. She turned out to be such a huge help that for the first time I enjoyed a visit with my children here without being exhausted by household complications.

So far I've been doing all the cooking, with a little assistance from Alicia, and we've been eating mostly vegetarian meals at home. Lots of soup. Chez Père Bise, the story is different. There we eat what we want. Milt is really enjoying the way we're eating at home and raves about bean salads and good bread with a minimum of margarine and a modicum of cheese. He may just be a reformed character.

How are the renovations going? I wish I could give you some of my enthusiasm for new spaces. It always gives me a lift to change things around and see things with new eyes. I'm almost sorry there's nothing more to be done to our place, though I'm sure Milt isn't.

I seem to have found a new career. I'm trying very hard to correct Alicia's English. The other day at lunch we took turns practicing verbs, me in French, Alicia in English, and Milt in Spanish. Then in the late afternoon, Assunta and I go down to the Auberge and she reads to me, again in English. I hope there's an angel up there somewhere recording all this, but just in case there isn't, I might have something delicious to reward myself with—a career as an English teacher...

The other night, for the first time since we arrived, I played a game of solitaire. Then I played another. Then another. And another. So I'm on my vacation. It's only taken how many weeks to relax enough to finally get here and settle down to vacation play? God bless my puritanical upstate farmhand ancestors and their long-lasting legacies. And that's after spending fourteen years living in California...

Milt has started driving around sightseeing in the last two weeks. (And that's after twenty years of coming here for vacations, speaking of slow starters). Last week he took Marian, her sister-in-law Connie, and Alicia to Mt. Blanc, while I stayed home and relaxed in the delicious silence. Maybe that's what started me on the solitaire. Marian's visit was a big success and we loved having her here. Connie was pretty shy, but extremely pleasant and nice to have around. Alicia did everything but the cooking, and I talked my head off after six weeks of no meaningless gossip in English. It was great.

Assunta and Jacques both send their best wishes—something to do with "amitiés," which I think means love or at least very strong friendly feelings. Another five years and I may be able to rattle those little French phrases off myself and actually know what I'm talking about.

In the meantime—*bonne journée,* and lots of love,
Rosemary

TALLOIRES 3

My head is ringing
avant, après, bonjour
fuddled by light wine
rouge et blanc
and incomprehensible questions
about my day, *ça va*

And the mountains thrust
their glory outside my window
worshipping
gris and cold the clouds
that cling

And *mon fils,* he waves
from the lake, over blue
and green beauty as he leaves me
for tomorrow

Et mon mari. He reads
a roman he would scorn
en anglais, hélas

July 17, 1991
Talloires, France

Dear Michael,
I've been thinking about you a lot in these last few weeks. It must be the return to Talloires. I'm feeling very well—much better than all winter. I'm psyching myself out of paying attention to my heart and its vagaries. If I have ten days, or ten years, to live, I might as well enjoy them without the constant attention to what I can't change.
    With Alicia here to do all the work that I normally feel pressured to do, I'm able to cook and read and just fool around

most of the time. It's given me time to find myself again in a good way. Fortunately, she is very nice and exceptionally discreet and intelligent, so it works very well. I thought we'd have her eat lunch with us and then eat dinner by ourselves, but after the first day I decided I couldn't do that. I just don't have it in me and she's nice, so we eat ensemble and it's just fine. The thought of her here in a country where she doesn't speak the language, and doesn't know anyone but us, was more than my conscience could tolerate, so we've become her family while she's away from her own. She's taking French lessons twice a week from Babette and loving it.

We had a wonderful visit with Jenny, Richard, and Elizabeth, who became the hit of Talloires when she learned to say "Bonjour, Monsieur Duclos" each morning when we went down for breakfast at the Salon de Thé. She repeats everything you say to her, and even caught on to saying "ça va" when he said it to her and almost charmed him out of his wits. I must say, she's pretty cute, and very good. And Jenny and I got along marvelously well...

I'm thinking of our mutual life together starting with me at eighteen and you at zero plus. We have happened into each other's existence at such good moments and stages. You were there in time for my first maternal urges to be awakened, just in time for me to practice combining my instinct with my little book learning about bringing up children, and I was there to love and listen to you with all my energy and love.

Then we met again when you were in your twenties and I in my forties. We both needed family that loved and listened again. You, because you were young and becoming an adult, and me because of losing Nana, and with her all my ties to my past family.

It's funny; we're changing, or have changed again. You're the adult now. You're the age I was when we found each other again in London, and I'm almost the age that Nana was when she came to live with Milt and me, going into another stage of life. One of pulling back, lying down to rest. A little out of the race. With a need to think, but only sometimes. A need to accept and stop struggling.

I won't know for six months, when and if I reread this, whether I've said anything at all. There's something to say, but I'm not sure I even recognize it yet.

I'm sorry about Colleen, but it sounds as if you were right. Too much talk is too exhausting. That's for younger years and other times. But most women need to talk a lot more than men. They like to confront problems and talk them out. Most men don't. There are even physiological reasons why men don't and women do. Somehow, with age, Milt and I have reached a middle ground. I don't need to talk things into the ground and he's now able to talk—minimally.

Love,
Rosemary

August 17, 1991
Talloires, France

Dear Dorothy,
I came across the enclosed passage from García Márquez the other day, and it's so beautifully expressed that I didn't want to put it aside without passing it on to you. I don't think I've read a more perfect description of a long-time good marriage. It's something Milt and I have tried to put into words to each other over the last few years without ever having said it nearly so well. I thought you might like it.

How is the renovation, or should I not ask? We'll see you at the end of next month.

Rosemary

She clung to her husband. And it was just at the time when he needed her most, because he suffered the disadvantage of being ten years ahead of her as he stumbled alone through the mists of old age, with the even greater disadvantage of being a man and weaker than she was. In the end they knew each other so well that by the time they had been married for thirty years they were like a single divided being, and they felt uncomfortable at the frequency with which they guessed each other's thoughts without intending to, or the ridiculous accident of one of them anticipating in public what the other was going to say. Together they had overcome the reciprocal nastiness and fabulous flashes of glory in the conjugal conspiracy. It was the time when they loved each other best, without hurry or excess, when both were most conscious of and grateful for their incredible victories over adversity. Life would still present them with other mortal trials, of course, but that no longer mattered: they were on the other shore.

-Gabriel García Márquez, *Love in the Time of Cholera*

ON BEING AN ARTIST

Strange December. I feel an overwhelming need to create something. I want to redecorate my nest. I want to see new things, new colors, and new shapes. I have the urge to make something beautiful.

In passing over the newspaper this evening, I caught a glimpse of a gallery ad for a painting of a nude, and I could smell the paint and feel the texture of it on the canvas. I wanted to be painting it myself.

The other day I told Jenny that I have the talents and instincts of an artist without the dedication and drive, without even the ambition and aspiration. Funny how many people you meet in your life who have no talent or aptitude for art, who have all the aspirations and even dedication, but whose output is no more than pretense and delusion.

Maybe they are lucky. I have just enough of the talent, urge, and instinct to feel pain at my failure to fulfill, my lack of dedication, and the fading of my life without being able to point to something that satisfied me fully, just once...

But in me somewhere, I feel this love of color and form and thought and sound, and I have no way to express it. Let the shell melt, Rosemary. Come out, come out, wherever you are. You're coming to the HOME FREE ALL.□

Journal
November 30, 1991
California

It seems years since I've written anything but names and addresses into the Rolodex and a new guide to TV stations. That and thinking about my health are about all that's been of concern. What a narrow way to live. I've been slowly boring myself to death. And probably everyone else around me.

I must change. Maybe I am changing. Maybe I have changed.

Jenny, Richard and Lizzie are here, along with the nanny Zoe, and Mavis, the ex-waitress from the Beverly Hills Hotel. All in all, a very full house out there in the extension. That extension has seen a lot of phases. There were Leah and Will and the army of incompetent, well-and-ill-meaning practical and not so practical nurses. Then came the emptiness for a while, then Michael licking his wounds and trying to find a new life for himself. Michael helped me while he was helping himself while I was helping him. He likes me. He made me feel likeable. I was his Aunt Mitzi who used to hug and kiss him and read stories to him, listen to him when he was happy or unhappy, and he was my nephew Michael, whom I once adored, who made me want children of my own to love. We were family together. He was my only relative left that I felt a kinship with. I love his brother Peter, but we probably don't understand each other at all.

Then came the renovation and the unused sports equipment, the sauna, etc., Peter, Sheila, Brook, and Murray, Assunta, Jenny, Richard and Lizzie.

Now a new incarnation. Full-fledged, four-bedroom apartment, stocked by family and help, new tables, chairs and dishes, commotion and life.

And I'm enjoying it. Jenny has grown up. She has a beautiful child, a loving husband, her career, and help. And now she lets us love her. She is to us now the person she has probably been to the rest of her friends for years.

I try not to wonder why she disliked or hated me for all those years, and just accept her for how she acts today. Maybe that's a part of why I don't want to write. I wrote so much of my pain for so long that I'm afraid it might spill out.

There's something about how I'm feeling now that reminds me of how I used to act around Jean. Dull, covered in gray fog. Distanced by opacity. Hidden behind the thick wall.

I'm bored by myself and by the people I know. They're nice, but I need some other stimulation that I don't have. I need to care about something and I don't. I don't care about writing any more. That's one problem.

I'm not a writer. Now I know why I could never call myself one. Like never calling myself a painter. I'm not one. I have all the needs of an artist without the drive and dedication. I have talent I don't use. I don't value myself, because to a great extent I live in the eyes of others. When there's no recognition there's no Rosemary. Part of the problem is the people I'm associating with. Probably nothing wrong with them and nothing wrong with me. We just have different interests. We moved to the wrong neighborhood when we came to California. And I've lost a big part of my life to it. I needed a less affluent community, and more reading. In order to be part of it even to a small extent, I've lost whatever it was that I was. I feel like Hoffman after he loses his reflection.

For some reason, I'm thinking of a woman named Lily Waters back in Queens Village. She was a friend of Aunt Vera and lived over the other side of the railroad track near 212th Street. She had messy hair and a parrot in a cage covered by a fringed black silk Spanish shawl with red, orange, and yellow flowers. My mother and I went along with Aunt Vera to have tea at Lily's house one day. She was very friendly and smiley but she looked as if she knew something we didn't, and it amused her. I'd heard my father say disparaging things about Lily, not unusual for him as he spoke that way about many people. I think it was the parrot and the shawl that got to him, but it may have been the state of her house and her clothes. They were as messy as her hair, and made little concession to community standards as the parrot did to performance on demand.

I thought she was fascinating. She seemed so mysterious with her funny way of talking and her secret laughter. I remember the china dishes she used for tea were colorful but chipped. I loved the colors of the parrot, though I'd have liked him even better stuffed. And I was excited by the Spanish shawl. It was so different from anything else I'd ever seen, foreign, exotic, gorgeously garish.

I wonder how other people in Queens Village saw her? I think she was a widow of a World War I veteran and a member of the American Legion, which would have been where my father knew her from and why he figured he could make pronouncements about her. I think she may have been a little eccentric, or a lot eccentric. In any case she didn't fit in, which may be why I'm thinking of her at this moment.

In order to fit in, I feel as if I've gotten rid of my Spanish shawl and parrot, I've washed the tea cups, and stopped smiling. And I hate it. Nobody has asked me to do it. I've done it of my own accord. Nobody to blame but myself. And I'm bored. And I don't know how to find my way out of conformity and blahness.

Shit!□

December 14, 1991
Alpine Drive, Beverly Hills

Dear Rose,
I know I sent you a Christmas card but this can be another missive to wish you a Merry Christmas and a Happy New Year. As I typed I could hear the melody of "We Wish You a Merry Christmas." Weird. It was as if I were typing on a musical instrument...

How are you my friend? I'm feeling rushed and a little harried, what with all the extra warm bodies in the house. Strangely enough, we seem to be adjusting very well, and Lizzie is a treasure.

Let me describe a typical day for Jennifer. She awakens at four o'clock in the morning and works (in her office, which is Andy's old bedroom minus the bed), talking to people in England and to her assistant there, until seven-thirty or eight when the baby wakes up. She takes care of Lizzie until nine, when the nanny takes over. About ten-thirty she piles the nanny and Lizzie into the car, and they go somewhere, to the park, a baby play group, or shopping. Then they eat lunch, either in or out. The baby goes to bed and Jenny works some more or goes out to her lab or gallery, then comes back by three and crashes for an hour or so, then takes the baby and nanny back out—not because they need it so much but because I suspect perhaps she needs it. They come back, and she crashes again. Then perhaps she and Richard go out for dinner or eat with us, and she goes to bed around eight or nine. It's all done nonstop. She lives and works the way she always has. She has a physical drive I can't comprehend. Milt says he's tried to talk to her about taking it easy, but he doesn't think she can comprehend that.

I try to mind my own business as much as I can and restrict myself to enjoying them all as much as I can. So far—all pleasure.
Love,
Rosemary

AN IMPOSSIBLE TASK

I must sit down and write, if only one sentence each day that has some meaning to me...

I cannot write about Rose because I cannot face her illness and soon death. I cannot write about my own illnesses, because I cannot face how many hours of my life I have wasted, and writing about my heart makes the contrast with my healthy years seem like a life almost lost.

And these are the months and years I might have wanted to write about. There are Lizzie and little Will, Julia, Andy, Jenny, Richard, and always my love, Milt. New feelings, good feelings, and, alas, sometimes, no feelings.

Tonight I'm going to the Heart Lifestyle group—boring dinner and group therapy with a bunch of heart patients. I enjoy these evenings so far. They make me feel not so alone with my unhappiness and fears. The only things I don't like about them are the plumber, that crazy bigot, whatever his name is, and the food. The group by and large is interesting and supportive, and I get a lot out of it.

The plumber—a short, round-headed, tough-skinned, mainly bald little man, smug in his ugly way that he survived Hitler's camps and Stalin's oppression—not inconsiderable feats—and religious in a simple, stolid, sanctimonious way—always, "I don't understand why people do this, do that, do the other, I never do that, never feel that, don't have the time for such luxury." I want to like him. I tell myself he's a simple man. But the truth is I don't like him.

Well, you can't make yourself like someone just because perhaps they deserve something extra after the bad things in life. You can wish them luck. Make your smile a little larger. Wave hello with your hand. And wish either you, or they, were someplace else.☐

CROSSROAD

"C'mon." My father held out his hand to me where I was sitting on the front steps. "Let's go around to the Hebe's for the papers. You can have a Popsicle." I tried to think of a reason not to go with him, one that would satisfy. "I have to do my homework," I lied. I never did any homework. I don't know why the nuns never said anything to my parents about it, but they didn't. I suppose it was because I wasn't failing anything so what was there to talk about?

"Homework! You can do it later. This'll only take a couple of minutes."

"Momma said I should do it now."

He laughed. "Forget the homework. I said you could come." Cheerful at having gotten his way, and happy to have found such convenient company, he took my hand and forced me to accompany him on yet another trip to the candy store to witness his continuing torture of its owner.

I walked slowly, and Dad, who shared the family fear that because I was so thin, I was doomed to consumption, thought immediately of my health, and asked, "Are you okay? Do you feel well? Okay, then walk a little faster. You want that ice cream, don't you?"

"I think I don't. Maybe I'll go back."

I started to disengage my hand from his as he sulked and said, "Don't you want to go with me? We're almost there."

"Please, don't argue with Mr. Sweigenbaum, Daddy."

He looked at me in surprise. As far as he was concerned, Abe Sweigenbaum deserved to be berated publicly for his slovenliness, and since my father didn't mind the job, he would do it. He spoke in a gruff voice, "What's it matter?"

"I hate it when you argue with people."

"Okay. Okay." We rounded the corner, Dad glum now, his steps heavy on the pavement and me hurrying to keep up with him.

Abe was a little man, his round head almost bald with grizzled tufts at the ears. His hands were stained from the ink of thousands of daily papers, and he wore a seldom-washed smock over his clothes, making change all day from its pockets. Though he had been in the country for years, his accent was still thick in his mouth.

The store was just a cutout between two other stores, with a window full of dusty toys and cheap magazines. Everything was dirty, the candy counter marked with children's fingerprints and the front windows hazy from lack of washing.

When we entered, Abe, his wife, and daughter were crowded in the back of the store. Mrs. Sweigenbaum muttered in Yiddish as Abe came forward, a false smile of hope on his face for a pleasant encounter with his least favorite customer. "What can I do?" he asked, looking warily up at my father as if expecting a gun or a club to appear.

"I'd like a paper, Abe, if you've got any," said Walter.

"I've got papers," Abe sighed.

"My daughter would like an ice cream."

I started toward the freezer and Abe's daughter Rosie heaved herself up from the canvas chair on which she was sitting. "I'll get it. Whaddyu want?" She was a fat girl of sixteen, with greasy hair and hands as grimy as her father's.

She was on her way to the freezer when my father said, "Your hands aren't clean." There was an expression of distaste on my father's face. "You don't want to touch food when they look like that. Let her get it herself."

"My hands are clean. If she wants an ice cream, I'll get it." Rosie hated my father. Abe's brown eyes narrowed with anger just held in check. Dad was a good customer. He might come in any time of the day or evening and buy fifteen kids ice cream, extras if somebody dropped one. Every penny counted.

"Rosie, the little girl will get it. Go ahead little girl." Abe nodded to me, and my appetite, never large, failed me by this time in the waves of hostility surging about the small shop. I moved to the door.

"The trouble with you, Abe, is you never clean this store. The place is filthy. Why don't you mop it once in a while?" Dad pointed to the corner. "Look at the floor. It's covered with junk. I'm surprised you get any customers, it's such a mess."

The little man held one hand in the other. "You're here, Mr. Primont. You come here. If it's so bad, why do you come in? Go get your papers someplace else." Abe was working himself up to his semi-annual rage at Dad, in which he would throw financial caution to the winds and invite him to spend his money elsewhere.

"Please, Dad, let's go." I tugged at his elbow. "I don't want ice cream."

He ignored me. "That's what's the matter with you Jews. Somebody tries to tell you something for your own good and you get angry. You can't take advice. I come here because I'm stuck with you. There's not another paper store for half a mile, and I don't see why you can't keep the joint clean for a change. It isn't decent. You sit here all day doing nothing. Then people have to wade through the dirt and you wanna know why they pick on you."

Mrs. Sweigenbaum and Rosie took their places a step in back of Abe. Rosie threw in a rude remark, while her mother contented herself with silent glowering.

We left the store without the papers or the ice cream. I hated it when my father argued with storekeepers, knowing afterward I'd hear him say, "Well, we won't buy anything in that place again."

"You said you wouldn't fight with him."

"I couldn't help it." He was the picture of abused innocence. "Did you see the place? It's filthy. They ought to close it down."

When he tried to take my hand for the walk home, I pulled it away. For the first time I made my dislike for him so evident that even he couldn't fail to see it. He was hurt. "You're silly. What's it matter what that slob thinks anyway?"

I walked next to him, head down, gray blocks of cement passing under my feet, thinking, I hate him. I wish I were somebody else. Then I wouldn't be his daughter, and saying aloud, "I'm going to Mary's for lunch." It wasn't true, but I wanted to get away from him. The corners of his mouth were down. If only the world could understand him, his face said. Why did everyone get so mad, when all he did was point out the truth that was right in front of their eyes? "Suit yourself." His feet were heavy on the pavement.

Ten steps further he said he was going to listen to the ballgame. Fifteen more steps and he remembered the leg of lamb in the refrigerator. He laughed. "Maybe I can talk your mother out of a few bites of last night's lamb for a sandwich while I listen. That guy Durocher thinks the Dodgers are going to win today, and I need a little nourishment to keep me going while the Giants mop the joint up with him."

I turned in at Mary's front walk and went into the house without speaking.▫

Journal
July 22, 1992
Alpine Drive, Beverly Hills

When you can't do anything right, stop trying. You might as well give up immediately, go to bed, sleep, get up the next day, and do something else. Screw it. It's not worth the effort.

I love having the second floor to just myself and Milt. I can come up here and do what I want. No one making faces. No one to irritate or be irritated by.

I must calm down and stop caring. The problem with thick-skinned people is that the things they say and do never disturb them. Only the thin-skinned around them are disturbed and unhappy and depressed. Upset.

That's me—disturbed, unhappy, and depressed.

Is that why I woke up unwell this morning? Probably not. Is that why I'm going to bed somewhat miserable and discontented tonight? Definitely yes.

I still don't feel well.

I must concentrate on the fun we had this evening. On how much I like Morty and Iris. On how much I love Milt. And oh how much he loves me.

And then I must go to sleep and rest and hope that tomorrow will be better than today. □

MEMORY

I thought that in music
and the fine black lines
of a moment in space
I would find life

but I don't believe it any more
than I believe
in the grand passion
of my dreaming virginity
or the divine moment
of insight
that would make me real

There is only memory
of the moments when we were
somehow somewhere

September 16, 1992
Talloires, France

Dear Michael,

Why does France always remind me so much of you? Not because of your stay at Taizé; that only registered to me in a way. You were still you to me and Taizé was just a place over to the left of Talloires. No, I think it's because the dirt and pebbles and gray stucco buildings of Talloires remind me of Hollis and Queens Village and my childhood, and your childhood was part of the end of mine. I find myself talking to you in my mind.

It's as if my imagination has been set free again after years of intense, inward, physical unease, and I feel free to let the world fall into all its pieces around me to be sorted out and tied together in whatever way strikes me as interesting—and who better to understand the connections than you.

Milt and I are having a wonderful time just doing any silly unimportant things that come to mind. Let's go sit down at the lake and have hot chocolate. Lunch at a new brasserie on the Rue du Sommelier. Dinner on the other side of the lake. Watch CNN. Do the crossword. Take that road over there. Pick out vegetables. Look up a word in the dictionary. Look at the sunset. Take a nap. Sleep a little longer this morning. Look at the stars. Talk to a cat.

I think two years of feeling ill have convinced me that I might as well smell the daisies while I can. Why did it take me so long? All those nuns telling me that Jesus died on the cross because I committed sins. My Aunt Nana making every pleasure seem undeserved. You may have been brushed lightly by Catholicism in your childhood, but your being was protected by a Mother with a huge smile who was probably pagan and thought you deserved every pleasure that came your way.

I wish you were here with us, and I'm sure you wish it too. It's quiet, serene, and today sunny, and we spent our morning trying (after five years of fumbling clumsily with appareils) to figure out the internal magic of our telephone system with the help of Pierre Chatelain, who is the godfather of our house and key catalyst for things that need to be done. The young man, who came from the company that sold us the telephones in the first place, spoke enough English, thank God—the good God, not the one who watches for my least infraction—to explain some of the mysterious workings of the French federal laws that prevent one from having a simple system that allows more than three phones to be connected on the same number simply by picking up any extension and talking at the same time. No, it's necessary to use a system of answering a call on one line and then transferring the call by pressing the number of the extension desired and hoping the person you expect to be at that extension is near enough to pick it up in twenty seconds, because after that time you lose the call, the caller, your temper, and possibly your sanity if you're at a busy extension. I am waiting to see how Milt manages to transfer a call (that he picks up lying down in his bedroom on the far side of the bed) to himself downstairs, where his papers are on his desk in the office. It's a very low bed and he's a very large man. I guess the thing will be for him to stand up first, get in the on-your-mark, get-ready, get-set position, then push the buttons and go as fast as he can without tripping on the stairs in his stocking feet, for he won't have his shoes on in bed I presume.

After that we drove to Albertville, last seen under a few inches of snow during the Olympics, to a restaurant that Assunta and I once went to that has at least one Michelin star and used to be pretty traditional. The ride was beautiful, the mountains beginning to change color, and we saw Mont Blanc for part of the way along the route. Our choices for lunch were not the best. I really don't like fish that has had any treatment other than grilling, sautéing, or poaching. In other words, I like fish unadorned and unencumbered, not sauced and flavored and surrounded by minute bits and pieces of cuisine minceur decorations pretending to be food. And poor Milt, his first course was something that sounded like soup with filet of sole, truffles, and the eggs of some bird but turned out to be four rather uncompromisingly rolled-up filets of sole, some shreds of truffles, and three or four smallish poached eggs of undetermined parentage and almost no broth, which was what he thought he was getting. His next course was small rolled-up portions of crab, langoustines, and crayfish (one of which fell off his smallish fish fork under the table) with teensy shreds of carrots and a few wispy leaves of tangy lettuce. It seemed so sad to see someone who was manfully trying to widen his eating repertoire of fish species dealing with stuff (even one-star stuff) that would have pleased a dieting Beverly Hills matron. However, dessert made up for the early shortcomings, and we saw Mont Blanc on the way back. When we got home I tested my blood sugar, which, despite eating a small portion of nut cake with sugar icing, was normal.

In the late afternoon we went down and sat by the lake at the Auberge drinking hot chocolate and coffee, me reading *The Herald Tribune* and Milt a book in French. The lake was calm and blue, and we had an hour or two of perfection.

And today all the polls seem to show that Clinton is doing well and Bush not so well, so we were in a mood to enjoy it all. The telephone chaos as I described it may have sounded irritating or depressing but it wasn't. It felt as if we had won a battle over incomprehensible electronic superiority, which set us up to enjoy the rest of the day no matter what.

I read a quote from one of Elie Wiesel's books about a man who went around for years trying to change the world to no avail. Toward the end he was shouting his ideas and no one was listening, and a small boy asked him why he bothered. He answered that he knew he couldn't change the world, but he kept on shouting so that the world wouldn't change him.

I hope we see you soon.

       Love,
       Rosemary

          December 8, 1992
          Alpine Drive, Beverly Hills

Dear Assunta,

I picture you on high (*Jet'imagine en haut*) in the snow and sunshine, and I envy you the beauty that you live in, if not the road you must take to get to it.

I spent a week in New York at the Randolphs so that I could see a dear friend, Rose Reitter, who is very ill, and who lives near them. It was a sad week, as I was with her nearly every day. I think it may be the last time I will see her. Rose and I met when she moved into the building where Milt and I lived the first year of our marriage. We have been friends through our early ups and downs (good times and bad) and over the years with husbands, parents, children, homes, dogs, cats, poetry, painting, pottery, books, and now this.

Someone said that cancer is one disease where you do your mourning before someone dies, and I think that must be almost true. I wish that she could go to sleep one evening in a peaceful frame of mind and just not wake up.

I think that perhaps Paula is correct in thinking that Canada would be a better place to move to. Unemployment is so high here at the moment that finding work would be very difficult. Also, if I were emigrating from another country, I might choose Canada over the United States. There are things in the Canadian character that I like. I think perhaps the pace is slower, and because the country is not a superpower, there is less of a superior/inferior mentality. The United States is always being criticized for doing too much or too little, and, who knows, maybe the criticism is deserved...

I'm already looking forward to our next stay in Talloires and missing your company greatly. Before I left Chappaqua on Saturday to come to Los Angeles, there were about two inches of snow that fell during the night and turned the world into a magic place and made me forget everything sad for a few moments. Then when I came home and looked at little Will, and he reached out for me with a smile, I couldn't help but be happy and know how wonderful life is sometimes, and feel how lucky I am.

               With much, much love,
               Rosemary

IT HURTS NOW

Every writer has to have a listener. Maybe that's why I've often only written letters. Most people like to get letters, and I know that someone I like will be happy to read the words I put on paper for them. If what I write is pleasant or humorous, they and I will enjoy it. I don't plan what I write beforehand. I write about whatever I'm thinking of at the moment, so in a way the letters are like a journal and I keep them the way I keep my journal.

Since Rose became ill with cancer I've had a hard time even writing letters. And I haven't written to her at all. I speak to her by phone. It would be too hard not to write truth to Rose. After people die, you can think, well, by and large she lived a good, satisfying life, but when they're dying, it's hard to see past the terrible part of what is happening.

That's how it was with Milt's father. I really loved Will. It would have been hard for anyone who lived with him not to love him. But all those long years of silent dying of Parkinson's became intolerable, and I couldn't think of him at all as good, intelligent, logical, kind, generous, loving Will, because that would have been intolerable. I could love him and take care of him, but I loved an ancient, invalided man who looked in on himself alone, and whose continued vegetative existence consisted only of the human need to breathe.

On the day of Will's funeral, it was as if everyone was free to love him for all the good things he was and for what he meant in their lives. It was a sunny day, and out under the trees in the cemetery a few people said what they felt about Will. Dan told about how Will first arrived in the United States after traveling from Russia by himself at the age of twelve, and how his boat had arrived two days early and no one was there to pick him up at Ellis Island. So the authorities kept him there for two days until a cousin came to get him. Will told Dan that he thought everyone had forgotten him. He said he would never forget the moment when they entered the railroad flat in Brooklyn where his father was staying, and at the far end of the apartment he could see his father crying, smiling at him, arms open to welcome him. Will said it was the happiest moment in his life. Somehow knowing he'd had that moment of joy was comforting to me, and I assume to Dan or he wouldn't have told it.

I try to think of Rose like that, but at the moment I can only think of her pain and how she wants to be with her family forever. My children are settled now with families of their own, but hers are younger and single and still closer to being the children they were. I know that after she dies I will remember the good days, but it's now that hurts.□

Journal
March 15, 1993
Alpine Drive, Beverly Hills

There are a few people back East whom I want to call today. I've been thinking about calling for a week or so, but now with the big snowstorm just over, it feels like the right moment.

I want to write something first. But what to write is more of a mystery than what to say...I got up at six-thirty and ate breakfast, with the intention of being in my office by seven-fifteen, but here I am, after eight, just beginning to warm up.

I spoke to Rose's friend Phyllis in New York yesterday, and Rose will probably die in the next few months. Phyllis said everyone expected her to die last month when she was in the hospital, but, in Phyllis's words, "she'd clearly bought herself another few months." It makes me remember how stunned I was when I realized that I would die someday, and then years later realized that it wasn't death I feared but dying. Then I watched my mother die and saw that it wasn't such a terrible thing for the dying if there is no pain, only for the people who will miss them.

I saw how when my mother knew she was dying she seemed almost relieved. Now it was over. Fear, unhappiness, loss, wanting, hoping—all the complications of living, with only caring for Jean and me still left. She was conscious but serene, her moments almost gone. She loved us but she was leaving and could say goodbye and she wasn't unhappy.

My father died a horrible death and my mother's was peaceful.

There are a lot of tears I haven't cried in the last few years because I've felt so terrible myself. Now that the medicine is working again and I have started to put words down on paper, I find myself weeping as memories of my mother come back. When I hold Will and Lizzie, I feel so close to her, and I wish so much she could see them. I know she would love them the way she did Andy and Jenny and Michael and Peter. It must be from my mother that I learned how to love. How sad not to have a mother who felt as she did. How sad not to understand that someone feels that way about you.□

THREE P.M.

When I came home each day
my mother met me
with arms wide open
like a great pink rose blooming
in front of the stucco house

She greeted me with apples
and vague questions about school
At her bidding I changed
into old clothes then we went
our ways till dinner

I remember
when I came home each day
my mother met me

WILL AT ONE

I just sat on my glasses...My reading (and writing) glasses. To what lengths will I go not to write. . .

I got up this morning about twenty to seven, determined to eat and run—into my office to type. It's now five after five, and having finished a day full of mostly trivia, ending with a half-watched program on the life of Ezra Pound while I did my hair and got dressed to go out for dinner, I am finally sitting down to try to put into words some of what I've thought today.

The only nontrivial thing I did was speak to Rose for a long time. She's going into the hospital tomorrow for more chemotherapy, and when I called she asked me to tell her something cheerful, so I launched into a description of dinner last night with the whole family, including Julia's parents. I guess I made it more convoluted and involved than it warranted but I knew she didn't want to be left to think. Recently she hasn't felt like talking because it tires her too much. Today was different. I know she is afraid of dying from the treatment. I wish I could be with her.

Will is going to be one-year-old tomorrow. Imperious, serious Will. I asked Julia's mother if there were any imperious (I refuse to use the word bossy) people on that side of the family, and she said no, not that she could think of. So I guess he gets it from my side of the family. It's interesting how much more objectively I can look at my grandchildren than I could look at my own children. I really couldn't see what they would be like, though I made some pretty good guesses.

Will has no discernable words yet to tell us what he wants, but he tells us anyway. With force, with determination, with outrage at our stupidity in not understanding him, with pleasure and appreciation when we're smart enough to know what he wants. Truly he is the great grandson of the five-year-old boy back in Hell's Kitchen in the year 1900, waving an American flag and shouting "Go home, you damn Yankees!" at soldiers marching in a parade.

Some babies whine for what they want. Some wail. Even at six months Will didn't plead with crying and tears, but commanded you to do as he wished. That characteristic wasn't evident for a while in the happy little body that only wanted nursing and food and holding and could always depend on someone to understand those wants. Now he wants so much more. He knows what he wants. Why don't we? We should, after all. His tone and body gestures say he WANTS IT, what's taking so long? He commands in a loud, hard tone, brooking no argument. He has spoken, loud and clear. I hear my father. I see his astonishment that anyone would question why, how, or what he wanted. Obviously, if he wanted it, it must have been right. This will be interesting to watch.☐

HERITAGE

Willed to the child the name of one
who would have loved him had they met
Gentle man of logic joined
to a small boy obsessed by trains and planes
Wheels of the ancient engineer transmuted
to love of Thomas and Claribel

And can the love that named him Will
bring ancestral gifts to brave another century
courage that led an immigrant boy of twelve
on the voyage alone to find a new home
goodness in manhood
wisdom in old age

And what's in a name?
What other grandfathers exert their wills
in hints of smiles and cantered gaits
as swift-footed this Will runs through his time,
creating his own logic
and making sense of his world

SISTER AGE
March 25, 1993

Happy birthday, little Will. My babies were very beautiful to look at when they were newborns. Andy was nine pounds and looked three months old, and Jenny had a whole head of dark brown hair that the nurses curled and waved so that the first time I saw her I thought she had naturally curly hair. I was pretty new to new babies then.

Little Will was so small and overwhelmed-looking that at first I didn't recognize him as one of the family. I wasn't feeling well when he was born and hadn't yet discovered that I had diabetes. That may have partly accounted for my feeling of strangeness. Also, I was in such bad shape I could hardly hold him for any length of time without getting shaky.

Here I am, as usual, saying it was all me, and it really wasn't. Let's say we didn't recognize each other, that's all. Will seemed so under developed. He was a very tense baby. He wanted and needed to be held all the time. Today he is very beautiful, not exceptionally tense, very commanding, very curious—all things perfect for a baby to be. He has an enormous smile and a wonderful chuckle. His favorite object, I can't say toy, is the remote for the television. And I would say he loves me, but love is the wrong word to use for what a baby feels. He likes me a lot. He likes how I love him and hold him. Being in my arms makes him feel good and he knows I'll probably give him something he wants. A very satisfying baby.

I'm reading *Sister Age* by M. F. K. Fisher. This is a book of short stories and anecdotes she wrote about the understanding that comes with age. Or she wrote with the understanding gained through aging. Some of it is extremely beautiful, some very moving, and some a little too bland to matter much. She's a marvelous writer. She sounds like someone it would have been interesting to know. But then that's the skilled writer writing.

I wonder how Rose is tonight. Today was the day for more chemo. She was terribly frightened. I remember one day, after I first met her, when I was about thirty and she must have been twenty-four. She came home glowing, sporting a gorgeous four-ply cashmere sweater that was just sitting on a counter in Saks Fifth Avenue "waiting" for her to come along. It was such a "great buy, only forty-five dollars." Just the day before she'd delivered a tirade about how her father, the optometrist, was always trying to buy her off, giving her money for luxuries she didn't need which prevented her from growing up and being responsible for herself. When I reminded her of what she'd said (as any thirty-year-old friend might do), she looked surprised and a little shocked. She didn't have a job so she didn't have any money, and her then husband wouldn't give her any, so who else was there but her father to pay for the sweater? Then she got mad at him again, because it was his fault she was so hooked on expensive department store shopping. But that's what twenty-four is.

And Rose's father is dead now. Dead of a brain tumor that took a long time to kill him, and Rose and her stepmother took care of him, a good part of the time at Rose's house, for that long stretch from diagnosis to death. They suffered with him and then Rose suffered with her stepmother as she died of cancer, and now cancer is killing Rose. How would I have reacted to Rose's luxury binges if I had known what I know today? Would Rose have bothered to buy that beautiful blue sweater if she had known? Or would she have bought it knowing that it would please her father to give her something so beautiful? She wore that sweater for years. It was soft and it kept her warm—she hates the cold.

In December, when I saw her, I gave her a large, soft, woolen stole. It was a thick weave in a cerise color, and when I gave it to her she wrapped herself in it with the same gesture she used when she was showing me the blue sweater years ago. The same glowing smile and cuddling into movement. It was right after her eyesight had begun to fail and she told me she could see the color, and seeing it and feeling its soft warmth made her happy.

I've been mourning for Rose for a year and a half now, though she's still alive. I am sad for myself but much sadder for her. She doesn't want to die. There's so much more she wants to do. And I can't help her to live. And there is no way to end this day's writing but to stop. □

LITANY

Rose of smiles
Rose of cheerful mien
Rose of good will
Rose of happy voice
Rose of faults
Rose of feasts
Rose of Loving

Rose of bread making
Rose of long words
Patron of pets
Patron of pots
Mistress of small mistakes
Mistress of Tai Chi

Mother of boys
Maker of poems
Rose of cheerful outlook
Rose of curling hair
Rose of deep set eyes
Rose of high cheek bones

Rose of friends
Rose of obligation
Rose of kindness
Rose of hope

Rose of pain
Rose of resignation
Rose of despair
Rose of dying

Rose

THURSDAY'S CHILD

I'm sitting here poised over the computer with nothing much to say this first day in May of the sixty-fifth year of my life. Strange that the story of my birth as told and retold by my mother's best friend, the neighbor I called Aunt Vera, about how my mother was still doing the ironing right up until the doctor came to the house and ordered her into bed so I could be born, has always been as or even more vivid, down to the colors in the room and the sunshine coming through the windows, than almost any of my other memories.

    I was born on June 29, 1928, fresh, sweet summertime in Queens Village, in my mother and father's bedroom. It must have been in daylight. My mother was doing the ironing, Aunt Vera was keeping her company, and the doctor was making his rounds, as they did in those days. My mother wanted to finish the ironing, but he told her not to waste another minute, I was about to present myself to the world; or, as I always thought of it, she was about to have me, I was to be.

    I see the room, sunny and bright, my mother scoffing at the rush, taking her good time putting away the ironing board, annoyed at having to leave some clothes in the basket still unironed. The doctor—I never see his face, just his back in a dark suit—bustling around, complaining about patients who wouldn't do what he told them to do, and Aunt Vera with her eyebrows pulled into an anxious frown and her lips pursed and smiling, as if to say, "That's my friend Rosemary for you. Doesn't want to stop even long enough to have the baby."

    Aunt Vera told me I was born practically the minute my mother got into the bed. She used to describe how beautiful I was and how they bundled me up and how she and my mother held me. The story always made me feel happy. I was born in my mother's bedroom, among all the things I knew and liked best in the world when I was little—the soft pillows, the dresser drawer with all her jewelry and nail polish, the button box, and her silky-feeling clothing. In June the maple leaves would have been new green outside the windows, and the windows open to the warm summer afternoon breeze.

Best of all, I was born to a mother who had life well in hand. She was taking care of things right up to the last minute. Even though the doctor told her to get into bed, and Aunt Vera clucked, my mother was the one who made up her mind to go to bed and have me. She was the strong one.

I was always convinced I was born on a Thursday. I don't know what Thursday's child is supposed to be like, but I believed I was a Thursday's child. I think I believed it because I liked the word Thursday. It had a smoky lavender sound. The beginning of the word sounds thin but soft, and I was a thin child. I thought Thursday's child must have an imagination and like to daydream.

Monday was navy blue, hard and practical, a hard-work day. Tuesday was beige-yellow and I didn't like the "ue" in the first syllable. Wednesday was blue-black, too much in the middle of the week, and altogether strange in its spelling. Friday was a rusty-brown word, all tied up with fish and religion and penance. Saturday was off-white, with unpleasant possibilities, and Sunday was pale yellow, no ironing on Sunday, a special day of church, relatives, arguments, and guilt.

I suppose I felt all the good things about my mother from the time I was very little, and the story Aunt Vera told me of my birth gave me a frame to put them in. The strong good mother who took care of everything in its time, making a home just right for her family. The story gave me a memory I couldn't have visually, but must have had from the time my mother first held me.

I guess my mother was the only really loving, secure relationship I had as a child. She loved me, even when she was angry with me, and I knew that. I never doubted that she loved me from the moment I was born. Her Thursday's child.□

LIFE

Let the child
cross the barrier
and begin the dance
of time
begun again

Let the music
wail its dirge
in keys minor
while sun blinds the eyes
of the beholder

Let the apple be
for eating
milk the elixir
the breast
comfort

Let all forget
sad trumpets
and remember
the sweetness
of bells

GREENWICH VILLAGE

Greenwich Village is a state of mind. A rite of passage, and a home for all those who didn't feel at home anywhere else. It's the place that everyone who really lived there remembers as "when I lived in the Village," and it was always more special, much better then, than it is today.

The first time I heard about life in Greenwich Village was from a whiskey-drinking, chain-smoking fashion editor called Prunella at King Features Syndicate when I was fresh out of high school. She was doing a fashion column under her own name and filling in on an agony column for a departed colleague. My job was to keep her in cigarettes and the racing form, and to screen out letters that were literate enough to be read and answered from the pile of agonized letters that arrived in the mail each day. And while I was deciphering the day's intake, she and her buddy, an alcoholic lady named Susy, whose job it was to sort through the fashion photos and invitations to showings, used to reminisce through the cigarette smoke about their good old days when they lived there and the Village was really The Village. Both of them were writers of a sort and used to wheeze and whoop about old pals and long ago drinking sprees and famous writers they knew back when. Then they'd get sad about how it was all changed and sneer at how deluded people were to think there was anything left to love about Greenwich Village.

Nothing in my recently released parochial school mind stirred with pre-recognition as they spoke. It never occurred to me that I might, if I chose, become part of that magic place, The Village. There wasn't much about Prunella and Susy I wanted to emulate, except possibly their extreme lack of care for what anyone else thought of them.

When I applied to The Cooper Union School of Art a year later, I was so lacking in sophistication that I didn't even know it was in the Village, or almost in the Village. But I found out soon enough, and like almost everyone else who has ever loved it, I felt I'd come home. It was my hometown. My heart's hometown.

Silver jewelry and handmade belts, baskets, posters, philodendron leaves, James Joyce and Hans Hoffman. It was wonderful. Cold-water flats, stray cats, elegant brownstones, Sundays in the park, espresso at the Figaro. My hair in a ponytail, my feet in sandals, my dresses balletic, I dared my boss in the Chrysler Building to complain about the heavy gray knee socks I wore in winter. He never did. He was a lawyer, married to a woman who had graduated from Cooper twenty years earlier, and he just laughed and told me about the Village when they were young and it was really terrific.

I moved to East Seventh Street, in the days before it was called the East Village, and each day I crossed the dividing line at Broadway and roamed up and down the streets, loving everything I saw. Each time I could, I moved to another, better apartment, and finally found a studio on West Thirteenth Street.

Dedicated Villagers always remind me of a fat old horse the man at the riding academy in Hollis gave me the first and last time I attempted to be a good sport about riding. The horse's name was Rosie, and Rosie had a mind, not a large one, of her own. Nothing I could do would keep her from her determined round back to the stables, starting fifteen feet outside the gate. That horse must have tried to go back after every twenty steps, with everyone, including the instructor, screaming at her and me to keep up. That's what Villagers are like. A day uptown makes them nervous. The Bronx seems like Siberia. And let them move to New Jersey for more space and fresh air for the baby, and you'll soon find the feet following the spirit on the shortest route back to Eighth Street.

In my days in the Village, the paper we all read was *The Villager.* That's where the serious advertisements were. No one listed Greenwich Village apartments in *The New York Times*. Along with apartment listings, *The Villager* reported on what the churches were doing, local political news, and school social activities. And jobs. Village jobs paid poorly, but for residents the benefits seemed enormous. We were like natives afraid to venture into foreign territory, and not to have to leave the area was considered the ultimate good luck.

Greenwich Village in my days was a small town, filled with the same variety of small-town stock characters that I'd left in Queens Village. That may have accounted for why it was so comfortable. We were a town full of parochial law-abiding anarchists. We were different and we'd gathered together to be different yet the same. You could spot Villagers anywhere in New York. There was always some giveaway feature: For the men, hair a little longer or disheveled, a beard, a casual reference to Baudelaire. For the women, a pair of handmade silver earrings, a look of disbelief at whatever was being said, or something as daring as my heavy gray knee socks.

We had gossips—somebody always knew someone who had a friend who was going out with somebody who'd been to an orgy. Given the fact that my mother was three months pregnant with my brother before she had the courage to ask one of her aunts how he was going to be born, you could say I'd come a long way, baby, even to be someplace where local gossip was about orgies, and that I had sense enough to ask what one actually was.

I went through a lot of growing up in the Village, from penny-pinching, cold-water-flat student to young, married, four-flights up, to young mother in the park, to single mother and child, to married again and entering the middle class with two children. The day I decided I was too grown up for the Village was one Saturday morning in the last month of my second pregnancy. I was sitting in Washington Square Park with Jenny and a friend. I was enormous, very nine months, wearing the one last maternity dress that still fit and a pair of presentable-looking bedroom slippers because even my feet had expanded. I was in a cranky mood after an argument with Milt. I felt fat and ugly and had thrown a temper tantrum from lack of sleep because of a backache. That's why I was in the park. I was trying to calm down and resign myself to the rest of the pregnancy, to say nothing of the delivery.

Next to me on the bench were two respectable-looking men, possibly Italian, one of them rocking a baby in a carriage, discussing the mob's new way of getting rid of people they didn't like by sticking them in the trunk of a car and then putting the car into one of those crushers that turns it into a small steel box in a minute. Not the kind of conversation to cheer you up after a fight unless you're contemplating using the method on an adversary, and certainly not the kind of conversation you want to hear when you're about to bring another human being into the world.

When I first moved to the Village, there were always a few drug addicts lolling in the park. Nobody, including the police, bothered them, and they didn't bother anybody. Think of any old cliché you want—live and let live, to each his own, one man's poison—and that was the motto. But this was the beginning of the sixties. Drugs were everywhere, and users very visible, and the park was becoming more theirs than anyone else's. Across from me, sprawled out on a bench, was a very drugged man and two of his friends. Since my last remaining maternity dress was green, he serenaded me with a wavering version of "In Your Sweet Little Alice Blue Gown" as he tried to convince me I should come over and join him and his friends for their Saturday morning party.

When I got up from my spot on the bench, I was no longer a Villager. I had already begun to reminisce about the good times when the Village was really great. And I hadn't even left it yet. If it hadn't been the crunched cars and my Alice blue gown, it would have been something else. I was ready for a change, ready for a picket fence. □

OLD FRIENDS IN THE VILLAGE

Twenty-five years is a long time
to live in Greenwich Village
not counting the years
of spiritual residence

Strollers in the hall
cold water flats, four flights up
Matisse beneath a paper lantern
and always philodendrons in a jug

Hiding for years behind dark glasses
in long skirts and sandals
a poet looking for a picket fence
with children trailing after

You know the Village
anything goes
anarchists become bureaucrats
and faithless wives are constant

June 29, 1993
Talloires, France

Dear Marian,
Well, this is it—the big sixty-five. I'm as old as my father was when he died, and a year younger than my mother was when she came to live with us. And I thought they were so old. When I catch a glimpse of myself in mirrors as I pass by, I think I'm pretty old myself, and it astonishes me every time.

Your new little dog sounds great. A beagle. Lots of energy. Likes to go its own way, as I recall. Very friendly, and nice to have around. One of our dogs, Sniffy, had a best friend who was a beagle. It used to call for Sniffy every day, and they'd go off into the neighborhood, part of an unthreatening canine corps. They hung around with the big dogs, but they definitely didn't count in the big growl department. I love the name Tucker.

I can't think of anything else to say for now, so that's all folks...
        Love,
        Rosemary

JUST DESSERTS

I don't need to look
In the mailbox each day
For a letter that says I love you
Bruiser's worth his weight in Purina
Now that he thinks I'm his mother

He sits at my feet
While I eat
He slobbers kisses
And he looks sad when I yell
And I say
This is what I deserve

August 6, 1993
Talloires, France

Dear Iris and Morty,

For some reason, I've been having a hard time sitting down to write. I'm having a good time, but I seem reluctant to put it on paper. However, we were very happy to receive your other fax, and equally happy to receive the one from today.

I can't wait to see the photos you took. I saw the ones that Shad took at the party, and we all look terribly together and in good shape, which was a great pleasure to see. I hope to get a few sets of those and bring them back to show you. It was a very interesting-looking group that night, and I may make an album just of those pictures.

Jenny will be forty in September, and I don't believe it. But if I'm sixty-five, she's forty, and Andy is thirty-one. Isn't that an amazing feeling? How can your children be older than you are? I ask you.

Our grandson now speaks a mixture of English and Spanish and has switched from kitty cat to gato, wawa to agua, and if he shows up calling Julia mamacita, we'll know we have to cool it a little.

Hope you are all rested up and haven't let the L.A. busy business catch you up too much.

I guess I should have known I'd be able to write to you tonight. I started doing a watercolor this afternoon, and there's no way I could do that and not be able to write. I mean, that takes a kind of self-confidence I don't usually have.

                     Be well, take care, and love,
                     Rosemary

August 6, 1993
Talloires, France

Dear Marian,

I have been having a hard time writing these last few weeks, partly because I had unhooked my computer from the printer so that both Michael and I could use it, and I ended up not using it at all. However, the real reason has more to do with mourning for Rose. This last week I've found myself beginning to cry over the slightest things—the doorbell rings, somebody honks a horn, I drop a book—not things one usually cries about. I haven't really let myself think about her death, and in my mind I can't merge my two images of her—one smiling and healthy, the other pensive, drooping, and so visibly dying. It's probably not a good thing to be unwilling to cry, or rather, to be willing myself not to cry, but I have a terrified feeling that once I begin, I won't be able to stop. Stupid, because I know that's an unreasonable fear. Maybe it's because it's Rose I want to talk to, to tell her how sad I am and how much I miss her being alive. And now I finally am crying.

Before we left to come here, there were things I wanted to say to you, Marian, but I felt so harassed, and even a little embarrassed. I wanted to tell you that I feel a friendship for you that for a very long time has gone far beyond the outward circumstances that bring us together each week. Losing Rose made me understand that I mustn't let time go by without saying the important things. I feel as if we are a community, you and Milt and me, and by extension Jim and my children. That you and I are friends beyond employer and employee, and even aside from Milt. I speak more directly to you than almost anyone else I know, and I hope that you feel as free to speak to me.

You are kind, honest, direct, loving, and good, and if I listed all the qualities about you that I like, you'd probably be put off, thinking I was trying to flatter you. I'm not.

Now I've cried, and I've managed to say some of what I wanted to say, and I hope it makes you feel as good as it's made me feel.

      Rosemary

August 17, 1993
Talloires, France

Dear Bob,
It would have been proper for me to have written to you immediately after Rose died, but my own feelings were so unhappy, I felt it would be an imposition on you to add to your sadness.

I was sorry not to be at the service, but it was a choice between coming in June when passing through New York, or coming to see Rose a few weeks earlier, then flying direct to Europe from Los Angeles.

This letter is saying nothing of the things I have in my heart, or of how I'm feeling about you and the boys, and about Rose. Everything I want to say seems presumptuous, because for all that we've known each other for thirty years, you and I haven't known each other very well.

What I hope is that life is good to you, and that you can find peace, comfort, and happiness as soon as possible. No one else can know how terrible these last two years have been for you, so no one knows exactly the right words to say or what comfort to offer. Take whatever comfort you find, and be glad for it, because life is all we have.
      Rosemary

ON GRIEF

So life goes on without Rose. I counted her one of my best friends. And I feel diminished by a third. I watched my mother as she aged, first taken from Queens Village, then from Hollis, then from Twentieth Street, and then from Chappaqua. She wasn't a woman who had many friends, just a few, but they mattered to her, and I guess I'm like her in that way. At the end of her life, they were all dead, or gone to other places as she was. In the end, since she wasn't a part of the community, it was her family who counted to her, and who either loved or failed her.

And Rose, who seemed so young and so vital, the one of us who would live to be ninety, still smiling her wonderful smile, making small noises of "that's life" and "isn't it terrible" over the bad things, but looking ahead with welcoming eyes no matter what. She was always there, at the end of the telephone, always with a lift to her voice when she said "Rosemary!" as if my call was a wonderful surprise and made her happy.

I heard that same lilt every time she answered a call from a friend. Even in her last conscious days, dying from the cancer that killed her. And what I heard was the same spirit, in a ghost voice of Rose, hoping that tomorrow would be better, tracing the character in Shakespeare who was not Iago, but the villain of another piece, wanting words looked up in the dictionary to better express what she wanted to say, telling me the tale of a neighbor who stopped by to bring her soup for lunch, liking being alive, wanting to live, hoping to live, wanting to see her younger son, wanting to see the autumn leaves, wanting to see tomorrow.

I loved Rose. And now she's gone. I am trying to remember her happy times. To forget the last two years, except for the good parts. And I'm so sad.

But I don't want to cry. I think my days for crying are over, and from now on I must carry my sadness within me until I grow old enough to forget. Not to forget Rose, but not to remember the missing.□

WHO'S ON FIRST?

There's no getting away from it, I'm having constant suicidal thoughts. That doesn't mean I'll do anything about them. Only that they're passing through my consciousness with increasing speed and regularity. Everything seems an occasion for ending everything.

If I exist in how I am valued by others, I don't exist if I'm not valued. When I worked at Cherry Lane, fifty people looked at me with fifty ideas of who I was. In the face of fifty concepts of myself, I was even more aware of the uselessness of all those ideas that weren't me. And who was I? Someone ephemeral who did things and had things done to she who doesn't exist.

That's what I am again today. An idea buffeted by other ideas, which I am not even sure exist as ideas. They are ideas that I think exist, but how can I know, since these are things seldom expressed as more than fleeting glimpses?

When I step out the door, I see people in their three dimensions. They are made of flesh and wear clothes of different colors, drive cars, eat food, and so they exist.

Does everyone feel this way to a greater or lesser extent? Like a ghost in a body, now up, now down, a shadow in varying colors depending on the warmth in others' eyes and smiles, frowns, indifference.

The closest I have ever been to another person is to Milt, who loves me for some reason. I don't know why. If I knew, I'd try to be that person all the time.

This is a bad morning.

Milt just walked in and we talked for a few minutes, and he made the day clearer, and now I'm Rosemary, Milt's wife. We had dinner last night with eight very intelligent, very funny, very likeable French people. All the conversation in French except for possibly twenty words, all very loud, all too fast, all exhausting. No wonder I'm not real today.

This morning, in an attempt to assert some inner independence, I did a few watercolors. Fast nothings, but something from within. Not good, but a start.□

LISTS

>What can you expect of a woman
>who spent years jotting down needs
>on scraps of paper
>carrying over one day to the next
>yesterday's unfinished living

SKIRT: Take Jenny's skirt to the cleaner
she's fifteen and pretty and we fight
maybe we will love again

PRETZELS: Andy likes them
he spills crumbs on his green shirt
laughing unselfconsciously as the Captain
makes silly mistakes on F Troop

MITTENS: They're out in the snow somewhere
I must find them before dark

ASPIRIN: In this weather
someone is sure to have a headache
or catch the flu

OREOS: At forty-three
Milt sits at the kitchen table
reading, eating, listening to music
chocolate and tears, *"Amor per me non ha"*

SHOVEL: Jenny and I will struggle on the driveway
over how to shovel snow the right way
cheeks red, eyes sullen
neither will win

KIBBLE: For the two black dogs running in great circles
through maples and hemlocks

YARN: My mother, too old for winter,
watches from the window
waiting for us to come in
so she can give us hot cocoa
The yarn is for the white afghan she knits
thinking I will need it
to remember her by

I SHOWED HIM MY POEM

I showed him my poem
the one about lists
and he said

You see I was right
There was something we had
In spite of misunderstandings
and not knowing what we were doing
that kept us together

And I could see in his face
that it made him happy
to remember

September 13, 1993
Talloires, France

Dear Iris,
Now I can't imagine why I was so nervous about minding Will. I'm not actually minding him very much. Assunta's niece, Emmanuelle, is so wonderful with him, and he is such a good-natured baby that it seems to be the smoothest of sailing.

In fact, I was happy to see Andy and Julia and Julia's parents take off yesterday. I began to realize that seven adults and one little baby is a lot more cooking, dishes and laundry than three adults and the same little baby. I did towels and sheets all day yesterday after they left.

I'd forgotten how much food eight people consume at a meal. I've made so much soup and vegetables this week, and they just disappeared in a blink. You know, when people eat meat, you don't have to do so much preparation, just fling it on the stove, make a salad, and they're happy. But now that we're all so involved with healthy eating, vegetables and all that, preparation time is quadrupled.

Everyone will be back on the weekend. I'm not complaining, just glad to have a breather.

When I walked into the guest bath off my office this morning and saw all of Will's toys stacked around the tub, I thought about how wonderful it is that at each stage of our lives there's something wonderful that makes it all worthwhile. Think back, to when you were little, and its ice cream and toys, playing, being loved. When you're a teen, it's still playing—at being in love, sports, favorite foods. In your twenties, there's sex, love, romance, and playing at being an adult. Then come the children and all the beauty and problems and hopes. They take you through to fifty, winding in and around and about important work, interest in culture, decisions about the world and politics, and, of course, making a warm home, a good marriage, and just hanging in there.

Then comes the next stage, the one you can't imagine being so good any time before it actually happens. I mean, you can't sit on the floor and cry your eyes out over anything that doesn't go the way you want it. You can't run and climb trees while eating innumerable hot dogs and Cokes or do two hours of the Lindy Hop. You can't fall in love at the wink of any eye across a room at a party, and being an adult doesn't feel like playing. Your children are bigger than you are, and they're making the important choices, expanding their lives, homes, and families. You could never have believed that living with someone for so many years could be better than everything that went before. All the delights of the past were no more wonderful than sharing a laugh or an interesting idea with someone you love more than anyone else. And then there are the toys around the edge of the tub, watching a baby eat and laugh, watching it play, and begin the whole process over again, and you know that, with luck, life can be very good.

So I must believe that even the next stage, the winding down of a lot of things, will still have joys and pleasures, pleasures that we don't know about yet. But I won't think about that right now. I'll go put the wash in the dryer, and get Will's lunch ready, and ready myself for a nice cup of decaf and a pastry down at Chez Bise later in the afternoon.

      Rosemary

YOU NEVER KNOW

What a wonderful gift—not to know. Each day may be a surprise. I still don't know how to paint. So there's something to strive for. Even hope for. There are books to read, movies to see, meals to eat, and friends to make. I don't even know how I know what I know. If I haven't solved that yet, I guess I never will, but it doesn't stop me puzzling about it.

My French is passable but I still don't know enough for it to be easy unless I use it every day. When we were going to France every summer, the people in the village where we stayed corrected my mistakes. I'd be trying to say how I wanted the lamb chops cut, and M. Bidal, the butcher (some American friends called him Gore Bidal), would wipe his hands on his bloody apron and explain the difference between agneau and mouton. Agneau on the plate. Mouton on the hill. Some days I'd lean my head against our front door before going out to shop and tell myself I couldn't face it. The effort to think and speak in French was too exhausting.

Leaning my head against the door in dread reminds me of the time in London when we were invited to a dinner honoring Plácido Domingo at the Spanish Ambassador's residence after a performance of Otello. I'd been depressed for about eight months, and I didn't want to go. But Milt was working with Plácido and he wanted to go. The Ambassador's social secretary had seated me next to a Spanish violinist. I wanted to sit with Milt. After hiding out in the lavatory, I emerged to discover that the Spanish violinist couldn't make it, and that I had been seated next to Harold Pinter. What luck! Harold Pinter! I introduced myself, and then told him that I loved his Proust screenplay. I had wanted to tell him that since 1977. It must've been the right thing to say to an author, because he became animated and we spent the next hour talking about books, books, books. I had a great time.

I don't know whether it was Pinter, the conversation about books, or the moment my depression was about to end anyway, but a few days later I realized that I'd put my feet on the floor two mornings in a row when I got out of bed without thinking, "Why bother?"

Not knowing must be what enables us to live. If we don't know, we can still hope. When I'm depressed, I know that sooner or later I won't be depressed. For years I could keep my fear at bay if I didn't dwell on death. Then I realized that it's not death I fear, it's dying. And I don't know when that will be, so most mornings when my feet hit the floor, I get up and live another day, and some days are nice surprises.☐

ON HER BIRTHDAY
November 27, 1993

Today is my mother's birthday. I still miss her and wish she were here so I could mother her. She would be terribly old, but then I wouldn't wish her back the age she would actually be, but the age she was in the few years before she died. Or any of the ages she was when I knew her.

I wish she were fifty again, with strong arms, cooking tasty meals, gossiping with friends on the telephone, sitting in the overstuffed chair on 213th Street, reading a book, looking up from the page, somber half-smile on her face, then looking back down again, lost in another place and time. Or I wish she was a little girl like Lizzie, in special pretty dresses provided by three fussy maiden aunts, making pies and cakes in the kitchen with her tiny, white-haired grandmother, not much bigger than she. Running up and down the stairs in the Brooklyn brownstone, an important little girl to the four frittery women who brought her up.

Or the strong young mother of lakeside picnics and the Fourth of July, cooking hot dogs and serving potato salad and cream soda to fifteen hungry people. Or the aged mother and grandmother of my children who loved us all; Jenny and Andy with forgiveness and generosity, me with a woman-to-woman understanding, always ready to put her arms around me and love me, always willing to let me love her.

I hardly speak to her directly any more the way I did for so many years after she died. So I know she's dead. But love isn't dead. It's only sleeping. It's not safe to let it awaken too often because it hurts. But I don't want to let today pass by without speaking of her.

If I were a religious person and thought she could know how I love her, I would never let a day pass without saying hello, but sadly, that comfort isn't for me. I'm glad I was so lucky to have had her for as many years as I did, and grateful to Milt that he learned to care for her too, and could let me have her live with us.□

IN MEMORIAM

>She gave me a gift
>I have it in my kitchen
>a folding file for recipes
>food mattered
>Meringues, soufflés, cassoulet
>they're all in there
>some in her own writing

>January 4, 1994
>Alpine Drive, Beverly Hills

Dear Assunta,
It's six a.m. and if I hurry, I can write to you now, before all the complications of the day distract me. My windows face the east and the sun hasn't begun to rise yet, so I have half an hour before day begins.

Will speaks more and more each day, and Lizzie is growing tall. She is old enough to know that Will needs to be watched over and taken care of, and her maternal instincts are beginning to show. They play together beautifully. It was a great pleasure to have them here for Christmas. We could relax without worrying too much that Will would eat the Christmas tree with Lizzie on watch.

The new baby should be born shortly, and we're all anxiously waiting to see whether it's a boy or a girl and that things are okay. It's funny. While Julia was carrying Will and Jenny carried Lizzie, I had no feelings at all about the babies to come, just a mild interest. They didn't seem real until after I saw them. And even then, it took time to begin to really love them. But I think I already love the new little one. I'm all ready to be its grandmother.

How did Paula and Shad do in Canada? Are they back yet? The weather there at the moment is dreadfully cold, with an enormous amount of snow. I hope they aren't discouraged, because it will be different in Vancouver.

Well, the sun is now up and the day is officially starting. Milt just got out of bed and is trudging (walking with a heavy step, *comme les soldats de Napoléon en retraite de Moscou*) his way to the kitchen, and that's my signal to turn off the computer and go be Mrs. Okun for a while.

Happy New Year. All my love to you and Jacques.
      Rosemary

             January 29, 1994
             Alpine Drive, Beverly Hills

Dear Madeleine,
There's nothing like an earthquake to put life into perspective. I'm sure that in time I will forget the horrifying terror of those seconds and begin to complain about things like the weather and poor service in restaurants, but sitting on the floor of a narrow hallway, bracing your back against one wall and your feet against the other, while you listen to the earth grinding its guts, your house seemingly disintegrating all around you, and items of glass and other materials falling and smashing, just as you think you will fall and smash, certainly makes you know what is important— and it ain't what the neighbors think, or even what you think.

It was the most frightening experience of my life. I've had painful experiences and sad experiences, and moods and unhappinesses that have lasted for long periods of time, but I have never, except for giving birth, felt my own helplessness and unimportance so intensely.

That feeling doesn't end with the shaking. It has continued night and day since the quake. And not just for me. Los Angeles is full of people suffering from a variety of sleep, psychological, and gastrointestinal maladies directly resulting from fear. It's nothing to start talking to someone, stranger or friend, usually a woman, whose eyes start to well up with tears and is very visibly shaken. Even men will express what they felt, though most of the men I know have more ways of suppressing the memory, and they play it much cooler. I suspect boys learn very early that showing fear is a good way to get yourself beaten up in the schoolyard, so they hold it in, and before they know it, they aren't feeling it. I ought to try a little of that.

Anyway, this letter is partly to thank you for your note of concern, and I guess, partly to let off a little steam and try to lessen my anxiety. Again, thank you for your note. It felt good to know that if the gods didn't care what happened to us, our friends did.

              Love,
              Rosemary

                                  January 29, 1994
                                Alpine Drive, Beverly Hills

Dear Jacques and Assunta,
In spite of three pretty big aftershocks last night—one of which was 5.4— we're in pretty cheerful spirits. We were so lucky not to have any serious damage. If we were religious, we would be thanking whatever god we believed in. As it is, we must be satisfied with gratitude for the fate that is ours and compassion for people less fortunate.

The building code in Beverly Hills is so strict (rigid, disciplined) that there was no real structural damage to buildings. However, there were many damaged chimneys *(coin au feu)* in the buildings constructed before the 1931 earthquake—over one thousand to be exact—and about three hundred had to be taken down. Many

people lost fortunes in sculpture, fine china, and glass objects.
Dans notre maison, pratiquement peu de chose comme cela arrive, parce que le code de les Okuns sont aussi très "strict." Presque toutes les choses délicates qui peuvent être détruite dans un tremblement sont dans des cabinets et tous les placards de la cuisine sont solides.

Also, our house seems to be very solid. We had an engineer make an inspection the other day, and we have only a few minor cracks around doorways that must be repaired.

Little Emily is now a part of the family. I've only held her once, while she was sleeping. Will thinks she is interesting. He likes her hands especially and thinks it's funny that her fingers wiggle and move just like everyone else's. So far he shows no signs of jealousy, but that will come later perhaps. Julia's parents are here to help, so Will gets plenty of attention at the moment.

So, except for being nervous about what the next earthquake will be like and when it will occur, life goes on much the same, at least on the surface.

    Love,
    Rosemary

        April 23, 1994
        Alpine Drive, Beverly Hills

Dear Mickey,

I'm having a hard time writing. Life seems full of chaos and confusion, though I'm not depressed actually. I think it's among the earthquakes, riots, fires and shootings; and fibrillation, bleeding, and bunions; and the good stuff like babies, bottles and cuddling; that I have lost my drive to write. There's just so much brain that operates at any one time and most of mine is occupied almost all of the time, including when I should be sleeping. I completely understood when you said you couldn't do your paperwork, even though I know how much it means to you.

I remember my mother at this age. We lived in Chappaqua and she was limited by not driving. She seemed to have endless days to read, watch television, cook, play with the children, go to the

Senior Citizens and play dominos with a few friends. I know it sounds mindless, but it also was very restful and full of love.

The question I ask myself all the time is, how did a child/woman/elderly woman who never had two pieces of paper to rub together suddenly at the age of forty-five begin to accumulate file cabinets full of papers, all sorted and serious? And that's just the stuff that's been, as it were, processed. There's that other paper monster that grows day by day, looming like a snowball rolling down a hill. I keep telling myself that if I died tomorrow, it would roll right by and no one would know the difference, so why do I bother—just because it's there I suppose. Stupid.

You have work you love. So do it. The promotion I guess you have to do. Jenny had some ideas for you that I think she will speak to you about herself. Think about visiting this summer if you can...

We are all excited about the quilts and can't wait to see them and make our choices.

                Love,
                Rosemary

                            April 24, 1994
                            Alpine Drive, Beverly Hills

Dear Hannah,
Rose has been in my thoughts very often these last few days. I miss her presence in life. Only now do I believe that it would have been good for me to go to her funeral. It wasn't possible at the time. I would have had to travel alone, and that just wasn't advisable for health reasons.

My father-in-law died at ninety-six after ten years of Parkinson's, during which time he lived with us for five years and in a nursing home for three years. The last three years were devastating to us all, since he ceased speaking, moving, or even opening his eyes. It was a nightmare to go to see him, how much more for him to be alive we couldn't tell. Perhaps he heard us, perhaps not. He was greatly loved by his family and friends. Most of his friends were gone, and the family scattered, except for Milt, his brother Dan, and myself. For years we were unable to feel anything but sadness when we saw him. It was a terrible time.

The strangest thing happened at the funeral. Suddenly, everyone began to talk about him as he was in earlier years, when he was the head of the family. And the family was large and very close then, with his brothers, sisters, cousins, and their children and grandchildren. Everyone began to think of him again as the loving and kind person that he was, not just dwelling on the illness he suffered for so long at the end.

The pain of seeing that reality was too terrible. Dan again told the story of Will's arrival at Ellis Island, and of being reunited with his father in a railroad flat in Brooklyn—one of the happiest memories of his life. That story made me remember the really good life he had had, all the love and respect that he deserved and received, and what a good man he was. The day of the funeral was sunny and warm and people were smiling as well as crying. Everyone was relieved that his life, such as it was at the end, had ended. Best of all was the flood of good memories.

I'm sitting here with thoughts passing so quickly through my head that I can't put them on the paper. A sense of reality has never been one of my strengths. I don't know exactly what it is or what it means. My friendship with Rose was an individual one, from long ago, when we were young. We didn't have mutual friends, though we each knew some of the other's friends. We spoke fairly often, but after I moved to California nearly twenty years ago we only saw one another for a few hours or days each year. So unlike my father-in-law Will, my memories of Rose, in later years, are of problems solved and unsolved, celebrations and important happenings, but not all the everyday bits and pieces of her life.

A friend of mine sent me photographs of pink roses in a garden that were taken and dedicated to Rose by another friend of hers. That was when my wavering sense of reality was shaken. It's one thing to know that we all see people differently and another to face the difficulties. As I looked at the photos I realized that if I thought about Rose in flowers, and it was almost inevitable because of her name, I would have thought of jonquils or Queen Anne's Lace, and if a rose, a deep red rose or a pink-and-yellow tea rose. Rose had such a beautiful smile. It was in every way like the best of springtime, or like wonderful chrysanthemums in the fall...

June 24

Dear Hannah,
I should have mailed the above, but I didn't feel it was finished, and then I caught the flu, the kind that keeps coming back for a day or two each week. Then we were busy preparing to go to Europe for the summer, and I thought I'd sit down and finish the letter there. So we flew to France and ten days later we flew back because Milt was ill...When I was writing in April, I didn't know exactly what or why I was writing. Rereading now, I see that I was trying to free myself of the last year of Rose's life, wanting to remember her as she was in her happier times. There's a part of me that wants to shake a fist at the terrible time she had when her father and mother were sick and dying. It doesn't seem fair that she gave so many years of love and care to people and wasn't rewarded with more years of unmitigated pleasure. And if I ask, do I really think that life is fair? — of course, the answer is no, but somehow I must always have thought that it would be fair ultimately to Rose.

    I'm glad you and I connected, Hannah. I need to be able to tell someone who loved Rose how much I loved her. I can tell my husband, because he cared for Rose too and he knows how I feel. We were all friends together. But it's different to speak to another woman. I wish I believed in God and Heaven and that I thought Rose did too. Then I could speak to her and believe that she heard me, but that wasn't one of the gifts at my christening. I hope you are well and happy, and when you have a chance, please write.
With affection,
Rosemary

DEBT

It must be eighteen years since we moved to California. I have never felt at home here. I've gotten used to it, but never more than as an onlooker, an outsider. But I would deceive myself if I pretended that I was ever a comfortable part of anything. I have walked through so much of my life pretending. Is that what other people do? If so, how do they get the energy to go on?

I miss my mother today. I need someone who thinks about me the way I think about my family. I just moved a small overnight case that used to be hers from one room to another, debating whether to keep it any longer. It's a pretty little floral tapestry bag, just big enough to hold a few things when she would go down to visit Jean over the holidays. It was a gift that I bought for her with love and that she used with pleasure and some pride. She liked pretty things and it always gave me pleasure to buy dresses for her. And to see her use the case. Now it's faded and dark and useless, but I have so few things of hers that I don't want to give it up. For a few minutes, in the odd moments that I see it or pick it up and feel its light empty weight, I remember all the times I saw her use it. I see sunshine and green trees, Milt in the car taking her to the city, the slight tension of her parting, and the pleasure of her return, Andy, Jenny, and me greeting her with love again.

I thought I'd forgotten her. I feel so old myself. I'm the age that she was the year my father died and she came to live with us. It was the year Andy was born. I try to give my children the love and help that she gave me. Do I do it for them, or for myself to try to find someone to love me as I loved her? I remember one time when I was little, maybe four years old, I was in the five-and-ten with her and she walked around the corner of the counter where I couldn't see her, and I panicked and began to cry in terror. It only lasted a few seconds but it counts as one of the worst moments in my life. The people around and even my mother made light of it and tried to reassure me, but I never forgot it.

I saw the same thing in Andy's face once when he was about seven years old. He had seen a program about an orphan boy in South America who traveled by himself for hundreds of miles to reach a shelter for children. Andy's face was twisted in pain when he cried out to me, "You mean there are boys who don't have a father?" He wanted me to say it wasn't true. This was some time after he accused me of not being his real mother, because if I was, I would never "leave" him. Meaning that I would never die.

And so I am always the lost child understanding the lost children. Like my mother and the child that Andy was, and may still be. And Lizzie. I think that Lizzie may be another lost child. With luck, Julia's children will be strong, like her, and the reign of family fear and loneliness will end.

My mother has been dead for twenty-two years and I have almost forgotten her daily presence and what it meant to me. Next year will be the centennial of her birth. A baby girl, full of the future, born a hundred years ago somewhere in Brooklyn to a young, dark-haired mother who only lived another three years to care for her, then left her to whatever terrors were in store.

When I die, someone will toss away the travel case, wondering why I kept such a grimy old thing. What I see when I look at it is a gift I could give that pleased her, something tangible in return for what she gave me.□

THE WORLD

I turned my head. Colors, a thousand shapes—toothbrushes, nail files, mirrors, candles, napkins, spoons, wire, candy, a smiling girl leaning over the counter—but no mother. I craned my neck to see above the counter. In a panic, I ran several steps crying, "Mommy!" I bumped into a lady in a dark dress with red and white flowers who looked down at me and said nothing, and then I heard my mother.

"Here I am, silly. Did you think you'd lost me?" Her round, warm shape emerged from all the others, solid and safe. She smiled and put out her hand. "I was right here all the time." I clung to her with one hand and wiped my eyes with the back of the other. "You're not crying, are you? You weren't lost." She turned to the girl at the counter to finish her purchase. When she had to get money from her purse, she pulled away from my fingers. "Let go now. I have to pay the lady."

We walked out of the store, her arms full of small packages, and me clinging to her skirt. Panic at being lost made me unable to speak. The five-and-ten was my favorite store, but it was dangerous, like matches and the gas stove, and I didn't want to go there again.□

MICKEY

Her real name is Marilyn
But the kids in art school called her Mickey
Her husband sometimes calls her Mick
I'm one of the former kids
So she's Mickey to me.

It's been a long life, a shared friendship
Between two unlikely traveling companions
One the daughter of a dancing woman
From a Coney Island shtetl
The other the daughter of a dancing milkman
From an Irish Catholic shtetl in Queens

How is it that someone comes into your life
And becomes family, part of your tribe?
Fifty years of shared food and telephone calls,
Laughs, children, husbands, parents, grandchildren,
Inner lives growing, changing, pain and joy
And long months between occasional moments
Together across three thousand miles

June 8, 1994
Talloires, France

Dear Mickey,

Well, we made it. Funny, every year I become convinced that this year we won't. I don't know why, but I think maybe it's my old Catholic schoolgirl indoctrination. I don't deserve Heaven because God and I know I'm not perfect and haven't repented adequately.

The flight was long and uneventful and we feel as if we've flown to the moon and back. However, the trip was worth it, because looking out at the lake has such a calming effect—at least on me. Milt is his usual calm self, only more so.

We had croissants and coffee down at Chez Duclos, and this afternoon will have our first pastry down at the Auberge.

Walking into the house this year was a heavenly experience. For the first time, there was somebody here to open it up before we arrived. Claudia Chiampo, Assunta's sister-in-law, came in and took off all the dustsheets and vacuumed and made the beds. All we had to do was flop our bags in the front hall, take out our pajamas, and proceed to relax.

For the first time in months, my heart sounds like a metronome. If I behave sensibly, maybe I can keep it going that way until I get back.

They have had a lot of rain here in the last month, so everything is super green and lush. And the plants around the house have finally matured nicely, so it's all tying together. It's lost that raw look that a new house has. There are a number of flowering shrubs that are beginning to bloom beautifully. We usually miss them because we come a few weeks later than this each year...

Maybe I should go take a good long look at the lake and think pain au chocolat thoughts and forget about everything in this life that I can't (or don't want to) control. Take care and be well.

Love,
Rosemary

HOLD THE MAYO

The kids are grown
the garden is green
the dogs like everyone
and my arm pressed
against my husband
feels warm

I don't care
if the plane falls
explodes or disappears
Just let it be fast

POSSESSIONS

That I am still here to write this collection of meanderings always comes as a surprise to me. By here I mean in Talloires again. I am always sure that we will not make the next trip. Even when I was in good health, it seemed impossible that I would be able to come to such a beautiful place...

Something has happened to me. It may be because I have turned a chronological corner, or it could be the feeling of constant ill health, breathlessness, and the waning of strength, but I no longer want to possess things. I can't stand to have around me all the small decorative bits and pieces that I always longed, perhaps falsely, to have softening the landscape of my life.

This state of mind has been coming over me gradually in the last few years, but it has reached a point where I have decided to give in to it. In California, my room will have only a bed, a television, a night table, and a beautiful armoire. Everything else will be in the closets.

In the kitchen downstairs, I am going to put everything off the counters as much as possible. I will train the new housekeeper to put everything away and keep it all pristine.

The dining room table will be stored or sold, and I will take over that room, with again a bed, a comfortable rocking chair, a television, a table for Milt and me to eat at, and some space for the children to play.

The living room will have only the few pieces necessary for the times when we have company, or want to sit in there ourselves. And on the walls of the rooms will be paintings, Mickey's quilts, drawings, and photographs.

I'm tired of living a life in which the things I own are my façade. I'm tired of trying to convince myself and the rest of the world that I'm a happy, ordinary, conforming person. I have as usual only conformed on the outside. Maybe everybody does. I don't know.

For example, why do I have a dining room? Past pleasures. I loved to cook and entertain. For a while, I had a caterer do the cooking, when I began to find it too hard. But I don't like having caterers. I don't enjoy the food. It cramps the conversation. And in Beverly Hills, few people our age invite people to their houses. Everyone eats in restaurants. It's as if personal lives, home, intimacy don't exist. Goodbyes are said at the doors of restaurants. There is no real hospitality. No offering of self. Only the informal chitchat that is warmer than cocktail conversation but usually doesn't go very deep.

We came to California too late to make the kinds of friends we had in Chappaqua. Not being joiners, finding people we like is difficult. You meet someone in a restaurant, friends of friends, and think perhaps they will be pleasant to know. Then there is the hassle of calling cold and inviting and coordinating busy schedules. The dinner, if it happens, well, it turns out that the couple who looked interesting and fun are conservative and too busy with the life they are leading, or whatever it may be. We have made exactly two friends that way...

I was pleased when people walked into our house and said how beautiful it was. For a moment I fooled them and myself into thinking that, yes, indeed, I was a warm happy person who lived a life filled with order and pleasant down-home beauty, with assorted bits and pieces of decoration to round out the image.

That's not what I am. Is it what anyone is? I don't know. But I suspect that there are more like me than not. And that makes me sadder than if I thought it was just me. So on to convent mode. Clean, neat, spare, and beautiful, if possible...If not possible, then just clean, neat, and spare.□

November 10, 1999
Alpine Drive, Beverly Hills

Dear Michael,
November is always a sad month for me. Not really actively sad, but a month that has always been misty and gray, probably just my reaction to the light that continues to lessen, to my childhood when by November the novelty of a new teacher was wearing off and the enormity of the eight remaining months of dreary unpleasant school routine loomed in my consciousness. All Saints' Day— All Souls' Day (I always preferred the word souls to saints)—family birthdays, Aunt Mamie, Papa, Nana, cold winds, quarrels, Christmas with its domestic chaos.

Since we've lived in California, I've been able to ignore a lot of the old memories, what with the sunshine and good green lettuce, but this year a cataract has catapulted me into a state of frustration big enough to take the place of my old November gray slumps. I have finally been driven to make an appointment to have the operation December 13th. I'm not happy thinking about it, though everyone tells me it's nothing. Of course, they're all passing on the information secondhand and looking at me out of their own perfectly grand, clear shiny eyes.

So, having all but given up using the computer, as well as being unable to read small print, thread a needle, or drive the car, I honestly believed I couldn't write you a letter. Not true, as witness this. Very complaining, and communication of another sort, but sent with love.

I've been quite cheerful since recovering from the operation on my thyroid. Very cheerful, but not manic in the least, something both Milt and I noticed. I mean, I feel good, better than I have in several years. The level of my thyroid hormone (if that's how one expresses it) after that operation put me in the terribly low range of hypothyroid, which means that I should have felt so fatigued that I couldn't move my legs, I should have been falling asleep, not able to think, very depressed, and unable to do anything. Instead, I feel cheerful, have done a lot, am always a little tired, but volunteered to cook a hamburger for Will the other day. As I was bustling around the kitchen, frying pan and spatula in hand, Will suddenly looked up from the train he was drawing and said, eyes shining and wonder in his voice, "You're cooking, Nana." He said it several times in just the same tone I would use to say, "What a good boy you are, Will," when he has put his toys away. Also, I took care of both children by myself for several hours here at home the last two Wednesdays, so whatever my thyroid was doing to me, it wasn't good, and I can happily do without it.

I just realized that a week ago I started taking a minute quantity more of thyroid hormone, and maybe that's why I have the courage, in spite of not being able to see the cursor terribly well, to write to you.

I found a jacket from Robinson's department store in my closet and I wonder if it is yours. It's a very nice dark wool sort of plaid, I think, and it's a mite too small for Richard, which puts it into your size range. Do you think it is? It was stored with all of our woolen clothes over the summer. Even if you don't remember it, I'll hang on to it in case it's yours or in case it fits you, because I can't imagine who else could be the owner.

I wish you were going to be here for the holidays. They promise to be quiet this year with three Sparkses in England and four Okuns in Massachusetts. Wait until you see the house...It's so clean and neat and beautiful, with shining floors, no dining room—the room is there but it's a kind of cozy playroom/sitting room—almost no furniture in the living room, and a different arrangement of artwork on the walls. I love it. I feel as if I've moved into a new house.

On the floor of the new sitting room, I've put the round purple rug that Nana hooked, and Will uses it especially to dance on, and that makes me happy. I like to think that Nana has done something nice for my little grandchildren. Will's dancing is a kind of primitive thank you to his unknown ancestor for giving him the gift of life and continuity. I know that sounds odd, but I often think of my mother when I look at the children and think about how she would love them, and about how she taught me to love them freely and generously.

Love,
Rosemary

JEAN

For so many years, the year 2000 seemed an impossibly far-off time, incomprehensible to one born in 1928. Now it's almost upon us...

Another thing that seemed impossible: Jean called me the other day and we had a long and pleasant sisterly conversation—not a hint of dislike or dissension in her voice. She said she called me because I always call her and she wanted to call before I did. It's the first time she has ever acknowledged that our relationship has depended primarily on me hanging in there all these years despite her jealousy, dislike, or resentment.

It's been a year since she stopped drinking, and this was the pleasantest conversation yet. Maybe the group therapy in AA has allowed her to look at her life through adult eyes, and to see me today as I am. She's still Jean, but she has relaxed with me. And it makes me very happy. All my life, I've wanted her to like me, to accept me for what I am, and not the younger sister she hated from the moment I was born, the one she cast in the role of bête noire...

Jean never saw that the things she wanted and didn't have were not the things I wanted or had. She saw me through such a haze of hatred that I never existed as myself to her. We're very different, but because we're sisters we have overlapping similarities. We are strange fulfilling prophecies of our parents, balancing one another out physically, here an ear, there a toe, a laugh, a tear, a dream.

I've always known those things, perhaps by instinct. I could smell them in the air we breathed. But Jean made a cage for herself out of dissatisfaction and jealousy, and it's only now that she has found a way to come outside. And it's only now that I can trust the change in her and let myself enjoy these moments when we speak. I almost said meet, because it's like meeting the sister I always hoped she would be.

Now that she's better, I don't care about the past. I don't have to build a moat and two-foot-thick walls to protect myself from ugly words and feelings that would hurt. Ex-Catholic that I am, I pray that her strength of purpose lasts. For her. For me. It's as nice as I always imagined it would be to have someone from my old life, my sister, from back in 1928, who remembers Mother and Dad and 213th Street, and who can laugh and sigh with me over those faraway times, when we were young, yet see them in the light of what we know now and are today.

I must celebrate this gift.□

November 27, 1994
Alpine Drive, Beverly Hills

Dear Michael,
Today is the ninety-ninth anniversary of my mother's birth. The older I get, the less I grieve about her death. Not that I'm not sad about her being gone, but it's as if I finally understand the passage of time and the transience of life—not in words and ideas, but in my body and whatever it is that is my soul.

When I was little, I thought a soul must be like a breath of air, the way it looks when it's freezing outside and someone exhales. That's what I thought happened when you died. The soul would come out of the body and drift away and disappear. Then I took comfort from the thought that when we died and returned to the earth, our bodies became part of the process of life in some form—plants, insects, just another kind of life. I thought we lived on in other peoples' memories, and maybe in some way our souls became a part of them, the way we take parts of the people we love and make them part of ourselves. Like the woman you defended in

Seattle who used to live over around Twentieth Street and remembered my parents. Like you and me.

I talk about Mother to strangers sometimes. It's easier to tell someone I don't know well how much I loved her and what she was to me. When Milt and I talk about her, we almost always cry and that hurts too much. I don't think Andy remembers her very much, and Jenny mentions her in passing. She loved her a lot, but she doesn't speak of her very often.

And so I talk to you, because you knew her, and you knew my family, and you're not afraid to remember...

Last week Richard said Lizzie was just waking up one morning when he put a question to her, did she want this or that, and she answered, "I can't tell you because my brain is sideways." And that about says it for the last week for me.

Now for your letter—thank you good friend nephew—for your good words and your love and thoughtfulness. They have meant more to me than I can tell you, many times giving me a warmth that I desperately needed. You help me know where I came from, who I came from, and what I have become. All necessary to remind me that today is today and there is always hope of something.

I think you can thank the good Primont ears, big ears, for your ability to understand Chinese. We may not always sing beautifully or even on key, but we are excellent hearers. Not for nothing did the generation before me stand around my grandparents' living room harmonizing song after song and playing their musical instruments at every family gathering. It was their family habit. Even Uncle Ed used to sing, with a funny small smile at the corners of his mouth...

Speaking of grandchildren, the tennis club has a Sunday brunch now (not magnificent, but only ten dollars), and we took everyone there today. Will has become imperious again. He has a frown worthy of a Chinese dragon. He puts his head down and slightly sideways a little— as if he were a goat, I'd say in a butting position—and says things like "don't eat my pancakes" and "I want that" through tightened lips. All with those amazing blue eyes and honey golden hair and eyebrows, making you want to hold him close and kiss him.

Emily sat in a high chair next to me smiling a hundred smiles with her many teeth and adding a lot to the fun. She ate ravenously and squirmed constantly. She's wonderful. Lizzie was calmer than usual, and spent a lot of time coloring and eating a mountain of eggs and bacon. Sometimes we have moments of pleasure and hugging, and sometimes she reaches out to tell me something or show me what she has made. She's a busy child. I think that after my operation, when I can drive again, I'll take her out, just the two of us, and see what happens then.

We've had a fair amount of windy and mildly rainy days these last three weeks. The air and skies have been beautiful, and there is a lot less dust coating all the greenery. It's cold for California, in the forties at night and sixties during the day. If it keeps up, we'll have a nice long winter. This is how I like it. No extremes. No mudslides. No fires. No riots. And definitely no earthquakes. Be well and take care of yourself.

      Love,
      Rosemary

            March 19, 1995
            Alpine Drive, Beverly Hills

Dear Peggy,
Well, I'll try again. I've got a new computer with a Windows program. I finished a long letter to you then zapped it right out of existence. Not there. Not here. Nowhere. It was all about how when I woke up this morning, I was thinking, "Dear Peggy, how are you?" I had the feeling I was back there on the, what was it, ninth floor of the Chrysler Building, and you were going to pop your head into the open doorway of my office and say, "What's that you're reading?"

It made me think about all those months I was involved in the world of Proust and how I loved it, and you kept looking at me as if I were some other species, to be liked and tolerated, if not really understood. You were pretty brave about reading him, I think for my sake as well as your own, and I really appreciated it. I have to tell you, not too many people have been that generous over the years.

Well, what I'm reading today is *The Cunning Man* by Robertson Davies—not his best, I think, but worth reading. I started a book group with some women at the Beverly Hills Tennis Club—a very down-home affair, just right for someone from Queens Village. We must have joined the only tennis club in the United States in a fancy town where they have to put pails all over the dining room when it rains. The first book we read was Anna Quindlen's *One True Thing*, which I loved but some found a real downer, so the next book will be *Cold Sassy Tree* by Olive Ann Burns. That ought to cheer them up. After that, they're on their own—unless they suggest something by Catherine Cookson, or what's her name who writes a new book every two weeks—Barbara Cartland, Princess Di's grandmother.

But back to Proust. I read the first book at least six times, the second three times, the third about four times, and the rest of the volumes one or two times, and when I started studying French ten or twelve years ago, I insisted on using *Swann's Way* for my reading and oral translating. All those years of reading it must have imprinted the English version on my brain so well that it was a cinch, much to my teacher's astonishment, given the fact that I couldn't get through a page of Agatha Christie without using the dictionary. A friend told me that it was because Proust's French was formally elegant and correct and just kind of sings itself along.

If doctors and psychiatrists back in the fifties had known about antidepressants and bipolar mood disorder, I wonder what kind of a life I would have lived. I could have been a Prozac lady, cheerful and outgoing, not looking back or in, but ahead and out. I wish I had been, but at the same time, would I want to give up all that I learned? I don't know. It's a good question. I know I don't want to live through another depression, and if I stumble into one, I'll probably try something swallowable.

I was born to be a grandmother. That's about the only thing I'm sure of. I love my three little ones, and feel that I know just how to behave with them because of my own mother's behavior with her grandchildren. I'm "Nana," and it's great. They learn that grandmothers are like presents. Or like Billie Dawn's mink coats. "He's nice to me. I'm nice to him. Three mink coats, I got."

Milt is watching the arts channel in the other room, and they're playing something by Stravinsky that's pushing me around a little. For this letter Satie would have been better. Oops, Milt says it was a piece by Maurice Jarre—shows you my musical limitations. Yesterday we saw *Don Pasquale* at the L.A. Opera. It was great. Music, singing, production— all wonderful. This all sounds like an endless round of culture, but it's not. Those are the highlights. The rest is just everyday frittering around, and I love it, and wish it could go on forever. I'm finding these later years, except for the usual falling apart, to be rewarding and pleasant.

It was really great talking to you again. I have thought about you often over the years and wish we could see each other. I know I asked you to let me know if you were coming out this way, or if you are going to be in France. We have lots of room. Anyway, you said you'd write, so I'll be looking forward to hearing from you. Be well and happy.

    Love,
    Rosemary

        March 28, 1995
        Alpine Drive, Beverly Hills

Dear Joan,
Time is roaring by. I picked your card of a year ago January out of the folder marked "to do" and couldn't believe it has been there unanswered for over a year. Or did I answer it during that time, and has the memory become part of the jumble? I used to remember things in relation to the school year—long hot days of summer; autumn cool and colorful; winter, cold, snow, wind, beautiful grays; and spring, new green. Maybe California has forever skewed my sense of time... Today time seems made up of innumerable weeks, more or less the same unless we travel or we're

in the middle of a riot, mudslide, or inferno. Perhaps that's what we Californians must substitute for seasons.

Five years ago I thought time was passing at an amusingly rapid pace, but today I feel I'm running just to keep up with it. I would worry, but many of my acquaintances tell me they feel the same way. As I watched my mother age, I had the mistaken impression that she had so little to do that her last ten years were quite serene. I realize now that she may have felt the same way that I do, and that her weeks and months went by in a rush of breakfasts, lunches, dinners, grandchildren, books, TV, friends, and pharmacies, not unlike my own.

How was your trip to visit Jane in Cameroon? It sounded awful, though I'm sure it wasn't. The truth is, at this point in my life, a trip to San Diego takes a lot of determination to organize. Milt and I are so alike that someday we'll probably be found curled up in little bundles in some cozy spot in the house that we haven't bothered to move from in the last few months...

Jenny and her husband and daughter, Lizzie, are here living in our house, in the wing we built for Milt's parents. We have all learned to merge just the right amount to be family, but not to interfere with one another. Luckily there's room for two of everything—kitchens, etc., and Lizzie and I are beginning to develop a nice grandmother-granddaughter relationship. Not possible much earlier, because she always had a nanny. Nannies today are young and run and jump and sit on the floor plus all the things that grandmothers do, so grandmothers aren't very necessary in a house with a nanny.

Andy and Julia have two children, Will, three years old, and Emily, a year and a few months. I take care of them (with my housekeeper, who can still get down on the floor to play) one day a week, and often see them more. Julia isn't working (she's a librarian) and is a wonderful mother. She's pretty unflappable and easygoing about most things, and the children are so sweet. Milt and I are ridiculously dotty and attached to them.

It's so interesting to watch young couples with their children today. Both Andy and Richard help out, and Richard takes charge of a good part of parenting. Andy works with Milt now so he's home a lot, and since Richard is a writer, he's home most of the time. I can't think of anything they don't do for the children as a matter of course—except ironing clothes—and they could do that with the same ease given the inclination...

I plucked up my courage and started a reading group of women here in Beverly Hills. I hope it works out, because it is certainly more convenient than the other group I'm in that meets in the evenings about half an hour away. I'll do both if I can, provided one or the other doesn't decide to read Henry James or, god forbid, *Crime and Punishment*. The last time I read *Crime and Punishment* I decided enough already with the self-flagellation. That must be the most depressing book ever written, except for Elie Wiesel's *Night*.

Jenny is working hard. As artists go, she is quite successful. I guess if you make a living in art, you are successful beyond most artists' dreams. She gets good reviews for her shows in Europe, but having arrived here during a big recession, things are pretty slow so far.

Chappaqua must be starting to get green and wonderful round about now. I have never stopped missing it and the friends we knew...

       Love to you and Bill,
          Rosemary and Milt

                       March 31, 1995
                       Alpine Drive, Beverly Hills

Dear Aunt Betty,
It was great to get your note, but embarrassing to realize that we missed out on sending you birthday greetings. It's not a good enough excuse, but I had a cataract removed, and, I'm afraid, was thinking only of myself. The operation was a grand success, but still haven't been able to find a pair of glasses that can bring my two now mismatched eyes into focus.

We're coming along fine, happy with our three grandchildren around us. We were both made to be grandparents; we love them so much. I can't imagine how we spent our time before they were born. And I also understand now the pride and love I always heard in your voice when you spoke of your grandchildren.

Julia and Andy's little one, Emily, is fourteen months old and the smilingest baby I've run into. She's a real cuddler and clings like a little monkey, smiling, the clearest picture of pleasure I've ever seen on a face. She's one happy child. I hope this is her lasting temperament and that she will go through life taking on the world just the way she does today. Will is a typical three-year-old, happy and cheerful when he gets his way, imperious when he doesn't, mad about trains, knows how to spell his name, and loves his grandfather and me. What else can we ask for?

Lizzie is five and a half. Yesterday she locked the bathroom door and slathered herself with my makeup and then wondered how I knew what she had done. She is determined to investigate our entire house and try out what everything does, especially the messy stuff. If I didn't remember pouring a bottle of red nail polish on my mother's dresser at just that age, I could be very irritated. She does an awful lot that reminds me of myself. On the other hand, she sits at the computer and shows me how to play games. The other day I asked what she was playing and she said poker, so I guess she takes after Jenny on that score... Well, happy belated birthday, Dear Betty. We send all our love and good wishes.

Love
Rosemary

LIZZIE

April 14, 1995

I've forgotten how I used to sit down and just write off the top of my head. I've got to start doing that again or I may give up altogether, and I need to write. It's the thing that keeps me knowing that I'm here. I have a need to look back and see that indeed I was here last year and last month and this is what I was thinking. It's the thing that gives a meaning to this second half of my life. I don't paint or draw anymore. I don't dance. I never could sing, though I sang a few favorite songs, mostly folk songs and lullabies, to my children. Young children don't judge creativity harshly. It gives you courage to open yourself up with them.

Last week Lizzie asked me to play the little toy piano so she could dance. She did a wonderful chaotic version of ballet dancing, with lifts, turns, and leaps. Then she wanted to play so I could dance for her, and after a second of hesitation, I did a dance not unlike hers, which delighted her. Then she danced and pranced again, which delighted me. It was one of our nicer moments. The movements of her hands are very graceful, and she has obviously watched classical dancers and ice skaters closely, where the positions of the hands are formalized and flowerlike.

It was fun to let go and dance in her almost ecstatic way. There was no obvious rhythm to what we were playing. It was dingbat banging, and it felt wonderful. It was forget about scales and forget about time and forget about everything but having fun and letting go. Yet she had ideas for her dancing. I could tell because she repeated movements and oriented herself in my direction. Next year, some lessons if she wants. And some tennis lessons, which she has already asked for.

Once she starts school in Beverly Hills, we can pick her up and let her do those things for fun and frolic instead of leaving her at playschool. That is, if she still wants to. I suspect she will. She's a funny little child, very serious in her own way. Below the hyper surface is a determined child. That's good but often difficult. She's intelligent, talented, and... what else? That's a question I may not be around to see answered. I hope life is good to her, and that she is good to life around her.□

WE WERE THERE

It's now the day after Easter, 1995. Not much relation to the Easters of my early life. Except that I called Jean yesterday to say Happy Easter and spoke to Mary Litchhult, now Mary Weiger, today.

It was strange to hear Mary speak today of how she saw my family. How much she loved my mother. How much she disliked my father. How when her mother, Vera, saw me walking down the street with my father she would say something like "poor thing," meaning me, when my family seemed to think that Mary was the poor thing because her father Andrew was so ill with sleeping sickness, and then died so young of Parkinson's.

I know that my father gave Mary's mother food and probably cash on occasions when she had none, and that he also sometimes paid for coal for her in the winter, but I had no idea that at the end of her life he was trying to borrow money from her when he had reverses at the store in Manhattan. Mary said her mother lent him money that he never returned, and I'm sure that's true, though I think it wasn't a lot because she didn't have a lot, and eventually she used Mary as an excuse not to give him any more by telling him that Mary had to co-sign to sell some of the savings bonds that she had. She was right not to, but I'm sure she felt angry and guilty for refusing him because he helped her out for years after Andrew died.

I played with Erna Lanza and Ann Guerin. We played in the yards, mostly ours since it was the largest, and ran around being queens and princesses, doing a lot of things that I think Mary missed out on, things that allowed me to forget everything and just let my imagination run about with my body in a kind of wonderful freedom from being who I was.

The disadvantage to Junior as a playmate was that he was much weaker than Mary, and she ruled the roost. She was an only child. Her mother idolized her. As a parent, I understand that, but it was hard on Mary. She had to be everything and fulfill all dreams, both constructive and destructive.

And though I was the youngest of three in my messy household, I was the strong child in my home. Somewhere inside there was strength, gleaned from all the family puritans, fanatics, and propriety-ridden prigs, tempered by my father's rashness and conviction that he was absolutely right, my mother's animal maternal strength, added to a talent for manual pursuits, a passion for reading, and a guilty Catholic conscience, and above all the understanding of my mother's love. Out of the mixture I have molded a life somehow and tried to maintain as much of a sense of reality as I can muster.

Mary told me something today that made me very happy. I wrote a story about her father from what I remembered of him, which seems to have been from the last year or two of his life. She told me how much she loved him and how they did things together all the time when she was younger and he was still well enough to get around. I always thought of him as an invalid, which he was to a great extent, because in those days there was no medication for encephalitis lethargica. But she has many happy memories of him, so her life was much richer than I knew.

Why do I call Mary now after all these years? I'd say it's because those years were real. I remember them. I've tried hard to understand what was and what wasn't true over the years. Some of the memories are so painful they take my breath away and some are warm and happy. There were hungers that grew in me then that have never been satisfied, and needs that grew and grew to make me incapable of behaving sensibly.

We live in the images that other people have of us. We see ourselves reflected in their judgments. We fulfill their prophecies and sometimes even our own of what we will become. And sometimes, successfully, fight to let ourselves be different, be what we might have been if left free to be.

We all try to make sense of our lives, sense of life, fit the pieces together like a jigsaw to complete our picture, and these may be the final years that I have the chance to do so. The fact that Jean and I can now finally speak to each other with generosity has given me the courage to reach out and speak to Mary, as the only child I was ever encouraged to play with before I was twelve years old, but with whom I had as incomplete an understanding as any two children would have who came from such different families and did not choose each other out of mutual interest but because their mothers were close friends.

I would like to think that now we can feel good things toward each other, without the baggage left over from that anxious time back in the thirties and forties when we were the love and pride of our parents and were living in a place that neither of us could wait to get away from, neither knowing how strong that feeling was in the other. We are two strangers who grew up in intimate proximity, who can look back and say, "Hey, we were there" and share our perspectives of what "there" was. It makes it possible for me to think of some of the good things, even about my father. It makes me remember the sunny days and the flowers and the good smells of food cooking.□

EASTER

Brought up in a Catholic home, I knew all about Lent and the Stations of the Cross, and that Easter was the day to celebrate Christ rising from the dead. The Depression meant that families had to economize on the annual outpouring of money for special clothes to wear to church on Easter. In Queens Village in the thirties, fashion was somewhat subdued, but almost everyone tried to wear something festive—a flowered hat, a new spring coat in a pastel color, dressy shoes.

Every year my mother bought us something new to wear. And on the Saturday before Easter we boiled eggs for the next day's egg hunt. I loved dying the eggs and eating them on Easter morning. That and the jellybeans, candy corn, marshmallow chicks, and big chocolate bunnies in the Easter baskets that my mother prepared for the three of us. All day Sunday, except for the hour we went to Church and while we sat at the dinner table, I had my basket next to me, poking around in it, rearranging the candies, eating as many as I could without getting caught. No candy before breakfast, so no candy before church and the eggs.

First, the chocolate ears. I always intended to be patient, but after the ears I would have to go back again, and then again and again, for just a little bit more. Then some jellybeans, always the licorice first, then orange and purple, then green, and last the pink, which I didn't like at all, but they were candy and if I couldn't trade with Mike and Jean for a flavor I liked better, I'd eat them.

Through the day the bunny got smaller, now the face, a leg, the tail, until only the base was left, and sometimes I felt too awful to eat that, so it waited in the basket until Monday. The little yellow chicks were best stale, so I saved those too if I could resist temptation. Candy corn was a problem. Everyone in the family loved candy corn with its three different stripes, and it was always gone the first day. Even grown-up aunts and uncles ate candy corn when the basket was held out with the invitation to "have a piece."

One Easter morning, next to my basket, I found a large plush bunny rabbit with a purple ribbon around its neck. I spent that day like all other Easters arranging and rearranging jellybeans, eating the candy. When bedtime came, I took the rabbit with me, the way I'd seen children do in movies and picture books. I may have asked for a plush rabbit, but this wasn't a friendly kind of rabbit. It wasn't soft and furry, but was stuffed with straw and very stiff. Its fur was thin and a faded lime-yellow green, and as I put my head against it, I could hear it rustle and crunch. I thought I'd feel tender toward the rabbit, but I didn't.

Just then, Mother passed by my bedroom door and, seeing me with my arm around the toy, called quietly to Dad to see how "cute she looks." I was so embarrassed by not feeling what I thought I should feel that I pretended to be asleep. I didn't tell them that the rabbit was unpleasant to hold. I didn't know why I didn't feel whatever it was those children in the pictures felt, but I didn't want anyone to know about it. After Mama and Dad left the doorway, I pushed the toy away. It was just a thing.

I took the rabbit to bed with me for a few weeks after that because I felt it was expected and I wanted to please them. I never asked for anything for Easter after that, but I always knew that my mother would fix an Easter basket for me until it was no longer necessary and she could give me the large chocolate bunny all by itself. That, and some candy corn and licorice jellybeans.□

AUNT VERA

Aunt Vera and Uncle Andrew Litchhult lived down the street from us. We weren't related, but in those days that's what children called their parents' close friends. Their house was slightly larger, with an extension on the back and a closed front porch. Inside the house, things were very different from ours. The furniture was well kept and there were some fine antiques inherited from Uncle Andrew's mother, a lady Aunt Vera was not sorry to see pass away, though she prayed for the repose of her soul with her eyes closed and her hands clasped together at the funeral Mass.

Aunt Vera's brother, Uncle Charlie, a gentle, bumbling, middle-aged alcoholic, lived with them and their daughter, Mary, a year older than me. Aunt Vera and my mother were best friends, having moved to the street about the same time. They were very different in temperament, but shared one thing in common. They both had a profound contempt for men. My mother found a few men in her lifetime whom she exempted from the rule that "they're all alike," but Aunt Vera never found any, except perhaps Uncle Andrew, who upset her deep conviction that none of them were worth the trouble. Poor Uncle Andrew probably escaped that condemnation by contracting sleeping sickness during the war and becoming an invalid, unable to work, spending his days sitting around the house reading the papers, and taking short walks to the store when he was well enough to do errands for Vera. Sometimes he worked in the garden. He could be seen ruffling around the flower-filled back garden with Blackie, his unclipped black poodle, carrying plants from one spot to another, filling bushel baskets with weeds, and smiling quietly if a neighbor spoke to him. Uncle Andrew usually wore a sweater buttoned down the front and a white shirt and a tie, like a respectable businessman going to work. But he often wore maroon felt slippers during the day, permissible because he was an invalid. His hair was grizzled and grew far back on his high rounded forehead, and his eyes were dark and shiny but not animated. I seldom heard him speak. Uncle Andrew and Uncle Charlie left most of the talking to Aunt Vera, which seemed to be the way she liked it. She ruled supreme in her own household, quick tempered and volatile. She was plump, with great dimples in her elbows and another in her chin. Her face could be fierce when she was irritated, though when it was turned toward me, it was usually soft and friendly.

I loved Aunt Vera. She held me on her lap and snuggled against my head. I could stick out my arm to be tickled and Aunt Vera laughed and obliged. There was always a cookie or a glass of milk for me at Aunt Vera's, and it was my second home. I never took liberties—it was understood that I had to ask for anything I wanted—but I was free to ask, use the bathroom, eat lunch, or call my mother on the telephone.

Aunt Vera sent away for things advertised on packages and jars. Mary had a blue Little Orphan Annie drinking glass, games, and code rings that popped open and revealed enticing secrets about characters on the radio. Mary would sit drinking Ovaltine or Cocomalt from the blue glass while I drank out of a plain one. She let me use the glass once, and I was surprised to find that it didn't change how the milk tasted.

Aunt Vera walked heavily on her thick legs in her college-heeled shoes and wore a small diamond-encrusted wristwatch on her left arm, a gift from her husband at the time of their marriage. Her hobby was collecting china—cups, saucers, small creamers—which she displayed in a glass cupboard in the dining room. Each year my mother gave her a china ornament to add to the collection. Since Mama's taste ran to the amusing rather than the refined, the items she gave Aunt Vera were put to use rather than into the cupboard. A teapot shaped like a doughnut. A cookie jar in the shape of an old man. China flowers in a basket. After growing up in her aunt's house surrounded by things one paid reverence to and used once a year, or never, because they were too good, Mama believed in practical gifts.

Mary was Aunt Vera's only child, born after several years of unhappy infertility. Then, as they were about to leave for a vacation, my mother gave Aunt Vera a black nightgown, saying, "Maybe this will do the trick." Mother claimed that it did, because Aunt Vera came back from vacation pregnant.

Mary was only allowed to play with a few children on the street. Me, because I was my mother's child, Junior Heiss, the pampered son of the neighbor across the Litchhult's back fence, and Albert Kudley directly across the street. Aunt Vera guarded her daughter's honor zealously. It could never be thought that Mary was less clever, less important, less strong than me. With two other children vying for attention and inattention, my mother was less concerned with my dominance and cared only that I got into no trouble and behaved pleasantly at Aunt Vera's house.

I always felt that Aunt Vera loved me, even if there were times when she didn't like something about me. I knew that it was right for her to love Mary the best because she was Mary's mother, just the way my mother loved me more, but it made me shrink a little when Aunt Vera looked piqued when I got better marks than Mary. I didn't work hard in school, and effort should have meant something.

The inside of Aunt Vera's house was darker than ours. Only the kitchen and front porch were bright and cheerful. It smelled of the wonderful food that Aunt Vera cooked, and it smelled best when she made cinnamon honey buns. She always gave me one if I stopped by. There were cucumbers soaked in vinegar and oil and a salad every day. Tea was the standard drink. Chocolate icing on cakes was very dark and thin instead of piled high and thick with butter. In summertime there was mint from the garden in the iced tea.

Mary was the most cherished member of the family, and all eyes turned to her when she spoke. She was the delight of the household and could say anything and be believed, though she didn't say much that wasn't believable. Her report cards were rewarded with treats of candy and quarters. Her baby teeth fell out to the clink of dimes instead of nickels.

Until Vera started working after Uncle Andrew died, there were only a few neatly wrapped presents under the tree at Christmas. Mary received presents from my family, the Kudleys, the Heisses, and other family friends, but there wasn't the same look of abandon under the tree as at our house. Aunt Vera was defensive about being unable to shower Mary with gifts, and always allowed a remark or two regarding the stupidity of people who overdid it at Christmas. After she began to work, the floor under their tree looked more opulent, and there was no more talk about the displays at other people's homes. She also began to buy more presents for Mary at other times, so that Easter often saw Mary with a delicate gold bracelet or ring along with new Easter clothes, and birthdays were more like Christmas.

Aunt Vera was an aggressive woman. Orphaned at an early age, she and her little brother Charlie went to live with an aunt and uncle in Missouri, her growth as a woman stunted by watching the misery of her aunt with her uncle, also an alcoholic. As Mary grew, she tried hard not to be influenced by her mother's bitterness, and to get out from under the pressure her mother put on her to hate and distrust men. Aunt Vera wanted Mary to be pretty, but when boys liked her because she was pretty, Vera became angry and hostile. She resorted to headaches, heart attacks, anything that would keep Mary at home, and when Mary went out with a boy, Aunt Vera sat on the front porch until she came home. Mary's embarrassment was dreadful. She hated what her mother was doing to her, but she was tied to her out of guilt over her mother's early widowhood and longstanding martyrdom with Uncle Charlie.

Apart from Uncle Charlie, it was an orderly, respectable household. And even he was a quiet, benign alcoholic, lurching silently into the house and up to his room to escape his sister's censure, and never making a public spectacle of himself. Every Friday night, Herman and Florence Bornaman came to visit Aunt Vera. I think my mother liked Florence, but she detested Herman and so did my father. Mary called them Aunt Florence and Uncle Herman, and was probably attached to them. They had children who were older than Mary, but I don't remember ever seeing them. After Uncle Andrew died, they were a permanent Friday-night fixture, and by the time Mary was ten, my mother was warning Aunt Vera to watch out for Herman. "He has his eye on Mary, Vera. I tell you, I know it. Watch out for him." To which Aunt Vera always replied, scoffing, "Don't be ridiculous. He's just being kind."

Herman was a small man, with small pink hands and small feet. He had an oily manner and eyelids that drooped slightly as if hiding some thought that his half-smiling lips couldn't say. Every now and then he brought a present to Mary. One that I remember was a manicure set. No nail polish, just scissors, a nail file, and an emery board in a leather case. Mary and I would sit in the kitchen on Friday nights doing our nails, with him sitting at the end of the table reading a paper and watching us, while the Friday night prize fights—a left to the chin and a right hook to the nose—rumbled on the radio.

Herman played the benign uncle, a father figure, and I think Mary liked him a lot. Her own father, who had been ill long before her birth, was a nice man, and kind to her, but almost absent in a way, even before his death, and here was this man who with her Mother's permission paid attention to her and made a fuss over her.

Florence Bornaman died when Mary was in her teens, and my mother said, "Watch out for him, Vera. He'll be after Mary now." Well, he wasn't, at least not noticeably. He was smart enough to wait until a short time after Aunt Vera died, when Mary was in her twenties. By that time, she was grown up enough to know he wasn't what she wanted. "I knew it. The old blister," my mother said to me.

Now that I think of it, it's interesting that my mother recognized lust when she saw it and Vera, the man-hater, didn't. Vera was simply worried about losing her beloved Mary. My mother knew that losing us was inevitable; she just didn't want Jean and me to get pregnant before wedding day. And she wanted us all, Mike included, to choose nice, suitable, respectable Catholics, but not too soon.□

LETTER TO MARY LITCHHULT

Dear Mary,
I was so happy that you were glad to hear from me. After not hearing from you before, I figured you either hated to write letters,

or were angry, or simply didn't care to be bothered. I was shocked to hear of Jean's refusal to give you my number in California, and it makes me wonder how many other people might have asked her for the number and been refused.

We have had an unlisted number for years because Milt used to get calls at all hours from songwriters or people who wanted to reach the singers he worked with. You can imagine what it's like to answer the phone at three a.m. to be asked if Milt would call John Denver the next day and see if he would do a benefit for saving whales, or if Milt would listen to a song the caller is sure will be a big hit. Those calls are infrequent in these last years now that Milt's not recording any more, but they still happen occasionally. At one point, even with the unlisted number, I started to get weird calls, not sex calls, just weird calls from a man whose voice I recognized but couldn't place. We had the number changed twice, and the calls continued, so it must have been somebody who had easy access to our number. I finally stopped answering the phone for some months, and then the last time we had the number changed, the calls stopped. So we've been leery about having the number listed.

You said that alcohol was to blame for Jean's refusal to give you my telephone number, but I find it harder to excuse than that. Long before alcohol became an entrenched part of her life, our relationship was sad. I'm sure in your lifetime you've wished you had a brother or sister to share the good and the bad times with you. But my life has been filled with a longing to be liked by my sister. My big sister. We don't change much from the children we were. We learn to wear our façades like overcoats. They may protect us from the world's eyes, and for some of us that may be enough.

I am still the daughter of Rosemary and Walter Primont who grew up in the small gray stucco house on 213th Street with a silent brother I didn't know or want to know, and a sister who didn't like me and never let a chance go by to let me know it. Her mythology was that I was a spoiled brat who never did any work around the house, when in fact I was handed a dust rag at the age of three or four, just as Jean had been at that age, and told to dust the bottom rungs of the tables and chairs. By the time I was five, Mike was washing the dishes, Jean was drying, and I was putting away. I made beds and vacuumed, washed windows, and folded laundry. By thirteen, when we moved to 215th Street, I did the family laundry each week, including Jean's because she was working, and from the time my mother went to work when I was twelve, I cooked dinner on weeknights. I also did the grocery shopping. She remembers none of this, because she doesn't remember anything that includes me in a positive way. The truth is that in our house, we all worked, including my father. Weekends when he was home, he often helped prepare the food and washed the dishes. The only thing I don't remember my father doing was ironing.

Jean's picture of her life is that of an orphan. I got everything and she got nothing. My mother used to say that from the time I started eating Jean counted every pea on my plate. What she never understood was that I wasn't hungry. I wasn't greedy. I was the kind of kid who just wanted to be left to one side and not have anybody call attention to me. I wanted to be loved, but not noticed. I'm still that same person.

Jean was a teenager at the height of the Depression, before my mother went to work, so there wasn't money for luxuries. We both paid a price for my father's generosity to other people, she because there was less money for nice clothes, and both of us in having to lie to bill collectors who came to the door and tell them that no one was home. But really the Depression was most at fault. I don't suppose Jean has ever connected that grand social event to mother's penny pinching.

I loved my mother. She was my anchor. I could count on her for love. Not necessarily for acceptance, but for love and protection and for arms that would hold me. I loved her as her child, then as her equal, then as her parent. But she was always my source of strength. Someone else could know her faults, as I did, but they were minor faults, no worse than yours or mine. For all that I was the one who loved her dearly, she never loved me more than Mike or Jean. She probably understood me less than she did Jean and Mike. But I was the one who didn't expect her to be perfect, so I was the one who loved her.

Mike was another story. He was always lost. He was her first child. Once, on the day of my last nap, Mother sang a lullaby called "Mighty Lak' a Rose" that she said she used to sing to Mike when he was a baby, and I could hear in her voice how much she loved him. Then she sang "Sail, Baby, Sail." I can hear her wavering small voice as she sang the lyric— "sail across the sea, only don't forget to sail, back again to me." I couldn't imagine not sailing back to my mother. We were in her front bedroom and she was trying to rock me to sleep. It was summertime and we could hear Jean and some of the other kids playing on the front steps. I asked my mother what lullaby her mother sang to her, and she said that her mother died when she was a little girl, so she didn't remember her. I remember how dreamy she looked while we were speaking and how I thought nothing could be worse than not having a mother. Maybe that was the day I decided I would always love her, because she didn't know how it felt to be held the way she was holding me.

As I walked up and down 213th Street, I was often the butt of unpleasant remarks aimed really at my father. He was bossy, opinionated, never hesitated to say what he thought, and didn't care what the neighbors thought about him. Jean may have had the same experience, but she was much more apt to speak out than I. She was much more gregarious. My problem was that I was shy, and I looked like him, and in those days people in a lower-middle-class neighborhood never hesitated to say what they thought in front of the kids, who were expected to keep their mouths shut. So I walked up and down the block, trying to ignore what was said, often feeling embarrassed and diminished by local disapproval. It took me years to understand that he had another side to him. He was often right, not tactful, but right. Abe's candy store around the corner was filthy. Henry Tiedeman's ice cream was terrible, until my father brought him some ice cream mix and went down into the cellar to show him how to use it. That was long after Henry refused in front of other kids to give me an ice cream cone and told me not to come back into the store. I may have been told to stay out of more stores than any other kid in Queens Village, and all because I looked like him. I certainly never expressed an opinion a storekeeper could have taken exception to.

Several days before Mother died, Jean told me that she had never loved her. Maybe I should forgive her that, try to understand. But I can't. I can tell you that she knew Jean didn't love her, and told me so once herself. I couldn't believe what she was saying and tried to dissuade her, but she just said, "I know it." Well, I've had enough experience to know that she was right and that when a child doesn't love you, unless you're deluded, you know it. But you see, if Jean didn't love Mother, I didn't love my father. I wanted him to be someone different. I saw their faults, but I only forgave my mother. I know now that my father, with his changeable moods, now ecstatically happy, now morosely depressed, had bipolar mood disorder, and I have inherited it. His moods fluctuated daily. He could go through them two and three times a day. It probably accounted for a lot of the friction he had in the neighborhood. One day giving lectures on neatness, the next treating all the kids on the block to ice cream, ten minutes later singing and dancing in our living room, then later sunk in a depression that made his feet drag and his eyes seem half dead. We never knew what his mood would be, and I lived always skirting around him waiting for the axe to fall.

So there we were—the Primonts—staggering along. I think Tolstoy said something like, "All happy families are alike. Each unhappy family is unhappy in its own way." My memory of that house is of broken furniture, fighting, and tension. The good things were reading, radio, good food, daydreaming, and always my mother. Even if she was scolding or disciplining me, she was there—dependable—and I needed that more than anything in the world. I needed one consistent thing to tell me who and what I was. If I was unhappy in school, and I was, and if I couldn't walk out in the street without being aware of the hostility caused by my father, I had one person who was always there for me.

I don't think Jean has ever realized that when you don't like someone, they feel it, and they can't help but react to it. So, if she didn't love Mother, then how could Mother be open and trusting to her? We can make ourselves vulnerable to someone else's hostility just so much and no more. If I could see, as a child, that Jean loved my father and forgave him everything, and forgave my mother nothing, certainly my mother could also see it.

And me. I've known Jean's dislike from the day I can remember knowing anything. But I was fourteen before I gave up trying to be liked by her and decided never to let down my guard with her. We were alone and having a pleasant time together, when two of her friends came to the house, and in a second she turned on me in front of them, demanding that I get out of the room and stop spying on her. That's the day I knew she couldn't like me and I had to let go. From then on, through good times and bad, I've kept my emotional distance as much as possible. I can't stop myself from wanting her love. When I get the urge, I call her and we speak, but during the last alcoholic years, I never spoke to her after noon California time. Even now, since she stopped drinking, when we've been able to have reasonable talks, I am afraid to scratch the surface. After all, the mythology didn't start with alcohol; it started with my birth.

I realize in reading this that I've spoken about my love for my mother but selfishly and childlike. I've not spoken about her, only how I saw her. She was orphaned at three when her mother died, and was separated from her two brothers, who went to live with an uncle who had several children, while she was sent to live with her three aunts and grandmother. She was brought up to be a lady, white gloves, chastity, everything in its place, the works. The stories she told of her childhood were mostly about her grandmother, whom she loved. Late in her life she told me that Nana had really acted as her mother. I don't know if you remember Nana. She was the sister who was the most openly chastising, a religious fanatic even in those days, a poor guilt-ridden unused woman, constantly in a state of trembling at the cruel justice of God's righteous anger. Then there was Mamie, cool, detached, saintly, and strong, and Julie, whom I only vaguely remember. She was the one who died early. I see her clearly, pepper and salt wavy hair, pink apron over a white short-sleeved dress, drying dishes and putting my father in his place, pleasant but tough, in the Hollis kitchen. Mother and Dad always said she was the lively one, with a sense of humor, and a history of being married once, to an alcoholic. A year of that was enough and she left him to return home, never to mention his name again.

We made fun of the three aunts, but as an adult, I understand that they were pretty tough women. They all worked and saved their money, bought a beautiful home, furnished it with taste, and maintained it in perfect condition. Everything in their lives was perfect, except for Julie's marriage, and that was swept under the rug perfectly. And they did all this without the help of anyone else in the family. They were independent in all ways except one. For love and attention, they depended on us. And my father, who appreciated their need, was as good to them as my mother, and with a true generosity.

So mother escaped the ivory tower and married a man who loved to sing and dance and be in a crowd. He was everything she probably thought she wanted to get away to. He was a Catholic, but he wasn't a fanatic, and it wasn't guilt that drove him anywhere. He was an empathic man. He felt people's pain and sadness and wanted to make things easier for them. And he tried to foster that in us. He was anarchistic and conservative. He was a Democrat who frequently voted Republican. He mistrusted all politicians, but was patriotic in the extreme, and supported the government the politicians created. He was intelligent and uneducated. I've grown to understand that he was a man of strong instincts at war within himself. And he was manic-depressive, sometimes both ten times a day.

My mother learned to deal with him as best she could. She loved him, and both admired and despised him. She'd had too much order in her life to bear it or the lack of it. He was what kept her from being Rapunzel in her ivory tower, and she probably kept him from total disgrace and debtor's prison. It was my mother who made ends meet with whatever money she could get out of him. He couldn't keep money in his pocket for ten minutes. He would spend it on anything. We were always behind on the mortgage, heating oil, electric, and telephone payments until my mother went to work and found her wings. She loved working. She had a responsible clerical job, counting, collecting, and reporting all the nickels, dimes, and dollars pouring into the cash registers at Gimbels on 34th Street. She even reached some supervisory capacity after a few years. What she loved as much as the responsibility was the respect of her cohorts and financial independence. Imagine, after a life of security and stability, having your food and shelter in the hands of a five-year- old, generous but without a thought to the next five minutes, much less tomorrow, because that's how my father operated.

Suddenly our house became brighter. Torn and battered ceased to be the main motif, and chintz and neat filled my mother with pride. She had some new clothes, and she bought clothes for Jean and me. Jean was working by that time and in a fog of love for Jimmy. It was too bad that the end of the Depression, the beginning of the war, and mother's independence all coincided with Jean deciding that Jimmy was the one she would marry. Mother and Dad detested him. I less so, but I was a child still and only saw romance. Unfortunately, that's all Jean saw, that and a way to have a savior from her mythical orphanhood. Jimmy would place her on the pedestal she deserved. He would stand up to the mother and father who deprived her of being the most important. Jimmy would show the world which one in the family counted the most. Jimmy I won't describe.

My mother didn't think Jimmy was good enough for Jean. And my father didn't think he was good enough for anyone. And both were right. But because my mother refused to go to the wedding, and didn't talk to Jimmy for several years, it took Jean twenty years to acknowledge to the family what she says she learned after a few weeks of marriage—that she'd made a mistake.

By the time Mother was able to swallow her dislike sufficiently to accept his presence, I was old enough to see that Jimmy was an ignorant fool. He was possessive and jealous of Jean. I was also a little afraid of him. I maintained a kind of reserve when I was with him, never criticizing or getting into any big arguments with him. I knew he had a gun and I sensed the seething quality of his hatred for almost anyone he thought he could frighten. Jimmy was a schoolyard bully with an explosive temper and a strong physique. Mother always spoke to him in a tone of sardonic contempt without being openly insulting. She had a special voice for Jimmy. He may have married her daughter, but she was stronger than he was, and they both knew it.

I knew my mother through the books she loved. When I started to read, she gave me her small collection of L.M Montgomery. She loved *Daddy Long Legs*. It didn't take long for me to understand that all the books she loved were about girls who were orphans, and who wanted to be something important when they grew up. They were independent, even though they loved and had families. They loved sunsets and the stars and books. Not a bad idea for a life to give to a daughter in those days. My mother had a social life of sorts, but her real life was solitary and thoughtful, lived behind her eyes when they were sad. Aunt Vera was the only friend she had that she loved. She had other friends over the years, but Aunt Vera was her best friend and my mother felt an undying loyalty to her.

I suppose mothers were always terrified daughters would become pregnant. And they were right—for their time. What a disaster that would be in lower-middle-class America, no money or know-how to end it, and certain disgrace if it was discovered. Also, our mothers knew that life could be painfully hard and deceptive, whatever the reasons. They hated to see us out with young men. Or any men. Each boy that I went out with was suspect. He was criticized and compared unfavorably to the last boy, the one I'd broken up with, the formerly despised young man, who was now held up as everything a mother could want for her daughter. It was like some kind of square dance of changing partners, with the new partner always said to be worse than the one he replaced, right up to and including Milt, though my mother came to love and respect Milt, to the point of always wondering how he could continue to love someone she considered as contrary as me. Because while I knew my mother loved me, she certainly didn't think of me as being without faults.□

April 19, 1995
Alpine Drive, Beverly Hills

Dear Jean,

Thank you for that article about Anna Quindlen. I'm glad you liked the books. I thought they were great. We read *One True Thing* in the new book group I'm in, but I think I was the one it spoke to most clearly because of the similarity of backgrounds. Some of the women found it too sad, maybe too much of a reminder of recent experiences. I'm looking forward to her next one with pleasure. Anyway, I'll make some copies of the article and pass them around to the others.

We had a nice, chopped-up Easter day. Will had a mildly upset stomach so we didn't go there for lunch as expected, but took Lizzie out for brunch, and then Milt and I went over to Andy and Julia's around four o'clock in the afternoon and had an early supper, Easter egg hunt, and big cuddle for a few hours, and then we came back and watched television. Have you been watching the Dickens *Martin Chuzzlewit* on PBS? It's so unreal that even I can stand the suspense.

I can't believe I'm actually sitting here typing a letter. Chalk it up to having a cup of decaf with an added half teaspoon of regular instant coffee. I've got Emily and Will for the day. It's my Grandma Day, Thursday, and usually by two o'clock in the afternoon, I'm sagging against the table and trying to grab a quick nap along with them. I'll probably pass out at four-thirty when they leave and won't be able to get up for dinner.

I read another good book, now out in paperback, *Having Our Say*, by two elderly middle-class sisters, one hundred one and one hundred three, now made into a play on Broadway, and it was really wonderful. Very simple, history spelled out in easy terms, a quick read. Really worth reading, and probably at the library if you're interested...I have the new P.D. James, and my kids have read it, so I'll send it on to you. That is, if you haven't read it yet.

Maybe it was Easter that made me think of Mary, so I called her again to see how she is. When I spoke to her a month or so ago, she sounded very depressed. It was strange to hear Mary speak today of how she saw our family, and how much she loved Mother.

I know that Daddy gave Aunt Vera food and probably a little cash on occasions when she had none while we were living on 213th Street, and that he also paid for coal sometimes for her in the winter, but I had no idea that at the end of her life he was trying to borrow money from her, when he had reverses in the store in New York. Mary said Vera lent him money that he never returned, and I'm sure that's true, though I don't think it was a lot because she didn't have a lot, and eventually she used Mary as an excuse not to give him any more by telling him that Mary had to co-sign to sell some of the savings bonds that she had. She was right not to, but I'm sure she felt angry and guilty refusing him because he helped her out for years after Andrew died.

Mary says she used to hide when Dad came down to their house because he was so bossy and made Aunt Vera angry trying to tell her how to live her life. How she ought to throw Charlie out if he didn't stop drinking. Mary says she understands now that he was right, but in those days she could only see how it upset her mother. And she understands why her mother couldn't put Charlie out.

She pointed out that she hardly ever came up to our end of the block because she wasn't permitted to play with the kids at that end. Her mother didn't feel they were nice enough. She was only allowed to play with Junior Heiss and Albert Kudely, both of whom were pariahs in the neighborhood—Junior who never was allowed to play with any of the boys, and Albert, who was a kind of born actuary. Junior never knew the kids made fun of him, but poor Albert was the butt of all the cruel boy jokes the kids like our brother could think of. Of course, Albert went to college, got a good job, married a girl named Astrid, had a couple of beautiful children, and for all I know, lived happily ever after. I wonder what happened to the kids on the block who were so mean to him.

What Mary didn't know was that down at our end of the block, I was also a pariah and felt great sympathy for Albert and Junior. With Daddy shooting off his mouth, and a good part of the time being right in his assessments, if not his right to broadcast them, we Primonts weren't the most popular of families. We were right down at the bottom of the list with the drunks and wife beaters and made it to plenty of storekeepers' lists of most undesirable customers. For most of my years, until we moved away when I was thirteen, I had to listen to taunts about my family being stuck up and walking around with our heads in the air, about Mike, but mostly about Daddy and who did he think he was telling everybody else what to do. If the neighbors' remarks ever bothered you, I don't remember you saying so. Come to think of it, I probably didn't say anything about it either, it upset me so. Maybe you were better able to fight back.

Mother wouldn't allow me to go into most of the houses on our block for the same reasons that Mary's mother refused to let her play with the children. Some of the women were slatterns. Some of the men drank. And mother had a healthy suspicion that little girls should not be encouraged to spend time in houses of people she didn't know, or didn't approve of.

The fact that you and I can now speak to each other more freely has given me the courage to reach out and speak to Mary, as the only child I was ever encouraged to play with before I was twelve years old, but with whom I had as incomplete an understanding as any two children would have, who came from two such different families and have not chosen each other out of mutual interest, but because their mothers were close friends.

I would like to think that now maybe we can feel good things toward each other, without the baggage left over from that anxious time back in the thirties and forties, living in a place that neither of us could wait to get away from, neither of us knowing how strong that feeling was in the other.

The call to Mary made me feel happy. We are two strangers who grew up in intimate proximity who can now look back and say, "Hey, we were there," and share our perspectives of what "there" was. It makes it possible for me to think of some of the good things.

                Love,
                Rosemary

April 28, 1995
Alpine Drive, Beverly Hills

Dear Michael,

Your letter came just in time to save me from a momentary (I hope) plunge into depression—you know, the kind of whining nobody-loves-me drone that bores even the whiner.

I woke up from an awful dream the other morning. I was back in Hollis taking care of little children. Will and Emily were part of my brood, and I was watching them for Julia. Then Will was either you or Andy. Suddenly I realized that Emily had disappeared. Panic. Rushing around explaining. Calling out her name. In cold, blue, late-afternoon slushy snow looking for her and then Julia returning, cheerful and happy, unworried, and me about to explain, thinking I would commit suicide if anything happened to Emily when suddenly there she was. I awoke just then, too soon to enjoy the end of the dream. When I was really awake, I remembered that it was in Hollis that I had the first awful depression of my life, the first prolonged suicidal period I experienced. It was there that I first understood death and evil, and where I lost the possibility of hope and the belief that things would be somehow better. I believed myself unworthy of being loved. I lost my belief in God, religion, and a way of life that was unsatisfactory but had given me some structure.

Why was it Emily who was lost? Emily is the quintessential, direct, happy, immediate, positive, loving, rewarding little creature who must represent to me what I might have been in a different garden. And it was in Hollis that so many things in me withered. Why am I burdening you with this? Who else, besides my therapist, whom I don't see until next Tuesday, will listen to me at such great length? And she will listen to me for money and you will listen to me for love.

See, now I feel better, and maybe I will not be depressed after all.

I loved your letter. I can feel China as you write, and I wish I were young and healthy enough to travel. But we hear such disaster stories about neighbors and members of the Tennis Club as they roam the world. They're always bringing them home prone after triple bypasses and oddball surgery on assorted body parts. I think we've already been forced to return home three times for Milt's various problems, and that's enough. China seems like taunting fate too loudly for me...

Last week Will got up, turned on the computer to a kid's program, made a picture of a train with smoke coming out of the stack, pushed the print button, turned off the computer, then woke Andy up to show him the picture. A few weeks ago, I heard the copier down in Marian's office whizzing away at about six-thirty a.m. and presumed it was Jenny. I decided to check and found Lizzie at work, making copies of a picture in one of her storybooks. I told her not to make any more, she had enough (thirty-three), and she said not to worry, because when the copier ran out of paper she got more from the cabinet underneath, and she was very careful to turn off the printer before she put the paper in, so it was okay. Right then and there, I decided that the next time Milt is having trouble with the copier, he could call on Lizzie for assistance. And Julia says watch out; Emily is already trying to get at the mouse to click away too.

Life can't be that bad with all the good things that are happening, right?

Love,
Rosemary

AFTER READING ANNE SEXTON

I don't want to write a love poem
singing out words of hate
I want to say that I'm alive
for a while
in a way
that I don't understand
and sometimes the green grass pleases

July 27, 1995
Alpine Drive, Beverly Hills

Dear Michael,
Your letter describing your young years made me want to cry. Even though we grow up and put things in some kind of perspective, inside we are still whatever we have been. I really failed you for a long time. I don't have any excuses. I loved you. But I couldn't take Mike. And I couldn't take Mike and Irene together. If I could have taken you to live with me, I would have. I used to fantasize about it. I loved you the way I love Will and Emily and Lizzie. And much as I loved you, I knew I couldn't make up for your parents.

Your description of going to that pool was awful, and I understood it completely. I was forced to go to every goddamn birthday party in Queens Village, usually in tears. I hated the games. I didn't like the sweets. I hated the birthday song. Everything about the occasion embarrassed me.

I hated school. Especially the schoolyard. Hordes of laughing, screaming, whispering, running, jumping kids, and no friends until I was eleven or twelve years old. And when I got home, my mother and father fighting. Mike silent or smirking, looking sly, and sidling. Jean a martyr on the attack. And me with my nose in a book hoping to be like wallpaper, please God, and not be noticed. Being noticed in my house was not good; in my neighborhood, not good; in school, not good.

I can't say I had a happy childhood. I can say there were happy moments. Walking and dancing along Hempstead Avenue, oblivious, on the way to school, the awfulness of what was to come put off until I made the turn, crossed at the light, and went the last few blocks to the off-white brick school, lucky if I timed it just right to get to the schoolyard at the moment the nuns started snapping their clickers to get us into lines to march up to class. Moments of walking under the maples and shade trees on 213th Street, fresh snow falling, listening to my father retell familiar stories, and reading, always reading. Listening to favorite radio programs. Dancing to music in the small living room—waltzes, rumbas, foxtrots. I loved my mother deeply, but I can't honestly say I have one really happy family memory except for my father telling stories. I remember colors, smells, the snow and rain and sunshine, trees, sidewalks, songs, the night sky and stars, the moon.

That was Queens Village to me, the good and the bad.

Love,
Rosemary

BICYCLES

"Bicycles are bad," Grandma said. No grandchild would have a bicycle if she could help it. Girls riding with their dresses up over their knees. Boys out in the middle of the road running over dogs, getting hit by cars. Disgraceful.

So in our house there were three-wheelers for children under seven, but no two-wheelers. Mike and Jean begged for a bicycle, one between them. Grandpa couldn't get Grandma to change her mind, and Dad didn't try. A bicycle cost money, and he had none. And they were dangerous he said, echoing his mother's argument, and with his vivid imagination he couldn't bear the thought of his children getting killed. Indeed, his mother's descriptions of their mangled bodies made him wince. How could he give them something that might destroy them?

Nana was willing to give us one but Grandma said no. Mike went around the corner with his friends and then hopped on the back of somebody's bike, his feet held up from the ground while the friend pumped off to another neighborhood. Whenever Dad caught him in this act, he was punished for disobedience. Mother cautioned him not to ride near the house but he continued to take chances. The lure of the two wheels was too great, and time after time he was caught. Jean did the same thing, but only in other neighborhoods and in the schoolyard.

Both children asked again and again for their mother to intervene and for their father to reconsider but Momma couldn't get her way. Dad was too afraid of a row with his mother, and besides, never having learned to ride as a child himself, he couldn't see the attraction so he put them off and blamed it on Grandma.

When Uncle Andrew died, he left a rusty red bike and Uncle Charlie fixed the flat tires on it. He gave it to Mike, who parked it in a neighbor's garage so Dad wouldn't see it. Mike paid two dollars, earned working at the stables on 212th Street, for a new chain and stand. Three weeks later, Dad discovered the secret, known to his wife and most of the neighborhood. He ranted and carried on until Mike tearfully gave in and produced the bike for Dad's inspection.

"Look at that thing," Dad said, his face turning red. "You'll get killed on it. It's not even in good shape. Get rid of it. If I hear that you've been on it again, you won't sit down for a week."

"Walter, it didn't cost you or your mother anything," Mom replied. "Why don't you let him have it? All the children have bicycles. Let him have one."

"No." Dad turned his cranky person in her direction. "I don't know what's the matter with Charlie. He was probably drunk. He knows Mike's not allowed to have one."

"He was sorry for him, that's all. He was trying to be nice to him." Her face was closed and hard against her husband but she hadn't the courage to let her son defy him. "You'd better get rid of it."

Crying and humiliated, hatred boiling in his heart, Mike slammed the door as he went out. He was thirteen. He didn't have a bicycle. His father never had a good word for him, hated everything he did. If he raked the yard, the pile of leaves was crooked. If he painted a door, the brush wasn't clean enough. If he washed his face, his ears were dirty. He'd run away, and this time they wouldn't find him. He'd go to the woods.

When Mike came home after selling the bike for a dollar to a boy around the corner, he went to the refrigerator and took out the peanut butter, a loaf of bread, and two quarts of milk and put them in a bag. He took a blanket from his bedroom and some matches from the box on the stove. Maybe he would die. Anything would be better than living here. He returned at midnight, cold and wet from a light rain and said no more about owning a bike.

I learned to ride on other people's bicycles like my brother and sister. Mimi and Edith Morgan and Marilyn Murphy had bicycles and they let me ride often. One day when I was thirteen, my father caught me and began to explain that I was not allowed to ride because it was dangerous. Grandma had disapproved of it. I interrupted him. "Grandma's dead now. Besides I like to ride a bicycle."

Mimi and Edith were standing with their bikes and chimed in, "Our daddy says it's safe as long as you go the right way on the one-way streets and stay off Jamaica Avenue. Can't she ride with us? We'll be careful."

"I like to ride and I'm careful." I looked at him, smiling hard with determination. "I'll show you how I do it." I got on Mimi's bike and rode around in circles in front of the house. "I'm a good rider. Can't I please, Daddy?"

I was smiling at him. He couldn't win. But there was more to it than that. I was going to ride no matter what he said. The next day I started a campaign to get a bicycle, but no amount of "Can't I, Daddys" worked. He said he didn't have the money. The truth was he didn't want to give in. He had a nagging suspicion that Grandma was right. Maybe I would be killed. But it wouldn't be on his money. He knew from looking at my face that I meant to ride so he didn't forbid it as he had with Jean and Mike. He knew I'd ride whether he liked it or not.

When Uncle Arthur visited us on my fourteenth birthday and asked what I wanted, my answer was, "The only thing I want is a bicycle."

"You don't have a bicycle? Why not?"

"Daddy says they're dangerous and he doesn't have the money, so I ride everyone else's."

"Does he let you?"

"I like to ride and I'm careful. I'm fourteen now. He's afraid I'll get killed and it will be his fault."

"Well, we'll see what we can do."

My mother stood by listening. She never told me not to ride, just to be careful. She had been disgusted with Dad for letting his mother provide him with an excuse for not doing what he didn't want to do anyway. It wasn't only his mother who prevented us from riding. It was his hostility to Mike and indifference to what Jean wanted, and now that his mother was dead he didn't want to lose face by giving in after all these years. Maybe Arthur could talk some sense into him.

Three days later, I received a call from Dad. He was in a bicycle store with my mother. He sounded ruefully pleased. He was buying me a bicycle. What kind did I want? I named the brand that Mimi and Edith had. The salesman suggested another more expensive brand. So he followed the salesman's suggestion over my mother's objections and my desires.

Uncle Arthur was the giver of the gift; a fact my father didn't tell me. Arthur, hearing the history of no bicycles in our family, was astounded that Dad had knuckled under to Grandma's wishes, and was surprised that he hadn't used better judgment where Jean and Mike were concerned. My godfather decided to give me the present I wanted.

Knowing his spending habits, he believed Dad had no money, so he gave Momma the fifteen dollars and told her to tell me it was from my father. Mother used the money to blackmail Dad into buying the bike. If he didn't buy it, she would tell me about Arthur's gift and blame Dad. He bought the most expensive bike in the store, not the one I wanted, so he could add ten dollars of his own money and have a basis for saying it was from him.

"Oh, thank you, thank you. What a birthday present."

Mom smiled grimly in the background, thinking of the other two children who hadn't made a dent in Walter's consciousness, who hadn't had a quiet champion who could shame her husband out of his arbitrary position, taken years before out of respect for a cranky old woman's whim. □

THE GROWLER

The oldest house on the street was a wreck down near the stores on Jamaica Avenue. Layers of peeling paint, rusty hinges, and unwashed windows with frayed curtains gave it the look of a ghost ship run aground on the shoals of the Great Depression. Every morning, Ma Fisher, shapeless in her house dress and felt slippers, came out the front door to send Pa off to work with sweeping motions of her broom as she made a feeble attempt to set some part of her life in order. The broom was worn by age and use the same as its owner, whose smile was more of a sigh and showed more gum than tooth. "Poor old soul," was what my mother and her friends said about Ma. "What can she do? Married to the likes of him."

According to my father, Ma could have done something. She could have washed the windows or cleaned the house. Instead, after her foray onto the steps each morning, she retired to a perch in the window by the front door. In winter she pressed her face against the glass with the curtain pulled to one side, only opening the window when some neighbor stopped by to ask how she was. In summer she sat in the open window and let the curtain float around her like an old lace shawl. She was like a faded figurehead in the front of the house, watching passively over the neighborhood doings.

"If she'd get out of that window and do some work," Dad would say, "the place wouldn't be such an eyesore. One of these days, I'm going to tell her so."

"You mind your own business, Walter." This from my mother. "What can she do, poor old thing? You know what he's like."

The neighbors called the Fishers Ma and Pa because they were the oldest couple on the block. They were also the poorest on the block. My father found out for himself just how poor when Ma leaned out of her window on a cold November morning to chat with him. "How come you haven't swept your walk this morning, Mrs. Fisher?" he asked.

"Oh, my arthritis is bad today, and my slippers can't keep my feet warm enough." He made the slighting remark he'd been wanting to make for a long time, that if she could get herself out of the window for ten minutes, maybe she'd have time to do something else, like put on her shoes. He was overwhelmed when she told him she hadn't any. The felt slippers were all she had to face the winter with. He pictured his own eighty-year-old mother, with her bunions and rheumatism, walking on the cold winter sidewalks protected by nothing but a pair of decrepit house slippers. So he told Ma to wait a minute, he'd be right back, and sure enough he was, with a pair of my mother's old scuffed shoes. They were ugly, but good enough to use until something better came along. She cried and invited him in for tea.

My father was a neat man, and he was horrified when he saw Ma's kitchen. The first thing he did was wash the cups and saucers for tea. Then, while he was at it, he figured he might as well clean up the rest of the kitchen. After that, he stuck his head out the front door and called to my brother, who was playing with two friends, to run home and pick up the chamois and ammonia. When they came back, he talked them into helping him wash the windows. Two hours later Ma sat looking through the sparkling glass of her front window, careful not to get so close that she steamed it with her breath, and now and then giving a swipe with her apron to polish it more.

Ma and Pa had children and grandchildren scattered around Queens and Brooklyn. Now and then, a grown child, or a grown child with a grandchild, would come for a visit. For the next week, Ma, in her thick brogue, slurred by lack of teeth, would tell anyone who stopped by what Patty was wearing, or what Neil ate, or how Ellen was doing since they gave her the medicine.

For all that Ma sat in the front window of the house most days, she seldom judged what passed before her eyes. The only one she judged—and in that she was like the other women on the street—was her husband, whom she called Bill. Bill Fisher still worked as a kind of absent-minded plumber. People only hired him when they were desperate. Ma saw him off at the door six days a week, lunch pail in one hand and a wooden box of plumbing tools in the other, and she was never sure he'd show up with both hands full in the evening. He, or one of the neighborhood children, often had to be sent to fetch his things from wherever he'd finished up. "There'll be no dinner for you until you bring back the lunch pail, Bill," or "Jimmy, will you be a good boy and go over to Mrs. Wagner's and see if he's left the pail there?"

Pa's problem with plumbing and forgetting wasn't caused by advanced age. He'd been famous for years for being a poor plumber. People were always talking about cold-water faucets that ran hot, sink drains left unconnected, or boilers that never worked once he'd tended to them. Pa's problem, and Ma's too, was that no matter how hard she searched the house, his pockets, and his lunch pail, she never found all the nickels he'd hidden so he could go around the corner to Murphy's Saloon to fill up on beer each day. Beer was the problem. Pa was a sad sight sober. In the morning, launched in flapping castoff overalls big enough for a man twice his size, his head down, his red-rimmed watery blue eyes flinching in the daylight, he'd snarl at anyone who spoke to him on his way to work. After lunchtime he began to find the world endurable. Around the corner to Murphy's, one beer, and his reddened face would work itself into a semblance of a grin, and soon he'd be shouting a few "hiyos" to the boys in the bar. "Hey, Pa, you'd better get back to work," they'd say. "The old lady'll be checkin' up on you." And if he was still there at two, Ma, with Pa's old dog Spot in tow, would stick her head in the door. "Bill, Mrs. Guinan is looking for you. You'd better get over there right this minute." The beer gave him courage to ignore her, so she'd go into the place long enough to poke at him with her old black handbag, while Spot whined and nuzzled expectantly until he was given a bit of beer to lick off the old man's fingers. After a suitable length of time to show he wasn't going to be bossed by anybody, and certainly not his wife, Pa would hoist himself off the stool and out into daylight, this time with a little less pain.

Pa was from the old school. Six o'clock found him putting in for home livelier than when he'd left in the morning. A stop at Murphy's en route always fortified him for the hour it took to eat dinner and listen to his wife before he could leave the house again to spend the evening with the boys. The neighbors always said you could set your watch by Pa's travel times each night, home by six and out the door by seven, with Spot marching sedately next to him, an empty covered growler—a tin beer pail with a handle—dangling from his tough terrier jaw. They had a sense of purpose, those two, and no man, woman, child, dog, or cat could distract them. Inside the saloon, Pa and the dog sated themselves on beer bought with hidden nickels, and by playing on the sentiments of the other patrons. Pa was always the oldest man in the bar, and always accompanied by Spot, who knew how to sit up and beg as well as anyone when it came to beer. At eleven Pa handed the growler over to Frank to fill for the journey home. That way there'd be one last beer to sweeten his dreams and get him ready for the next day's battle with the wrenches.

As soon as Spot had a good grip on the handle, the two of them pushed off, rounding the corner by the light of the moon if there was one, or the streetlamp if there wasn't, the old man singing and humming. As they neared the house, Ma would lean out the window, hushing and complaining until they mounted the steps, the growler clanking on each one. "Be quiet, you fool, you're wakin' the neighborhood."

That was the routine of their nights, with one prominent exception. Two toughs showed up at the bar one night looking for one of the regulars. When they couldn't find him, they decided to look for trouble instead. Pa was there, down at his end of the bar, with Spot sitting in the sawdust at his feet, and both of them enough sheets to the wind not to see a storm when it was coming. At eleven o'clock, Pa drifted between the two strangers and reached out for Frank to hand him his pail of beer. One of them said something insulting to Frank, and before Pa could hand the pail to Spot, there was a shout and a shove and the pail overturned. The beer poured down the front of the pants of the man on the left, and in the excitement, Spot, full of beer, let loose on the leg of the man on the right. Everybody started shouting. "Pick on someone your own size! Leave the old man alone! If you wanna fight, fight me!" In a second the strangers were gone, and everyone was laughing and patting Pa and Spot and calling them heroes. Pa was inconsolable over the loss of the beer until Frank gave him a refill. Then he and the dog took off for home with only a misty notion of what had happened.

Ma kept busy in the window for a week talking it over and Pa came in for his share of praise each night at the saloon, as if he and Spot had known where they were aiming. Within a week things settled down to normal, Ma sweeping him down the steps in the morning and complaining him back up again at night.

They were the neighborhood old couple for a long time. Children and grandchildren still came by for visits. My father kept Ma supplied with old shoes and sometimes a packet of tea. And often, as Pa got older and the plumbing took too much of his energy, he'd send Spot by himself to get the night's ration of beer. The dog became a familiar sight with the growler dangling from his jaw. Cars stopped as Spot crossed the street at an angle and disappeared around the corner, measuring his steps to keep time with his invisible master. If you could set your watch by Pa's comings and goings, you could check its accuracy by Spot's, since the trip to the saloon and back took him exactly six minutes.

One Sunday in November, after Spot had been gone for six months, Pa died of pneumonia. Ma buried him, and then died herself two weeks later. The neighbors shook their heads and said, "Poor old soul. Maybe it's for the best. He was difficult, but after all those years, she wouldn't have known how to get along without him." □

September 10, 1995
Alpine Drive, Beverly Hills

Dear Michael,

I sat down an hour ago to write to you, and Lizzie walked in and we started playing a game together on the computer, and now I don't recall what I was going to say to you. Some little bit of trivia perhaps...

Oh, now I remember—I don't know about the Mirthas, but the Godsils, my mother and your grandmother's family, were an addictive lot. I never thought of it that way until last week when I was having fits about Milt taking so much codeine. The doctor turned to him and asked, "Are you from an addictive family?" Well he isn't, but my answer for myself had to be yes. My great Aunt Mamie, who died when you were two, spent the last seven years of her life zonked out of her head on morphine listening to soaps on the radio.

The phone just rang, and there you were, China to Los Angeles, you to me, us, now you and Milt, and I writing to you.

On to the addicts: I believe that my mother's father and definitely one brother were alcoholics. I remember their complexions—lots of little spider veins, very ruddy for such washed-out, blue-eyed types. One of my cousins, the son of the alcoholic uncle, may also have been one. I never before connected that with Jean and alcohol, but there it is.

And me. It was only my weak stomach that saved me from being an alcoholic, something you and I share. Three glasses of wine and I start quivering internally; four drinks and I have a headache; five drinks and for twenty-four hours I cannot bear to be alive. Stomach quivering, mind invaded by depression and grungy fuzz, a headache that no painkiller touches, a tongue like Forty-Ninth Street and Tenth Avenue during a street cleaners strike, and the general feeling that, like Lady Macbeth, I have become something that water can't wash.

But the temptation has always been there. One glass of wine and I laugh and make jokes. I feel wonderful. If there's music, I begin to dance. Two drinks and I'm very happy. I can talk to strangers and socialize. Unfortunately, my tongue loosens a little too soon if the wine goes down too fast, and I'm very apt to say more than I want to.

If I'm happy to start out with, all is wonderful. If I'm depressed before, I have some moments or half hours of reprieve, and then I am very depressed. Alcohol is not for me, or only in small amounts. Though I love it. I've read that it's a kind of self-medication, something that isn't talked about much. I think my father probably reacted to alcohol in much the same way, and he used it sparingly for such a gregarious man.

I guess Jean wasn't so lucky in the stomach department. For me, it was like having a built-in Antabuse pill. So, I did have one good failing.

Lizzie just came in for her supper—peanut butter and jelly on a baguette...I have some funny stories about Will. The first day in France, he kept asking his parents, "Are we on France now?" The other day he told Assunta that one of her desserts was "unimprovable." Andy says he can't believe that Will has understood what he said, and I say, why not? The other day Andy called and said that he had been telling Will about the earth being round and how it was daytime in some places and nighttime in others. He said Will had a question to ask me: "What time is it, Nana?"

"It's noon here, Will. Daytime. Alicia and I are having our lunch. What time is it where you are?"

"It's dark." Then Andy came back on the phone.

"He's standing by the window now, looking out at the dark. Will, Nana says it's lunchtime in Los Angeles and the sun is out." And then I hear a small solemn voice in the distance saying, with what might have been irritation.

"You're giving me a headache."

Is he going to be an engineer? He is certainly logical, like Dan and Milt. And sensitive, like a lot of us. His other grandfather, Doug, is an engineer. Did you know that it takes an hour to eat a peanut butter and jelly sandwich, and then another half hour to go to sleep after numerous trips to the bathroom and to the kitchen to see what I'm doing?

Milt is snoring in one room, Lizzie is squirming herself to sleep in another, and the two cats are creeping around doing cat things in the living room. This missive started about five hours and a hell of a lot of activity ago, and it's time now for me to go fold the laundry.

Love,
Rosemary

THE BIRTH DAY OF MOTHERHOOD

I almost typed 1953. That's the year on this day that Jenny was born. I remember the sun shining through the green leaves I could see from the hospital window. I remember the joy of her, of holding her all wrapped in a flannel blanket.

It seems longer than forty-two years ago. I seem to be much more than forty-two years older than that young girl who gave birth. I wasn't even a woman then, despite my twenty-five years. Just a dumb kid doing what nature intended, thinking I'd decided it all by myself. How do we survive?

I was a wreck—conscientious, terrified, loving my child, doting, single- minded. And what was her father? I didn't know then and I certainly don't have any better perspective now. All I know is that we weren't good for each other.

Strange that we take a course in life that is so important, that becomes our life, that is our life, and we do it as stupidly as if consequences counted for nothing. I married, had a child, divorced, remarried, had another child, and spent my life as a consequence of those decisions. Spent is a good word for what happens to life.

I look at Andy and Julia and I wonder what they will think when they reach sixty-seven. And Emily and Will. And Jenny, she lives the consequences too. All the bending and twisting, the pressure and activity— I wonder what she will make of it when she comes to reckoning.

October 9th is coming next, the anniversary of my mother's death. It's hard to believe that she doesn't know about my grandchildren, yet it's almost as if she is here somewhere watching and loving them with me. Maybe she is the part of me that loves them so and makes the effort to be with them and take care of them. I can be close to her again as I do for them the things she did for Jenny and Andy. □

JENNY

> Born to October turning
> red apples crisp and sweet
> broad clouds soaring
> smiling sky telling of children
> born to vision

November 29, 1995
Alpine Drive, Beverly Hills

Dear Michael,
In my file in France I found a whole batch of journal entries from 1978 and 1984. I carried them on the plane and started to read them, then gave most of them to Milt to read. He was so moved by some of them that he was in tears, and for the first time I realized that the things I write about are part of his life as well as my own, just told from my point of view. So I fell in love all over again.
   Love,
   Rosemary

May 1, 1996
Talloires, France

Dear Marian,
The grass is Crayola green and the mountains are spotted with dark pines. The roads are empty, the supermarkets full of native French people. Low, foggy gray clouds float close to the surface of the lake, and my soul, which I'm convinced at times like these that I have, is becoming more tranquil by the hour.
 It's true. I do believe in souls. My Catholic upbringing took hold on that score. It's just that in the stress of so much commotion and so little serenity, I don't often notice that it's there...Be well, take care of yourself, don't go near the cats, and have fun on the long weekends.
   Love,
   Rosemary

May 5, 1996
Talloires, France

Dear Lizzi,
How are you today? Absolutely great, I hope. Yesterday, we were in the bookstore in Annecy and I found a copy of *La Petite Sirène* in French, or, as it's known in English, *The Little Mermaid*, so I thought you might like that for a birthday present. I can't quite figure out what to do with it. Should I mail it home to you right now? Should I leave it here at the house so you'll have it when you come in July or August on vacation? Shall I bring it home and give it to you when you return from England at the end of the summer?

Give Daddy a big hug from me and tell him that breakfast at Père Bise this morning was wonderful. We are having our first really sunny day today, and are getting over jet lag finally. Things are looking good.

Love,
Nana

May 11, 1996
Talloires, France

Dear Will,
Thank you for my wonderful Mother's Day message. Those drawings of the rocket ship and space shuttle and the very tiny rocket were so good.

The next time you draw more ask Daddy to fax them to me so I can learn all about space too.

The moon was so bright in the sky the other night that it made the lake shine and I wished you were here to see it.

I had a chocolate croissant yesterday morning in a coffee shop in Annecy where Granddaddy and I went to read the papers.

Then we went to a computer store and I saw a computer game that was for children from four years old to seven years old. Do you think I should get it for you and Emily to play on Mommy's computer?

Have lots of fun today.

Love,
Nana

XXXXXXXXX

All the X's are hugs and kisses from Granddaddy and me.

May 11, 1996
Talloires, France

Dear Emily,

I liked the little drawing that you did that Daddy sent to me. I'll save it and put it in my album.

Granddaddy and I really miss hearing you sing "Down by the Station" and "I've Been Working on the Railroad" when we're driving around France. I hope you remember the words until we get back in June and then you can sing those songs for us again.

There is lots of wonderful bread here in France and I know you would like it a lot. Maybe we can bring some home for you when we come back. But in the meantime have fun eating olive bread.

Have you been watching Winnie the Pooh or Barney on the video?

I have to go make lunch now. I'll write you another letter soon. Have lots of fun today.

Love,
Nana

XXXXXXXXX

All the X's are hugs and kisses from Granddaddy and me

May 11, 1996
Talloires, France

Dear Andy,

When I was writing to the children this morning, I realized that today is our anniversary. I was pleased that this year I was the one to realize it first, so I could wish Milt a happy anniversary before he could remind me.

We have never been sentimental about our anniversary, and I always felt, not guilty, but puzzled by that. You know—I failed car pool twice, and anniversary every year. Then this morning I started really thinking about it and I realized that every day that I live with Milt seems like the most important day of our lives, much nicer, in fact, than the day of our marriage, which was fraught with the feeling that maybe it was all a mistake, and maybe we would be sorry the next day, if not two hours after the ceremony.

The wedding itself was nice, in spite of the cantor, Jonas Javna, who lectured me on how he didn't know me very well but he knew Milt and (I'm paraphrasing) he hoped I would be as good to his friend as he so justly deserved. While Jonas didn't include it in the wedding ceremony, he was also hoping that Milt would hire him to sing on one of his future records. Heaven knows how flowery he would have waxed if he had known how successful Milt was going to be. I mean this was back in the days when Milt was earning something like thirty dollars a week and even I was making more.

All the relatives, save Beth, were very loving and pleased with me. I felt I was becoming part of a warm, friendly group who wanted me as Milt's wife and for myself. They were nice people. As for Beth, her first words of greeting, before I could get up the stairs and into the apartment, told the story, as P.G. Wodehouse would say—"I'm so sorry you and Milt are getting married. It was nice to have him all to ourselves."

The food was great. Leah's famous meatballs, overdone and delicious, and her incredible chopped liver, the secret of which even she didn't know. I used to think she wouldn't give it to me because, after all, it was a claim to fame, but now I believe she didn't have a recipe. She just closed her eyes and made it, and it was perfect. There might also have been turkey and ham, and there were salads. I remember especially eating a lot of rugalah, those pastries with ground nuts inside. In the two weeks before the wedding I went from a size twelve to a size ten, and the wedding feast gave me a good start for putting the weight back on.

We were so puzzled by being married that we had no idea what to do after we left Milt's parents' house in Brooklyn Heights where the wedding took place, so we went back to my apartment, now our apartment, changed into more comfortable clothes, and went to a movie on Broadway. I think we were suddenly made so shy by the change in our civil relationship that we didn't have a word to say to each other beyond, "What shall we do now? How about a movie?"

Andy, you almost didn't become. Two days before the wedding we went walking in Greenwich Village with our witnesses, Bob and Louise De Cormier, to buy a ring, and Milt was so sulky and awful that night that I told him we could call off the wedding if he was so miserable, but that if he still wanted to get married, he'd better shape up! How was I to know he behaved that way anytime he got near a store where it took more than thirteen seconds to buy clothes, food, jewelry, hardware, furniture, a house, a car, and almost anything else, even if, or maybe especially if, it was for him. His demeanor on those occasions is that of a cranky seven-year-old with better things to do. Anyway, he shaped up and I have spent the next thirty-eight years shopping—alone, if possible.

I didn't think of myself as a bride on my wedding day. After all, I didn't have a white dress and a veil. And to me, weddings were always the trappings—churches, music, people wiping away tears. I was thirty, divorced, and had a four-and-a-half-year-old daughter, and I was old enough to know that it could be awful no matter how right it seemed at the moment. No, I felt like a bride a few months after we were married, when we settled down to being a couple and were so happy to be in love and together.

The bride feeling lasted a long time, and after it was over, I always expected it to come back, and it did, from time to time, always a wonderful surprise, always with a rush of love, made up of time remembered, and time present, and all the time of our being together.

So today, after I beat Milt to saying Happy Anniversary, we went down to sit and read and have coffee and a croissant at Sophie's cafe; then to Mireille's boulangerie for bread and a big cheese puff pastry; then into Annecy to walk around and see if we could find a hardware store so I could buy deck varnish, a paint brush, and masking tape, and then to eat a salad and wonderful crêpe for lunch. After that we stopped in at Fidèle Berger to sit and read and have another coffee and a bite of superb bitter chocolate.

Now that we know it's our anniversary, we will go to Père Bise for dinner. The day couldn't have been better if we'd planned it this way, and it has come as a nice surprise.

Love,
Mom

May 11, 1996
Talloires, France

Dear Julia,
This has been one of the nicest anniversaries we've ever had. Nothing planned, just pleasantness and pleasure all day.

We just got back from Père Bise, where Milt had truffle ravioli for an entrée, just three or four in a very fine Italian pastry, with only the juice from the truffles and a tiny amount of butter coating the pasta, and I don't think I've ever tasted anything quite like it. It was wonderful. Obviously Milt was kind enough to let me have one. We had plain (Père Bise plain) roast chicken, green salad, and a plate of about fifteen different baby vegetables. Then the petit fours. Then home to digest.

We were surprised to find that today was our anniversary. Fortunately, when I wrote the date on the letters to the children this morning, I sort of shook my head and said to myself, um, May 11th, why does that date sound familiar? Thirty-eight years familiar. Given my inability to remember numbers, it's fortunate that we were married during the summer I turned thirty, so if I know how old I am, I know how long we've been married.

I found a pretty blouse that I hope you will like. It can be washed by hand or dry cleaned, so maybe you can get Andy to take it to the dry cleaner when he takes his shirts.

The house and the view of the lake are so serene, and I am so calm for a change that I feel great. The only problem is that I am eating a lot, and I will have to try to cut back. Milt is behaving much better than I am, so I can't say that it's his fault for leading me astray...I finished a book on the trip over here—*Behind the Scenes at the Museum*—that I'll bring back with me. I think you might enjoy it.

I miss you and Andy and the children very much. For the first time ever, I think I'm a little homesick. A very mild version of what I felt in Spain. Very mild, but a feeling of missing something important.
       Love,
       Rosemary

       May 18, 1996
       Talloires, France

Dear Julia,
This morning as I awoke, you were in my dream. I think Jenny and a few other people were there too, but you were the one I focused on. You were smiling and healthy, very pretty because you were happy, and beautiful because you were very present and very three-dimensional for an awakening dream.

Yesterday when I received the card from the children I wanted to write and tell you how much it means to me when I receive cards and notes signed by them, or by you and Andy. I know it's you who has really been the moving force behind them. Sometimes I'm afraid to tell people how much I love them because I think that I might embarrass them. I've been very lucky in my life. I found Milt and we've been happy together, and now Andy has found you, and in finding you, Milt and I have you to love too.

Julia, I don't just love you because you're Andy's wife. That was our introduction. It's you that I love and admire. I could list all the things about you that make me feel that way, but maybe I can express it better if I say that I feel as if our three generations of family have finally convinced me that the chain of unhappiness that was the family I came from has been broken, that it hasn't continued through me.

And your presence in the family that we are—your kindness and generosity—has given me the chance to feel wonderful. There's no other word for it.

       Love,
       Rosemary

                  May 26, 1996
                  Alpine Drive, Beverly Hills

Dear Michael,
Well, we're back in Los Angeles a month earlier than we expected. Milt wasn't feeling great, possibly a recurrence of last year's back misery, so I suggested he call the travel agent and buy a ticket back on the Concorde, with one for me to follow later in the day. The final outcome was that they don't know but he's feeling much better. I think the fear of pain and discomfort was worse than the actual pain and discomfort, but to a woman who put off having a foot operation for thirty years until her foot started walking off in another direction, fear of pain is real indeed.

I've developed a new philosophy. I'm soon to be sixty-eight. I love the people I love; I like the people I like; and since Milt and I haven't too much good healthy time left, I don't think I'll let the loved ones, or the liked ones, and certainly not the hardly cared about ones and the ones I don't care about at all, affect (effect) how we live. That's probably how most people live anyway so I don't suppose it's such a startling idea.

A few nights before we decided to come home, I walked out on the patio and looked up at the mountains and down at the lake, and was struck by the obvious truth that I am not the same person who built that house; not the same person who rushed around doing all that cooking, cleaning, shopping, laundering, and caring what other people thought about what I was doing or who and what I was.

There's a lot I just don't care about anymore. As soon as I realized that, and accepted my limitations and my age, I felt suddenly unlimited and free and really my age. I could feel burdens leaving my being, my past limping away from me, all that stupid caring about being like other people, something that has plagued me all my life—the need to conform to what I think other people expect me to be, to what I expect me to be. I don't wish to be unacceptable, but I don't think I'll set up so many obstacles to being comfortable, to letting myself do as I please.

    Love,
    Rosemary

              August 3, 1996
              Alpine Drive, Beverly Hills

Dear Diane,
I think it must be nineteen years ago that we met at Immaculate Heart. That day, the sunshine, sitting in the shade on the steps eating our funny anti-hypoglycemic lunches, and, I think, sharing a few almonds—it makes me think of two shipwrecked sailors clinging to each other on a rock, not in a storm, but afraid there might be a storm out there on the sunny horizon and thrilled with the prospect of a buddy to share it with. It was the greatest luck. There wasn't another person I could have made friends with as I did with you, and it happened on the first day. And yet, I always wondered why we were friends. I was so much older than you. And you were so much more intelligent and capable than I was. I never understood how you could operate on two such different levels: on one, with your staggering abilities and intelligence, and on another with such genuine tolerance and generosity in the face of your friends' lesser abilities.

I'm not unintelligent, but my intelligence has the scattered quality of a person who hasn't the energy and concentration necessary to pursue interests in great depth. It's as if I let life pour over me and ideas rise to the surface if they will—as if my chin is just above water and treading is the extent of what I can do a good part of the time. I have aspirations but not too many pretensions.

Who are we today, Diane? You're in your prime, and I'm sixty-eight and in another kind of prime. I forgive myself now for all the things I haven't done, except, perhaps, for the things I haven't said to the people I cared about, out of laziness, or out of shyness and fear. The trouble with telling people who aren't family or lovers what they have meant to you is that it may not be the right moment for them to hear it, so you hope that they just know without the telling...

Things have gotten better for me in many ways. I now understand myself and my problems with depression and elation for what they are. They've been blunted with time. And therapy has helped. It's given me a mirror to see myself, or to know myself in my three dimensions, with as much a sense of reality as is possible.

Jenny and I have found a meeting ground, which is certainly better than not at all. My therapist has suggested that while I am of a depressed nature generally with short periods of hyperactivity, Jenny may well be almost one hundred percent activity, which would explain her pace and drive, her obsessiveness about her work, her play, or what she calls relaxation—until she drops. It has made me more tolerant of her, though I try to avoid her pace as much as I can. Given our history, and Jenny and her family living in the extension, we do relatively well together.

If it sounds as if I've become a Valley therapy nut, it isn't so. Jean Holroyd, my therapist, is very intelligent and sensible, and I see her once a week. We just talk—sometimes about uncomfortable things, but usually about books, kids, movies, aches and pains, friends, doctors, dogs, cats, clothes, family, bread, mountains, anything at all. And she has nearly as much to say as I do. Even when I'm a little depressed, we don't necessarily talk about that. I know all about my depressions. I know what words I think during them. I know the feelings I have. I know that they will be over with eventually. And I know now that they are in part chemical and genetic. I use therapy to clear the air, to put myself into some kind of perspective in relation to others. For a while I felt guilty about going, then I realized that since I started, I've been on a pretty even keel. This is my mink coat, my personal trainer, my annual trip to wherever.

Andy and Julia's children, Will and Emily, are a delight—bright, open, amenable. They love me and they let me love them. Seven-year-old Lizzie and I are becoming good friends. Up to now in my side of the house, I was only someone who prevented her from doing what she wanted. Now that she's calming down, we are doing more things together, like sewing, talking, and going out to lunch. I think she looks to me as someone who can teach her things her parents aren't interested in. She's very intelligent, hyper, short-fused, and like a lot of only children, very impressed with herself. She's going to The Mirman School for Gifted Children this fall, which I hope will be challenge enough for her.

And Milt? Well, he's still Milt. He's enjoying himself enormously on the Board of the L.A. Opera, the only one on the Board, I think, who is a professional musician. He's still watching sixteen different sports on television, while he reads financial reports and prospectuses, does the crossword puzzle, snoozes, and talks on the telephone, all at the same time. Andy and I convinced him to get a computer, which sits on his desk, and after he gets tired of Solitaire, I know he'll branch out to Free Cell, then Tut's Tomb, and then the stock market reports. After that the world, right?

We were having lunch yesterday and some incongruous difference of interests came up, I forget what, and I asked him suddenly whatever got us together in the first place, and we both laughed out "sex" at the same time. And it's true. It was great. But it's funny how you lose sight of that after a while and think it was all the other reasons that only became important with living together. Sex isn't what has kept us together. Luckily, the thing Milt and I needed from one another was exactly the same for both of us. We each needed someone who would love totally, unquestioningly, loyally, and unendingly, no matter what differences we had inside the walls of our marriage. No matter what, we would be there for one another with love. That's what has kept us together.

I hope all is well with you. I think about you often. I wanted you to know that you are one of my good memories, Diane, and your friendship is and was important to me. You're approaching the age that I was when we met, back when I felt so old and didn't understand how young I was. Now I feel younger than I did then, not physically, but freer to be whatever it is that I am, less concerned with what I think someone else may think, even less concerned with what I think.

I wrote a poem a year ago about being like a dog, circling around in one spot to make a nest to sleep in. I think it's what I'm doing in a way now, and it's not morbid or depressing, and it isn't about death but old age. I'm making this comfortable nest for myself, and whenever I get a chance, I curl up in it and doze off. Then every once in a while I open one eye, take a look at the world out there, and murmur something like, excuse me, but I'm feeling a little tired, so you take over now, and let me dream my dream for a while.

          Love,
          Rosemary

GETTING CLOSER

    I've returned to my twenties
    and I know now what I know
    I'm done with middle-age
    that was for finding the school girl
    I never was

    Finished with being mother,
    some stray ends to weave into wife
    the hostess seems to have gone
    the way of the reader,
    intent on making her way to Heaven
    gold star for classics blue for romance

Next the carefree teenager
I feel it coming.
will I sit dreaming over chocolates?
breakfast, lunch, dinner
lighting up my day?

And after that
the long dream before the dream.
I must hurry
and like a dog turning in downward circles
carve myself a haven

August 17, 1996
Alpine Drive, Beverly Hills

Dear Michael,
Milt and I had a nice morning. It's Saturday and we had the house to ourselves. I didn't get dressed until five minutes to eleven, when I flew upstairs to throw something on so we could get to Toscana before Andy and Julia and the kids and order the pizza so it would be ready and waiting, cool enough to eat, before they arrived, thereby avoiding the usual whining and bread-eating session, which would mean the kids were ready for dessert before the pizza even arrived.

They were wonderful. Will had on a bright red-green-white-blue- striped Mickey Mouse shirt that made his cheeks look the color of ripe peaches. That sentence doesn't do justice to the glow of his beauty. And when he leaned over and told me quietly that he was "happy to see me," well, I ask myself, what more can there be in life to love?

Emily, dressed in green and purple, ate three pieces of pizza and two spoons of tiramisu, drank apple juice from her sippy cup. She held my arm for a moment and gave me a significant look, meaning what, I don't know, but she was half smiling with her blue-ringed Primont eyes, and I knew that we knew something together.

I spoke to your mother last week, and she sounded good. I'll call her in a few days to see how things are going.

Assunta's sister Paula is now dying in Vancouver. Assunta is flying there on Monday at the suggestion of the Canadian oncologist. There are things to think about. How long might she have lived if she had stayed in Talloires instead of going to Pakistan? If she had known she would die so soon, would she have left when she did? They were told flat out that she would probably not survive the move for very long, and in fact, they've only been there since mid-May.

Milt and I will offer to go up to Vancouver to help Assunta in these next few weeks. She can only stay there until September 11th because Jacques has organized a very large auction and needs her help to get him through it. I think I told you that he had some kind of heart problem, probably a narrowing of an artery, and spent several weeks in the hospital recuperating and being tested. He's on a strict regimen of diet and exercise, so there is no question of him coming with Assunta.

I look around and I see all the real problems that people have, and I add guilt to the depression I already feel for myself and all humanity. Michael, I live so much in my mind that I don't know what reality is. Jean and I were talking the other day (Holroyd, that is), and she was saying that my state of mind and lack of body consciousness at present (if I understood her correctly) is a state of being that many people try to attain, though without the element of depression, through religion or meditation. She lent me a book called *Sacred Sorrows* with an essay that she thought might be of interest. Just the name plunges me further into the pit, but maybe the essay will give me a leg up.

Anyway, I should be over this in a few months if it runs true to course. In the meantime, if enough little children love me, my nephew remembers how much I love him, my son pats me on the back, my husband stays with me and smiles, really smiles at me, at least once a day, and if my daughter and I can communicate like civilized adults, it won't be all bad. When I read that list I think, "How can I be depressed?" and that lasts until the next morning when I put my feet on the floor and feel a mumble in my soul, my primitive prehistoric voice grunting something about "why get up, when it's all nothing?"

Be thankful, Michael, for the genes you didn't get.

This is, if not a cheerful letter, at least a letter, and I'm sitting up to write it. If one can still feel it's important to edit mistakes out, one can't be too sad.

Lots of love,
Rosemary

DAD OLD

I'm going to describe my father, my father as I knew him. Not an easy thing to do, since I both hated and loved him, and in equal measure. I must have loved him as a very young child. After all, he was my father and I didn't yet understand the burden of being the youngest in the family and his favorite. I was only his favorite because I was the youngest, though my sister and brother never understood that. He was like a huge five-year-old himself, so it wasn't strange that he was constitutionally incapable of paying attention to any but the youngest child in sight, providing it was up and around, running on two feet. Infants were left to their mothers. My judgments of him were gleaned through the unclear vision of an unwilling favorite, and by the time I was five years old I had begun to dislike him intensely, and by six, I learned to hide at his approach.

My first memory of my father was the day of my third birthday. I was in the backyard with my mother and some neighborhood children at my birthday party. The party was almost over when my father appeared carrying what seemed to me to be a large box. He was smiling and pleased as I opened it. It was a Patsy doll, about twelve inches tall, dressed in a pink organdy dress and black cloth Mary Janes. Patsy had a Buster Brown haircut just like mine.

My mother lost her temper and started yelling at him. I don't know how much Patsy cost in dollars, but I know what she cost in birthday tranquility. It was 1931 and there was no money for dolls, or not enough for such a grand doll. She wanted him to take it back, and he refused. When she said I could keep it, but only take it out to play with on special occasions, he turned and left, his day spoiled, her day spoiled, my day spoiled. The other kids kept right on eating, and then they left and probably forgot the whole thing. My sister and brother never forgave me for that doll. If he had thought about it, he would have brought them something equally grand, but he never thought about anything. He probably just walked into the store and Patsy was the biggest doll, or the first doll he saw, so he bought it.

My father was thirty-two when I was born, and by that time he weighed about two hundred and fifty pounds. In spite of his weight, he was a handsome man, and carried himself along with a light step. Because he was six foot and heavy, and because he was outspoken at all times, he was never called on to use force to get his way. Which was lucky because he wasn't a fighter. I think he had the fearlessness and belief in his own power that are the most valuable possessions of any tough street kid.

They were possessions he needed when he was young, for he was born on the Westside in New York City's Hell's Kitchen, third child of five, to Gus and Maggie Primont. His parents differed sharply in style. His mother, Maggie Donahue, daughter of a farmer near Syracuse, was tall, stern, and religious, and was married in a navy blue taffeta dress with leg o'mutton sleeves and one hundred and four self-covered buttons on the back. His father was a short, cheery man, son of French immigrants who landed in New York in 1858 and somehow made their way up the Hudson to Syracuse, enabling Gus and Maggie to unite in what may have been marital bliss, which lasted over fifty years until death separated them.

My father's three brothers and one sister were each of them all of a piece. Arthur, the oldest, was consistently kind and gentle, the nicest man I knew as a child, and indeed, I have never met a nicer one yet. He was six-foot-four with soft brown eyes and a quiet voice. The next brother, Gus, was dreadful—sarcastic, overbearing, alternately glowering or grudgingly near pleasant. Arthur and Gus were New York City policemen. Arthur had a reputation for honesty, insisting on paying his fare on buses and trolleys, and Gus, when he died, left a cache of pilfered pencils and stationery all bearing the markings of the Police Department. That and eight cases of Spam he'd hoarded in case the Germans got as far as Staten Island.

Ed, the third child, had the misfortune as a boy to be run over by a trolley car, which cost him half his right leg. With a new wooden leg and the settlement from the trolley car company, he and the family set off for the suburbs. Ed was the quintessential accountant. Maybe the experience of trading half a leg for a different social position gave him his basic numerical outlook on life. His words were measured, his humor doled out dryly. He saved string and silver cigarette paper and rolled them into even-sized balls. And every seven years he painted the outside of the house, starting at the northeast corner and ending three weeks later at the same corner, having known from the beginning to the drop how much paint, turpentine, and time he would need. And every night he cleaned and washed his brushes.

Elvira, the fifth and youngest, cynical, musical, and innocently streetwise, was a Dominican nun with a tough Westside accent and a very direct manner, which I suppose was muted in the convent but given free rein on her infrequent visits home. The family doted on her and never called her anything but Babe. She was good-humored, bigoted, and very conservative, and was more like my father than any of the others. Except that she had more sense of responsibility.

My father, the fourth child, seemed caught in a chaotic conflict made up of all the strongest aspects of the collective family temperaments. From my grandfather, he had a good sense of humor and a desire to please and be pleased. From his mother he absorbed efficiency and fanatical neatness as well as his cynicism. Like Arthur, he was generous, and like Gus, he could be terrible tempered and sarcastic. He was bigoted, conservative, and logical like Elvira. With Ed he shared almost nothing, except a facility for numbers and rigidity in his personal habits.

In my father, all these traits were taken to extremes and in such rapid succession that it was hard for us to know what would happen next. And I am not sure he ever wondered about his changeability. Does a five-year-old think that far ahead?

If his family had one unifying trait, it was a sense of infallibility. They had an absolute conviction at all times that they were right. None of them ever questioned the rightness of their opinions, though they were humorously tolerant of other points of view, dismissing them with a quick New York sarcasm often painful to outsiders but comfortable to themselves.

It may have been a joke that my grandfather wanted to name my father Napoleon, but Grandmother won out, and they called him Walter. It was too bad in a way. Napoleon would have suited him. He was a born general. If he couldn't give the orders, he wasn't interested. And he was always right, or so he believed. When confronted with evidence that he was wrong, he dismissed it with a laugh and a shrug that implied, "Well, I can't be right all the time." Then he forgot at once that he had ever been wrong.

With a consistency worthy of Uncle Ed, the accountant, he was always neat. His clothes were always clean. He wore dark blue suits, white shirts, and either blue or maroon ties. His socks were black with blue clocks, and he kept a handkerchief in his upper left-hand pocket. In winter he wore a fedora, and in summer he wore a straw boater. And in the rain, he refused to wear galoshes. Every morning he brushed his teeth before he went downstairs, and then drank three cups of coffee, cooled in the saucer, to wake him up.

When he was twelve years old, he left school to work for a family friend who owned a milk company. It was a good job for him. He was by nature a fastidious person, and given the precarious state of refrigeration in those days, a milk company had good use for someone who watched over the products it sold, like an English governess raising a crown prince. At home my father insisted on the same standards of cleanliness with food preparation and with dishes. He often offered to help wash the dinner dishes, and even on Thanksgiving or Christmas, when there was a mountain of dishes, we tried to discourage him, because he worked with such a furious concentration that someone always left the kitchen shouting, or if one of us kids, shouting and crying.

But if he was rigid in matters of cleanliness and appearance, he was erratic in everything else. He never got up, left the house, or returned in the evening at the same time two days in a row. The most consistent thing about him was his inconsistency. He nearly always acted on impulse. The blue suits and maroon ties were probably what held his life together and kept him from flying off in a hundred directions. His moods were unpredictable. He swung from gaiety to gloom and back again at the smallest provocation, or with no provocation at all. One moment he would be humming a foxtrot or singing a vaudeville tune, leading the partner he happened on in whatever room he was in, or an imaginary partner if the real thing wasn't available, smiling, eyes gleaming with pleasure, when a word or an unwanted thought would jar his mood. The dance would stop, and his face turned glum, his huge body dragging. The partner would be forgotten and slink off, knowing better than to stay around to see the gross ill humor that could succeed melancholy. Then, as often as not, a few minutes later he was smiling and proposing a drive to Hempstead or an ice cream soda for everybody.

He was a man of irritating excesses. If he decided to wash the windows, he commandeered everyone in sight, even neighbors, into the project. Within minutes, buckets, pails, brushes, ammonia, squeegees, chamois, newspapers were in the hands of the unwilling recruits, and Walter was firing commands, now cheerful, now sarcastic, as competence and incompetence demanded. And the windows might not even be his. They might be the neighbors' if he took it into his head that they were in need of a good washing. According to him, with a little bit of good will the job could be done in no time—or two hours, or ten. He didn't care. He plowed on until the end, working with rapid efficient motions, often getting angry as the others drooped and dropped from exhaustion.

My father was indiscriminately generous, giving food, money, time, energy in about the same spirit that other people smile or say good morning. And he gave without thinking of consequences or return. Of course, he often gave what wasn't his to give, so the consequences were sometimes unpleasant. When there was just enough food for the family, he invited friends. If he had two ties, he lent them both to friends who needed them; sure he could always get another. He treated strangers in bars, paid for little old ladies on buses, took all the children in the neighborhood to the corner store for ice cream pops on hot afternoons. If his children asked for money, he cleaned out his pockets, leaving nothing for his wife, or the gas company, or the next day. If he bought roller skates for his six-year-old, he bought skates for her friends. He even gave things to people he didn't like, if they looked as if they needed them.

This was during the Depression, and no one understood why he did such things, least of all him, I suppose. In those days, generosity was more the style than it is today, so no one looked for ulterior motives. My mother was often bitter, telling him that charity began at home.

During the worst days of the Depression, Dad only brought home a few dollars a week, when his boss, Charlie Malone, divided whatever money came in equally among all the men who worked in the dairy. That is, he brought those dollars home if he made it there before running into someone with a hard-luck story. Like the young man selling King James Bibles, which, as Catholics, we were forbidden to read, and which Dad bought two of. "But he was so thin, Mary. He really looked hungry." Certainly none of them felt the urge to question their good luck or the motives for his generosity.

Not all of his gifts were so extreme. Sometimes, if he was doing the grocery shopping, he would pick up a few items, coffee or butter, maybe eggs, for my mother's best friend, Vera Litchhult, a widow who lived down the street from us, or he'd drop half a dozen sugar buns off at her house so she and Mary and Uncle Charlie could have a treat. She thought he was crazy. She would not have done it for him. But she blushed with pleasure while she scolded him, and I saw how her eyes watered more than once when he was good to her.

My father could never resist a tale of woe, especially if it involved money. He cosigned notes for hundreds of dollars in bank loans for good friends who immediately lost their jobs, only to regain them a month after my mother had scraped together enough money to pay off the notes. He used the phone money for movies, the electricity money for beer, and the mortgage money for something else. If my mother sent him to the A & P for half a pound of ground chuck, he came back with a leg of lamb, a chocolate cake, and a dozen cigars. He never meant to be short of money for necessities; it was just that the necessities for him included many things not on the standard list of things needed by most families of such modest means.

The only time anyone could remember him using good sense about money was when Charlie Malone, his first employer at the milk company, now turned inventor, wanted him to invest in a device to stop automobiles in an emergency. It consisted of six stakes like the fangs of a predatory beast that were meant to be fastened along a car's front bumper. When the brakes failed, the driver could push a button and the teeth would drop down and jam into the road. It looked fantastic, and Charlie assured my father that it would make their fortune. Fortunately, my grandmother's cynicism and Uncle Arthur's tender nature were dominant in him at the moment, and he snorted as he thought of the fortune, and winced as he thought of the broken skull of the driver, if the device actually worked.

Every Sunday after Mass, if any friends happened out the door of the church at the same time as my father, he would invite them back to the house—for dinner, for brunch, for coffee, he didn't care. Then he would drive to Hollis and pick up my mother's three aunts and his mother and father, and my mother would settle down to catering for everybody, while my father disappeared up the street to visit someone else. Or he'd go out and mow the lawn. Or he'd go to sleep. Or listen to a baseball game.

He loved baseball, and above all, he loved the Giants and Babe Ruth. He had an incredible memory and remembered every game he ever saw, all the batting averages of every player, and the history of players on almost any team. He was so good at math that he could add up long three-figure columns in his head as he looked at them, but the only place he got to show off his facility was in grocery stores and sometimes at work. After years as a milk salesman in New York City, he knew the stores that occupied almost every corner from the Battery to 86th Street and from the Hudson River to the East River. Not only that, but he knew the owners in most of them, and even where the telephones were located in the stores that had them.

My father's family was musical. Grandpa played the banjo. Uncle Arthur and Uncle Gus played mandolins. Aunt Elvira played the piano and accordion, and Uncle Ed played the accordion and banjo. My father, too erratic to settle down to lessons on any instrument, played the piano by ear, and was the singer in the family. They all sang rather well and in tune, but he had the pleasantest voice, and was a tenor, unusual for such a large man. Whenever his whole family was together for dinner or a holiday at Grandma and Grandpa's house, there was always an hour of singing before the day ended, and my father always sang harmony. No one ever performed alone. There always had to be at least two for music to happen. And no one, except possibly Elvira, who was the only accomplished musician, was ever treated as better than the others.

Sundays and holidays were the only times we saw my father during the day. He went to work between seven and eight and got back when he got back, sometimes at six, sometimes at eight, sometimes at midnight. No one, including him, ever knew what time it would be. If it was late, he had some excuse, and if it were early, he would pick himself up after an hour or two and leave to meet friends at the American Legion or at a bar where he could sit and talk.

He spent most of his spare time at the American Legion clubhouse. I think he may have been one of the founders of the Queens Village club. He certainly acted as if it was his invention. He loved the noise and the card playing, the easy sentimental patriotism, the singing, bugle playing, arguing, fundraising, elections, bingo, parades, commotion, uniforms, badges, poppies, dinners, breakfasts, beer parties. I don't think there was a single thing about the American Legion that he didn't like. It was one big party for him. A party where someone with a loud voice, a stinging tongue, and a lot of opinions could be a very big frog in a small pond like Queens Village. He held every office a man could hold in the town and county in the Legion. He was the drum major and led every parade with a big brass baton. He was chairman of this and chairman of that, and it all succeeded.

Because he was Catholic, half Irish, and lower middle class, he was a registered Democrat who went occasionally to the local club meetings and always spoke as if he was a mainstay of the Democratic Party. That is, he was a Democrat until he got into the voting booth at every election, when the urge to vote for a Republican became overwhelming. He had no use at all for politicians, and he must have felt that there was at least a chance that the ones he didn't know might be honest. The Democrats at the local club kept trying to get him into politics, so he already knew about them. When his Republican friends heard his views on the Democrats, they invited him to join the Republican Party. He went to one meeting and became so uncomfortable that he left early, coming home to confess to my mother, "I'm a Democrat. I can't join the Republicans."

The inconsistency between what my father did and what he said was never more apparent than in the matter of his friends. There wasn't a race, religion, nationality or profession that he didn't have a sarcastic epithet for. Except the Catholic Church, and there he confined himself to loud grumbling about their failure to send to the poor the money they collected from the rich, among whom he numbered himself.

It never occurred to him that it was ridiculous to declare at five in the afternoon that all Italians were "wop spaghetti benders," then spend the evening with an arm around the shoulder of his good friend Joe Luciano, cousin of Lucky, singing "O Sole Mio" before they sat down to one of Josephine Luciano's marvelous spaghetti dinners. If anyone called this to his attention, he looked surprised and said, "But Joe's different."

All his friends were different. Lawyers were shysters, but Tom Pastor, his friend, was honest, and never tricked anyone with the small print. Butchers always put their fingers on the scales when they weighed the meat, but his friend Louis Wagner didn't. Louis never cheated anybody in his life. Baptists were a bunch of mealy-mouthed psalm singers, but Jim Savell, our next-door neighbor, was staunch and stalwart, even if he did happen to have a beautiful tenor voice that could make a person cry when he sang his favorite Protestant hymns.

The Irish were a bunch of shanty sentimental sots, except for Howard Murphy, another neighbor and friend. He never drank to excess, was neat and clean, and had a generous good nature. Proof of this was the time he and my father decided to plant a vegetable garden together. They dug up the soil, prepared the beds and planted the seeds. Two weeks later, my father arrived home early from work and decided to do a little weeding. When he finished pulling up all the suspicious-looking plants in the garden, there was nothing left but a few stray seedlings from the four o'clocks for Howard to laugh over. From then on, Howard played gardener and my father did the watering.

All Jews were dirty crooks except Stanley Berger, who came to our house to eat roast pork and bacon because his wife kept kosher at home. He was a fine man, also an exception to the rule about insurance men, who robbed you blind selling policies you didn't need and then presented themselves at the door like leeches each week to collect the premiums.

Jim Larsen the sign painter was very intelligent, not like the family three doors away with whom my father wasn't acquainted and whom he judged to be a bunch of "dumb Swedes." Then there was Charlie Hrostoski, who was in construction. He was a recent Polish immigrant, the builder of the new American Legion Hall. His loose-toothed mouth always held a soggy cigarette, which didn't help his unfathomable accent, but his talents as the only honest builder and decent Polack my father ever met made Charlie an invaluable friend, especially when the drains clogged and the garage door fell off.

My father's best friend, and the most telling exception to all the rules about foreigners, was Vic Chavoushian. I don't know what ugly thing my father had to say about Armenians. The subject may never have come up, since I think Vic was the only Armenian in Queens Village. Vic emigrated from Armenia to the United States before the war, fought in the army, and joined the American Legion with my father. Over the years he became part of the family. He was a mechanic. My father said he was a genius, but then my father could hardly swing a hammer without wrecking something. He would start a job and then Vic would walk in and save face for him by saying that my father was doing it "very good" but he would show him something a little better for next time. And my father would stand back and admire him. The fact that Vic lived with a Greek woman named Mrs. Paul, the deserted wife of an old friend of his from whom he had been renting a room at the time of the desertion, never raised an eyebrow in my family. Living in sin, if that's what it was, wasn't sin when one of my father's friends did it.

When my father was fifty-one and my brother, sister, and I were grown up and working, he quit his job at the milk company and bought a soda parlor on Eighth Avenue and 20th Street in New York. What had been an Irish neighborhood the year before was by 1945 half Irish and half Puerto Rican, and like all New York neighborhoods in transition, it was a mess. Why he bought that store, of all the stores in New York to choose from, was a mystery. Eighth Avenue was seedy and run down, full of petty thieves and poverty, and he had lived for too long in the suburbs to remember how to cope with tough city living.

The first year the store made money. There were many longshoremen living in the area, and they ate a lot of banana splits. Then there was a long strike, and then unemployment, then further deterioration of the neighborhood. The store stopped making money. My parents probably didn't make twenty dollars a day over expenses anytime in the next fifteen years. Through it all, my father managed to play host to the hundreds of thousands of people who came into the store, and he made friends of some of them. He gave away ice cream, coffee, and Danishes, invited people to stay to dinner with him and my mother in the back of the store. He was robbed by countermen, deliverymen, and health and fire inspectors. He laughed and joked and made ghastly bigoted remarks, then got insulted if anyone took offense. He slipped from high humor to gloomy depression without apparent cause, and made his more timid customers fearful that they might have hurt his feelings. And every day he opened the door to the store with an energetic crash and washed the place down from front to back as if he was going to get a gold star when he was done. He never bothered going to a bar or to the American Legion again once he had the store. He didn't need them. He had that long Formica counter, and if he stayed open until two in the morning, he had sixteen hours of company a day, on his own territory.

Of course, he went bankrupt. He was such a terrible businessman that it was inevitable. The problem was that he should have gone bankrupt after three years when it was obvious the business wasn't there. But he kept right on making seventeen flavors of ice cream, and polishing mirrors and glasses. He just didn't pay his creditors, chief among whom was the Internal Revenue Service. There was no money for anything.

His last illness was the only thing in his life that he couldn't ignore. The strong constitution that had let him barge through life, pretty much without tripping, became at the end a liability. He struggled against death, in a time when there were no medications except morphine to help him. And that didn't work for long because doctors were afraid to give enough to kill the pain and possibly cause someone to become an addict.

Before he died, before the lobotomy they performed to try to prevent him from remembering the pain he was feeling, he told me that he was sorry for all the terrible things he had said in the past "about colored people." He'd never known any except the nursemaid who took care of Elvira when she was a baby and he was a five-year-old. I remember him telling me about her when I was little, joking that it was a wonder her color didn't rub off on Elvira. And when we drove through Harlem, he always had plenty to say about the lazy coons and shiftless niggers hanging around looking for a handout. But in the VA Hospital where all the orderlies and most of the nurses were black, he discovered that there were all kinds, no different from everyone else, and he was ashamed. And for once, he didn't say that they were different from the rest, he said he was sorry.□

August 19, 1996
Alpine Drive, Beverly Hills

Dear Michael,
Older people, myself included, develop a philosophy that sometimes blunts their sensitivities about death. Not that they are unfeeling—they may be terribly sad and feel the loss of friends and family deeply—it's just that in order to accept death for themselves, they have to accept it for other people. It's not that they want to die, but they have to see life as transient. Maybe it's important not to let oneself think too empathically about death. It's more than seeing it; they know it completely—physically as well as intellectually. It is almost sad to see old people who don't reach that stage. It's the only way to begin to remove yourself from the fray and from the fear of death. And it's not that you don't try your best to stay alive and breathing. You can still love the sunrise, but let go of it for someone else the way you know that others will let go of it for you; the way you are trying to let go of it yourself.

In answer to a few things in your letter of July 20th: You wrote that you think your mother sees you as weird and unreachable. If she could love and accept me when I was young, and she did, think of it—you're her son whom she adored as an infant and boy growing up, who then grew up to be a lot like me, especially in what you might call the weird and different department.

When you and Peter were little, I used to fantasize that something, whatever, would happen, and I would be your mother; I would have two little boys I could love and keep for my own. When you came to live with us in California, I felt guilty for my old sin of envy and covetousness, as if finally, I'd stolen you for myself, even though you were now forty years old and free to be where you wanted to be. I still loved you dearly, now as family, a friend, a nephew, and an equal. But there was always guilt, even though I knew I could help you in ways your mother couldn't and ways that you needed.

But I know how much she loves you. And I probably even know how she "criticizes and complains." I've been lucky to see Andy a lot after he grew up. I've watched him become an adult, then a parent, behaving responsibly, and I've finally given up all the old mother habits of telling him what he should do, when he should do it, and most important of all, why!

Irene hasn't been that lucky. She hasn't seen you weekly being who you are year after year, so it's no surprise that she reverts to treating you somewhat the way she did when you were young and in need of direction. After all, no one else lives exactly the same way, and parents are always trying to pass on their habits of living along with their genes.

I remember that when you were a little baby, she used to say things like "give it to Mommy, dear," and so you called her "Mommy Dear." That always seemed appropriate to me because when she spoke to you her voice was so loving, like the whole earth opening up and offering you everything wonderful.

There's a part of her that remembers all those feelings and I hope you can somehow find them too. She knows you're okay and that you're a good person and all that, she just doesn't have the vocabulary to tell you. You and I find it easy to speak of our feelings, but many people can't speak so freely in that way. So she falls back on the old ways of communicating, or not communicating, from when you were a teenager before you went into the army. That was the last habit created between you. I saw this happen with many of my friends after their children went away to college. They couldn't change while their children were changing and there was always friction when the children came home, even years later.

Michael, you have given me a kind of love that no one else has, as I guess I have you. We've been really blessed, haven't we?

     Love,
     Rosemary

September 5, 1996
Alpine Drive, Beverly Hills

His playing is that of so fine a pianist that one is no longer aware that the performer is a pianist at all, because his playing has become so transparent, so imbued by what he is interpreting that one no longer sees the performer himself— he is simply a window opening upon a great work of art.
—Marcel Proust, *The Guermantes Way*

Dear Plácido,
Marcel Proust didn't hear you sing last night. If he had, I think he would have said that you are both the window and the art.

With deepest thanks for being the perfect performer and artist that you are, and for giving me some of the most memorable experiences of art possible in a lifetime of searching for meaning.

I'm thanking the talented man who has worked and studied so hard for so many years, but it is the art, maybe even the search for a universal human soul, for which I feel an unending gratitude.
Sincerely,
Rosemary Okun

Journal
September 29, 1996
Alpine Drive, Beverly Hills

Andy is thirty-four today. When I called to wish him a happy birthday this morning, I tried to tell him about how Milt looked, so glowing and beautiful, when I woke up from the anesthesia and Milt turned to me; I remember him leaning over and telling me how amazing and beautiful Andy was, but it was Milt, amazed and beautiful, who I saw.

There are things you never forget, and that look of the greatest love Milt could ever feel tied me to that moment forever. I knew that this time, the father of my child, our child, would love his child forever, and I was tied to that gift of love in Milt's heart.□

HAPPY BIRTHDAY

I was destroyed by pain
the first time I saw you
and in my exhaustion
made you mine

Somewhere in those years
of watching you grow
there was so much to see
all the disjointed steps we took
and the harmonies we heard
made a pattern not known to us

Journal
October 3, 1996
Alpine Drive, Beverly Hills

Today is Jenny's forty-third birthday, and Saturday was Andy's thirty- fourth. I remember their tiny bodies so well. At Jenny's birth in 1953, I was in Montclair, New Jersey, and outside the hospital ward window were wonderful maples and oaks in full fall color. It was a glorious northeastern fall, and my baby was as beautiful as the whole world outside and my heart was huge with love. No young mother could have been more in harmony with the universe than I was the moment I saw her...□

LETTER TO AN OLD FRIEND

Dear Joan,

I woke up fifteen minutes ago writing a letter to you, reminded of a poem, "Lists," that I wrote when I went back to school twenty years ago. It says better than anything else I could write how much those years in Chappaqua meant to me. In a way, they were the teenage years again, so much better than when I lived with the family I was born into. They were years filled with the color and beauty of the setting, of physical love with Milt, of love for my young children, of love and caring for and being cared for by my mother, of good health and vigor, of springing out of bed in the mornings, dressing in three minutes, of housework done in half an hour, of reading hours a day, and spending hours with good friends over coffee and lunch...

It wasn't that I was always so happy in Chappaqua. Today they have a name for my problems, bipolar disorder, explaining but not blotting out the bad times. Even without the explanation, I had begun to learn how to sit out the lows and look to the highs, my highs being equivalent to most people's normal good days. Fortunately, the manic side, which was more pronounced in my father, isn't too far out of the ordinary in me.

The seven years in Chappaqua were filled with beauty that I can go into myself and remember, looking north into the distance at the crest of Hardscrabble Road at the winter colors of the tree bark and evergreens against snow on the hills under the late afternoon sky; I can hear the snow falling, feel it under my feet. Or think of heavy, hot summer days and cool iced tea and the flower garden outside our kitchen window. Dinners with friends, cooked and served almost effortlessly, pleased to be together. And reading. Reading so many wonderful books. Hearing what other people understood from them. Reading so much that when I went back to school, I discovered I'd read more than most of my instructors, if not more intensely in any subject other than Proust or Joyce, certainly a wider range of literature.

Back in those Chappaqua days, I didn't know that I was intelligent. I thought I was practical and I liked to read, but I knew

I couldn't do math and had "only" gone to art school. I never had a teacher who didn't complain about me, my work, and my effort. No one was satisfied. Not even in art school... When I lived in Chappaqua, I thought of myself as a failure, not smart, only a practical somebody who scraped along, uneducated, a kind of female Leopold Bloom, full of made-up theories, unaccredited by the establishment, opinionated without cause undegreed in a world of the BA'd and the PhD'd. I remember mentioning something like that to you toward the end of those years, and you looking at me with skepticism, saying, "You don't really mean that. With all you've read? Why, you just finished reading..." I was amazed when you said that. It was possibly the first direct compliment I'd ever had. I felt like a fraud because I thought you were fooled by some exterior pretense I made of being smart like all my friends. I never made the connection that being intelligent was a part of why I had those friends.

When we moved to California and I was looking for an avenue of work, I went to a class for women who wanted to find out what they were capable of doing. There were over a hundred in the class, and one of the exercises was to describe ourselves, another was a verbal test, and another a test of what our interests were. My adviser asked why I felt I couldn't go back to get a degree. I gave her my old list of failures at all levels of school. She said that didn't matter. I got the highest score on the test, a mark that put me at the level of gifted student for Stanford University. Milt said that the difference between us was that I was "intelligent" and he was "educated," which I didn't take as any kind of compliment, though I get it now.

According to my interests, likes, and dislikes, the occupations I was suited to were what I was doing (staying at home, reading and doing what I liked), teaching English at the college level, writing, or speech therapy. I would have loved to be a speech therapist. I have a great ear and find it easy to explain and demonstrate how to make different sounds. But to be a qualified speech therapist in California, one has to take math and statistics, and if one has trouble getting one's own address and telephone number straight, and had to copy everyone else's algebra tests in order to pass and get a high school diploma, one is not going to be a speech therapist.

So I went back to school, and got a B.A. and an M.A. After the ceremony I came home, finished sewing a dress for Jenny, and cooked a party dinner for forty people. But I needed those two degrees. I needed public recognition that I was intelligent so I could feel good about doing what I liked to do. It sounds crazy, doesn't it?

I'm still at home. I write a journal, thanks to the computer. Like almost everyone I know, I accumulate innumerable pieces of paper. Occasionally, I pick up a paintbrush and do some little thing, which often ends up in the trash for reasons of discretion. I love my grandchildren passionately and see them every week if I can. They came for a sleepover the other night, and while I was fixing dinner, Will, Andy's four-and- half-year-old, looked over at me with his beautiful smile and asked, "Nana, why do you love us so much?" My answer: "Because you are my grandchildren and you're so wonderful and I took care of you when you were babies and that makes you always love someone so much." As I spoke, he shook his head, as if to say, "Yes, yes. That's right, I see."

Milt isn't nearly half-retired yet. He still reads, eats, watches television, and occasionally listens to music, all at the same time. He's not playing tennis at this point, so he has begun walking and doing exercises in the pool. Andy works with him, studying, analyzing, advising, doing a lot of the legwork on investments and our music publishing company. Andy and two working reporters have begun a periodical of show business litigation for attorneys, which he does in his spare time. Julia has opted to stay home with the children, which is great. She's a librarian, but I don't know how outdated her training and experience will be by the time she goes back to work. That will be quite a while, since the children will have to go to private schools if they continue to live in Los Angeles, and they'll need ferrying back and forth.

Jenny goes on working, just the way she did when she was a child. She's talented, organized, and obsessive. She's a lot like Milt in his middle years. Not much else matters to her besides her work. She loves her husband and her child and her social life, but she lives for her work. We have called a truce, which generally works quite well. Only now I have learned how to demand that people keep out of my way. Let me be the teenager again, free to use my space and time the way I want.

I've been at this since seven-thirty and it's now ten-thirty, doing my thing for as long as it pleased me. I forgot to eat breakfast. I didn't take any of the three thousand pills I take each day, thereby setting up any number of weird things in my innards I suppose, so I'll end here. I'm enclosing a list of the books we've read in our book group. Another that I've read and thought was excellent was *Angela's Ashes* by Frank McCourt. Also, *Bastard Out of Carolina* by Dorothy Allison—incredible writing on a subject that isn't always so well done.

I was really happy to get your letter yesterday, Joan. Write again when you get the urge. It's hard to go in different ways and lose friends with the passage of time. We only know each other as the younger people we were, but with some people, I feel that at any time we could meet and find mutual interests in our present mellower, more understanding phase. Give my love to Bill, and Milt sends his too.
    Love,
     Rosemary

         October 25, 1996
         Alpine Drive, Beverly Hills

Dear Michael,
I've had a hard time writing too since I heard about your mother's illness. I know how much she loves you and Peter. Don't be fooled by her turning to the television before you leave the room. Some people know how to anesthetize themselves in the face of pain. And sometimes they can't let go and just weep.

I think it would be a good idea to write to your mother and tell her how much you love her, and why you love her. Maybe you could recall some good times, ones that you especially remember of your life together that weren't spoiled by my brother in some way—something especially good that she did or said. I am sure there were important moments— possibly not at the time they happened, but now, if you think about them, maybe you can understand how much she loved you, not just that you loved her. If you let her know that you understand what her love meant to her and to you and Peter, I'm sure that would be a great gift to her.

Do you remember the two wonderful cakes she used to make? One was a many-layered yellow cake with chocolate icing in between the layers and hard caramel candy on the top, and the other was an incredible, light, delicious nut cake. I know she didn't like to cook, but when she baked those two cakes, there couldn't be any better baker.

She may have a long time to live, Michael, and the chemotherapy may help give her some good time. I hope so. I'm sure you will see her again, and you have to make sure that Peter knows he has to get you back in time while she is well enough to take pleasure in your presence.

It's almost hard for me to identify with you in your feelings for her because I had Nana with me for so many years before she died. We had an almost uninterrupted warm relationship and she was so important to me all my life. I couldn't have made it without her. Or if I had, my life would have been even bleaker than it sometimes was.

I wrote a description of my family in its entirety the other day, and I realized that while I've written about us piecemeal over the years, it's the first time that I ever told the truth about us as we were, or as I saw us. It wasn't overly long; it was just the description of what today would be called a dysfunctional family. It wasn't about why we were that way, just that we were, and the word I used to describe us best was "broken." After I wrote it, I realized that none of us ever did get repaired. I probably come the closest to having patched myself together in a presentable manner, but I'm not really sure of what I am. All the mended seams still feel uncomfortable, like scars that heal with a ridge, and they are very sensitive to the touch.

We have that history in common, and thank god we have a love in common that comes from my having cared for you as an infant and young child. We both need that. The difference between us is that I'm a woman and you're a man, and women are allowed to be conscious as they grow up, if they wish to know how much they love the people around them, while young men somehow transfer love to other things and people. When most women have children they suddenly become members of the larger community of women, and they understand how much their own mothers have felt for them. Not all of them have that experience, but very many do, and I was lucky to be one of them.

This is rambling, but what else is there to do but ramble when things are not going well? Take care of yourself. You are needed.
   Love,
    Rosemary

         October 31, 1996
         Alpine Drive, Beverly Hills

Dear Michael,
Just typing the word Halloween made my mouth begin to water. Oh, those miniature Hershey chocolate bars! Those days in the past when I could eat all the candy I wanted!

In my day, we didn't go trick or treating. At least, girls didn't. Only some of the boys went out, and I don't think they ever waited to collect a treat. About a week before the big day, we would all begin to ring doorbells. You usually rang the doorbell of a grownup no one particularly liked, then you ran and hid in the bushes until they came and opened the door. There was a lot of snickering and shuffling in the shrubs, and some gasping if the person came out the door and started shaking a fist.

Real courage was going back and ringing a second time in five minutes, and then we all just ran away. Halloween night, though, was for the boys. The girls stayed home and hoped that the boys would ring their doorbells, so they could open the doors and be indignant when no one was there.
   Be well, and lots of love,
    Rosemary

DÍA DE LOS MUERTOS

If October is
red golden leaves
a moon yellow and great

If brisk winds
brush to glowing
pumpkins smiling plump

Forget the last sad day
the sad and lost
the unspeaking
when the last leaf
clings to bare limbs
after midnight

                        November 2, 1996
                        Alpine Drive, Beverly Hills

Dear Michael,
Will and Emily are sitting at the kitchen table eating cereal and bananas. They had a sleepover by request with us last night, and this morning they climbed into bed with me and we snuggled and chatted for a half hour—a sublime way to start the day for a grandmother. As I recall, it wasn't my favorite way to start the day with my own two kids, but I probably would have loved it with you and Peter. I was twenty when you two were babies, and am now forty years older than my two.

    Emily was very pleased with the breakfast menu, Will less so. "I don't like bananas," he murmured quietly and definitely with a sideways look, as if to say, "I don't have to eat it, do I?" And following that, a look of, "I'm not going to eat that." I explained to him that when you cut the banana across in little rounds it tastes sweeter. At least, it seemed that way to me. He ignored me and went on watching *Pinocchio* on video. So I pushed a little harder, but nicely, saying, "It's almost as if you put sugar on them. Would you like to try it that way? You know, sometimes as we grow we begin to like something we never liked before."

He turned from the screen, narrowed his eyes, and said, "I'm telling the truth of me, Nana. I don't like bananas." So I apologized and told him that if there was anything I believed in, it was trying to listen to people when they say something and not to keep on insisting they do something they don't want to do. And that made everything okay.

I looked away for a minute and then saw that he'd taken a bite out of one of the rounds. He smiled angelically at me, and without saying anything, still smiling, ate another round, and then we gave the rest to Emily, who munched them down. I guess my apology was profuse enough to convince him that I understood he had a right not to like something, but he could also be generous enough to give it a try and show that he forgave me.

Love,
Rosemary

Journal
November 9, 1996
Alpine Drive, Beverly Hills

Milt and I had Will and Emily most of today and took them to Borders Bookstore in Westwood, then out to lunch at the club. I AM TIRED! But it was a happy day, because we found that now that Emily is three and doesn't need to be picked up we can manage quite well. Milt becomes more and more enamored of them each time they visit. Today, I found him in the playroom, sitting at the table reading a book while waiting for me to get ready to go out.

After we came back from lunch, Lizzie came over to play. She was wonderful. They were wonderful. I, on the other hand, had to sit in the kitchen with my head held up by my hands, trying to stay awake, except for the time that Emily sat on my lap and I could rest my head on the top of hers so I knew without any doubt where she was.

Will assured me today that he loves me more than I love him. I didn't want to get into a contest about it so I just said that would be hard. The greeting they gave me when I opened the door to let them in this morning was what all of us think we deserve but almost never get.

Weird, weird thing: I just realized that it's 6:30pm and Jenny, Richard, and Lizzie are paying a visit to Dick, Jennifer's natural father. Jenny ran into him and his wife at a shopping mall about a month ago. He and Jenny didn't recognize each another, but his wife remembered Jenny from fifteen years ago. Jenny said the meeting was a little bizarre. Just a few days before, she had told Lizzie that Milt had adopted her after he and I got married and was her real father, because the person you live with who takes care of you is the real father. She was prompted to tell her because Lizzie has a friend who is adopted and having a problem with who is her real mother, etc.

So somewhere along the line she decided that she would let Lizzie meet Dick. When she told me yesterday, I was in shock, and I'll try to explain why. From the time Dick and I divorced and I married Milt, I felt as if our paths simply went off in different directions, or rather, that my path went straight ahead and Dick sort of wandered off to the side and gradually disappeared into a fog. I've known for all the time we've lived here in California that he was in Venice, but it never seemed real. That person I knew was gone; the person he knew was gone; the life we lived together was nonexistent, so nonexistent that I never even worried about what I'd say if I met him. I simply didn't think about him.

Now, suddenly, there's this person, old, and probably as decrepit as I am, somewhere a half hour away, and what never occurred to me before is that we actually have something in common—Lizzie. It's a shock. I never felt that Jenny was a connection to him, or that if she was, it had nothing to do with my relationship to her. He never wanted her; he wouldn't have had a child if I hadn't insisted; and he asked to have Milt adopt her.

Dick and his wife suggested that Milt and I come too, but knowing how little I would enjoy that, and Milt's definite disinterest, Jenny said she didn't think so. She was right. She says Richard is similarly unenthusiastic, but he's going anyway to keep her company, and I suspect, to keep an eye on Lizzie. I've probably said enough to Richard to make him suspicious of Dick. And he's right.

Laughing, Jenny said that Dick told her he still takes acid when he paints. I'm sufficiently interested to want to hear the report, but no more than that. It comes under the heading of gossip, I think. I'm allowed that, aren't I?□

December 3, 1996
Alpine Drive, Beverly Hills

Dear Michael,
I spoke to your mother the other day and we had a nice, long teacup conversation. We could have been back in Hollis leaning on our elbows on the old white porcelain table, looking out the window at the apple tree. The house in Hollis, the white table, the apple tree, and even the teacups are only there in my heart, but they couldn't be any more real.

Your mother is a very wise woman, Michael. She made sure to tell me that she loved me, just as we were saying goodbye. I could hear in her voice, her long ago young woman's voice, the love that we both feel for one another, even though we haven't seen each other much these last many years. She thanked me for all the things I've done for you and Peter, but it's as much I who should be thanking her for the gift of you in my life. And I knew what she was doing, consciously or unconsciously— trying to tell me, while she had the opportunity, that I was someone she'd known in her life, who counted to her. And that means a lot to me.

Love,
Rosemary

January 4, 1997
Alpine Drive, Beverly Hills

Dear Carol,
The photograph *Legorreta Yellow*, on our Christmas card this year is a triptych of photographs of a building by Ricardo Legorreta, an architect who Jenny says always uses yellow. I've been telling everybody who asks that Legorreta was the name of an architect, but I wasn't sure since Jenny was in Europe and I never got around to asking her. She does photographs of buildings almost exclusively, so it was a pretty safe bet.

When I got your letter talking about your sister and her problems, my mind was so full of things I wanted to say. In my adult life, I have been in therapy with three different people. About a year at the age of twenty-eight with a dogmatic little Polish woman who didn't mind sticking her Freudian two cents in now and then but helped me get out of a difficult first marriage and behave sensibly enough to know that Milt was the right person for me.

Then before Andy's birth and through most of the years in Chappaqua, I saw another woman, this time a well-educated, intellectual, artistic Austrian, who, as I put it then, helped me keep my head out of the oven. I went back to her again when we returned from Europe. I suppose I saw her on and off (mostly on) from the age of thirty-two to forty-seven. The problem was that every time I went through a good period, I thought I was "cured" until things became rough again.

After we moved out here, I tried it on my own, and went through a really bad depression, so bad that though I certainly should have been in therapy, I couldn't bring myself to look for a doctor. Some years later, I became depressed again, not so severely this time, but at the end of it I went through a marked manic state that went on for some months. That was a first.

It was almost funny. At least some aspects of it were. In the first six weeks, I decided to learn bread making. I bought all kinds of equipment, cookbooks, oven tiles, bread pans. That was the fun part. Milt was ecstatic. Anyone who walked through the kitchen left with bread under his or her arms. Friends were sighing with pleasure. I suppose in six weeks I made a hundred loaves or more of all kinds of bread. You name it, I made it. Milt started talking about opening a bakery.

One day, mania stopped being fun. A switch flipped. No more bread. When happy bread making subsided, rage took over twenty-four hours a day. I decided I had to stop. I was making myself sick with hate. I stopped—another flipped switch. I didn't know I was manic, so imagine my surprise when the minute I decided to stop hating I began to eat. Every waking minute, I ate. I ate so much that within a few weeks I gained seven or eight pounds. I didn't bake bread. I just ate.

Once before, I'd gone on a thirty-pound eating binge that was stopped by one visit to a hypnotherapist. So that's what I looked for— and found—a doctor at UCLA whose specialty is hypnosis, usually for patients preparing for surgery. When I explained what was happening, she agreed to see me, and I've been seeing her ever since. The eating stopped but the mania continued, put to good use by working for CARAL, the abortion rights league here in California. I made hundreds of phone calls, raised money for them, had a fundraiser at the house, and then with great relief, left for France for the summer and left mania behind. By that time even I understood I was manic.

I don't handle medicine very well. I'm one of those people who gets all the weird side effects, as well as the usual ones. Anti-depressants make me manic unless I take them with something to keep me down, like lithium, yet lithium is no help for depression, so on the advice of the doctor in charge of psychiatric medicine at UCLA, I don't take anything, but will consider it if ever the depression becomes so bad it's intolerable.

I have had three severe major depressions in my life, and now that I am writing all this, I realize that all three were during periods when I was not in therapy. Just being in therapy with a sympathetic person to hear me speak, to help me feel real, to let me be what I am, to be a witness to something I can't describe in words—my existence, whatever that is—takes the edge off the depressions and helps me make it from week to week until suddenly the filter changes and I see colors and sunlight again.

I used to feel I was a failure because I had to be in therapy. But in the last few years, as I've read more and more about manic depression, I've been able to accept it better. I tell myself, no one would think twice if I said I had a personal trainer who came and helped me work out— that's healthy. I could spend the money on restaurants, fur coats, cars, books, going back to school, cruises, traveling around the world, and there would be someone to say "great—right on." So if being in long-time therapy is what makes my life healthier and better, then that's what I'll do.

What I want to say, but am taking a foolishly long time doing it, is that I hope your sister can understand much sooner than I did that being in therapy can be a constructive thing, can be the best thing. It's nothing to be embarrassed about. I used to tell Jenny that being dyslexic was like having green eyes or red hair. Well, being a depressed person is pretty much the same thing, only not so pleasant. I hope the drugs work for her. Each day they invent new ones. I'm not sure it helps to know you're not alone in your depression. You haven't said exactly, but I assume she has times when she's not so depressed. If she does, maybe she will learn to concentrate on realizing that those better times do come. It may sound Pollyannaish but that's what I try to do when I'm depressed. I even have a mental image for it—a kind of glow, far off, but not so far that I can't see it.

Your letter made me so sad for her that I wanted to offer something to help. I'm a stranger to your sister, but sometimes strangers are easier to bear than friends because they have no expectations, and you have no expectations, of what they want from you.

Anyway, I'm here in California. Tell her, if you want, that I've been there. I know how it feels. If she ever feels like talking to a stranger, just a voice on the phone, I'll listen to her. I say that because when I was thirty-two and overwhelmed, I heard of a suicide hotline in Sydney, Australia, one of the first of its kind, and I was so desperate that I would have called them if I'd had the number.

To bring you up to date, Jenny and I now get along quite well. We do not have the relationship I would have liked us to have. We have what we have, and as long as neither of us asks too much of the other, things work quite well. They have been living here in a separate wing of the house for about five years, so it's workable.

I don't know if you've read any poetry by the woman who won this year's Nobel Prize for Literature. Her name is Wislawa Szymborska, and there's a book of her poems called *View with a Grain of Sand* that's remarkable. I haven't yet read *The Unconsoled* but will. Just finished *Beloved* by Toni Morrison a second time, and another very interesting book, *Stones from the River* by Ursula Hegi.

Be well, and give my best to Bill.
      Love,
      Rosemary

THE GRANDKIDS

Milt is awake in the next room hoping I'll go down and fix some breakfast for him—just cereal topped with walnuts, raisins, and banana, and some brewed decaf for a pickup.

Poor Jenny, I must go down and see how she is this morning also. She thought she had a toothache but the dentist she went to for a root canal says he thinks it's neuralgia, and she went to bed in awful pain.

Lizzie ate dinner with us last night, and she was so good. She's going through the six-year-old girl stage a little late. In a girl, round about six is almost as nice and pleasant as it gets. I was complimenting her on something, then noticed I'd forgotten to tell her to wash her hands before coming to the table. And I said, "I'm not a very good Grandma, am I?" "Not very," she answered, while absent-mindedly fussing with her food. "But I like you anyway. Actually, I love you." So I told her I loved her too. This has taken years to come. And effort. Probably on both our parts. It's the first time she has said it, though for the last four or five months she has been running to hug me and be kissed when we meet.

In Will, there is a quality of directness in his concept of himself, and he has a concept of himself, that he doesn't give up. You can get him to do things he doesn't want to do, if you can present them in another light with a little sleight of words and images.

Emily—verbal, articulate, positive. Wants everything pink and pretty. There has always been some little thing around the eyes that reminds me of my family, so she may look like us somewhat. I think she has always looked like Julia's sister Amy.

Lizzie—impulsive, hyper, full of imagination and courage. The courage must come from Jenny. Inside Lizzie there is a person with a need for order, form. She is determined to have her own way.

All three grandchildren are very intelligent, and they'll be who they are with or without anyone's help. To me it's fascinating to watch them grow and develop, and I love them for their differences. I love just looking at them. They're so beautiful, not only for what they may be, but for what they are at this minute. Life has sometimes been tough even without the problems so many people have of poverty and loneliness, and I don't always want to live, but when I look at them, I forget that. They make everything worth the effort.□

March 29, 1997
Alpine Drive, Beverly Hills

Dear Michael,

It's six-thirty and I'm up, fed and drinking my coffee. Doesn't that sound energetic. Mornings are getting lighter now and I will have to put down the awnings to keep the sun out of my eyes. I thought of calling your mother, I almost went out into the garden where the grass and the plants are still shimmery with dew – it's the only time I enjoy being out there, before the sun is too bright and everything is quiet – but I caught myself in time to turn on the computer to write to you.

My letters have been so gloomy, but that's how I was feeling. Maybe the morning good cheer will sustain me for this one. I realize that so far I haven't seen Milt this morning, and maybe that's why I can think about writing.

This week he had a number of bad tests, all of which gave normal results. No details, but bad stuff. He has been knocked out by them.

Yesterday, I started to treat him as if, yes, he has a pain, but he will live through it. Now, I've felt and known that before, but I've let his pain tyrannize over me. Not him, but the pain. It's not easy, none of it. I feel unkind and guilty when I'm tough and think of myself, and exhausted and near suicidal when I let it run me into the ground.

I said this would be an up letter, and really it is. Yesterday was quite different. I didn't let him and the pain get to me. Enough with being grateful for how he has put up with my depression in the past. He was kind to me, but he didn't miss a meeting, a lunch with a friend, a beat, in fact. He was kind to me around the rest of his activities, whereas, I've stopped all activities, because whenever I was out for any length of time, I'd come back to find him worse.

I have to face that he isn't worse when I come back, he thinks he is. And then I give up going out. I also have to face up to the fact that possibly our lives will have periods like this from now on, and we're going to have to have to live through them with some kind of grace and perspective.

What you are hearing is Michael/Rosemary/Primont resolution. Weekends are the worst with no one to share the weight. Jenny, et.al. are in Santa Barbara for three days, and today Will is having a fifth birthday party with twelve children arriving to play Power Ranger run around shooting, so Andy is occupied. Therefore, I will go to Gelson's at eight o'clock – I already have the oven timer set to go off at seven-thirty – do my shopping for Will's birthday celebration here tomorrow; then go to the gym to exercise my knees and little old lady muscles. When I return, I'll give Milt a hug and kiss, mess around for a while and invite him to join me in a small walk somewhere, maybe a trip to Brentanos, who knows. If he grimaces and says no, I swear I am going out even if I sit on a bench down on Santa Monica Blvd by myself reading a book and checking out the local derelicts. Better that than sitting home hating being alive and losing loving someone out of resentment.

I make a lousy martyr. Weeping, complaining, grunting, grinding teeth. I do it all. Making martyrdom a lost cause. I think it has something to do with enjoying the euphoria connected with good deeds, doesn't it? Not my scene at all.

The other day I muttered something about the necessity of submitting to the machines to the trainer at the gym, and he laughed and said I was about the least submissive person he'd ever met. I was able to tell him that not being submissive was what got me out of Queens Village and a lot of other shit in life, but I was only going to be there another fifteen minutes and knew I couldn't even begin to explain what I meant.

What you hear is the starch in my back crackling. My intentions are firm and good, right? Right!

Be well there in China. I think of you often.

        Love,
        Rosemary

Just read your letter about opportunism and it's lack (Smith) and impression (Gore). My little Michael. I'm impressed love, hugs and kisses, said the aunt. Queens Village was never like this.

Journal
May 31, 1997
Alpine Drive, Beverly Hills

All night long I have felt ill from eating too many sweets, and in between mild bouts of nausea I've been listening to Anthony Trollope's autobiography. It's interesting—not the biography, but what he writes about. He tells of his miserable childhood, talks about writers he's known, and gives details about every book he's written—dates, payments, publishers—but offers almost nothing personal. We hear about the post office, where he must have been an exemplary, if not amiable, employee. Right now he's going through the major English writers of his century, analyzing the structure, grammar, and reception of their work. I wonder if he will speak of his family, or if the few sentences at the beginning about meeting a young woman in Ireland and marrying her will be as much as we get of the inner man.

I woke up thinking I should write about how I don't care much about living, though I suppose I would struggle like anyone else if breathing became a challenge. Words began forming in my mind as I fixed a cup of coffee in the sitting room. Just then, in the semi-dark, Lizzie trotted in, reminding me that she slept up here with us last night. So I invited her to read in my room while I write. She went down to her room, put on shorts and a cute shirt, grabbed a book, and came back up. She's a foot away from me, on the bed, lost in a book.

How can I write about not wanting to live under these circumstances? Andy called last night after arriving in Nantucket, where he and Julia and the children are vacationing. His voice sounded sweet. Isn't it strange that the qualities people have as infants and young children, with luck, don't change much and surface again and again? Andy was sweet as a young child, and he is kind and nice as an adult, and now and then that same sweetness, the truth of him, comes out in his voice. The thought came to me that this too should make me want to live, but it doesn't always. I don't want to get old, and I don't want to watch Milt getting old. I don't want to see bad things happen to my children and grandchildren. I don't have the courage to face the bad things in life. I don't suppose anyone has enough courage. We just do it. But some people are able to look beyond the pain and suffering and get on with it with grace...Having Lizzie here beside me prevents me from writing too many depressed thoughts. There is nothing like an eight-year-old girl curled up sideways on a bed, one arm on an elbow, face too close to a book, body wiggling in all directions and hair hanging down in her eyes, totally engrossed in what she's reading, to banish such thoughts.

My computer is teaching me to spell, and I'm learning all kinds of spelling rules I thought were gone out of my life. If I could learn one new thing every morning that changed me somehow, perhaps I could be happier. It's when you think you'll never be anything but what you are, in all your imperfections, that it doesn't seem worth going on. Has learning always cheered me up? Yes. Then learning is what I should concentrate on.□

June 17, 1997
Alpine Drive, Beverly Hills

Dear Michael,
I finally brought my laptop upstairs to my bedroom, have it right next to my bed, and when I get up in the morning the first thing I do is turn it on. Then I go into the sitting room, where you slept last time you were here, and make a cup of coffee, then go back and sit down and type.

I don't worry about what I will type. I just type. And I'm back to keeping a journal, something that will be necessary next fall, when Jean Holroyd begins to do some serious traveling. In fact, I think she may have been trying to prepare me for her retirement a few weeks ago when she spoke of her plans. She says her husband retired earlier than expected, and that has given them the freedom to travel more.

Naturally, that makes me glad for her and sad for me, but I only have to look at how things go at my age and Milt's to encourage anyone who has the opportunity and desire to travel to do it while they can. I will miss seeing her very much. It's hard to give up someone to whom you can tell the truth without either one of you flinching, and it takes years to reach that point. I should be used to this kind of relationship, since she isn't the only one I've had it with. But she is the one I've had the most interesting time with. She reveals enough about herself to be not just a mysterious rock of support, like many therapists, but also like a willowy tree with soft green leaves who can offer solace as one human to another who is often in need. She gave me the names of therapists to call when she isn't in town, and I suppose I will call one of them when she leaves on the first extended trip. But I won't do it happily. She was away for a few weeks while Milt was sick, and then for another few weeks after the operation, and it was almost too hard with so much that was stressful going on.

The amount of help I've needed over the years just to get by, alternately depressed and mildly happy, has been discouraging. At first I thought, okay, so I need some help, so what, a lot of people do. Who knew it was something that would last for life? I keep thinking that each bad depression will be the last, but I'm worried. I'm reaching the ten-year mark, and somewhere around every nine, ten, or twelve years, I have another bad one. The minor ones have been mitigated by talking them through with Jean, using her like a backboard so I can talk my way into getting the ball through the hoop now and then—a way to check myself against someone else's reality and see my feelings through someone else's eyes.

You will undoubtedly start getting letters from me like mad when Jean retires, but I don't think you'll mind, as long as I don't expect you to answer all of them. You and the journal will have to be my source of strength, my strong trees on the island in the real world that I sometimes can't find to put my feet on.

          Love,
          Rosemary

ORIGINS

I've flown over New York
fifty times
and never known
Queens Village
was down there
over to the right

July 28, 1997
New York, NY

Dear Mickey,

I just wrote to my nephew, Michael, about what you and I were talking about, or rather moaning about, the other day, and I thought you might be interested in some of it. No doubt you and Steve could add tons of different observations. All current and former New Yorkers could. So here's what I wrote early this morning in July, before I went out and attempted to take in yet another sliver of New York:

I'm sitting here in a fancy hotel in New York, barefooted, six o'clock in the morning, trying to get over some of the jet lag in Talloires before it happens. New York is a shock after a ten-year absence. My memories of the city begin about 1932 when I was four years old. I remember the dairy somewhere on Ninth Avenue between Fortieth and Fiftieth Street where my father worked as a salesman. I can still see the men rolling the barrels of milk on the loading dock. They were probably heavy aluminum in those days, and they rolled them on the round rim at the bottom, which made a funny crackling metal noise on the rough concrete.

The dock was always wet from being washed down constantly, and there was a lot of smelly wet burlap and big blocks of ice used to keep the milk barrels cold. My sister and I, being girls, weren't allowed to go near the dock in case we might get in the way, but I do remember my brother up on the dock trying to roll one of the barrels while the men laughed and joked with him. My father worked in dairies from the time he was twelve years old, and probably started out as one of the barrel rollers, but by the time I was born, he was one of the important ones, or so I thought. And maybe he was. He certainly gave orders to everyone around as if he was important. Must be where I get my bossiness from.

So here I am, sixty-five years later, sitting in my hotel room on Fifty- Seventh Street between Park and Madison, looking down on a city that has changed as much as Beijing just in the last ten years. Maybe not to a stranger, but to an old New Yorker, it's almost earth shaking. Other people talk about how New York has changed, but they mean the reduction in crime, less garbage strewn in the street, fewer panhandlers. I haven't seen Forty-Second Street, and probably won't, but I can believe it's changed now that I've seen Fifth Avenue. Maybe the word should be "exchanged." They have exchanged Broadway and Forty-Second Street for Fifth Avenue and Fifty-Seventh Street. All those gaping tourists are now a block away and right downstairs. Thousands of people in sneakers and drag-assed clothes haul themselves past the few remaining elegant stores sandwiched between Disney, Victoria's Secret, and a ghastly chain of extra-large convenience stores going by the amazing name of Duane Reed.

Fifth Avenue was just as much a fantasy to a girl from Queens Village in the first half of this century as Disney and Victoria's Secret are to those hordes who mill about today. Only it was beautiful then. Windows were filled with clothes and articles, beautifully crafted, most beyond the reach of anything but dreams for most of us, though the people who could afford them could be seen walking and chatting, impeccably dressed, on their way to whatever business or leisure occupied them.

Ordinary people walked, talked, and acted more politely when they were on the corner of Fifth Avenue and Fifty-Seventh Street. It was expected. That could and would be interpreted by radicals as good old American worship of money, but I choose to think of it as awe in the face of the beauty and order that people saw could be a part of life.

In the Forties and Fifties, beautiful Fifth Avenue began at Thirty- Fourth Street. There were some bleak spots before you hit Forty-Second, but above that, elegance was almost uninterrupted. By the Sixties, elegance began somewhere above Forty-Fifth, and then gradually each year more and more trashy tourist watch and camera shops and going-out-of- business shops with marked-down prices crept up and up, until now they might be the most elegant things around.

I visited my friend Mickey in the Village last night and drove down Broadway below Fourteenth. All the years I lived in the City, that street was dark, deserted, and dangerous. It is now lined with shops and bustling with people, and I mean bustling. Almost like

Sixth Avenue in the Village in the Forties to Sixties. The City is like a large body with neighborhoods breaking out here and there like spots in a rash. They come and go, get bigger and smaller. I see almost two-thirds of a century of changes, and for the first time I'm amazed. I was always philosophical about changes in New York—you know, things change, and you have to accept them...

Chelsea went from Irish to Puerto Rican to the beginnings of upper middle class in the twenty years I lived in New York. The cold-water railroad flat I paid nineteen dollars a month for on Seventh Street and First Avenue in 1950 rents for over a thousand dollars a month in its current renovated state. Presumably the toilet is now inside the apartment. When I lived there the neighborhood was mostly immigrant and first-generation Poles and Ukrainians, plus a smattering of artists and students from NYU and Cooper Union. The bread was great and freshly baked around the corner, and you could hear polkas pounding on the radio when the windows were open in the summertime.

Greenwich Village in the twenties and thirties was crammed with intellectuals, writers, and artists of all stripes. It was a haven for people who felt and often were different in their aspirations and behavior from the more conforming and respectable population at the time. By the time I found it in 1948, its glory days were pretty much over according to former residents in the Twenties and Thirties. It was still the most benignly friendly neighborhood in New York City, still full of artists and writers, and it was safe for a woman to walk alone at two o'clock in the morning—a little city with its own dress and behavior codes, clearly understood by the residents if not by the rest of the city.

By the time I moved to the suburbs in 1964, the Village was a walking drug scene. Washington Square was impossible, playgrounds fenced in and no adults without children permitted in them. No women walked the streets at two a.m. unless they were working. It probably got much worse than that, but I didn't wait around to witness it. Ten years ago, I went to a publisher's party on Eighth Street, where I used to wheel Jenny in her stroller going to the Eighth Street Bookstore and the Art Theater. As I walked down the block from Fifth to Sixth Avenue, I was appalled to see that in a majority of the doorways to stores and buildings there were drugs being sold and used by slumped-over, tragic-looking human debris. They weren't being furtive, not hiding their actions. This was Eighth Street. Drug Street. In my time, it was a street of book and record stores, bakeries, bars, and groceries, handmade jewelry and antiques, restaurants and sandal makers. It was our main street. It was where we walked on Saturday night and shopped at Christmas.

I can accept change, though sometimes with great nostalgia, but now enough time has elapsed for me to see the astounding changes that mass media, buying from catalogues, and the influence of nationwide conformity of interest have made, and this in a city where anything can "go." I know it's still a city of great cultural possibilities, but at the same time it has become like a grand shopping mall, with the same successful stores found in any mall in Peoria or Duluth.

Maybe the world will finally become safe from wars when the entire population can sedate itself by shopping in the same stores, wearing the same clothes, eating the same mass-produced food. There will be no Fifth Avenue and Fifty-Seventh Street beauty and craftsmanship to envy and struggle for. Maybe the opiate we're searching for isn't religion at all. Marie Antoinette may have been right. Let them eat cake—in this case, McDonald's or Famous Amos.

I just looked out the window, and New York above street level is as magnificent as it always was. Sun rising, golden light gleaming on the upper stories of buildings, the air clear and fresh after a day of rain; below, one or two people now in sight, walking to work, the hum of occasional buses and cars. Memories come flooding in, sights, sounds, smells. I have over sixty-five years of memories of New York, and they capture me for long moments. I'm all those years of living here. It's what I am. Starting with Queens Village, right up to today, a New Yorker with a Californian perspective, a Californian with a New York perspective.

It was such a pleasure to be with you and Steve and the Beusmans. You have beautiful grounds, Mickey. The olives and cheese were great too. Did I miss anything? This is a somewhat bizarre thank you note—you know, like when the bride tries to describe how much she loves the salad bowl and all the ways she and the groom will mix the salad in it.

        Love,
          Rosemary

STREETSCENE

Sometimes I'm overwhelmed by all the faces
I want to kiss and hug and stare at
all of them busy with worlds I don't know about
but they all look the same different
from me and mine and I want to tell them lets
all live now forever and never die, right here
on 51st Street where we're all hurrying away from

THE MORE IT CHANGES

In the nineteen thirties, 213th Street in Queens Village was like an Ellis Island at the entrance to the American Dream. There were always new arrivals, some from Europe, lots of couples with children, and lots of misunderstandings. It was a dowdy street, but the neighbors tried to keep things looking neat. Most people there expected to move to a nicer place after they made enough money. Some houses were wood frame, some two-story attached, and there were about a dozen small stucco houses built close together. I lived in one of those.

At one end of the block, there was a ramshackle yellow house, part of one of the old farms that Queens Village used to be. It was unheated and in terrible condition, and no one lived in it for very long. People who needed a place to sleep sometimes walked in and stayed until someone threw them out. It was a chronic source of irritation and discussion among the adults in the neighborhood. Treelike weeds grew all around the house, and when it was empty, its dark windows were covered by tattered curtains. The neighborhood children pretended it was haunted. On Halloween, our favorite dare was to see who had the courage to run up and knock on the front door.

The year I turned five, a large Italian family lived in the house—two brothers, three sisters, and a collection of wives, husbands, and children. Among them was an old woman the neighbors supposed was the mother of the middle-aged children. They called her The Mother because no one knew the name of the family and they couldn't call her Mrs. Somebody. One of the brothers spoke English, but no one else in the family could communicate with their neighbors on the street. My father struck up a friendly enemy acquaintance with the English-speaking brother, and during their first conversation he let him know that the neighbors hoped the house would be put in shape as quickly as possible. He listed the improvements that could be made indoors and out, giving estimates of the little time and energy it would take on the part of so many people to get the work done. The man nodded and smiled, and ignored everything my father said.

The youngest child in the family was a three-year-old girl with soft curly brown hair who sometimes wandered down to play with me. I treated her like a baby and felt my first stirrings of maternal pleasure. She was better than a doll. I didn't know her name, but I could take her hand and lead her around the yard and tell her when to stand up or sit down. It wasn't a problem that we didn't speak the same language. She was amiable, and I could arrange her into almost any shape I chose. One afternoon, I was sitting on the back steps blowing bubbles with a three- bowled bubble pipe that my mother had given me the day before. I was having a good time filling the pipe and blowing bubbles that floated away and broke on the rose bushes next to the steps. I had been playing for a long time when the little girl came into the yard. Even though I was happy to see her, I didn't want to stop my game. So I took her by the arm, sat her down on the step below me, and continued with the bubble pipe until I had used up all the soapy water.

I called through the screen door to my mother who was working in the kitchen, "Mommy, can I have some more water?"

Mother came out the back door to pick up the bowl and smiled at the little girl. "I see your friend is here. It's too bad we don't have another bubble pipe. Wait a minute, I'll get some more water."

She returned with the bowl of soapy water and watched the first few tries. "Don't get yourself wet," she said, and disappeared into the kitchen.

I felt very important. "Now, you sit still," I said. The little girl was fascinated and watched every movement I made. "Watch the bubbles," I said as they drifted away over her head. A few drops of translucent, soapy blue water fell on the girl's curly hair. I put my hand out to wipe them away and found that they had soaked into her hair right away. I held the next pipeful of water closer to her head, and when the pipe was empty, there were more drops waiting to be rubbed in. She was so docile that I blew some bubbles into the curls. I dumped the next pipeful on without any preliminaries. By this time there wasn't much water left, so I poured it straight from the bowl onto her head. I was scrubbing her scalp, keeping soap out of her eyes like a good mother, when my own mother noticed the silence and came out to see what was going on.

"My god, Rosemary, what are you doing?"

"I'm washing her hair."

"You can't go around giving other people's children shampoos. What made you do a thing like that?" She forgot that only two days earlier she had offered to wash Ann Guerin's hair. Ann lived next door to us. Her hair was unwashed for days at a time, and my mother was afraid I might get lice if I played with her. "Quickly, go and get the big towel."

Sensing disaster, the little girl started to howl.

"There, there, child," my mother said, "you're all right. No harm done. Come, let me dry your hair."

Mother gave the little girl a cookie and a glass of milk while she set to work on the curls. They were damp dry when the child ran home, and I was given a lecture on not washing other people's hair without getting their mother's permission.

Ten minutes later there was a loud noise in front of our house. When my mother went to see what was happening, she was faced by a two- hundred-pound woman shouting in Italian about the terrible thing that had been done to her helpless daughter. At least, that's what my mother and the gathering neighbors imagined she was shouting. The woman pointed to the child dramatically, plucking at the clean hair with anger as if to show that the little girl was permanently disfigured. She was wild-eyed, clutching and waving the little girl's arm in her fat hand, and looked apt to do her more damage than the shampoo.

She carried on for some minutes, shouting and pulling the child back and forth, as her huge bosom heaved and she continued gesticulating toward the neighbors. Mother did her best to smooth things over. She pleaded with the woman to be calm and not to make so much noise. She explained her philosophy of not getting into an uproar over children's mischief. The woman screamed at my mother, and then shook her fist in my direction to show what she would like to do to me.

That did it. My mother was conscious of the watching neighbors and had been trying to calm the woman with logic, but at the sight of the raised fist in my direction, she lost her temper, and making the kind of gesture that Moses may have used to part the Red Sea, commanded in her loudest voice, "Keep quiet! And stop this nonsense! You're making more noise than an army, and all over a wet head." Her voice was filled with scorn. "It didn't hurt the child and you were probably going to wash it today anyway." She pointed. "Look at her. You're out here shouting your head off and she's ready to play again."

It was true. At the beginning of the fight, I cowered behind my mother. But when I heard her start to shout, I knew everything would be all right. Nobody could stand up to her when she was furious. So I circled around and mingled with the bystanders and edged toward my friend. We smiled at each other. When her mother saw this, she held the girl close and scolded her for having anything to do with crazy people who washed stranger's heads. But her voice wasn't as loud as before. The volume subsided once my mother took over. They were like two sopranos coming to the front of the stage for the big aria, first one, then the other, the center of attention, all high notes and intense drama, while the neighborhood chorus waited to see who would win. Fortunately, the baritone, the brother who could speak English, made his entrance. With a woman on each side pleading her cause, he reacted with anger to the woman's tale, and then relayed my mother's side of the story. There were suspicious looks from the woman and exasperated harrumphs from my mother until finally a peace was made.

Mother invited the couple to have a cup of tea, but the woman refused to enter our house, so they were served tea, plain with sugar, out on the sidewalk with rows of children and adults watching. My mother was determined to calm the woman and kept talking and smiling at her, and in the end, she made her laugh. No one but the man knew what the woman laughed at, but it satisfied my mother and she went back into the house to finish making dinner.

The little girl never came back to play again. I'm not sure she was allowed out at all after that. For a long time, I rushed past the yellow house when I walked around that corner, afraid that the woman would come out and shout at me. Once she did come out, but she smiled. The Italian family was the last to live in the yellow house. When they moved out, it was torn down, and all that remained was an empty lot covered with the descendants of the weeds that had grown there before. The owner put up a wooden fence to keep the children out, and a few years later he built a faceless white brick three-story apartment building on the property. At first the neighbors were pleased when they heard about the new building. They thought it would raise property values. But they were never pleased with the building itself. It was so foreign. It didn't fit in. It had no front porch or yard, so the tenants had no place to congregate or meet the neighbors. The apartments had only one bedroom, so the building was filled with people who only passed by on the way to and from work. Everyone complained for years about the property. Some even said it was better when the yellow house was there, and some said it was better as a vacant lot.

In July of 1967, I was driving out to Montauk Point at the end of Long Island with my two children, Jenny fourteen and Andy eight, and I saw the exit sign for Springfield Boulevard on the parkway.

On an impulse I asked, "Would you like to see the house where I was born?"

Jenny, sitting next to me, turned and asked, "Is it far from here?"

"About ten minutes away." The area near the parkway had changed in the twenty years since I had been there last. What used to be woods and scattered houses were now rows of garden apartments and attached houses. I wondered if my old neighborhood would still be the same. As we got close to 213th Street I felt uneasy. My children were growing up in a large house with an acre of lawn and trees and they might think my first home depressing. I drew my breath quickly, thinking to myself how it would hurt if they didn't like it. I hadn't seen it for years, but to me it was home, the beginning of the world.

When we turned into the street Jenny asked, "Which house did you live in?"

I drove three-quarters of the way down the block, stopped the car and pointed. "That one."

"Who lived there with you?" Andy asked.

"Nana, Papa, Uncle Mike, and Aunt Jean."

"It's so pretty," Jenny said, "you never said it was so pretty."

I looked at my daughter with love. It was pretty. The tall maples were gone, but there were other trees. The small stucco house was freshly painted, and flowers bloomed in the yard. When this was my home, the Depression had turned much of the country dim and gray, with no money for paint and not much for more than a few flowers. Suddenly, I could see it through my children's eyes, without the past.

"What's that boy doing?" Andy asked.

There was a boy of about four playing the game I'd played so often when I lived there, balancing on the narrow raised cement border surrounding the tiny front garden.

"He's balancing on the ledge. I used to do that too when I was a little girl."

It was a wonder the ledge hadn't worn away from all the children's feet that had made their way across it over the years. When he reached the far side of the plot, he jumped across, as I knew he would, to the cement ledge that bordered the next garden, and balanced there. I could feel the sensation in my feet as he landed, and I tried to help him, gritting my teeth and shifting on the front seat of the car, when he turned and jumped and was near us again.

"That must have been fun," Jenny said.

"Hello. Do you live in that house?" I asked.

"Yes." He looked serious as he came toward the car.

"I used to live here too. I was born here. Up in that room."

"That's my Mommy and Daddy's room."

"It was my Mommy and Daddy's room too."

A dark-haired woman came out onto the front porch wiping her hands on her apron. She came down the steps and stood right where my mother stood the day the Italian woman came to yell about me shampooing the little girl's hair. "Is there anything you want?" she asked. Her voice was harsh. She was understandably suspicious of anyone in a parked car talking to her child.

"I was just showing the house to my children." I smiled to reassure the woman I meant no harm. "I was born here in 1928, up in the front bedroom."

"In this house?" The woman's face relaxed. "No kidding?" She turned and called to a woman who appeared at the window of the house next door. "Hey, Ethel, this lady was born here."

"Whaddya know?"

The woman in the apron turned back to me. "That's exciting. Has the neighborhood changed a lot since then?"

"No, everything looks pretty much the same, only nicer, and with more flowers."

She put one hand on her son's shoulder and motioned with the other toward the house. "Would you like to come in? It's probably different now."

"Oh, thank you. It's really nice of you, but we're late. We're on our way out to Montauk, and we have a long drive ahead of us." I didn't want to go inside. The house was too real to me, and I wanted to remember it the way it was.

"Well, any time you feel like having a look, just stop by."

"Thank you, very much." I started the car. I waved to the woman and the little boy, and we pulled away from the curb and headed toward the parkway.

As we drove past the corner where the yellow house once stood, I saw that the white bricks of the three-story apartment house had aged to a grubby yellow, and weeds still grew in the narrow strip of dirt around it.□

IT'S A MYSTERY

Last night was the second time since the beginning of menopause that I slept through the night. It happened once before, but I don't remember the occasion. And it was an occasion. Why last night? If I could just figure that out. It's a mystery.

We ate early, at five o'clock. I forgot to take my glucophage; blood sugar was way up; took the pill; ate a plum at ten-thirty; went to bed at eleven-thirty; woke up at six. Amazing! Not only did I sleep without once turning the tape over, but when I awoke and figured out what day it was, I was really up and ready to start the day living. Why was this night different? And where's Elijah?

He's the one they always put an extra chair out for at the Passover dinner table. Is he the Prophet Elijah? I always assumed he was, but never asked when I was at someone's house eating the noodle pudding and matzohs.

Passover dinner is so much more fun than the Catholic mass. It's like Christmas dinner without the toys and tinsel. Everyone gets dressed up. The mother of the family spends a lot of time making special foods, some that take hours of preparation. The male head of the family gives the children coins (or are they hidden?) representing...what? I have forgotten. Did the Jews buy their way out of Egypt? No, I think Moses saved God's people from a plague, or a lot of Heaven-sent miseries, and then they were freed. The matzoh may be required because the Jews had only unleavened bread to eat when they were fleeing Egypt. So, while eating a little matzoh to commemorate that time, everyone eats a little or a lot too much and swears not to do it again next year.

And then there's that empty chair waiting for Elijah. He hasn't eaten too much. I have this weird feeling that Elijah may be the Messiah who hasn't yet arrived. If that's true, I'm glad I didn't figure it out until today. My Catholic training would have sat an imaginary Jesus in the chair and spoiled the mystery of Elijah. The Jews didn't accept Christ as the Messiah, and according to legend, killed him during Passover (wasn't the Last Supper a Passover feast?). I'm getting everything muddled.

Every morning in second grade we opened our catechisms, a child-size book with a light blue paper cover. The text was in the form of questions and answers—positive answers.

Question: Who made the world?
Answer: God made the world.
Question: Who made God?
Answer: Nobody, God is a spirit.
Question: What is a spirit?

That's when it got sticky. I forget how the answer went, but it was always explained to us that it's a mystery, and when you came up against a mystery, you just have to accept it (accept what you were told without asking questions) so we did. But that was when we were seven and about to make First Communion. As the old Catholic saying goes, if you get them by seven, you've got them for life.

It's true and not true. I'd like to think that I got their claws out of my skin, but there's stuff inside me that's not so easy to extricate. Maybe I shouldn't even want to, it's so much a part of me.

I may not be sure who Elijah is or why there's an empty chair, but I don't regret believing that while I may be able to fool some people, God and I know when I'm telling the truth.

Anyway, how and why I slept last night is as much of a mystery to me as Elijah or what a spirit is. I think it can be summed up in my old friend Maureen's remark, "I don't believe in souls, but I'm always so happy when I meet someone who's got one." I think I'll just enjoy my sleep feast and not worry about the empty chair.◻

August 29, 1997
Talloires, France

Dear Jean,

I really want to answer your last letter. It's sad, isn't it, the things we remember that hurt us, even things that gave us great pleasure and maybe hurt at the same time?

The house hasn't been sold, but it will be empty by next week, so from our point of view, it's as good as gone. Yesterday was magnificent after a heavy rainstorm. It cleared the air, and the sky and lake were incredibly blue with great white clouds racing across the sky. You hardly see those colors anymore because of the pollution, which the locals don't even see. It's been such a gradual thing.

Okay, sitting down at the computer has given my feet a little rest and I can think better, so I'll try to tackle sweet sixteen. First, I'm so happy that you wrote to me. Maybe email will be our line of communication. I start from the proposition that no one in the family was happy most of the time. That's how it always seemed to me. Sometimes when alone or reading by myself, I was satisfied, but that was living someone else's dreams and imagination. Or if I sat somewhere, my mind in some outer space, daydreaming or just puzzling things out, or even just looking at the shapes and colors of things, I may have been content.

Loners are supposed to not need people, but I did. I just didn't have the talent for being with them. I really didn't have friends until I was about fifteen or sixteen, or if they were friends, I didn't know it. Maybe that sounds strange to you, but when I went to high school, I thought of it as going someplace where no one knew me. I could reinvent myself into someone likable.

I had a terrible time in grammar school. High school was better, if not with the nuns, at least with the other students. I didn't fit in at grammar school. I suppose there were others like me, but they may have hidden it better, or more likely, I didn't notice their problems. In high school, with a hundred girls in each year, there was room for almost any type of person, and compared to the girls who had much worse social problems than mine, I was not too bad. The problem with reinventing yourself is that you feel like a hypocrite—like someone at a masquerade who has to keep feeling the mask. The expression is hardly ever natural.

I was depressed at the thought of my sixteenth birthday. I think you asked me the names of some of my friends, so I thought you were going to give me a sweet sixteen party, which terrified me. I'd only had a few dates up to that time, and I couldn't imagine why anyone would want to come to a party for me. And I didn't know why you were giving a party for me. We didn't get along too well, and it all seemed hard to understand and frightening to face. The party was in the garage and the yard, and I was "surprised" not that it happened, but that people came and I was able to talk—not a lot, but at least a little. You name it, I was shy, unable to talk, and clumsy in social settings, said the wrong things when I did talk, and was more at ease with a book than at a party.

When I read your sixteen experience, I understood what it meant to you, even though we were so different. My image of you was that you had a lot of friends and loved parties. You laughed and talked and dated. So you gave a party for me when I reached sixteen. Life isn't fair, is it?

We can't change things once they're done. And we can't change who we are, try as we might. You gave me what you didn't have, and the 'I' that I pretended to be couldn't enjoy a party; I knew I was just masquerading as a happy person.

Maybe that was one of my first bouts of depression, only at that age, the things one is depressed about sound so banal, and after a few years they pale beside broken hearts and mishandled love affairs. I wish I could pour some balm on the painful experiences that we had, but I know there isn't any to pour. I don't think it would ever have occurred to Mother to give anyone a surprise party. I think she was more like me. She certainly wasn't a social person. She had friends and acquaintances, but I think her social life was dictated by or, better still, was an adjunct of Dad's. He went out and made friends and she got to know them.

As for Dad and the book of "isms," who can explain that? His mind must have been somewhere else that day. I know that like me, but in a much worse way, he had what is called bipolar mood disorder, in plain layman's English, manic depression. So if he was manic at that moment, he was certain it was exactly the book a sixteen-year-old (who read books all the time the way you did) would love to have. Or, if he was depressed, he was in a fog and couldn't think of anyone being happy over anything, so he bought the first thing that came in sight.

I've gotten presents like that often in my lifetime, and it's hard to understand why anyone would give you such a stupid, unlikeable gift. We try to grin and bear it, but it's almost unbearable. If it's any help at all, think about how old he was when you were sixteen. You were born in 1923. He was born in 1896. So he was twenty-seven when you were born and forty-three when you were sixteen. What were we like when we were forty-three? What with premenstrual depressions and chronic depressions, it would be safe to say that most of the time I was depressed, trying very hard to be like everyone else and not quite making it. Elated at times, if someone seemed to like me or if I succeeded at something ordinary. Always unsure of myself, and trying all the time. Just trying.

Dad and Mother were a mess. And so were we. None of us could help it. There we were, all of us at odds with one another. That was the life we could have. It wasn't the worst that anyone ever had, and looking at it that way, we were pretty lucky. I wish you could forget how you felt at sixteen and try to remember that I'm happy you wrote about it because it made me understand a little better why you had a party for me when I turned sixteen. The party was really a gift that didn't end on that night. You invited Eileen Casey and one or two of her friends, and I got to know them and hung around with them after that, so I did have a good teenage experience, thanks to you. I dated and went to parties at their houses, and there were times when I felt really happy to be part of a "crowd." I was lucky that I had that, because by the time I was eighteen and in love for the first time, the shit really started flying. But that's another story and it's now midnight, so until some other time.

      Love,
      Rosemary

September 13, 1997
Alpine Drive, Beverly Hills

Dear Michael,
Hard to believe we were in Talloires and now hard to believe we're in Los Angeles. Where are the croissants and where is the Reblochon? And Jacques and Assunta and Claudia? And the view? I only saw the view one day. It was an alternately cloudy, rainy, sunny day, sometimes mysterious, sometimes joyous, wet, dry, with the view of the lake constantly becoming something other than the last time one looked. I will miss the changing lake more than everything else about having had that house.

We came home with eight suitcases, seven of which contained clothes that had to be dry cleaned or washed. Fortunately there were five weeks of General Hospital tapes to be watched, matching exactly the number of loads of clothes to be washed. And my motto was—wash and watch, wash and watch. It even sounds like the washing machine if you say it fast. It took care of the first half of jet lag. And getting up early to write will take care of the second.

Milt has done remarkably well. He's feeling wonderful, was even up to going to the opera with Jenny, and came home ecstatic about Plácido's performance. We're going to the Sunday matinee if we can get tickets, and also to one of the free performances for schoolchildren next Wednesday morning.

Our new secretary Margaret seems quite nice and pleasant to have around. The doors between the office and the living room are now closed, and I have so much more privacy. She's in that office and Marian is in the next room, and almost everything goes on between those two rooms and Milt's office.

This time I'm being much smarter. I've been giving her stuff to do from day one. No more apologies for asking for work, as if it were a favor. When Marian started working for us, Milt was still in the middle of a good part of his career, and any time I asked for something, which mistakenly wasn't much, Marian acted as if it was irrelevant. That was probably my fault, not having the habit of delegating to others. It took years to get her to understand that telling the plumber what to do was as, or more, important than almost anything else that went on in the house, and that included most of Milt's calls, appointments, and lunch dates. Fortunately, Marian finally accepted that as part of the job, but there were some tense moments. Now that she's training Margaret, that part of the job is being passed on nicely, and I see that Margaret is handling that side of the work with a smile.

Murray is coming out for a week to work with Milt on a number of things, not the least of which is what to do with all the old papers that we have in the files. I'm hoping by the time he leaves to have five hundred thousand fewer sheets of paper in the house. Milt and Marian are sitting at a big table in the middle office, going through box after box, weeding out stuff. I did that in Talloires, and now someone else is doing it here. We should reach near stufflessness in another month or two. That's what I deserve.

Sadly, I also feel I deserve a lot of chocolate. I can't eat as much chocolate as I did in Talloires and go cold turkey like this, so yesterday and the day before I went and bought myself two Hershey bars with almonds. It's not great chocolate, but in a crisis it'll do.

I'm glad your time in Talloires was restful and a little sad mine wasn't. However, the relief I'm feeling about never having to clean up the house again is more than reward enough. I guess the thing to do in life is to know when something is over and act on it. That's hard to do when you're married or living with someone.

For the last three years, I've felt oppressed by the responsibility for the house in France. This year was different. Sometime during the winter, or maybe on the day when we had to leave in a hurry last summer, I decided I was finished and that I was not going to go there anymore. I would go back one more time, take what I wanted, and leave with the idea that I would probably not go back again to stay there for more than a few days. I didn't put it exactly that way to Milt, though I made it clear that if he had to return to L.A. before I was finished with the job, he could go back but that I wasn't leaving until it was done.

I know you know all this, but now that it's done, I have to write it out to be finished finally with it. I could write it in my journal, but then I wouldn't be writing to you, and I wanted to say hello.

I'm afraid my letters to you are filled with whatever trivia is passing through my fingers at the time I'm writing.

I want to remember the fun times we had there. The sunsets and sunrises, rainstorms, clouds, my beautiful Cedar of Lebanon tree near the patio, the wonderful smell in the morning, my morning walks around the path and all that food. We'll go back to the Auberge and Albert's and eat cheese and chocolate and watch the lake, and I will sit and read and think and remember—and be happy to be there.

I'm just superstitious enough to be uneasy about that last paragraph. But then I remember that I was sure the house would never be built because that would be too wonderful and I didn't deserve anything so wonderful. So, there's more proof—too much wonderful is too much. Right?

I'm a little concerned and trying not to know it. Andy is feeling unwell and they can't figure out why. And he and Julia and the children are leaving for three weeks, one in Massachusetts and two in England. I haven't seen him yet, but will today when they all come over for some late afternoon fun and then supper.

Have fun, try to be rested, and we'll write.
Love,
Rosemary

Journal
September 15, 1997
Alpine Drive, Beverly Hills

Andy. Andy doesn't feel well. Is he ill? Is he depressed? Is he depressed because he's ill? Is his stomach upset because he is depressed? I don't feel any answers popping up anywhere. He and Julia and the children are going East for a new nephew's christening, then on to England for two weeks. He's lost about nine or ten pounds in two weeks from lack of appetite, so I don't think it's a great idea. If it's some kind of infection or malady other than depression, then traveling with or even without two children is not a good idea.

He says this happened once before, right after the second Rodney King trial. We all went to Campanile for breakfast, and he went home and threw up and didn't eat much for another week or so, losing weight, and I guess feeling down just like this. He says that lasted for several weeks, and then he got over it.

When I spoke to him the other day after coming back from France, I could hear it in his voice. He sounded down. So knowing my history and that of my father, and after hearing that all the tests taken by the doctor show nothing physically wrong, depression is the next question.

After the usual maternal probing and sonly rejection, we both apologized, me for being the knee-jerk Earth Mother, and him for rejecting my interference. I made the call, but we both apologized at the same time. I promised to drop the subject. That was on Friday. Saturday they all came over to play, swim, and have dinner. When Andy went off to speak to Milt, I asked Julia, bluntly, if he was depressed. She didn't want to say, and said I should speak to him. So I told her being depressed wasn't something to be ashamed of, even though it had taken me four years to use the word with the first therapist I went to, I was so ashamed. It seemed such a failure in life. I failed happy.

I also told her it was something she must know. That it runs in my family and it's important to be able to talk about it. I went into Milt's office and talked to Andy in front of Milt. I told him I knew. I promised not to interfere again, but that I wanted to talk about myself. I told him briefly about my depressions, more clearly than I ever have before, and about my father and mother's depressions, about the malaise and lack of energy, the feeling of the general pointlessness of doing anything at all. I talked about how I've learned to look ahead to the time when I'll feel better and how that gives me some relief. And that the time always comes when I realize I haven't felt depressed for a few days and I know it's over.

I gave him Michael Gitlin's number and told him not to take any drugs that a regular doctor prescribes for depression without consulting Gitlin or someone like him, and he accepted the number. His attitude during this conversation was interested, perhaps to placate me. He understood the ramifications for his children and possibly for himself and said he should know about depression and family background. If Andy is depressed, and if this is something that will occur occasionally, it will make things difficult for him and Julia. For Andy, because he is depressed, and for Julia because she has probably never experienced depression up close before and her first thought is to take it personally. She talked to Jenny about it and said she was afraid that maybe he wasn't interested in her anymore.

When I was talking to Andy, I told him one of the reasons Milt and I were able to live through all my depressions so well was that Milt was able to ignore them. He was unhappy that I was depressed, but he didn't take it as personally. That was a huge help to me, because it was just what I needed—someone who could love me when I was feeling sad for a reason that had nothing to do with him.

Unfortunately, as a woman, and a woman with no experience of depression or living with someone who is depressed, Julia is taking Andrew's feeling as how he feels about her. I did exactly the same thing every time Milt came home and was distracted or irritated by what happened in his work or just within himself.

If it's depression, I hope it goes away soon. If it isn't, I hope traveling doesn't exacerbate it. We've suggested several possibilities. That they go to Massachusetts and leave the children here; that they take the kids, come back, then take a vacation and let us mind the kids. I don't think they will. They're too young not to consider that a kind of defeat. They will do what they will do, and we can't influence their decision. Milt wouldn't even try. He didn't want me to talk to Andy at all after Andy's first rejection, but that worked out well because I followed my impulse to call and apologize. And after speaking to him about myself and my depressions yesterday, he was just as direct and friendly as usual, maybe even more so.

It was strange. Milt can't meet things head on. I spoke to Andy in front of him, more for Andy's sake than Milt's. The way we were sitting, I don't think Andy could see that Milt had cocooned himself in reading some papers, but his body was there and that was what I wanted. I didn't expect Andy to speak about whether or not he was depressed, but I wanted him to hear depression spoken about openly with just the hint that maybe that was the problem at the moment.

Why do I think that writing all this will make my life somehow more worth having been lived? I don't know. Maybe I think that by doing this every day, I will prevent depression in myself. I'm worried about Andy, and that's exhausting me. I feel my small reserves of strength ebbing and the need to cover my head and not think. I know we have children because nature drives us to it. I know we get so much joy from them when we love them and they love us, but it's a hard bargain with life. Instead of the fear of the unknown, it's the fear of the timing of the known that terrifies us with its inevitability.□

ANIMALS WITH A DIFFERENCE

I've been reading Szymborska's poetry this morning. It was worth it to me for her to have lived her life of anxiety and introspection, so that I can profit by feeling that I'm not so alone. I think that of all the writers I have ever read, she speaks more clearly than anyone, and with more humanity and depth.

As I woke up the other day, I was thinking how we live two lives, one as an instinctive animal and another in the tribe—clothed, licensed, categorized, consuming, stratified, and seemingly conscious. But what we seem to be unconscious of is that the complete animal life of scratching, copulating, eating, defecating, and birthing that goes on, driving everything we do in our clothes and categories, goes on even if we have no clothes or categories. It has been going on since before we had categories to stratify in.

No one ever tells us as we're growing that we're just animals with a difference. Not the only animals that think and love. Even our pride (and ignorance) in our superiority over all the other animals is probably not unique. Tell me what animal thinks another's way is better than its own. Instinct drives us all, from anthills to calling cards.

Maybe that's what's wrong with me. They did their best to make me ignore, make me ashamed of, and make me separate myself from the animal that I am, and I couldn't accomplish the job sufficiently and comfortably. I feel my animal feelings, covered in hats and teacups that don't mean anything to me, and I know the falseness of the things I say and do that have no connection to the life in me that laughs and cries and groans, while my face pretends.☐

October 20, 1997
Alpine Drive, Beverly Hills

Dear Michael,
I hear from Jenny's friend Lance, who is also staying at the house in London, that Andy is in great spirits and that the children are wonderful, so I'm quite happy.
We came back from Denver and Aspen yesterday afternoon. Friday there was a service for John Denver in the church in Denver that John's mother attends. It was a very sad day. Then on Saturday we flew to Aspen where there was a big outdoor service, more a kind of celebration and memorial with people talking about John and showing him singing some of his songs. Milt spoke both times, very well, after thinking that he couldn't possibly even go, he was so upset.

We both were. I should understand shock. The morning I heard my father was dead after a grim dreadful illness of more than eight months, I had a friend over for a visit—a cousin, Sue Bender—and I remember her expression of astonishment when I mentioned, in conversation, that my father had died early that morning. She asked why I hadn't called to tell her not to come, and I remember saying something like, "Oh, there was no reason to." It wasn't until about four o'clock that afternoon that I suddenly understood he was gone. My doctor was out of town and I desperately needed something so I would be able to sleep that night. I charged around the corner to the drugstore with my eight-year-old Jenny in tow and begged, demanded, that the druggist give me a pill, just one pill to get me through the night, promising to get a prescription for it the next day. We were customers there, so he and his wife knew me, and after a hard look at the two of us, and hearing the pressure in my voice, he gave me a tranquilizer. I remember holding it like a treasure all the way home.

John's death in no way compares to the depth of the pain I felt when my father died, but I see that sudden death also has an element of shock that cannot be dealt with all at once. Thirty years of knowing someone, depending on and being depended upon, for all kinds of nameable and unnameable elements of acquaintance, advice, and friendship, of being an audience for his art, and for Milt, the years of collaborating with John on his music. This was a great loss. Losing the living sound of a voice that is better known to you than your own and can be called into being internally at any time at will, singing songs you've heard so many times. It's hard to believe.

We heard the news about John at ten o'clock on Sunday night, and while neither of us slept, we didn't really cry until the next day when Misty, the girl who does the flowers in the garden, came in and told us how sorry she was, and then we both fell apart. Each day it got worse instead of better. The phone didn't stop ringing. We took most of the calls but not all. I fielded one and decided not to put it through to Milt, fortunately, since the first words the caller spoke after the usual condolences were, "Was it suicide?"

It wasn't suicide. John was doing really well and seemed to have his life in better control. But it was a stupid plane from my point of view, a stupid plane for him to fly, given that he had an eight-year-old daughter. I guess pilots never fear flying or they wouldn't be able to fly.

Someday Milt or I will tell you of all John's personal generosity to us, as well as to other people who worked for him. Even you have benefited directly and indirectly from Milt's association with John. He was the single most important person in Milt's career over the years, and the only one who never once betrayed Milt. That sounds melodramatic, but it's an accurate description of their working relationship. Milt was John's mentor from the day John started to work with the Mitchell Trio. He always turned to Milt for advice, and though he often didn't listen, he gave Milt the respect and loyalty Milt deserved and that was so lacking in his relationships with many other singers. And I think Milt gave John the respect that he deserved for his good nature and generosity, and especially for his music and great talent as a writer.

There are many ways that we measure our lives. We measure by friendships, by illnesses, foods we eat, and films we see. For you, the first year at Taizé, the time in Vietnam, Hollis, high school, California, and now China.

For Milt and me as a family, we measure by the ages of our children as well. Andy was one when John joined the trio and Jenny was ten. I met him for the first time in Washington, where the trio was singing, and we had the kids and my mother with us at the Shoreham Hotel. When Andy was four, he played in the snow with John outside the kitchen window in Chappaqua when John came to do a concert at Milt's request at the high school. When the concert was cancelled because of a snowstorm, he ended up singing for an hour in our candlelit living room at a party for our good friends. That was in the middle of the Vietnam mess. I remember when Andy and John came in out of the cold and took their socks off to dry, I found out that John was missing two toes on one foot and that was the reason he hadn't been drafted.

Andy was thirteen when we flew to Colorado to see John in concert at the Red Rocks Amphitheatre. John came to Jenny's wedding in Gloucestershire and charmed a village, the year that Andy was twenty-one and had just met Julia.

Milt and I have gone from brown-haired to gray, from young and energetic to old and slowed down, while John, on his way from talented, ambitious kid to muddled middle age, wrote, sang, and became a star, made a lot of people love him through his music and a lot of people grateful for his generosity. He made plenty of mistakes, but they were his mistakes to make, and mostly they were mistakes of determined denial. I don't think he could face it that anyone he knew and trusted would want to do him wrong. How could they if he was good to them?

You can call that childish or childlike. Maybe John wrote about children and nature so much because if they hurt you, it's not from dislike or intentional. It's an accident. They're there to be loved and admired, like superb works of art. It's ironic that it was the sea that destroyed him when something went wrong, when he collided with it.

I'm glad it was quick. I'm glad his life was going in a good direction again and his last weeks and days and hours were happy. It will make listening to him sing about the good things in life a pleasure, the way it always has been.

John wasn't sophisticated. He wasn't an intellectual, so he didn't have to pretend to be cynical and above the herd to prove his superiority. He could reach millions of people with simple poetry about the most important things in their lives: Love. The sun that warms us and gives us life. Our home, the Earth. The children who are our future. And he sang that poetry to melodies he wrote that we could also sing. His gift was our gift.

I didn't intend to write all this but I'm glad I did. I won't feel better until somehow I get it all out. I think when I cry, I'm crying, like so many other people, because John touched a chord in me that is my better side. I am sophisticated and cynical, but I'm also still enough of the child I was, wondering at how beautiful a cloud can be, or a leaf, or a baby, loving the days when I'm happy, hoping something good will happen. Wanting for everything and everybody to be at ease. Meanwhile, mourning, as you know, is not a full-time job. So we laugh, eat, work, and read. Then every once in a while, there's a fleeting thought and watering eyes.

    Love,
    Rosemary

          October 26, 1997
          Alpine Drive, Beverly Hills

Dear Jean,
These last two weeks since John Denver died have been an emotional roller coaster. Much worse for Milt than for me. There were so many feelings related to John, associated with him and Milt...I loved many of his songs and lyrics. I think performers must

be the unhappiest of creative artists... Very strange. It took nine years after Mother died for me to accept that she was dead. I had a dream that she was standing at the rail of a boat. The light was an intense rose and yellow color, like a tea rose, and she was looking off into the distance. I was so happy to see her that I went over to her and picked up her hand. When I looked down at it, it was all dried and dark like meat hanging in a butcher shop. I dropped it and for the first time I really knew that she was dead. I woke up and for the first time I gave up hoping and feeling in my heart that surely she would somehow come back

     Love,
      Rosemary

Journal
November 5, 1997
Alpine Drive, Beverly Hills

I started to write a letter to Plácido in my head. I found the small folded list of the prayers and music from John's funeral, with the song "Perhaps Love" listed. I knew it so well. I remember the first time John sang it for Milt in our living room. It would have been hard not to love it from that moment on.

  Then I remembered the day at the studio in New York when John and Plácido recorded it. I thought they should change the last line that said, "My memories of love will be of you," because they were two men singing. I was probably the only one in the country who was bothered by the line, and wisely, Milt ignored me.

  I remember how beautifully John's voice came through with Plácido's, and how surprising that seemed. I couldn't imagine the two voices working together, but they did; Plácido's dark, infinite possibilities, and John's direct, perfectly placed, and sure; two men, strangers until that moment, singing one man's truth become art.

  That song is so filled with human truth about human experience and human emotion that it is art in the word's best sense. It is that which gives us time suspended, time to be a part of all life and understanding. A few moments of saying to ourselves, "Yes, I see.

I see. That's what I believe," of believing that we know we exist, if only for the exquisite joy of being a part of truth.

Art doesn't need to be complex or obscure, the sole property of an elite cadre, above and outside the rest of us. Art is not passive. It needs to nourish us and bring us joy. The artist creates it because he needs to, perhaps even unconsciously. Someone comes upon it and, if the moment is right, responds, and it is the creation and the response that is art.□

PERHAPS LOVE

(Duet with Plácido Domingo)
by John Denver

(Plácido sings) Perhaps love is like a resting place
A shelter from the storm
It exists to give you comfort
It is there to keep you warm
And in those times of trouble
When you are most alone
The memory of love will bring
you home

(John sings) Perhaps love is like a window
Perhaps an open door
It invites you to come closer
It wants to show you more
And even if you lose yourself
And don't know what to do
The memory of love will see
you through

(Plácido sings) Oh, love to some is like a cloud
To some as strong as steel
(John sings) For some a way of living

For some a way to feel

(Plácido sings) And some say love is holding on
And some say letting go
And some say love is everything
And some say they don't know

(John starts joined by Plácido)
Perhaps love is like the ocean
Full of conflict, full of pain
Like a fire when it's cold outside
Thunder when it rains
If I should live forever
And all my dreams come true
My memories of love will be
of you

(Plácido sings) And some say love is holding on
And some say letting go

(John sings) And some say love is everything
Some say they don't know

(John starts joined by Plácido)
Perhaps love is like the ocean
Full of conflict, full of pain
Like a fire when it's cold outside
Or thunder when it rains
If I should live forever
And all my dreams come true
My memories of love will be
of you

November 8, 1997
Alpine Drive, Beverly Hills

Dear Jean,

I was going to call you to tell you that I'm glad you received the rolling cart. I have reached the stage where I hardly carry any weighty thing back and forth in the house. I just toss it on the cart, or them on the cart, as the case may be, and away it or they go to someplace else.

Yesterday I moved the laundry from the hampers to the laundry chute on the second floor, then to the washer on another cart on the first floor. Later I emptied the contents of the dishwasher to the downstairs cart and wheeled them to the other side of the room to be put away. After that I used the cart to weed out books Milt's giving to UCLA music library. I've decided I have to work out a way to do things that doesn't put any pressure on my feet or my back both of which are fading fast from my list of usable assets. The carts have alternated as adjuncts to my desk wherever and whatever that happens to be, or a server at dinner when all the kids are here, and pulled up by the table to hold pieces of jigsaw puzzles.

Let me know when you find any more things to do with them. I have a vision of myself as a little old lady surrounded by nothing but rolling carts. If I could figure out a way of sleeping on them, I could have a constantly changing bedroom at the flick of a whim.

I'm so happy you're back online, as well as happy that you love your new home. I took a nap and woke up close to unable to get out of the bed suddenly depressed. Believe me, with no reason, but then my depressions are almost always without reason. We had Will and Emily here for an overnight. They have to be the best little children in the world. Not that they never fight, but they are so reasonable and have easygoing natures. Lizzie "babysat" for them to help me, which consisted of almost spilling apple juice while attempting to fill their sippy cups but she read to them before they went to bed and she came over this morning and spilled some more juice to help me. Will and Emily adore Lizzie so much that I can't think what will happen when she gets a little too old for them and can't be bothered. Maybe it won't happen.

My chin, instead of being on the floor, is now somewhere about waist level. Now I need a few good movies like *The Full Monty* where people have a real problem; they solve it, and it all ends up terribly funny. That would put me in a good mood and get the chin up to level and maybe more. Otherwise, I think I'll just try to be sensible and get out of the house for a while. Isn't this the mood they used to say women went out to buy a hat to conquer? If only they still wore hats or better yet if only I didn't hate hats so. Hats could be my strongest reason for living in a warm climate.

Now I'm babbling.
                Love
                Rosemary

                                November 18, 1997
                                Alpine Drive, Beverly Hills

Dear Michael,

I think my gloom and doom has changed. I'm feeling better in every way, except talking to people. That hasn't improved. In fact, it may be a little worse. I don't wake up thinking I wish I were dead. And I've started dabbling with little watercolors, doodles, just smearing and blotting, but in colors. Not art, but an expression of something that I'm sure someone else could volunteer interpretations for, though I'm not stopping to figure them out. Except for a very ugly one, which is a picture of depression.

Jean Holroyd suggested another therapist, a woman, nice ex-Catholic, Irish background, a little younger, so I guess that's who I'll be seeing when Jean retires or travels.

I woke up dreaming this morning that I was studying French in an Alpine setting, all snow. First, I was outdoors with people and then gradually found myself in a medieval room made of snow, sitting by a window carved in the snow, a French textbook in my hands. My friend Mickey Randolph came into the room to chat, and I suddenly realized that the entry wasn't a door but a small opening, like the entrance to an igloo. I tried to make her understand that we had to be very quiet and leave immediately or it might cave in, and as I was saying this I noticed that it had. I told her to follow me, and I began to burrow through, clawing the snow away, not frantically, but with purpose. After five or six tries, as it became more and more difficult, the blockage finally gave way, and I felt, with my hands, the freedom of empty space on the other side and I woke up.

Yesterday I tried several times to speak to people, but I heard my voice as if it were someone else talking, saying frozen-stiff words and feeling weird and outside everything. Very unpleasant, like being at a cocktail party with strangers and no reason to be there but you're talking desperately to no end.

My first thought this morning was that depression is a frozen room with no way out, but you're trying to learn a language that isn't your own so you can communicate with the outside world. It isn't easy to find your way out, but you have to try.

I awoke before I was completely out of the room, just my hands and the feeling of weightlessness in the space outside. And as I wrote that I realized that I've started to paint a little on small watercolor pads, and I've begun to write in the mornings again, as witness this letter. So my hands have begun to live in the sunshine again. And that's funny, because the first thing I had the urge to paint, and did paint, was an image of the sun, very bright and very yellow-orange, which eventually, with a lot of scratchy black ink lines and purple, became an ugly image of depression. But it was an image outside myself, not an inner one, so I guess I'm on the way to feeling better. No, I am feeling better. Not perfect, but better.

I received a note from my sister Jean the other day saying that she has to have some invasive test done this Friday for an arterial blockage that's affecting her feet and ability to walk. They will decide what to do after the test. She says that if they don't do something, she will end up in a wheelchair. Not good.

Email may actually allow Jean and me to have a relationship without pain. I hear from her every week or so, and sometimes it is very warming. I spoke to her on the phone after her note, and realized writing has cleared away some obstacle between us. So I made a light remark about how it was a shame we didn't have email all these years, something that would have made her bristle in the past, and she just sighed and said, "You're so right."

Everyone is well. I'm faxing you a copy of a thank you letter that Lizzie wrote to John Dupont, who sent her a present. This is the little girl who lined up her first set of blocks according to color, shape, and size. I wonder what she will be like in twenty years. We're getting along much better now. She has a determination that matches Jenny's, and I wonder where it will take her.

    Love,
    Rosemary

NOVEMBER

All the Novembers of my life come crowding into my memory this morning. Young Novembers in tan lisle stockings and scuffed shoes walking along Hempstead Avenue to school. Holding my mother's hand to cross streets, holding on to her to put off the moment of leaving her at the corner to walk into the schoolyard alone, or with my sister, waiting in the cold for the bell to ring so we could get in line and enter the school—apprehension a daily diet. The coldness of the day, no colder than my hands or my heart at being there.

November at ten years old, on the way to school, but walking there I've learned to treasure my time. If it's raining, I can look at the reflections and dance from puddle to puddle. I sing and see. On sunny days I can smile and dream. I dream and think and see everything. I read as I walk, if a book is hard to put down, avoiding pitfalls with peripheral vision, though I don't know the word. Two blocks from school, I start to worry about whatever work I haven't done. It's too late to do it, but if I worry about it, I think at least I've done something, even if it's only to find an excuse for not having done it.

November at fourteen. The last year of grammar school. I'm still dreaming as I walk, but this time the walk to school takes a different path. We've moved to another, nicer neighborhood, and along the way I pass well-kept houses and stores on Main Street full of interesting things, and two movie houses with their colorful posters. I still don't do any homework, no more than a few lines a day, and my life is in movement, seeing and reading. And sometimes I draw, the one accomplishment that has gained me any credibility in all my school days. Novembers in grammar school always appeared in turkeys, pumpkins, Indians, Puritans—and praise from the teacher when in the second grade I drew a turkey, suitably impressive, and then proceeded to scribble all over the page. They only gave us one piece of paper each week, and I never knew when to stop. I couldn't just sit still at the desk. I had to be doing something, and the crayons were there, the piece of paper was there, and I was there. When the teacher saw what I'd done, she asked the inevitable "Why did you do that?" It was the question I never could answer, and was asked all through my school days. The November chill wasn't just outdoors as she made an example of me to the class and to the teacher who came into the class to see my drawing.

November was the birthday month. The sad month. It started with Halloween and the dead to be remembered. It was my mother's birth month, November 27th. My father's was November 11th, Armistice Day. He had the luck of an important day in my mind, very apt and easy to remember. Aunt Mamie was November 25th.

After I graduated from high school and went to work, it was dark in the morning when I left the house and dark when I returned. There were the family holidays and Thanksgiving, Christmas to come, none of them promising much pleasure. I'd given up expecting much by then, but there was always a small hope that this year would be different.

Manhattan is not especially pleasant in November. I lived there for sixteen years. It's cold and gray. The leaves on the few trees turn brown and fall and only the store windows are filled with color. Novembers in Chappaqua were beautiful. My children brought home pumpkin and witch drawings, without, I think, the associations I had with hell, death, and suffering. We had jack-o'-lanterns, and pumpkin pies, beef casseroles, apple cider, and split pea soup. There were beautiful hemlocks to make up for the lack of leaves, and I didn't send them out to play in the rain. I didn't stop them either, if that's what they wanted to do.

Novembers in England could be like any other month, big clouds racing overhead and lots of rain. But London has a lot of trees to look at and interesting stores and museums, so there was always something to do. In California, I miss the seasons. I miss October and the maples changing color. I miss Christmas and the promise of snow, January and waking up in the morning to the world covered in snow, April's spring and jonquils and daffodils pushing up through the dormant grass, and the excitement of summer arriving with time at the shore, feet in the sand, grilled lobster, and farm-fresh corn.

Here in California, I don't miss November. I hate Halloween and its myth of the walking dead. I am too old to prepare a turkey dinner by myself, for my family, though I'm happy to go to Andy and Julia's house that day, knowing I'll enjoy being there and will love the food.

I'm sad when I think of all my aunts and uncles and my grandparents. They were all part of November to me. I'm sad that we weren't a happier family. There were always the undercurrents, as well as the open hostilities. I know those things are a part of life, but that doesn't make them less sad to experience. Why couldn't life be like all those walks to school when I was ten, ignoring the bad things, dreaming and dancing, reading books, just letting life that was right around you happen, however it was happening, without worry? Wouldn't that be nice?

NOVEMBER DREAM

Yesterday it felt like November
and I cried
for my mother dead
to all but me

November is dark
leaves withered
like the arms of my mother
sailing on the sad ship

Dead gray November
joining tears and rain

A GIFT FROM ROSE

I just put a small pottery vase on the shelf in my desktop. It's there, just slightly in front of my vision. It's very beautiful, something my friend Rose Reitter made. It's the only piece of pottery she made that I really liked. I didn't see everything she made. Her pottery just missed. Often it was the concept that was at fault, as if this very intellectual, artistically inclined, sensitive person had a vision problem that prevented her from seeing the pots and bowls that she created. I don't know if they were beautiful to her. They must have been, because she showed them with pride.

    Almost everything Rose made, except for her cooking, seemed slightly off, and she never noticed. But not this small vase on my desk. It's so naively happy and perfect. It's asymmetrical, unassuming, and accidentally perfect, with the quality of an unfurling rose. The color is an oatmeal tan and I think it may have been an extra bit of clay left over from some more ambitious work, something Rose felt more enthusiastic about, more her own, and more creative to Rose's way of thinking, and she pressed out this little bowl, so fresh and free of interference that when I look at it, I think of Rose's spirit, the soul of Rose.

She gave me several pieces over the years that I couldn't tell her I didn't like. How can you tell someone you like so much that you don't like a gift they have made especially for you and presented to you with eyes all smiling in expectation at your pleasure? The truth was that for all the years we knew each other I never told her that I didn't like her sense of design. It wasn't terrible. It just missed. I don't have the words for what it missed, but I recognize myself in that flaw. It's how I miss when I try to paint. I have talent. I can draw. I can use one color, at the most two, but I am not a good painter. What I have is a good eye, so no one sees the bad stuff, the misses. It's the art that counts for me, not who did it.

Rose gave me the little bowl when I went back East to see her six months before she died. We were sitting at the kitchen table looking out at a cold winter day, cool sunlit sky, and the bowl was sitting on the counter along with a handful of other small pieces, and when I picked it up and admired it, Rose said indifferently, "If you like it, keep it." She didn't give me its history, never said when she'd made it, or even if she'd made it. She did have a few other artists' pottery around the house, so it might not have been made by her. But when I look at it, I hear her voice, smiling enthusiasm, and affection for the person she was talking to. She had a capacity for friendship greater than anyone else I know: she was empathic, sympathetic, loving, spontaneous, compassionate, and I counted her a good friend, as did many others.

And the little bowl is like Rose. She was a pretty woman, whose face, until she became ill, hardly changed from the time we met when she was twenty-four until her death at sixty. She was pretty, but looked beautiful, because her good will and enthusiasm shone in her expression. She wore her inner qualities just the way the little bowl does. She was spontaneous, open, ready to hold good things as well as bad, pleasures and sadnesses.

Sometimes when I look at the bowl, I cry. Life didn't treat Rose fairly. She was often unhappy, and with reason. Two years of suffering in the process of dying was not the reward she deserved for cherishing her family, for the years of loving and caring for two parents who, one after the other, died long painful deaths, for ten years of watching an anorexic son try to kill himself through starvation, and for living with a husband who could not have been easy.

But somehow, unhappy as her life may often have been in her later years, she was always able to find the energy to think of someone else, to write another poem, to please herself and others, to love someone. She loved her dog and cat, her sons, her husband, her friends, and the children she taught poetry to. Things didn't have to be perfect for Rose to love them. And that was her perfection. Like the little bowl, more beautiful in its imperfection than something too planned and worked over.

I've heard that a sculptor must try to find the form that exists within a piece of stone for the stone to come to life. That's what happened to this little piece of clay-become-bowl. To me, it is Rose, a reminder of my friend. It doesn't matter if she made it. It has her spirit in its shape, and I cherish it.□

January 9, 1998
Alpine Drive, Beverly Hills

Dear Michael,
You're lucky to be elsewhere at the moment. Everyone but me has the flu or a cold. Los Angeles is gradually taking to its collective bed. People are sneezing and groaning in a loud chorus. Either that or staring dully into space as they contemplate life through stuffed noses. I'm quaking, waiting for my turn, swallowing pills and thinking positive Zen thoughts whenever I can muster them.

Crazy heavy rain yesterday for most of the day, an overcast sky right now at seven a.m., and cool enough to need my woolen bathrobe. Maybe it's the unexpected dampness, but the last three nights have been non-sleeping nights. On one of them I listened to seven of the twelve tapes of Dickens's *Great Expectations*. That's a bad night.

I don't think anyone, single, terribly interesting thing has happened since you left, except that one day I called Andy and he mentioned that Will was in an exceptionally happy mood. Andy suggested that we might like to come over for a while. We did. He was right. Will was so happy and cheerful, not high happy, just smiling, loving, leaning happy. And Emily too. The both of them were such a pleasure to be with. I always love them. They're always my grandchildren, to be loved and cherished, but they're not always so loving. That was the difference. It was great.

Well, overcast, gloomy daytime is here. The road is wet though it isn't raining. Milt is coughing and feeling crummy. I read two mysteries in a row, played solitaire, and edited a bunch of photographs on the computer. The gray has seeped into my brain and all the little cells are swollen and sagging. If this was 1940 and I was somebody else, I'd go out and buy myself a new hat. That may be the single best thing about 1998 that I can think of. No hats.

You don't remember the hats. They were bizarre. A milliner would start out with a kind of vaguely formed hat shape of felt, poke it and prod it and steam it into the latest style, then decorate it with buttons, bows, sequins, and netting until it became its own distinctive thing. Then some depressed woman, driven by a compulsion to be like the rest of the women she knew, would go into the shop and try the hat on, along with twenty others, the hat lady hovering behind her, cooing and murmuring encouragement until the customer bought something, anything, but generally nothing she needed. A hat.

When that happened to me, which it did very occasionally, I would buy a hat, the least obnoxious, take it home in its hatbox (the best-looking item in the transaction), get in front of a mirror, try it on, and realize how stupid it was, how little like anything I was, and proceed to dismantle everything the milliner had attached to it. Off with the ribbons, the veil, the sequins. I may even have once or twice tried to unshape it by steaming. When I finally made it completely unwearable, a kind of pre-Annie Hall fedora, I'd give up, stick it in the hatbox at the top of the closet, to be thrown out at some future date when I could console myself over the price I'd paid for it by saying, well, I'd learned my lesson, and if I took it out to the garbage pail scrunched up in a paper bag, even the garbage man wouldn't know what it was. And the hatbox would come in handy for storing socks, and I'd start collecting them right that minute to prove to myself and any saints or dead relatives who happened to be watching that I was really pretty practical after all.

I was twenty-one the last time I wore one of those hats. I was in Cooper Union at the time, just moved to the East Village, and an old high school mate of mine was getting married. The wedding was filled with people my age from the suburbs, all intent on marrying and duplicating as closely as possible the lives their parents led and cheerfully drinking themselves into wedding abandon. A girl was there I'd never met named Rosemary Guiney, who through four years of high school was referred to by friends and strangers as my double. As we went into the restaurant for the reception, we were introduced with comments from people around us like "at last you meet—look at them." She didn't look exactly like me, but watching her was unnerving. Her gestures were so like mine. It was like looking into a distorted mirror. I stayed just long enough to eat dinner, took one last glance in her direction, found her looking at me, and left. When I got into the subway station, I threw the hat in a trash can and swore I'd never wear another.

Until this moment, I hadn't realized that it wasn't just the hat I was throwing away. It was Queens Village, the Catholic Church, all the conventions I'd been brought up to think were the be-all and end-all of living. Not that I wanted to be rid of everything Catholic in me, or that I would ever be from someplace other than Queens Village, but that I wanted to choose bits and pieces of a different life, without any voices asking me why I wanted to do this or that, why I wanted to go outside their "norm"...

We don't really change much, do we? My impulse is still to throw anything out that I don't want. (I salve my conscience by giving it all to the Salvation Army, telling myself at least it's not wasted.) And I still get crazy when someone asks me "why" I did or said something, as if to make me feel suspect. And by 1998, I've lived long enough to be the conventional one.

For some reason this all reminds me of a cartoon that my Cooper Union friend Mickey Henrion sent me some years back. It's a line drawing that shows four elderly women sitting properly on a sofa in a primly antique-looking interior. Three of them are kind of frumpily dressed and the fourth has on a striped apache shirt, black skirt, and ballet slippers. She's skinny with a Buster Brown straight haircut and her feet are turned out in a ballet fifth position. The caption reads, "Myra Hennessy once danced naked in the moonlight on Nantucket Island. The past is a treasure to be infinitely cherished."

She's such a picture of the Villagers that Mickey and I were, so daring, so different, so conventionally what we were, but so happy finally to belong somewhere. Rebellion was so safe in those days.
          Love,
          Rosemary

GREAT DIVIDE

Forget problems
Let them disappear
Think California

This isn't Maine
where life grows
in glorious green profusion

Or New York
where people scurry
in timetabled cultural activity

This is California
where it will never end

INSOMNIA

I've been listening to *Pride and Prejudice* on tape. It's one of the easiest things to listen to on long interrupted nights. I know it so well I don't have to stay awake to listen, but if I should be awake it washes over me with the soothing effect of a mild tranquilizer.

Listening to books on tape during the night has changed my existence. I used to hate nighttime. Whenever I woke up I would begin to worry, always nervous, always afraid, maybe of the dark, maybe of all the cumulative fears of my lifetime. I used to think that if I had to be alone at night I would die very quickly from fear, from lack of sleep and relaxation, and I think that might be true.

I began listening to tapes when we came back from England to wean myself away from the BBC. When we lived there, Milt and I listened to the World Service all night. It was wonderful. They broadcast plays, music, news, and discussions all night long. After we moved back to the States, we met an Englishwoman who did odd jobs, and the odd job she did for me was tape eight or ten programs a month, usually plays and things like "My Music," and send them to me in Connecticut. I listened to them over and over, and they became my security blanket.

I wore out those tapes long ago. Almost had a memorial service for them when I finally threw them out. It seemed disloyal to be rid of them. By that time I had begun to build a library of taped books. I used to rent them, but I found that listening to them at night meant that I missed so much while I was sleeping, and I had to play the same tape over a number of times in order to hear the whole thing. Also, if the book was interesting, not unpleasant, well written, I could listen to it more than once. In fact, some of my books I listen to once a year, a few even twice a year. So I have become a collector of recorded books, most of them nineteenth century and long-winded. The nineteenth century specialized in nonviolence or leave it to the imagination violence, not too much suspense, romantic pain if any pain at all, and for the most part, social manners.

Of course, I've bought a number of lemons, things that would have fascinated me at twenty-five, like *The Brothers Karamazov*, or at thirty-five, like Falkner's *Light in August*. Both defied listening to. They sit in their plastic-covered volumes accusing me of a lack of seriousness of purpose and accomplishment, not understanding that my purpose in the middle of the night is to be not serious, not accomplishing anything but peace of spirit. If I have a spirit, a soul, I don't want it to be awake wondering what's under the bed or breaking in a back door. I don't want it wringing its ghostly hands over war in Africa and poverty across town. I don't want to be obsessing about the plumbing that's leaking and what time I have to be at the dentist the next day. I want to be lost in a place where all the problems are solved by the next to last spoken page—and I already know the solution—preferably in beautifully crafted ideas and sentences. And if it happened a hundred and fifty years ago, that's even better.

I know that it probably dulls my mind and takes the edge off some of my own creative thinking, but like an addict, I can't give up the pleasure of nights without fear and unease. If I didn't wake up every hour and a half with hot flashes, giving me half a dozen opportunities each night to wake up and worry, it might be better. If I could sleep through the night with just a time or two awake, I probably wouldn't bother with the tapes.

I was a thumb sucker. Finally gave it up at six years old, under great duress. Emily and Will are too. The thought just crossed my mind that somehow evolution has done us wrong. It's too bad we don't continue to suck our thumbs to go to sleep. How wonderful to have this quick ticket to sleep, no need for pills or tapes. And do we give up the thumb because the sucking instinct lessens and fades away, or is it society that forces us to, by teaching us that only babies suck their thumbs?□

March 16, 1998
Alpine Drive, Beverly Hills

Dear Joan,

Thank you so much for your nice, nice letter. It made me feel good. Life has such a weird fleeting quality, and we live so much of our time in memories. It's wonderful to know that the memory you are to another person is good... The book I've read most recently is *The God of Small Things*. I read it with two book groups, and found the second time amazing, the language even more beautiful. What a writer. Perhaps that's the test of a great book. All the books I've really loved—*The Leopard, Wide Sargasso Sea, Portrait of the Artist*, Proust—I've read over and over, always taking the same or even more pleasure than on the first reading.

I passed on your compliment to Jenny. The attention her work is getting is something she deserves after twenty-five years of hard work. She has everything it takes—talent, obsessive drive, and good luck. It might be better to say that she has enough creative talent for ten artists, enough obsessive drive to succeed for all ten, and she makes her good luck happen. My father-in-law said two wise things: "If she has a cold, keep her home from school. She'll graduate the same year," and, "The harder you work, the luckier you get." So I kept her home and she graduated, and she works harder than almost anyone I know, artist or otherwise.

Milt and I keep hanging in there wherever there is, grumping over each new twinge, but not letting it hinder the fun stuff. Neither of us was ever terribly athletic. Perhaps Milt with tennis, but that was an isolated activity. He doesn't play tennis any more, and he's beginning, finally, to realize that he has to move a little more than his finger on the remote or his hand to turn one page to the next. He works with a physiotherapist for his back, and has expanded to a forty-minute routine of exercises.

I putter around on a hundred unimportant things, enjoying most of all the visits with my grandchildren. I enjoy many things, but they make me happier than all the rest. I'm my mother's daughter. Milt sends his best to you and Bill, and so do I.

                              Rosemary

ABOUT LOVE

> My mother, too old for winter now,
> watches from the window,
> waiting for us to come in
> so she can give us hot cocoa.
> The yarn is for the white afghan she knits,
> thinking I will need it to remember her by.

I know my love for my mother wasn't unique, but it was unique for me. It remained the one constant in my life. The love I've felt for other people has always changed in some way, through time, anger, boredom, indifference. It changes as circumstances and interests change.

When romantic love is new, it's intense and fascinating. Then, almost without knowing, it becomes companionship and necessity. Later, it becomes part of the cement and bricks of your life, an intimate partnership. The "ship" in that word is significant, because it is as if, in a long-time marriage, you are together, at sea in a small boat, not always sure of how to deal with the winds that blow in unforeseen directions, yet always knowing the ultimate direction.

Love for children is the most altruistic, the best of all love. The reward is the immediate pleasure to be gained from the beauty of a face that turns to you with some need, or, better, with pleasure at your company. A clear-eyed smile, a happy physical response. Arms to wrap around you unselfconsciously. Eyes clear and direct, emotions not hidden. I love you. I hate you. I want you. Come. Go. Hug me. Feed me. Give me. This is for you. No doubt at all about love for little children. But that changes. They grow up and become adults, and you love the memory of them as children. Your love for them changes to fit their age. An adult can't elicit the same love as a child, something that's often hard for your own children to understand. It has to change to a different love and respect; where once you respected them as children, you need to be able to respect them as teenagers, then adults. And they need to behave as adults toward you to earn respect.

As long as I live, I will always remember my mother with love and longing for the comfort and cherishing she gave me, for her letting me comfort and cherish her in turn. I still feel my arms around her, and hear her voice trying to hide her pleasure at being loved so openly. How lucky I was to be her daughter!□

BEFORE THE STORM

I hate to believe that I might be depressed, but perhaps it's some form of very mild depression that's sitting on my tongue, stopping me from using my fingers to write anything meaningful. Maybe it's because I finally wrote about Milt. And Jean. How did Jean reconcile her sexuality with her religion? I never did. I never reconciled anything in my life with anything else... As I've written before, I have this strange sense of us all being two creatures. First the animal that we are, chewing, swallowing, digesting, urinating, farting, defecating, hiccupping, twitching, grimacing, smiling, fucking, hopping, itching, scratching, sleeping, blinking, all of it. And then the other creature living its life of electric switches and fancy cars, six kinds of underwear, and a blank expression while pretending that none of that animal stuff is happening. It's all a Bond Street pretense, sweet-smelling soap and flowery china.

What's real and what's not? I try to hang in there not thinking, but it doesn't work. I've had this one life to live, and things outside and within me seem to have screwed it up. Milt is so blissfully unguilty, and I am plagued and uneasy, like a lake on a gray day when a storm may break, with always a sense of the water in a little too much motion. I can't blame the Catholic Church, but I do, rather than blame my parents.

What did they know? And Jean and Mike? They were what they were, but the dislike and disgust lingers. Lingers? It's the foundation on which I'm built. It's the pain of rejection by Jean, the fear of pursuit by Mike, and the terror of the child in the face of the looming hell of Catholicism that curdled my spirit. So the best the civilized "I" that I am can do is scrape along, trying to pull myself together and watch myself pretending to be comfortable.

Meanwhile, I've been listening to the autobiography of Mark Twain during the night. Bad mistake. I find I have absolutely no sense of humor late at night, and unless I'm completely awake, it all seems dead serious, so I'll listen to it in the car. Staying awake to see the amusing side of his writing defeats my purpose in listening. He isn't ha-ha funny, he's bitter funny, and maybe bitter funny is the cure I need for this mood. □

LIST OF INGREDIENTS

Sunset and sunrise—the change from first dawn to sunrise is so rapid. It happens so quickly. You look and the sky is barely gray with only the faintest lightening at the horizon, and one minute later there's a hint of rose, above it a faint yellow, and above that, luminous pale night blue. At least that's what I see out my window right now in this early morning dawn over Los Angeles.

We've had a lot of rain lately and the skies have been clear, but this morning, after a day and a half of fierce Santa Ana winds, I can see that the smog level is also rising. The pink is turning to mud gray—or is that smoke I'm seeing through? There were brush fires out Glendale way and who knows where else. I won't listen to the radio for fear of finding out. Better to start the day not knowing...

In my old age I have begun to feel maternal toward my own father. I can understand how hard it was for him to be who and what he was: alternately and without discretion too openly happy and too depressed; someone who always wanted company but often wasn't fit for it; bigoted in principle, generous individually. Shamed at the end of that bigotry by the kindness and care that was given to him by the black male attendants in the VA hospital in the months before he died, and needing to confess it. We Catholics have our special needs.

I don't come from nowhere. Into my special recipe goes my mother's fierce maternity, her sadness, and her love of books. My father's quick mind, his manic depression, but, thank god, not high and low ten times in one day, the way it was for him. His lightness of feet and love of music, his good ear, his ability to be elated.

From my mother's aunt, Nana, comes worrying. From Mamie, stubbornness, living things before they happen, and a need for perfection. From Aunt Julie, the ability to say "no," since she was the only one besides my mother who had the nerve to say no to my father, openly and with scorn, if he tried to tell her what to do. From Grandpa, the ability to love people. He was just a nice gentle man. I don't like the portion of me that Grandma gave—the hardness, the inflexibility, the rightness. The long-legged bony gawkiness of me. The suspicious cranky old lady I'm becoming. Please let Grandpa win out. Let him be my flavor.

From Aunt Vera came grudging love. I could never be her daughter, Mary. From neighbors, except for Aunt Francis and Uncle Jim Savell, the knowledge that I would always be an outsider. From the Savells, kindness and cookies.

From the priests, knowledge of Hell and damnation. From the nuns, the knowledge that I was always lacking something.

From Jean and Mike I learned not to trust, not to hope, always to be on guard.

Not a bad life, really. Pretty good compared to many. So I'm not complaining. Just describing. In my old age, I couldn't or possibly wouldn't change any of them. They are what I am.□

WOMEN AND BOOKS

I woke up in a pretty good mood. That is to say, I wasn't sad, saggy, or convinced that I needed another hour and a half before I could get out of bed. I wonder what made this day different. I hear a pulsing downstairs that I think means Jenny is on the treadmill at ten after six in the morning. That, or there's something in the house that goes bump, bump, bump in the near dark. I wonder about that too.

Before I got out of bed I was thinking about the tea I went to the other day. Ruth Coleman invited a number of friends to meet her son and his French wife and six-month-old daughter who were in town for two weeks. There were perhaps thirty people, most of them women. The son was handsome, the wife cute, and the baby very bright. Ruth's daughter was in from New Hampshire with her ten-year-old daughter. It was interesting to see a family fleshed out and loving. Not just Ruth speaking about phantoms...

The thought I had shortly after opening my eyes, spurred on by the memory of Ruth's tea the other day, was that it's easier to read a life than to live one. That may be the reason readers like me carry books around, ready at all times to whip one out and disappear into it. At the tea I met half a dozen women, and I only really spoke to a few people, and all of them were in book groups. And they were reading very good books.

A social gathering would normally have sent me into my invisible closet, incoherent, unable to think of anything to say, struck as dumb and clumsy as at any party when I was eleven, when I first found out there was such a thing as a social gathering. Instead, everyone talked about books when the subject came up, and since Ruth introduced me as the leader of our reading group, the subject always came up. It was great.

When I was little, my mother, also a reader, read with a group of women in Queens Village, hardly a hotbed of intellectualism. They were wives of men in the American Legion. Seven or eight of them met in our small living room, sitting around and having coffee and cake and talking about that month's book. And they probably read pretty good books. I remember a green copy of a Faulkner novel sitting in the living room for a while, either from the library or the drugstore lending library. Mother and Aunt Vera used to share the cost of renting books, and took turns reading them.

That would be sixty years ago. I joined a book group when we moved to Chappaqua, one of two in the town. That was thirty-four years ago. It was a great group. When we came to California, I lucked out. We went to dinner at the home of a music business lawyer, I think he was, and I said I hoped to find a book group. The hostess said that a few women had just started one and I could come to the next meeting with her. I did. She never came to another meeting, but I've been going to them ever since, and that was twenty-two years ago.

About five years ago I started a book group over at the Tennis Club. They all read the books, but they don't always make it to the meetings. They love the books generally, and all say they're reading things they never would have read without the group, but sometimes it's an uphill battle. The thought I had the other day, listening to how the women spoke, was that if they weren't in a group, they would still be reading. The difference is that they're reading books and analyzing them, questioning, comparing ideas and experiences, and making themselves heard. They're validating publicly what they think and feel about the art, content, and success of someone's work. It's not in the closet anymore.

We may be among the largest number of educated and intellectually assertive women in the history of Western Civilization. My mother and her friends loved the books they read, but they thought—and their husbands didn't hesitate to tell them publicly—that it was just women stuff, frivolous, to be done after everything else was taken care of. The women in Chappaqua didn't think what they were doing was frivolous, but a man walking in might have made a crack about a coffee klatch, and we would have laughed and pretended he was funny.

Milt was different. He saw it for what it was. He wasn't typical.☐

April 2, 1999
Alpine Drive, Beverly Hills

Dear Michael,
Shall I be truthful or shall I be socially acceptable? Should I say I had a wonderful time in New York? I can tell you the truth, right? It wasn't fun. I was depressed and my stomach was a little off before we left L.A., and both conditions got worse in the Big Apple. How far can I go with the truth and not bore you? The weather didn't encourage walking and my poor feet were hurting after all the work at home before leaving. They took a week to get better, so basically I was in the room a lot the first five or six days. We had dinner with Peter and Sheila and that was pleasant, and I

had dinner with Sheila one night toward the end while Milt and Peter were out on business.

Then there were Steve and Mickey. The first visit in Chappaqua was pleasant and almost a relief, as we were able to act rather naturally and Steve was in a pretty good mood. Then came Steve's operation, and Mickey suggested that he might like a visit from us in the hospital. However, before we arrived they discovered that he'd caught an infection, and he was off getting tests. He was in a bad way when he came back, and then Mickey was in a bad way. One son was there with her, and after the infection took hold, she didn't talk to anyone, us included, which added to my normal depression. In the limited surroundings of the hotel, there wasn't much to distract me. Perhaps I should be honest and say that it was the limited surroundings in my head that kept me down. Nothing helped, and I finally confessed a strong desire to return to L.A. and not stay the whole three weeks. As soon as we got on the plane, I felt considerably better. I don't really like traveling any more, and traveling when depressed is not a good idea.

The University of North Carolina is establishing a chair in Dan's name, and Milt is going down for the dinner and ceremony on April 23rd. I'm not in shape for that many airports, plus my sister-in-law, Beth, seems somewhat less friendly than my sister Jean did in her preadolescent, adolescent, and drinking days. Beth has been Dan's good wife all these years, so in a way it's her big day too, which she justly deserves, and I don't feel like putting a crimp in it by being there. So Milt will go on the twentieth to New York, then to Chapel Hill, back to New York on the twenty-fourth, to Paris on the twenty-fifth, then on to Geneva, where I will meet him for a ten-day stay at Père Bise. That will be our trip for this year unless he goes to Salzburg for the festival with Harold this summer. I trust my mood will be better by then.

I wrote the poem about Grandpa when I went to college after we first moved here about twenty years ago. You and I may be the only ones who think it's telling.

          Love,
              Rosemary

GRANDPA

When I was a child
Grandpa looked at the switch on the wall
and said
It's a miracle, girl
you push the button
and the lights go on
just like that

He had a radio
given him by his children
On Sundays he sat in his old chair
listening to a voice from Chicago
Grandpa said,
Don't touch it, girl, it's a radio.

Astronauts visit the moon
on television
Not the moon outside
the one the cow jumped over
That one, flat and mysterious
shines down on my world

I laughed at Grandpa
And I laugh at me
And I laugh at my children
laughing at me
and their children laughing at them

April 6, 1999
Alpine Drive, Beverly Hills

Dear Michael,

I was afraid of death until I watched my mother die. Then I knew that if you could cope with living, it was the dying, not death, that was to fear. And if the dying was painless, that would be something to be grateful for. I have a vision of all the bones of all the people who have died and become part of the earth. It doesn't make me feel sad, just gives me a sense of the rightness of it, and the continuity that I will be a part of.

But as to the pain of facing the loss of any person I love, I haven't much perspective. I'm very subjective. Today I called Mickey, and when she asked me if I'd had a good vacation in New York, I decided to tell the truth and said "no," that I'd hardly left the room I was so sad and unhappy about Steve. It made it easier to talk to her than if I'd lied. Lying is hard unless it's unimportant.

I still have to answer your letter about the century. I see it differently, but that's because I'm twenty years older than you. I think my century starts with the marriage of my grandparents, somewhere about 1880. Their influence and that of their generation formed my parents, along with all the history and culture that formed my generation. Electricity, mass production, cars, planes, the beginnings of modern medicine, women's suffrage, comfortable clothes—that all started to become a reality during my grandparents' adult years. They formed my parents.

By your way of figuring, Will and Emily would be people of the twentieth century, since they were born in 1992 and 1994, whereas my mother and father were born in 1895 and 1896. I think of my grandchildren as being strongly influenced by Milt and me, by Barbara and Doug, and by our predecessors, but I think of them as of the future, the twenty-first century.

When I think of the future, I'm sad for all the music I won't hear. The delicious food I won't eat. The flowers and trees and mountains I won't see. Moving things I won't read. I don't care a lot about the inventions, wars, important occasions, stars. I am pessimistic about the capacity to destroy all life and civilization that we humans possess, and the fact that given man's drive to make "progress," we haven't seen the worst yet. I hope for my children and grandchildren that they have health, food, shelter, and whatever good things they can, and that they don't suffer unmercifully.

I understand you liked the Lewis and Clark book. Ex-active housewife that I am, it seemed to be a succession of something like suburban weekly shopping lists, substituting bison and flat boats for hot dogs and roller skates. The only thing I found really fascinating was the length of time it took to get a letter from Ohio to Virginia in the middle of the eighteenth century. Of course, they were brave, and they were inventive and skilled, but that book needed an editor. Be well.

Love,
Rosemary

THE COOPER UNION FOR THE ADVANCEMENT OF SCIENCE AND ART

Dear Michael,
I've been watching a program on Dashiell Hammett. Enjoying it immensely... Seventy-one. I made it. Creaking all the way, but I'm now officially seventy-one and a day. Julia called to say that Emily, who finished school last Friday, said that Will got to lunch with me one day when she didn't, so she wanted a turn to go to lunch with me without Will. Then Milt and I had dinner with the Holdridges. It was a happy day, but as usual, I ate too much. The irritating part is that no matter how much less you eat as you age, you hardly lose any weight.

Oops. Hammett's in trouble with the McCarthy crew for being a Communist, or at least a sympathizer. Jail. Hellman runs out on him. I think his biographer is madly in love with him. She's gushing about him as if he was a darling poster boy, and maybe he was. But all on his own, I guess he fried his brain in alcohol. He didn't write much of value for the last thirty years of his life and died at sixty-six.

Today was great. Milt and I went to see a movie based on Oscar Wilde's *An Ideal Husband*. I can't tell you how much I love going to the movies before noon. I'm so awake and energetic. If I could always go to the movies in the daytime, I'd go once a week—if I could find fifty-two good movies to go to in a year. It really gets me into a great mood.

We donated a group of prints and paintings to The Cooper Union in Will, Dan, and my names. We removed them when we painted the downstairs, and I decided I didn't want them back up. I was tired of them, and I didn't want them up just to impress. I'm done with impressing.

And I owe Cooper Union a lot. And the Okuns do too. Will came from Russia at the age of twelve because as a Jew he couldn't go on to secondary school. After high school in Brooklyn, he got into Cooper, which was one of the two or three top engineering schools in the country. Then Dan went to Cooper during the Depression and went on to a wonderful academic career. I went there for two and a half years, before I had Jenny, and it changed my life. Just as Vietnam, living in and out of France for ten years, and now five years in China have changed you, opened up the world to you, Cooper Union did even more for me. I was so limited in my outlook, by the parochialism of town and church, by the Depression and lack of money, by the idea that girls didn't need to think about anything but getting married and knowing how to take dictation, and at eighteen I was at the end of the line. I was like a blank piece of paper with a few faint lines on it.

I heard about Cooper from a painter who used to come into Papa's store. He taught there, or one of his friends did, and somehow I found out that it was a free school and I could take a test to get in. My parents were sort of horrified by the thought of my going to an art school. Artists had bad reputations for being bohemians (think free love and Communists), and they rued the day they'd let me speak to the painter.

For a six-dollar-a-year registration fee, I learned a lot about art and more about the world, religion, society, and literature, met people from all kinds of countries, states, and counties in a school where no one from the dean to the dumbest student ever asked me that horrible question I'd heard all my life: "Why did you say that?" I could do and say anything I wanted and not be thought strange. It's a measure of how unstrange I really was that no one noticed me except as a pretty and kind of shy girl who hung around the edges of things, whereas back in Queens Village and Hollis I was usually considered weird, a little out of step.

My children owe a debt to Cooper, though they're not conscious of it. My training helped me to see Jenny's talent very early on. So she had chances she might not have had if she'd had other parents. It made me more tolerant of people's differences than I would have been. It helped me see beauty in places and people I might never have noticed. I hate to think of what I would have been if I had stayed in Queens and married some clerk or shoe salesman I fell in love with after a few drinks, had three kids, and gradually turned into a sad turnip of a woman sipping beer on a Saturday night. What a crazy letter this is. It's the outside of my life. I feel as if I'm writing about somebody I once knew.

    Love,
    Rosemary

    January 11, 2000
    Alpine Drive, Beverly Hills

Dear Michael,
Milt and I loved your letter, and I kept thinking I'd answer it, but before I could, I acquired some kind of intestinal hoo-ha that you don't want a further description of, and it's left me weak and uncommunicative. Except that I do want to communicate and say how nice your visit was this year.

How nice to have someone who never expects me to be anyone but who I am, and of whom I expect nothing more than loving nephewhood. Thank god we got to know each other again at my mother's funeral. Just when I lost the most important person from my past and all that love and acceptance, I found someone who could help me remember who I am and where I came from and that there were good things in those days too.

For an ailing aunt, that wasn't too bad. Take care of yourself—health being on my mind at the moment.

    Love,
    Rosemary

AT THE OPERA

I spent some time yesterday and today trying to imagine writing about opera without adjectives and adverbs. Opera lovers fall in love each time they see a wonderful performance and carry on during intermissions and after the last curtain call like a bunch of excited kids at a pop concert. They stop short of climbing onto the stage and fainting, and they never try to tear the clothes off their favorites, but I suspect that some of them would tear off their own clothes if their favorites asked.

Women are more obvious than men in their backstage idolatry. They love male singers, believing they're the heroes they play onstage. Women wait backstage for the singers to appear from the dressing rooms, hoping for a moment of attention. They check their clothes, hair, and makeup in any surface that gives back a reflection. I saw a woman in a revealing cocktail dress pour perfume down her massive cleavage when a manager announced that a favorite male singer would be out in thirty seconds to meet the fans. That was a bit over the top even for an opera fan in a crowd of sixty people.

Men are more subdued backstage, but you can feel their passion just the same. They stand in line, use the same clichés and superlatives as women. A handshake from the star, a smile, five seconds and the opera night is done.

People who don't go backstage may go home with music still ringing in their heads. Some try to sing parts of arias. They imitate the gestures of the singers struggling to hit the notes. Sometimes it takes hours to come down from an opera high.

Opera fans compare musical experiences the way gourmets compare restaurants. They talk about pitch and phrasing. They compare productions of the same operas. Conductors, sets, and composers. Each fan has favorite singers to laud and defend. I find I can talk about opera fans, but if I wanted to tell you what I thought about the production of *Faust* I saw the other day or the production of *The Queen of Spades* at the Met last spring, I don't think I could do it without using adjectives and adverbs. Lots of them. This is a very hard exercise. Oops.□

THE VIEW FROM HERE

I listen to the different things that people in class write, and I see that age makes a difference—that my age makes a difference. If I had known that I could write at twenty, I think I know what I would have written about. I remember twenty very well. But I'm not interested in my twenty-year-old self any more. And I've written most of the things I wanted to tell of my childhood and the town I came from.

I'm more interested in yesterday, today, and tomorrow, and things from the perspective of seventy-one. I was with Andy in a room full of women the other day, and he said something about all the estrogen in the room giving him a headache. That irritated me, except the truth is I was one of those who had migraines all the time back in the days when estrogen ruled my moods. I could say the same thing about a roomful of men and all that testosterone...I've never been happier than in the last ten years. That's strange because so many bits and pieces of me are deteriorating. Arthritis, heart, balance. I put effort into staying as healthy as I can without making a fetish of it, but I understand limitations. A woman in class wrote a piece about an older woman with Parkinson's who was happy to be in a sanitarium because there was always someone there to help her when she needed it. A phrase came up: "I'm not ready." When I heard it, I thought, "I'm ready."

I say I'm ready, but I don't want to die right now. It's truer to say that I'm getting ready. I know I won't like dying. I'll hate it, especially if it's painful. When I think of being dead, I hate that I won't hear music again or see flowers and trees or colors. I love my husband and children and I adore my grandchildren, but I don't want to know their future.

I've changed in these last few years. I'm choosing to relax now. I've stopped worrying about most of the foolish things that disturbed me when I was younger. I've learned to do that watching my grandchildren go about life unconcerned with what other people think about them. I'm saying yes and no when I mean yes and no. Even to myself.

In these years that will be the last part of my life, I want serenity and acceptance of being. I had an image of human bones layered beneath the surface of the earth. They were the bones of everyone who had ever lived. It comforted me, made me feel what I will be a part of when I die my not very special death. I've come to think of the end of my life not as a personal death, but just the end of another person in a long human tapestry. I can think of it that way for myself because I know I won't have to mourn for myself.

I'm seventy-one. I'm selfish enough to want to die before the people I love. I don't want that pain. I'd like to die while I'm still enjoying living. I've had my share of everything. Had my choices and chances. It's time for others.

I like the view from where I stand today.□

Journal
January 31, 2000
Alpine Drive, Beverly Hills

I've moved my laptop to a desk in my bedroom, and on top of the desk are four family photographs with different stories to tell. There's Milt sitting at a table at our favorite restaurant in France. He doesn't have much gray in his hair so it must have been taken about fifteen years ago. Next comes Jenny in her backyard in London. She's pretty and she's cuddling Lizzie, one year old and angelic. Then come my two nephews. I took care of them for years after they were born, and we're still close today. I'm like both of them. And they couldn't be less like one another.

The fourth picture is of my son. It was a school picture taken in London when he was nine years old. When he was eight he had a class assignment to write an autobiography, and his started out, "I'm a boy. I'm eight years old, and I have rough hair." And there he is at nine, eyes and teeth too big and rough hair growing every which way over ears that stick out, my attempt at a Beatles cut gone wrong. At thirty-seven he's long grown into the eyes, teeth, and ears, but his haircuts still look like I do them. Rough hair is hard to cut.

I moved my laptop upstairs because my daughter Jenny and her husband and ten-year-old Lizzie have moved to a house of their own, leaving their part of the house to me. Eight and a half years ago they came to stay for two months because Jenny and Richard wanted to see if they could get their careers going in the States. Now I have the equivalent of a small apartment all to myself and I'm in the process of moving my kitchen office and hallway art into it. In the meantime I need a place to work, so this desk is it.

How I am like my two nephews could take up many pages. Peter is intelligent, dependable, practical, creative in business, has problems with numbers, handles people well, and is CEO of a growing music publishing company. He's married to the girl he began to date at the age of thirteen.

Michael is intelligent, dependable, impractical, creative, and unmarried. He's learned six languages since high school and is always convinced he's right. He was a monk in France for ten years. He started a newspaper for local residents when he lived in Hell's Kitchen in New York. At forty he came to California and went to Stanford for a law degree. He worked for two years in Seattle as a public defender, but said he liked the clients better than the other lawyers. He's been in China for six years working for the music publishing company. He speaks Chinese fluently, proving that he has a good musical ear. He writes great letters and sometimes poetry. He lives in apartment buildings that only rent to Chinese and has a number of Chinese friends. The State Department calls him for advice and invites him to business and political meetings that happen in Beijing. He thinks he'll be there for a long time. But I think one of these days he'll wake up and decide he's ready to go on to the next thing.

I'm intelligent and creative in business in a most impractical way, which I discovered when I went to New York and ran the music company on horse sense and intuition. Like Peter I have trouble with numbers and like Michael I have a good ear for voices. When I had my first child, I was forced to be like Peter—dependable and practical, when by temperament I'm more like Michael. I can have a long-time interest in something and one morning I wake up and I'm done with it. It's over. I like change. I like to savor everything I can about a new situation. Make it a part of me. And when it's done, I like to pack my bag and go on to the next thing. And like Michael, I'm convinced that I'm right. If someone convinces me differently, it's okay because I don't mind changing my mind—then I can be right again.

One night I had four friends over for dinner. One of them said she had different personas. First there was one she called Gladys, the one who always cleaned out the refrigerator and made the bed, even on Sundays. Jill was the one who wrote music and lyrics for children's records. There was Pat who went to meetings and signed contracts for the records. Then there was the one who went around the country having affairs with men who were handsome and interesting. I asked her what that one's name was, and she purred Yum Yum. The other women looked at her as if she was crazy, but I understood.

And the picture of Milt. He's the constant of my life. I look at the photo and try to think in words how I feel about him. I remember the shirt he was wearing and the tennis jacket hung over the back of the chair. He was playing tennis in those days. I know because I can see that his right arm is more muscular than his left. His chin is in his hand and his elbow on the table. A familiar pose. If I enlarge the picture enough, I'll be able to see who took it in the reflection in his glasses. His mouth is a little open. Had he just said something? Or was he about to? We've lived together for forty-one years. We've laughed and cried, made love and made breakfast, brought up two children, been elated and sad, felt passion about politics, music, and books. We've loved and buried parents, aunts, and uncles, and I can't think of how to say how much he means to me. I ended a poem that I wrote about him years ago with the lines "I am Eve and the apple and the snake/ and you are the garden." Maybe that's what love is. A feeling that things are right, a place to feel safe and be what you are.

On a shelf beneath the photographs is a glazed clay vase. It's only two inches high with a rolled asymmetrical rim like the clipped and jagged petals of a flower. As I've written in the past, my friend Rose gave it to me six months before she died. She was a poet and a potter. She gave me other things over the years, but they weren't as good as this. I loved her, and the question is, "What do you do with all the love when someone dies?" I have the little vase, and I keep it where I can see it.□

Sunday, July 14, 2000

Dear Michael,

I'm happy you arrived safely, if two hours late. The description of your trip made it sound as if it was going to be about fourteen hours late. Nothing much has happened here. I hope getting the Olympics does great things for China and the rest of the world. Mazeltov.

I looked at a picture of Milt, Jenny, Andy and me when Milt and I were in our early forties. Andy was about five years old and when I looked at him with his big wondering eyes, I thought, who could not love him. I have a picture of you and Peter when he was about a year old. Sheila gave it to me. Every time I look at it I have to laugh. You two look so happy and I remember those days so well. I want to hug you both. Be well and write when you can and I'll write too.

Love,
Rosemary

MY SELF

It's hard to take yourself seriously after a certain age. Maybe I should break the word "yourself" in two. That would express more of what I think I'm trying to say. Yourself. I remember the moment when I understood that myself wasn't unique. All the attention I'd paid to it over my lifetime didn't make it much different from the millions of other selves thinking they were unique, just like I thought.

I was sitting at my computer by the window facing the garden, and I'd just written a poem, "In Desperation," about the advantage of not having a brain to think with. I wanted to be as unconscious as the flowers in my yard. I wanted to be one of the thousands of things living without a self to bother about. And then, epiphany. This self I was making such a fuss about was nothing more than all the other selves, similarly concentrated on by the uncountable masses of people outside of me, starting right in the next room, and reaching back in time and forward into all human tomorrows.

When you're born into a family you don't fit into, into a religion you can't believe in, in a milieu that counts conformity the greatest virtue and you fail that too, perhaps the only refuge is in thinking you're unique. It was a shock. If I wasn't special, what was I? Had I spent a lifetime supported by the idea that I was somehow special without defining how I was special? Now I was facing life as just one more in the parade. Gradually that knowledge became a door into the comfortable room of growing older, though it took time to feel the relief of being free from trying to impress. My first feeling was despair. Why compete in a pointless race? Why set goals that can't be met? Why bother?

When I was young I felt sorry for old people. I thought youth was the good time. I loved the old people in my family, but I couldn't imagine being like them and being satisfied. In my twenties, thirties, and forties, there were the pleasures of sex and motherhood, and the pains that go with both. There were all those judgments I made about myself and everyone else, and the responsibilities I thought I had to be accountable for. In my fifties I began to realize I was aging. And then came the realization that I was not unique, not special, not even to myself. How could I face aging without that crutch?

    Instead of being lost, it feels good. I can't say I feel like a marigold, more like a tall pale tree, still standing, not too supple, but able to look out at life with less anguish and more generosity than when I was that unique self of my fantasies.☐

IN DESPERATION

I bought flowers today
with my man-made money
and planted them
right in the middle of my depression

Saying to myself, a marigold
has a reason for being
that I don't know and
it doesn't know either
but sitting there red and orange
next to the delphiniums
it doesn't worry about how it failed
to be blue

Along with geraniums and pinks
and something purple
I don't know the name of
I made the world more pleasing
and if they flourish and spread
covering the bare brown dirt
I will feel I've done something good
with my life

December 27, 2000
Alpine Drive, Beverly Hills

Dear Marian,
I love your letter. I'm finding it hard to write letters these days. I've started writing in earnest now, trying to put all this stuff I've been doing for the last forty years into some kind of shape to leave to my children and grandchildren. I'm really plowing into it and having fun, which surprises me a lot.

It was just Milt, Michael, and me for Christmas this year. We didn't bother with presents, a tree, lights, or even dinner at home. We celebrated at Julia and Andy's with just presents for the children and a lovely dinner, since the kids were all going back East or to England. So when Christmas finally came, I had the feeling it was about the 10th of January. Why were there still decorations in the stores and on the streetlamps?

That was not an election; that was a selection—by the Supreme Court. I'm not happy. And I don't think it will be possible to be happy with how things will go for the next four years. I've stopped reading the paper at the moment. I get too upset when I see the people being chosen for important jobs—like an Attorney General who hates, not too strong a word, I think, everything the people I respect stand for. Ugh!!!

       Lots of love,
       Rosemary and Milt

August 1, 2001
Alpine Drive, Beverly Hills

Dear Michael,
All the lush greens and colors of spring and summer are a little faded and I am having my annual bout of mid-summer blues. No reason to feel blue, but it happens every year and catches me unaware each time. I never expect it.

If only we were perfect people. But that's my mistake. Being blue is probably just as much part of being a perfect person, if being real is being perfect, like being happy, or angry.

I think I've found the clue to my ocular migraines: a combination of the drug I was taking for tremors plus caffeine. Even the caffeine in decaf caused a problem. And chocolate. Ah, misery, even that has to go. So now my hands are shaking (I'd forgotten how inconvenient that was when eating soup or peas), and if I'm tired, I'm tired, and I just go to sleep, no matter the hour, without a splash of caffeine to stir me up. I don't make appointments far from home after lunch lest I fall asleep driving on the way home. And chocolate has now gone the way of shellfish, raw berries, and mango. Maybe that's why I'm blue.

I've just exhibited another aspect of a perfect person. The need to explain everything, as if we can know everything there is to know in a reasonable way.

Love,
Rosemary

August 10, 2001
Alpine Drive, Beverly Hills

Dear Michael,

I'm trying to figure out what to say to Lizzi, twelve today (she now spells her name without the "e" at the end). I like it. It's as if she's making a declaration of independence by that omission. I hope it's all part of her new phase of being terrific and pleasurable.

Now that I've given up coffee in all its incarnations, I need something to comfort me. I'm way too old to find hot milk soothing.

You wrote a beautiful paragraph in your letter of August 7th that you should save for some future story: "the air was soup thick and soup hot," and ended, "that I was loved and that all I needed would be there when I got home." It really says it for everyone.

I have run out of things to say. George W. Bush—stem cell research. Ugh. Israel—Arabs. Ugh. I've lost four pounds. Ugh. You get the picture. Cranky Aunt. Double ugh.
    Lots of love (that part's not ugh),
    Rosemary

        September 8, 2001
        Alpine Drive, Beverly Hills

Dear Michael,
Tuesday we're going to New York for about twelve days so Milt can work and I can spend some time at the Metropolitan Museum. We'll be right across the street at the Stanhope Hotel, which I hope will be more fun than down at the Four Seasons, just because of the location. More green trees, more paintings, and EAT right around the corner.
 I just wolfed down a whole box of fancy chocolate-covered wafers and I'm paying for it the way I once did when I ate too much fois gras. Some people never learn.
    I miss you.
    Rosemary

        September 12, 2001
        Alpine Drive, Beverly Hills

Dear Michael,
We didn't make it to New York today. Terrible day. There's nothing to be said. Since this was meant to be a pleasure trip, naturally it's off. It's unbearable to think about, and there's no way not to think of it.
    Love,
      Rosemary

HABIT

I was convinced by nuns and others
of the Hell of Bosch and Blake,
of the saintly Christ,
the just God judging
the sin of being born.

They taught me their truth
was all that mattered
between me and their God.
But I lived with the God within me
and counted truth the air I breathed.

They were surprised at half-rejection,
appalled by half-acceptance,
wanting compliance until time and habit
wore me down.

But when the great world shakes
or thousands die in peaceful starvation,
or when bombs blast and God's men
claim righteous privilege
to make others die

I still cry out to the forsaken God
who is not there, and cannot save us.
The nuns have gone.
So have others.
Leaving only habits.

September 15, 2001
Alpine Drive, Beverly Hills

Dear Michael,

The entire country is in mourning. Even the people who don't know it are exhibiting all kinds of strange behavior. And I am with them. The thought of all the families that have had their existences abruptly cut off. The lives lost. The homes that will be lost. Families thrown in other directions. Faith lost. Love with no place to go.

The sadness is overwhelming. I suppose only a psychopath can remain untouched by this stupid human folly and useless carnage. Like so many things that men do, it was there to do, so they did it. God forbid they ever have atomic capacity. They will use it. They are absolute believers of absolutely something.

The only thing one can say for the Americans and Russians at their worst was that they understood if either one blew up the other, they'd both go, and now we're faced with a group that doesn't give a shit one way or the other.

After Will saw some of the footage, he asked if they would rebuild the Trade Towers, and when told that some people would want to, he said, "Then they should build them shorter and fatter."

I hoped that I wouldn't see the terrible things that could happen in the twenty-first century. I wanted to die before they began to happen. I lived with the terrible aftermath of the First World War, the Second World War, Korea, and Vietnam. That's enough for one person. I wish you were here. Maybe we could cry together. One of my thoughts the other day was that I'm glad neither my mother nor father, nor Milt's parents, knew about this.

Buildings as big and as in-your-face as the World Trade Center Towers right at the front door of a country shows a chutzpah before the gods. What's the first thing little boys do to anything that's piled up really high? I'm sick.

Love,
Rosemary

October 25, 2001
Alpine Drive, Beverly Hills

Dear Michael,
I'm so glad you're coming.

I need to remember the good things about Hollis. The apple tree outside the kitchen windows. You and Peter as little babies and how I loved you. Nana and Papa and how their faces looked when you kids were in the room. Grandpa and Aunt Mamie. Being a grandchild, a great niece, a daughter, and an aunt all at once. Being twenty-one. And you're part of that even if you don't remember it. Somewhere in you those memories exist in smiles received, in food given with love and hugs and kisses.

Aunt Mitzi

April 25, 2002
Alpine Drive, Beverly Hills

Dear Michael,
Milt and I spent a week in New York with Sheila and Peter. At the last minute, I decided that I didn't want to spend a week alone in this big house. They were so kind and generous and we had a good time with them. Milt loves going into the office and all the meetings. I only went to the Metropolitan Museum once with Mickey Randolph, but I got to spend an afternoon with my other friend Mickey and time with Sheila that was pleasant and very satisfying.

After twenty-five years in California, I'm not a New Yorker any more. I suppose if we'd come here when I was young, it wouldn't have taken so long. Perhaps it's because I've become less capable of walking in hurrying crowds without losing my balance. And people's faces looked so strained and tense.

I'm past wanting to use my energy to hurry. My needs are less pressing—read a little, listen to tapes, see an opera now and then, draw a little, eat a little. Exercise when necessary. Nothing to excess...

I'm just beginning to get back from the trip East. It sure takes a long time. The laundry room, hall, and bathroom aren't finished yet, but the rest of the house is returning from its long siege by the workmen....

This is a very dull letter. What can I say other than that I've been going to some art classes and my mind seems taken up with sorting out colors for the flowers in the garden and catching likenesses of models in a shabby classroom. I'm not in verbal mode at the moment. Anyway we love you and look forward to seeing you.

    Rosemary

          August 18, 2002
          Alpine Drive, Beverly Hills

Dear Michael,
Please forgive me for not writing sooner. I seem to have only one gear at this point. Painting and drawing. That's two, I guess, but I count them as one. Also the migraines happen very infrequently now that I'm not spending so much time on the computer.

I loved receiving your letters, but somehow I couldn't sit down and write. This has been a summer of more downs than ups in my mood. I think it was because my younger generation, from you and Peter to Emily and Will, were away and I missed you all.

Jean hasn't been well. Another stay in the hospital and what I hear in her voice is something close to exhaustion of spirit. I've been trying to call her more often but the truth is that by the time I remember at the end of the day, it's too late. I'm going to send her a box of books tomorrow. I think I'll call Donald to get a straight story.

    Love,
    Rosemary

March 5, 2005
Alpine Drive, Beverly Hills

Dear Rose,

I miss you.

There have been times I have wished for death, but not the death that claimed you. A death quick and unexpected was what I wanted. Not a long, painful, frightening death.

I see us young taking steps we didn't understand, middle-aged yet still hopeful, and then the decline, fast for you and slow for me. Each day some new piece of myself aging beyond repair...

If you were alive today, I see you cheerful, concerned with your boys, who must now be in their thirties, perhaps with their own children. You would have loved to be a grandmother, and your grandchildren would love you so. It would have been payment for everything that never was in your life.

And I would hear your voice saying my name, "ROSEmary," each time I called you to chat. How did we not become the people we aimed to be? Were our dreams just impossible fantasies meant to be forgotten?

All the poems you didn't write. All the words you mastered that never went on paper. All the bread you didn't bake, the clay you didn't form.

I miss the life you haven't lived. I miss it for me and I miss it for you. You helped make life bearable for me in my worst moments and beautiful when I was able to be open to beauty. Dear Rose, I miss you.

MYSTERIES

I've been awake since 2:30—a.m. that is—and with the onset of the first leg cramp decided it was time to give in and get up, not for the day but at least for an hour. Typing will make the time less irritating. Maybe I'll find out that I'm thinking something interesting.

For years I've berated myself for not being more adventurous at choosing new mystery writers, so I picked out a dozen books at Dutton's, making sure they were by authors I'd not read before. Well, I've read five of them. One was good, by a writer who has written about forty others. Clever—lots of literary references and smart-ass jokes. Another was by a medical pathologist, a good-enough mystery, but with more blood and guts than I would like; one was some weird psycho nonsense about a dysfunctional family of super nutty sisters. Bad writing, a waste of time—only leg cramps could be worse; I've forgotten the others...Now I know why I always rely on recommendations.

I need good mysteries. I need pleasant jigsaw puzzles, a good cup of coffee, and a well-made croissant. I need those things to keep me from thinking about the kind of stuff I thought I'd write about when I came in here, like what I really think of being human, what I think life is like. Maybe I even needed these less-than-satisfactory mysteries so I could come in here and bitch about them. It ain't easy to get away from yourself if you don't get cooperation. Maybe I should go back to Nancy Drew.☐

Journal
March 2, 2006
Alpine Drive, Beverly Hills

I've been lying in bed, my brain in a fret, enough to prevent me from hearing the tape I'm listening to. We made an offer on a small house today and it was accepted. It's frightening and exciting because it made me feel that maybe Milt and I will find new ways to enjoy living together...☐

BEDROOM

When I was little I loved my mother and father's bedroom. It was the biggest of the three bedrooms in our house, and the only one with matching furniture—a tall walnut veneer dresser for my father, a longer and lower one for my mother with a large mirror over it, and a big soft bed with a curved headboard and footboard.

There were so many interesting things in their room. There was a tall wooden clock on top of my father's dresser, and a wooden box with a carved dog on it to hold his cufflinks and tie clasps. He kept his change in there too, so I took that out and put all the pennies in a row. In his top drawer there were handkerchiefs and little suspenders to hold up his socks, pencils, a few more pennies, tickets, shoelaces, and cigars with a picture of a lady on the ring in a humidor. I picked one up and smelled it through the cellophane. I saw the nail clippers and tried to use them on my chewed nails.

But it was my mother's dresser that fascinated me, and I always went there first. In the top drawer there were lipsticks, bottles of nail polish, hair nets, slip straps, embroidered handkerchiefs, bobby pins, safety pins, needles and thread, nail files, all of them asking to be picked up and examined. I saved the button box for last. It was a large, round, red tin with painted flowers on top, filled with a treasure of odd buttons from the sweaters, blouses, skirts, shirts, trousers, and winter coats of my mother's married life. They made funny clattering noises against one another. I picked out some of my favorites and set them in front of me. Rhinestones, mother-of-pearl, clear blue—I knew them all by heart.

And, of course, there was her jewelry. A few dainty, ladylike semi- precious stones set in antique silver, false pearls, and a zircon necklace that she wore on formal occasions, along with dozens of earrings from Woolworth's—pearls, stones, plain red, plain blue, and single earrings in different colors, saved in the hope of finding their mates. Her only piece of gold jewelry was her wedding ring, which she never took off.

The top of the dresser was covered with a hand-embroidered dresser scarf, curling flowers and green leaves neatly stitched by a steady hand. There was a delicate rectangular porcelain tray decorated with flowers hand painted in soft hues by Mother's Aunt Nana. There was perfume to sniff, a round box of talcum powder and a smaller one of face powder, and even some rouge. Everything seemed so different from the things in the other rooms. The lady on the hairbrush with her powdered wig and lacy mantilla looked up at me with gray-blue eyes, and I picked up the brush and ran it through my short, brown hair. I looked at myself in the mirror, dipping my chin low to make my eyes look bigger.

Under the scarf, the top of the dresser was stained with a small, hardened puddle of nail polish. In my heart I always thought that I had spilled it, and it may have been me. Mother let us play in the room, but always warned us not to touch the nail polish. She seemed to know whenever I was there, no matter how quiet I was, and let me play for a while before I got into real mischief, calling up to say it was time to do something else.

And the room held my past. I was born there on June 29, 1928, and on that very bed. I knew that because Aunt Vera was there and told me about it.

"What was I like?" I would ask, knowing the answer.

"You were a pretty baby," she said, "all pink and smiling, not the least bit red and crabby like most babies. Your mother was so happy to have you. The doctor let her hold you before we put you in your crib."

"Rosemary, what are you doing? Are you in my room?"

I shut the drawer with a thud and scuttled around the bed and out of the room.

"Not now, Mommy."

"Well, stay out of there dear. I don't see what you find so interesting anyway. Get your coat on and go out and play. Go call for Mary." □

Journal
July 1, 2009
North Crescent Drive, Beverly Hills

My ten-year-old granddaughter, Lizzie, and I are on a broken escalator that's not going up at the Westside Pavilion. We hear a shout. On the other side, on the moving escalator going down, an old woman has fallen. Arms clinging to the moving railing. Helpless body descending. Just like her life. Down, down. Bumping against the serrated metal steps.

I turn and run down the steps shouting for Lizzie to follow. Lucky for the old woman, there were three women to grab her – one at the top of the escalator who ran down after her and caught her under the armpits. Another who ran over to meet me, and we each took a leg. Mine was the left leg.

A big adventure at the Westside Pavillion. What's happening? Who knows? Life comes together for us in between floors on that escalator. Like most rescues it isn't smooth. No Superman. Just a little old woman, white hair askew, being hauled off an escalator like a half-empty sack of clumsy stones with legs. Three woman holding her up telling her, "It's okay. You're okay now. We've got you."

But she doesn't want to be gotten. She wants us to leave her alone. "Where's my pocketbook? I can walk. I'm fine." We're afraid to let her go. Maybe she's been hurt. What if she falls on the first step she takes? What if she broke some bones?

"No, we're going to take you over to that bench." So there she is looking vague. She knows her name is Sylvia. She looks eighty-five, maybe more, and she is vague. She knows she lives near Beverly Glen and Wilshire and she has children, but she doesn't know their telephone numbers. She doesn't drive, she took the bus, and now she wants to have her hair done. She doesn't know where the salon is, points over to the left where there is nothing but doors to nowhere in the underground parking. She wants to go that way. Where she can get her hair done.

One young woman, the one who grabbed the right leg, wants to leave. I can see it in the way her body is tensed, on your mark, set. But the go hasn't sounded yet. We have to decide what to do. We're adults. We're responsible. I have my ten-year-old granddaughter with me. I get the parking attendant to call Security and that feels like the right thing to do. The third woman says she's associated with the medical profession and starts to check whether the old woman is hurting anywhere. There were going to be some pretty big bruises, but they haven't shown up yet. She does have a gash on the side of her knee so the medical woman, black and gentle, used to little old ladies who don't want to be fussed over, talks her into putting some antibiotic cream on the gouge. But no doctor. "I don't need a doctor. I want to have my hair done."

I'm also used to old people who don't want to be fussed over. My mother used to get into scrapes like climbing up on a counter to get something out of the top shelf of the cabinet and then not being able to get down again. My husband had to go to the rescue that time. My grandfather insisted on his eggs fried in bacon fat and wouldn't hear of anything healthier. And I took care of Milt's mother who had Alzheimer's. So I'm used to getting around old people who don't want to give an inch. They want to do what they want to do. They don't want to help. They want to be left alone. And this old woman wants to get her hair done. She's getting cranky. Maybe she's forgotten the escalator.

The security man comes and acts as if he'd never heard of someone falling on an escalator. He doesn't have a pitch like an Encyclopedia Britannica salesman, but I bet they give them lessons on how to look innocent before they give them the uniform. He pulls out a Band-Aid and announces to one and all that he's not putting any ointment or salve on the cut on her knee, just putting on a Band-Aid. By this time the old woman isn't having any doctors, salves, or Band-Aids, and says, "No, no, I don't need that."

She does need it. It's a good sized gash, not too bloody, but enough to get infected. While she is protesting, I remember a time in London where we spotted a drunk wandering up and down a curb where there was heavy traffic. We stopped and tried to convince him to sit down against a building. He was about as vague as the old woman but happier, and tried to convince us he was just fine, no problem, couldn't be safer. He asked me who I was, and I said, "I'm somebody's mother and you have to sit down." He slid down and said, "Thank you, thank you," and curled up to go to sleep.

So I put my face up close to the old woman's face and said, "I'm somebody's mother, and you have to have a Band-Aid on that cut,"

"Oh, okay," she responded.

The security man has a car, and he wants to get her out of the building. The medical woman offers to go with him and the old woman to try to find the hairdresser on Pico Boulevard where they might know who the woman is. Lizzie and I climb up the escalator that still isn't running, and proceed to eat lunch and do our Saturday errands.

It reminded me of "The Bridge at San Luis Rey," minus the disaster, with all of us converging on the scene to play out our parts, and then going on to live our lives elsewhere. It also made me wonder what might have happened if Mrs. Hitler had put her face up close to her son's and said, "Adolf – I'm your mother, and I'm telling you, stay out of Poland."□

A WOMAN

who thought
she wasn't thinking
and seldom planned
who she would be
never knew
what she would say
until she said it

and found herself
in realms uncharted
sitting at a typewriter
spilling words
telling what she is

why is not in question

ACKNOWLEDGMENTS

I am profoundly grateful to my nephew, Michael Primont, whose questions about our family history planted the seeds of my desire to write. Our friendship has been a constant source of nourishment and encouragement, as evidenced not only in Michael's Foreword to this book but throughout our long correspondence.

Many thanks to my friend Cheryl Wade, it was her enthusiasm about the pieces of my writing that I read out loud to her which made me begin to believe in the possibility that people might enjoy my book.

I wish to thank Anna Sklar, who typed old letters and journals into the computer when I first thought to organize this material for a book, and Cathy Allison, who spent many hours reading and rereading for interest and choice of materials. Special thanks to my first editor, Garrett White, who read years of writing and helped me to find a path through it in the beginning of selection.

I am particularly grateful to Mickey Henrion, who has read most of this material in one form or another through all the years of our friendship. It was Mickey who gave me the courage to publish a book of poems and art made over sixty years, titled *An Imperfect Life*, and then helped to create that project. Another great influence on that project was my daughter, Jennifer, who arranged the physical form of the book of poems and let me sit next to her and give directions as to how I wanted the words and drawings to appear on the pages. Also for this book, she has helped with the design and formation of the cover.

I want to acknowledge as well the support given to me by the late Peggy Josephs (1932–2012). We read many books together, notably Proust, beginning in the early days when we both worked in the Chrysler Building. I was also helped by my close and loving friend Rose Reitter (1934–1993). We spent years reading and critiquing each other's work, and I miss her vital presence immeasurably.

Thanks also to my nurse, Catherine Cook, who shares her life experience of excellent reading and has been willing to take time to proofread my manuscript

Great credit for the layout of this book is to be given to Kerry Grimes, whom I was lucky to hire as my computer consultant in order to relearn the computer after several years of ignoring it. I discovered her creativity and ability to accept suggestions as to how I would like the book to look and her agility to make that happen making this book easier to read.

Thanks also to Marian Baird, Milt's secretary of many years and my good friend. When Marian retired, Margaret Thomas came to work for us. Also a good friend, Margaret continues to manage many important aspects of our lives.

Thanks as well to my son, Andrew, for his love and attention. As always, I owe the biggest debt of gratitude to my husband, Milt, who read the manuscript several times. My most trusted reader, he also shared so many of the days and experiences I have tried, however imperfectly, to express in these pages.

—Rosemary Okun

Made in the USA
San Bernardino, CA
30 March 2017